Strive for Insight

Strive for Insight

Into Your Local, National, and World History

Ted Warren

Scranton, Pennsylvania
The Teenage Edge & Company
2025

Strive for Insight © copyright 2026 by The Teenage Edge & Company. All rights reserved. No part of this book may be reproduced in any form whatsoever, by photography or xerography or by any other means, by broadcast or transmission, by translation into any kind of language, nor by recording electronically or otherwise, without permission in writing from the author, except by a reviewer, who may quote brief passages in critical articles or reviews.

This book was created entirely by human authors without the use of generative AI. No part of this publication may be used in the development, training, or enhancement of artificial intelligence systems without the express written permission of the publisher.

The Teenage Edge & Company
Scranton, PA

ISBNs: 978-0-9915847-7-2 (hardcover); 978-0-9915847-8-9 (paperback); 979-8-9930514-0-6 (ebook)
Cover and book design by Mayfly book design

Library of Congress Catalog Number: 2025924748
First Printing: 2026

This book is dedicated to the once and future teenagers
of the Lackawanna and Wyoming Valleys

Contents

Preface ix

Part One: Modern History xiii

Chapter 1: The Twenty-First Century 1

Chapter 2: The Twentieth Century 1900–1945 21

Chapter 3: The Twentieth Century 1945–1999 45

Part Two: Ancient History to the Nineteenth Century ... 79

Chapter 4: The Great Valley 81

Chapter 5: The Native Americans and the First Europeans 89

Chapter 6: A Civil War Within the American Revolution 105

Chapter 7: Political Revolutions in the Eighteenth Century 127

Chapter 8: Science and Colonization in the Seventeenth and
    Eighteenth Centuries 147

Chapter 9: The Industrial Revolution in England 167

Chapter 10: The Industrial Revolution in America 183

Chapter 11: The American Civil War 199

Chapter 12: Reconstruction and the American West 217

Chapter 13: Colonial Empires in the Nineteenth Century 233

Part Three: History Powered by Electricity to This Day ... 253

Chapter 14: The Commerce Revolutions 255

Chapter 15: Land, Labor, Capital, and the Great
    Anthracite Strike of 1902 273

Chapter 16: The Information Revolutions 289

Chapter 17: The Financial Revolutions 305

Afterword 325

Bibliography 327

General Index 337

Index to Ideas 341

Notes 355

Preface

History moves like two powerful rivers. One river flows continually from the past into the moment and forward to the future. The other river flows from the future into the moment and then back into the past. These huge rivers of time converge in our consciousness in the moment we learn about history. To raise your consciousness, you must pay attention and connect with reality.

I wrote this book for teenagers. It is the background material I would use if I were still teaching grades nine to twelve.

The book begins in the 21st century and moves backwards in time. It is important for teenagers to begin in their own moment of history and then enter the past. As a teen, you are discovering opportunities coming towards you from the future. Who will be your friends, your partners, your family? Which careers will you pursue? What will be your true passions? Which skills will you develop? Will you unite yourself with important ideas that become your ideals for the rest of your life?

Each generation has their own music, their own technology, and their own attitudes. You work and play differently. You find new ways to experience nature. You improve sports. You create new dances, new books, and new science. You learn differently. Strive to discover what is new!

You are also confronted with conflicts coming from your historical past. These conflicts have evolved over many centuries. They are unavoidable and often overwhelming. The conflicts in history challenge you to discover the context in which you are living. This gives you a foundation in the reality of the moment.

Strive for Insight

When we take part in historical events, we enter the local stage, the national stage, or the world stage—much as William Shakespeare noted in his play *As You Like it*:

All the world's a stage,
And all the men and women merely players;
They have their exits and their entrances;
And one man in his time plays many parts.

The soldier who enlists locally enters the national and most likely the world stage. College students enter the national and often the world stage. The same is true when you become employed. This book will help you discover the stages you are experiencing today. Which players are entering and exiting? And which parts are they playing?

In history, you observe millions of people who are able to fulfill their destiny and millions who do not. Many are betrayed. Others meet tremendous obstacles.

In your own life, you have a particular starting point. It is a combination of your thinking, feeling, and willing, your family, gender, culture, and education. These factors are very important, but even more important is what you create out of them. Making mistakes is a necessary part of your learning process. The most important thing is to learn from your experiences. Not everyone learns, nor do countries always learn. Instead, people stop thinking and repeat their mistakes.

To make changes in your life, you need civil liberties and human rights. Millions of people before you fought for their liberties and rights. They also fought for you. For their sacrifice, we can be humble and thankful.

This book is based on my experiences teaching history to teenagers for the past thirty-three years. I am a history teacher, not a historian. In this book, I use a very direct writing style so teens can read it on their own. Teens who read history should be critical of facts and numbers. Take the time to check important topics with other sources.

And remember that the people who make history are responsible for their actions. Pay attention to the key players who make the big choices

Preface

that shape history. Some make good choices, while others make bad choices. Try to figure out their desires and their goals. What can you learn about their real personality?

On the stages of history, you learn to deal with your family, your community, your nation, and the world. When you strive for insight, you learn to deal with the limitations of your local, national, and world stages. Then you can overcome those limitations.

PART ONE

Modern History

CHAPTER 1

The Twenty-First Century

The Local Stage

Flying into Scranton, you look out the window at heavy forests and old wooden buildings. When you land at our international airport and enter the building, you discover it is called the Wilkes-Barre Scranton Airport. It serves a 500-square-mile valley. This is the Great Valley. Within it, two separate valleys and two cities have evolved. The City of Wilkes-Barre is in the Wyoming Valley, while the city of Scranton is in the Lackawanna Valley.

How is that possible? Starting in 1847, as the Industrial Revolution in America emerged, the dynamics of trade, industry, and culture split the valley in two. Wilkes-Barre sent her coal down the Susquehanna River south to Philadelphia. Scranton sent her coal east via the Hudson River to New York City. Close to 95% of the anthracite coal in the United States lay under the Great Valley.

The first thing many people think of when they hear you are from Scranton is *The Office*, an NBC sitcom. Fans give you a big smile! The show made Scranton one of the most well-known small cities in the country.

Strive for Insight

Today, the Great Valley is the center of Northeastern Pennsylvania (NEPA)—an industrial and cultural region bordering the New York City metropolitan area. The valley lies directly west of New York City, two hours by car.

Community Life

Scranton has small-town charm, low crime, little traffic, and a relatively low cost of housing. Genuine and intact communities are some of the major strengths that have evolved from generation to generation in the valley. Neighbors, friends, and family are the spice of life. Festivals, parades, and sporting events are enjoyed year-round.

Residents in the Great Valley are proud of the lifestyle they enjoy. Everyone has a car or two. The local Harley Davidson store in Dunmore is well known far and wide. Unlike most bikers in the world, many Pennsylvanians do not wear helmets. Families enjoy golfing, skiing, biking, kayaking, swimming, and hiking. Camping, hunting, and fishing are always popular.

Many young people come here for college and post-graduate degrees. In 2007, the Geisinger Commonwealth School of Medicine opened in Scranton, joining the University of Scranton, Wilkes University, King's College, and eleven other excellent universities and colleges in NEPA.

One local challenge is to generate knowledge to improve the quality of life and prepare the local workforce. This attracts new enterprises. To retain our children in the valley, we need better professional opportunities for them.

Some talented people leave the national stage to take responsibility on the local stage. Originally from Beaverton, Oregon, Mayor Paige Gebhardt Cognetti took office on January 5, 2020. She is the first female mayor in the history of Scranton.

Local individuals also enter the national stage. Scrantonian Judith Ann McGrath was named chairman and CEO of MTV Networks on July 20, 2004. For seven years, McGrath oversaw their channels—MTV, Comedy Central, and Nickelodeon. She joined the board of directors of Amazon in 2014 while also serving on the board of the Rock & Roll Hall of Fame.

Breaking Benjamin, a heavy rock band from Wilkes-Barre, is on the world stage.

The local stage is filled with professional sports. The Scranton/Wilkes-Barre Railriders are affiliates of the New York Yankees. The Scranton/Wilkes-Barre Penguins are affiliates of the NHL's Pittsburgh Penguins. Pocono Raceway holds two NASCAR races each year. In 2001, Mike Munchak, from the Hill Section in Scranton, was inducted into the Pro Football Hall of Fame.

More importantly, the area is filled with great athletic programs at all levels of high school competition. There have always been many top young athletes in the valley.

In January 2022, Scranton shed its designation as a financially distressed city after thirty years. Despite urban sprawl and the loss of their industrial bases in the 20th century, the towns and cities in the Great Valley have prevailed.

The Middle Class

The valley has the highest percentage of middle-class population of any area in the USA. As of July 2017, the Great Valley encompassed roughly 528,104 residents. For 165 years, NEPA was a melting pot of immigrants from thirty European countries. Now the Hispanic population is growing.

All presidential candidates come here to prove to the rest of the country that they connect with middle-class Americans. On November 3, 2020, Scrantonian Joe Biden Jr. was elected the 46th president of the USA.

What does it mean to be middle class? For many, it means almost always being broke but just able to pay your expenses. If you are lucky, you have a good landlord who keeps the rent low and covers some of the utilities. You have no savings. Employment is unstable.

In Northeastern Pennsylvania, where the cost of living is relatively low, middle class falls within yearly earnings of between $25,000 and just under $100,000. About 32% of households have an annual income between $35,000 and $74,999. In Lackawanna and Luzerne counties, a one-parent family with two children must bring in $55,080 annually, according to a 2016 report by the Institute for Public Policy and Economic Development. A single adult must earn $19,558 annually, according to the institute. These annual incomes are far higher than the 2017 federal poverty guidelines, which say any single person making $12,060 or less, and a family of five making $28,780 or less, is impoverished.

Family Businesses

Family-run businesses have filled the valley for more than 260 years. Martz Trailways, Gertrude Hawks Chocolates, and Tuxedo by Sarno are well-known examples today.

The local touch was exemplified in Ralph's Barber Shop on State Street in Clarks Summit. By 2016, Ralph Marasco had cut hair for sixty years. I asked him how many haircuts that may be. He estimated eight haircuts per day. With no vacations, but two days off per week, that is roughly 124,800 haircuts.

One notable family-owned business in Carbondale has developed important businesses on the national and world stages. Gentex Corporation is a global provider of personal protection and situation awareness products, systems, and platforms. Specifically, the company provides aircrew life support systems, helmet-mounted displays, ground soldier protective equipment, high-performance textiles, and communications equipment.

Local Industry

Warehousing is the largest private business in the valley. Tobyhanna Army Depot is the largest industrial employer in NEPA. It is a center for army electronics, avionics, missile guidance and control. The US Air Force Technology Repair Center supports communications and intelligence.

In 2008, a Penn State University study revealed that 50 trillion cubic feet of natural gas lies locked inside the Marcellus Shale formation in NEPA. Natural gas producers flocked to NEPA, including Chesapeake Energy Corp from Oklahoma and Statoil from Norway.

Oil and gas are removed by a technique called fracking. Chemicals are placed in millions of gallons of water and injected deep into the earth at high pressure to extract the oil from rock. The oil and gas industry is not required to disclose the chemicals they use in the fracking process, yet many are known to be endocrine disruptors and carcinogens. Methane gas leaks from the sites. Where there is fracking, property values decline and agriculture is lost.

Landfill of garbage is another major industry in the valley. Traffic on the highways adds up to 126,672 garbage trucks and 35,568 tractor-trailers per year. Keystone Landfill receives 7,250 tons of waste per day, mainly from households in Pennsylvania, New York City, and nearby states.

On June 3, 2021, Keystone Sanitary Landfill received permission from the Department of Environmental Protection to increase their disposal area by 100 acres and to operate uninterrupted in the 42-year extension of the 714-acre landfill. Capacity will triple. The *Sunday Times* tells us landfill will bring in 94 million tons of additional waste, or about 188 billion pounds, into the 2060s.

Residents wonder how many more garbage hills will be built within city limits. Grassroots organization Friends of Lackawanna is appealing. Residents are concerned about the length of the expansion, lower property values, public health, and environmental issues along the Lackawanna River. The kids in nearby schools can already smell the new mountains of trash. The garbage facility has a wastewater treatment plant, a methane recycling operation, and a liner system designed to keep waste from leaching into the groundwater.

By law, landfill operators must capture the waste gas they produce, especially methane. Keystone Landfill consumes half of its methane in flares at the landfill and pumps the other half to PEI Power Park plant in Archbald to generate electricity.

Four miles to the south, the Lackawanna Energy Center is a natural-gas-fired combined-cycle power plant with three General Electric 7HA.02 air-cooled gas-powered combustion turbines that burn natural gas to generate electricity.

One and a half miles away, another natural-gas-fired power plant has been completed, the Meadowbrook Renewable Natural Gas facility at Dunmore. The plant converts gas from decomposing garbage at the

Keystone Sanitary Landfill. The gas is sent through the interstate pipeline to be used as compressed natural gas.

Pennsylvania Power and Light Corporation (PPL) carried its first kilowatts of power along the Susquehanna-Roseland transmission line on May 12, 2015. It is the most powerful transmission line in the country. It originates near Berwick and runs to Newark, New Jersey. The 280-kilovolt line enters the Great Valley at Pittston, where it crosses the Susquehanna River. The line runs along Bald Mountain before it stretches over the notch at Chinchilla and crosses over the city of Scranton at Archbald. How much more powerful will the line become?

The World Stage

As teenagers, you are heavily influenced by what takes place on the stages in your life. Why learn about the world? It expands your sense of reality and helps you connect with humanity. You learn how different people interact according to their language, landscape, climate, religion, industry, education, and sciences.

The Peoples Republic of China

No other nation has more forcibly entered the world stage in this century than China. In 2000, only five countries counted China as their largest trading partner. By 2020, more than one hundred countries did so, including the United States. The state-dominated banking system, run by the Communist Party of China (CPC), enables the government to control capital markets and the flow of money. They can easily steer money exchange and interest rates.

In 2004, China joined the World Trade Organization. They held the summer Olympic Games in Beijing in 2008, further opening the country to the world.

In October 2010, China surpassed the USA in car production. One year later, they passed the USA as the world's largest producer of products. Cheap labor wins!

China saves roughly 40% of the Brutto National Product (BNP) to invest inside the country. It also invests large sums of money abroad. Which country is the largest foreign owner of US bonds? China.

President Xi Jinping started the "One Belt, One Road" initiative to invest $1.6 trillion into infrastructure throughout Asia, Africa, and the Middle East. Take Africa as an example. Just north of Swakopmund, Namibia, Chinese radar dishes track satellites and space missions. Twenty-five miles south, in Walvis Bay, China has built an artificial peninsula for ships. Chinese trade flows through the port. China's first overseas military base is in Djibouti. They built an $8 billion high-speed railway in Nigeria. In Central America, a canal across Nicaragua is expected to cost $50 billion.

Technology is another major factor in China's dominance in world markets. In July 2017, the State Council decided to make China an Artificial Intelligence innovation center by 2030.

By October 2018, China's two tech giants, Tencent and Alibaba, became exclusive $500 billion tech companies. Since then, Tencent lost tremendous value when Chinese authorities limited the amount of time users can spend on computer games. By October 2020, China had launched more than 700,000 5G base stations. This technology drives smart manufacturing, health, energy, and agriculture.

China's dominance also extends to the military. With 350 ships and twelve nuclear submarines, China has the largest navy in the world. This compares with 293 battleships in the United States Navy. They have launched aircraft carriers and have 1,250 land-based missiles, as well as ballistic missiles and cruise missiles based on normal warheads. These missiles can reach targets from 310 to 3,418 miles away. They now have roughly 500 nuclear warheads.

China's space program is part of the military. In 2020, China landed a robotic spacecraft, Chang'e-5, on the moon. The probe spent two days gathering rocks and dirt. In the 2030s, China plans to build a moon base for astronauts.

Many Chinese cities are installing nuclear energy to reduce air pollution from coal. The China General Nuclear Power Corp (CGN) expanded its supply of uranium for national and worldwide civil projects, tripling its capacity between 2010 and 2020. Operating in twenty countries, CGN has agreements to develop nuclear energy in Canada, Australia, and Namibia.

The country has removed democratic processes in Hong Kong. People who do not agree with the government in China quickly lose their civil rights. Over one million people, mostly Muslim Turkic minorities, Uighurs, Kazakhs, and Kyrgyz in Xinjian, Northwest China, have been put in re-education camps without due process.

The Middle East

Two historical conflicts are ever-present in the Middle East. One is the permanent conflict between the Sunni and the Shia Muslims. This goes back to the year 632, when the Prophet Muhammad died. Who should replace him? The Sunni Muslims declared Abu Bakar the rightful successor. The Shia Muslims chose Ali. The Sunnis and the Shia have disagreed, developed different beliefs, and fought each other for close to 1,400 years.

Roughly 85% of Muslims all over the world are Sunni. They live in Algeria, Egypt, Indonesia, Morocco, Pakistan, Saudi Arabia, Tunisia, Turkey, and Yemen. The Sunni are in conflict with Shia Muslims, who have the majority population in Azerbaijan, Bahrain, Iran, and Iraq. There are Shia minority populations in Kuwait, Lebanon, Yemen, Qatar, Saudi Arabia, and Syria.

Modern Saudi Arabia

Where did modern Saudi Arabia originate historically? In 1744, Muhammad ibn Saud allied with Mohammad ibn Wahhab to create an absolute monarchy with fundamental Wahhabism as its ideology. They demanded complete acceptance of their political and religious beliefs, including old desert traditions, tribal behavior, and gender segregation.

Saudis believe that a Muslim who does not accept Wahhabism can be sentenced to death. The Saudis have taken hold of the entire Arabian Peninsula. In the 1970s, the Saudis mounted a global propaganda campaign to spread Wahhabism. They financed religious schools and mosques to preach Wahhabism. They translated the Koran and added women-hostile comments. This led to new conflicts between supporters of different forms of Islam. Fifteen of the nineteen terrorists involved in the September 11, 2001 attacks were from Saudi Arabia.

The Saudi royal family's estimated worth was roughly $1,400 billion in 2018. They are heavily invested around the world in real estate, casinos, personal planes, yachts, and professional golf. They pay into foundations in the USA and hire lobbyists. They invest in oil refineries, banks, think tanks, and universities in the United States. The US exports 33% of all global arms yearly and 10% of that goes to Saudi Arabia.

In the desert of the northwest corner of the country, Prince Mohammed bin Salman is building a new high-tech region called Neom. By 2030, he wants to make the country independent of oil. His goal is that green hydrogen will be the new energy source in a carbon dioxide neutral state of the future.

Israel and Palestine

The other permanent conflict in the Middle East is between Israel and Palestine. Israel considers Jerusalem its capital. They want the entire ancient city. The Palestinians want East Jerusalem as the capital of a future Palestinian State.

In 2000, the Palestinians launched the second intifada, which lasted until 2005. Israel controlled the West Bank and the peace process stagnated. In 2002, the Israeli government completed a wall around the West Bank. In 2004, huge natural gas fields were discovered under the Mediterranean in Gaza. There may be more.

Not until 2013 did the United States revive the peace process between the Israeli government and the Palestinian Authority. The talks were stopped when Fatah, the ruling party in Palestine, formed a government with Hamas in 2014. That summer, the Israeli military and Hamas fought for two months in Gaza. In the spring of 2018, weekly demonstrations took place on the border of the Gaza Strip, where Israel continues to develop settlements.

On October 7, 2023, Hamas militia broke through Israeli lines, killing 1,000 and wounding another 2,600 in the deadliest incursion on

Israeli territory in its history. Hamas took roughly 250 hostages back to the Gaza Strip. Israel shut down the food, water, and electricity supplies into the Gaza Strip while bombing civilian areas.

Israeli forces separated Gaza in two and blocked the roads running from north to south. Farmland across the width of the strip was bulldozed, and major roads have been torn up by the constant movement of tanks. Huge craters and rubble are all that is left in many neighborhoods. During intense Israeli bombing in Gaza, a doctor at the hospital in Gaza City, knowing he would soon be killed, wrote on the message board "I did what I could."

Israel wanted to destroy Hamas and prevent anyone from using Gaza to attack. The boycott of food, medicine, and gas has left half of the Palestinians in hunger. The Israeli military estimated about 14,000 Hamas combatants in Gaza had been killed or captured. Millions of Palestinians are now refugees in Gaza. Tens of thousands have been killed, tens of thousands are wounded, living without homes, clean water, or medicines.

The war reached another front where Israel is fighting Iran and its other proxies, Hezbollah in Lebanon and Syria, Islamist militias in Syria and Iraq, and the Houthi militia in Yemen. The Hezbollah in Lebanon and Hamas in Gaza are Sjia Muslims. Iran is Sjia.

Besides crushing its own women seeking greater freedom of thought and dress, Iran is effectively controlling four Arab states—Lebanon, Syria, Yemen, and Iraq—through its proxies.

Islamic State

When Saddam Hussein's dictatorship in Iraq was destroyed by the Americans in 2003, a strong Shia-dominated government came to power. Ten years later, the Sunnis, who were pushed aside by the Shia government backed by the USA, became an important recruitment base for the Islamic State (IS).

At the very beginning of 2014, IS wrested control of the city of Falluja in Iraq's Anbar Province. On June 6, a band of 1,500 IS fighters entered the western suburbs of Mosul. Within a couple of days, tens of thousands of Iraqi Army forces fled in panic. On June 11, IS rolled into

Tikrit, capturing billions of dollars' worth of American advanced weaponry and military hardware. They controlled population centers of some five million people. IS had removed the Sykes-Picot border between Iraq and Syria to create a new caliphate.

On July 21, 2015, the *Toronto Star* told the story of two half-brothers, Assad and Amjad. One of their mothers and some of their siblings had escaped to Germany, where they saw an IS propaganda video and recognized their boys.

Assad and Amjad were captured on August 3, 2014, when 500,000 Jesidisics fled to the Sinjar Mountain. The boys had two choices—either convert to Islam or die.

In April 2015, they were transferred to an IS training center for suicide bombers at Tal Afar, outside of Mosel. IS reported about one thousand volunteers at the institution. Many were children. The brothers were taught that they were ignorant. In a video, they said they wanted to kill non-believers.

Assad and Amjad were fourteen years old in January 2017, when they were filmed jumping into their car filled with explosives in East Mosel, Iraq. They smiled for the camera. Looking through a tiny window, they drove down the street to Iraqi military vehicles. Iraqi soldiers and international journalists ran for cover. The car exploded. IS filmed the explosion and their family watched the film in Germany.

At the beginning of 2016, IS controlled land the size of Texas, where they wanted to establish a Sunni state.

The Arab Spring

The Arab Spring began when a fruit seller in a poor Tunisian town set himself on fire after a policeman slapped him. Protests quickly spread. The masses lived in poverty and corruption, while the rulers were rich. After Tunisian protesters forced Zine el-Abidine Ben Ali into exile, demonstrations erupted in Egypt, Libya, Yemen, Bahrain, and Syria. In Libya, the United States and allied countries bombed the forces of Muammar el-Qaddafi and backed the rebels.

In Egypt, the Arab Spring began on January 25, 2011. People were angry about the daily repression. Hosni Mubarak had been president for thirty years. Two weeks later, he was ousted. Six months later, Egyptians voted for a new parliament. The Islamic Muslim Brotherhood won the election. Under President Mursi, crisis after crisis evolved. On August 14, 2015, Egypt's first democratically elected government was overthrown by the military.

In Syria, the uprising became a civil war that destroyed entire cities, opened the door for jihadists, and sent millions of refugees abroad. President Bashar al-Assad remained in power after inviting Russia and Iran to intervene. Syria was destroyed. On Sunday, December 8, 2024, a coalition of rebel forces took over Syria and forced Assad into exile in Moscow.

Refugee Crisis

In 2015, a worldwide refugee crisis arose, including nearly 30 million children who had been driven from their homes by war and persecution. To reach Europe, migrants worked with human trafficking agents, a modern form of slavery. Three hundred thousand migrants fled violence and hunger in countries such as Syria, Iraq, Afghanistan, Libya, and Eritrea, and poured into Europe. In 2010, the number of migrants worldwide was 43 million; in 2020, the total was roughly 82 million.

Scientists predict that by 2050 more than 50 million climate refugees will have fled northward to escape areas of the globe made uninhabitable by soaring temperatures, droughts, famines, and the chaos of failed states.

Covid pandemic

In January 2020, the World Health Organization (WHO) declared the Covid-19 virus an epidemic. By February 24, 79,000 people were reported infected, mostly in China. Apparently, it started in November 2019 in Wuhan, China. The virus spread to South Korea, Iran, and Italy.

According to Johns Hopkins University Covid Resource Center, by January 14, 2022, there were 324 million cases reported in the world, with 5.5 million deaths. Throughout the world, millions lost family members, jobs, homes, or businesses to Covid-19. By February 2022, 400 million cases had been reported worldwide.

For teenagers throughout the Western world, school lockdowns resulted in a loss of education and skills. Students did not learn as well online as they did in the room with a teacher.

The Invasion of Ukraine

Ukraine is a country of 44 million people. It feeds 400 million people around the world, mostly grain and sunflower seeds. Poor countries like Bangladesh, Sudan, and Pakistan receive roughly half of their wheat from Ukraine. The same is true of Egypt, Turkey, and twenty-two other countries.

The River Dneiper flows through the capital, Kiev, in the north to Kerson in the south, where it empties into the Black Sea. The Danube River flows along the southwestern border of the country. The Donets flows through southeastern Ukraine. At the mouth of the Kalmius River, on the coast of the Sea of Azov, lies Mariupol, with 430,000 citizens. It was a center for the worldwide grain trade.

On February 24, 2022, President Vladimir Putin of Russia invaded Ukraine. From one day to the next, normal life was shattered. One hundred thousand Russian troops crossed the border. Bombs fell on Kiev. Massive firebombing terrorized the people.

The people of Ukraine made a stand for their country and their democracy. President Volodymyr Zelensky and his government remained in the capital. The Russians met a determined army that had been at war since 2014, when Russia annexed the Crimean Peninsula.

In the first week, Kharkiv was continually attacked and Mariupol was surrounded by Russian separatists from Donetsk. Two weeks later, grain export to the rest of the world was stopped. In less than one month, 3 million refugees had crossed the border to Poland, Hungary, and Romania. Russia was still earning one billion dollars daily on sales of oil, gas, and coal to European countries.

Although Russian forces greatly outnumbered the Ukrainian Army, the Ukrainians ambushed them with Javelin anti-tank missiles, Stinger anti-aircraft missiles, anti-tank weapons, and tactical drones. The Switchblade drones were carried in a backpack and flown directly at a tank or a group of troops.

Strive for Insight

The Ukrainians were operating in units, usually between eight and ten soldiers in size. They were armed with smart weapons and could take out heavily armed tank units and armored convoys. Civilians with iPhones called in the locations of Russian units, providing real-time, actionable intelligence. By the third week of the war, Russian advances stalled near major cities. The war turned into genocide as the Russians killed civilians with long-distance rockets and artillery. Directly targeting civilians with any kind of weapon violates the Geneva Conventions.

In Mariupol, Putin bombed the university, the maternity hospital, schools, and apartment buildings. Two hundred thousand civilians were hiding underground with little food, no electricity, water, or telephone contact. Thousands were killed and buried in mass graves. Ninety percent of the homes in Mariupol were destroyed. The Ukrainian 36th Marine Brigade held out.

In November 2023, the brutal winter war began. Russia had bombed energy distributors throughout the country. Most of the people were without electricity and water. The UN estimated that 7.5 million people had fled.

By January 1, 2024, time was working against Ukraine. The counter-offensive of the previous summer did not meet expectations.

The National Stage

On September 11, 2001, flight AA11 was highjacked outside of Boston with ninety-two passengers on board. It crashed into the north tower of the World Trade Center in New York at 8:46 a.m. Seventeen minutes later, another passenger flight, UA175 from Boston, hit the south tower. At 9:37, flight AA77 from Dulles Airport crashed into the Pentagon in Virginia. The fourth plane, flight UA93 from Newark, hit the ground outside of Shanksville, Pennsylvania, near Pittsburgh, at 10:03. They assume it was headed for the Capitol Building or the White House in Washington.

A total of 2,996 people were killed in the Al Qaeda attack, the deadliest on our soil in US history. Osama bin Laden from Saudi Arabia led the attack. To hunt down bin Laden and remove Taliban control of the land, President George W. Bush invaded Afghanistan on Oct. 7, 2001, marking the beginning of Operation Enduring Freedom. In August 2021, the twenty-year-old war ended when the USA pulled out and the Taliban took over the country. The USA and NATO allies deployed 150,000 soldiers at the height of its engagement in 2010. By 2018, the war had cost an estimated 110,000 lives. Almost 2.5 million Afghanis were registered as refugees, another million were unregistered in Pakistan.

The Patriot Act

On October 26, forty-five days after the attacks on September 11, 2001, the Patriot Act was passed by Congress and signed into law by President Bush. The new law expanded the authority of US law enforcement agencies to fight terrorism at home and abroad. The agencies could now search telephone and email communications, medical, financial, and other personal records. Since 9/11, Americans have been stripped of essential civil liberties. Americans are videotaped in public places. Surveillance drones are flown over American soil.

The US Treasury could now regulate financial transactions. Law enforcement and immigration officers could now detain and deport immigrants suspected of terrorist activities. Terrorism now included "domestic terrorism." Domestic terrorism was defined as mass destruction, assassination, kidnapping, and activities that are a violation of the criminal laws of the US or of any state.

On March 20, 2003, President Bush, together with his neoconservative administration, ordered the United States to invade Iraq, a country ruled by dictator Saddam Hussein, who had nothing to do with 9/11. This was the beginning of Operation Iraqi Freedom. Before the attack, Foreign Secretary Colin Powell showed evidence to the United Nations that accused Hussein of hiding weapons of mass destruction in Iraq. This proved to be false.

The ground war took less than a month. Freedom did not break out in a shattered Iraq—a civil war did. In September 2010, President Obama turned Iraq's security over to a Shiite government under Nouri al-Maliki.

Maliki was an authoritarian. His government held little legitimacy in the eyes of minority Sunnis and Kurds. By December 2011, almost all US troops had left the country.

Between 2012 and 2014, the USA spent approximately $3 trillion in Iraq. By 2017, some 7,000 American troops were killed fighting in Iraq. At least 250,000 Iraqis were killed. Why did the American Empire start the Iraqi War? Was it to promote democracy or to make money on the oil fields of Iraq?

The US Prison System

According to the Vera Institute of Justice, we spend $31,000 a year for each prisoner in the United States. The Federal Bureau of Justice Statistics states that we have 2.2 million people incarcerated, including 1,300 at maximum-security prisons. To see the full impact, we need to multiply that number with the families left behind.

Between 1975 and 2005, the rate of incarceration in the United States increased from 100 inmates per 100,000 citizens to more than 700 per 100,000 citizens. This is one of the highest rates in the world. Though Americans make up only about 4.6% of the world's population, American prisons hold 22% of all incarcerated people in the world. Who are the Americans sitting in prison?

Prisons, like the rest of the society, have been privatized. For-profit prisons and detention centers, in which private citizens may invest, have been established. The corporations, which make billions off the prison system, run phone services, food services, medical services, and commissaries.

Black Lives Matter

Police violence against young African Americans continued week after week. Some of these killings were caught on videotape, yet, in most cases, the police were not charged. In 2014, Black Lives Matter (BLM), a civil rights movement, started demonstrating against the deaths of young Americans such as Dontre Hamilton, Tamir Rice, Antonio Martin, Akai Gurley, Eric Garner, and many more. In August that year, BLM supporters marched in Ferguson, Missouri, following the death of Michael Brown.

The Twenty-First Century

In May 2015, a protest by BLM in San Francisco was part of a nationwide protest against the police killing of black women and girls, including the deaths of Meagan Hockaday, Alyana Jones, Rekia Boyd, and others.

George Floyd, a forty-six-year-old Black man, died on May 25, 2020, in Minneapolis as the result of a Minneapolis police officer kneeling on his neck for more than eight minutes. The federal government brought civil rights charges against all four officers involved. One was sent to prison for twenty-one years. Three other officers were sent to prison for three years.

That month, 450 protests were held in the USA and other parts of the world. On July 24, President Trump sent federal security forces in unmarked vehicles to stop Black Lives Matter demonstrations in Portland, Albuquerque, and Chicago. Violence broke out in Washington, D.C. when people rallied against racial inequality and police brutality.

In America, we must all have freedom and equality. No justice—no freedom.

Climate Crisis in the States

The environmental movement arose in the 1960s because we had removed the healthy water from our rivers and polluted our farmland. The eagles left our skies. Today we have the climate debate and a movement for global climate crisis management. Floods, hurricanes, heatwaves, and wildfires threaten large populations, resulting in disturbed food supplies and lack of water. It is our responsibility. Young people like you are leading the way to change.

The Western states are running out of water, both in the reservoirs and the ground water. In the summer of 2021, reservoirs were down 50%. Lake Mead delivers drinking water to 25 million people. Less snow in the Rocky Mountains and less water in the Colorado River has left the lake with only 37% of its water. Ground water has also disappeared. Will the Central Valley still produce fruit and vegetables for the entire United States?

One Tenth of the Top 1%

As of 2024, the population of the USA was roughly 345 million people. One percent of the total population was 3,450,000 people. One-tenth of 1% of the population in America was 345,000 people. The richest one-tenth of 1% of the population, or merely 345,000 Americans, own almost as much combined wealth as the bottom 90%, or 310,500,000 Americans. This is a serious imbalance.

A 2015 report entitled *Billionaire Bonanza*, from the Institute for Policy Studies, showed that the richest 400 Americans have a combined net worth of $2.34 trillion, which is equal to that of the bottom 61% of the US population, or about 194 million people. According to the report, a mere twenty individuals in America now control more wealth than the bottom half of the population, which is 152 million people living in 57 million households.

Nearly two-thirds of all working-age poor are actually working but unable to earn a living wage, forcing them to rely on food stamps, which only provide about five dollars a day per person for meals. In addition, over 83% of all benefits going to low-income people are for the elderly, the disabled, or working households.

The Institute on Taxation and Economic Policy (ITEP) found that, in 2015, the poorest fifth of Americans paid, on average, 10.9% of their incomes in state and local taxes. The middle fifth paid 9.4%. But the top 1% paid states and localities only 5.4% of their incomes in taxes.

Most state and local governments rely on regressive taxes—particularly sales and excise levies. Poor and middle-class people pay more, simply because they have to spend the bulk of their incomes just to cover their costs.

Our inequality is already high because of the low minimum wage, the weakness of unions, and very high levels of private-sector compensation at the top.

We redistribute money through taxes less than other countries. We also have lower taxes on the highest incomes, especially income from capital. By taxing the wealthiest so little, states lose income to provide services to all citizens.

The Twenty-First Century

January 6, 2021

On January 6, 2021, President Donald Trump incited supporters to overpower the democratic process on Capitol Hill, where lawmakers were counting the votes of the Electoral College. The president campaigned to overturn a free election guaranteed by the Constitution. Trump urged a mob of 30,000 supporters to march to the Capitol.

Around two-thirty in the afternoon, the wave of Trump supporters pressed past police barricades near the west side of the Capitol. On the east side of the complex, the mob rushed through the entrance. Thousands walked into the Capitol Building.

As debate progressed in the House Chamber over a Republican protest of Arizona's Electoral College votes for President-elect Joseph R. Biden Jr., few lawmakers knew of the attack. But Capitol Police officers were quietly locking down the building, instructing everyone in the hallways to shelter in place. The police closed the gallery doors. Congressional leaders were ushered out as staff urged lawmakers in the gallery and on the floor to remain calm. Aides scurried back to grab hold of boxes containing the Electoral College certificates, making sure that the mob could not literally steal the results of the election.

When evening fell, the Capitol Police, aided by F.B.I. agents, squeezed protesters from the building. Then lawmakers resumed counting electoral votes. Early the next morning, Vice President Mike Pence certified Biden as the nation's 46th president. Within three weeks, 750 rioters would be arrested.

January 6, 2025

On January 6, 2025, Congress ratified the election of Donald Trump as the 47th president of the United States. There were no riots, a peaceful transition of power was restored. Two weeks later on Martin Luther King Jr. Day, January 20, 2025 inside the Rotunda of the Capitol Building, Donald J. Trump took the Presidential Oath:

"I do solemnly swear, (or affirm) that I will faithfully execute the office of President of the United States, and will, to the best of my ability preserve, protect, and defend the Constitution of the United States." (Article II, Section I. of the Constitution.)[1]

Cosmology is Changing

NASA's James Webb Space Telescope was launched on December 25, 2021. It records images of galaxies and stars that are forming planetary systems. The scientific goals for the Webb are to act as a time machine to see the first stars and galaxies that were formed, to better understand how galaxies and planets formed, and possibly how life has been built outside of our universe.

In 2023, astrophysicists consistently received data from the telescope that forced them to develop new models on how fast the universe is expanding. They may have to change their concepts of the components of the universe, as well as the nature of space and time.

Webb studies galaxies at the edge of our universe, measures star formation rates, and creates maps of cosmic dust. Using ultraviolet light, it captures images of distant galaxies, young stars, and planets. It is designed to study how new stars, solar systems, and galaxies form and change over time. Galaxy clusters include thousands of galaxies. Gravity pulls the galaxies together. Gas and dark matter are heated when they fall into the clusters. Scientists study the images each day. A revolution in science has begun.

CHAPTER 2

The Twentieth Century

1900–1945

Was the American national stage progressing in 1900 or were the decision-makers hindering progress? Maybe it was moving both forward and backward? You will be able to answer these questions for yourself at the end of this chapter.

The Local Stage

At the turn of the 20th century, the anthracite coal industry was strong and the flow of immigrants swelled the population of Scranton to 102,206.

Child labor continued in the coal mines and the textile mills. In February 1901, Mary Harris "Mother" Jones came to the valley to help girls between the ages of twelve and sixteen strike against local silk mills from Carbondale to Scranton. The girls earned minor concessions.

The entire valley had excellent public transportation systems. From 1896 until 1954, the Scranton Railway Company operated electric trolleys. City lines ran in Scranton and Dunmore. Suburban lines ran from Forest City in the north to Pittston in the south. At Duryea, there was a connection to Wilkes-Barre. In 1900, the railway carried 10.5 million passengers a year and operated more than one hundred cars. By 1912, it carried 24 million passengers a year.

Strive for Insight

The Scranton-Wilkes-Barre Laurel Line was built in 1903 by the Wyoming Valley Railroad. The line received its name from the wildflower growing along its nineteen-mile route. The three-rail electric interurban line operated commuter train and freight service between Scranton and Wilkes-Barre. Following the Susquehanna River, the line originated at Scranton, continued southward to Rocky Glen and Moosic, and finally reached Wilkes-Barre. When the mining industry was strong, it carried as many as 4.2 million passengers a year.

One lesson learned from the Coal Strike of 1902 was the need for a state police in managing 150,000 strikers, strike breakers, private eyes, secret societies, and the public. In 1906, Pennsylvania became the first state served by its own police force when the Pennsylvania State Police was founded.

The Friendly Sons of St. Patrick of Lackawanna County was also founded that year. One of the founders, Edward Blewitt, was the great-grandfather of President Joseph R. Biden Jr., who was born in Scranton in 1942.

The Tunkhannock Viaduct opened in 1915. It is the largest concrete railroad bridge ever built. It soars 240 feet over the surface, with ten huge arches, each 200 feet wide and 200 feet high, topped by eleven other arches. The whole viaduct carried a roadbed for several tracks. It reduced passenger-running time from Buffalo to New York by twenty minutes, freight trains by a half-hour.

In 1916, the Scranton Button Company expanded its production lines when Thomas Edison asked them to produce his records. Frank Marquardt was hired to manage record production. In 1929, in an $8 million deal, Scranton Button formed the American Record Corp.

The local *Times-Tribune Newspaper* tells us that in 1917 there were 175,000 people working in the mines. Total coal production was 100 million tons. The garment and textile industries had 150 plants and mills in Lackawanna County, employing 15,000 people. The railroads employed another thousand people.

Marcus Frieder had created silk-throwing operations in the Lackawanna Valley by building the Klots Throwing Company in Carbondale. Just before World War I, the company had silk mills in Archbald, Forest

The Twentieth Century

City, Scranton, Maryland, Virginia, and West Virginia. By 1916, Frieder had full control of the General Silk Importing Company, with operations also in Asia.

Next in line was his son, Leonard Peter Frieder, who travelled to Japan and China in 1916 to meet the people who worked there. General Silk built a major silk mill in New Bedford, Massachusetts, and produced cartridge bags made of silk for soldiers in WWI. In the 1920s, the Frieders continually looked at new engineering applications for the materials they made. Though the silk industry collapsed in the early 1920s and the General Silk Corporation was forced into bankruptcy during the Great Depression, the company survived.

Women's Suffrage

On May 21, 1919, Congress passed the Nineteenth Amendment to the United States Constitution. The amendment prohibits the United States and its states from denying the rights of citizens on the basis of sex. One hundred and forty-three years after the Declaration of Independence, women finally had the right to vote.

National leaders such as Susan B. Anthony, Mrs. Elizabeth Cady Stanton, and Francis E. Willard fought for equal rights for all people. They used civil disobedience, parades, vigils, and hunger strikes. Local leaders encouraged all women in the valley to register to vote.

The year 1920 represents the city of Scranton's economic apex. Anthracite coal production was strong. Then two major anthracite strikes broke out in 1922 and 1925. Coal operators chose surface mining instead. This increased productivity as machines stripped the earth and fewer laborers were needed.

Then consumers stopped heating their homes with anthracite coal. The oil and gas industries began heating homes and fueling vehicles. The coal industry and electrified public transportation collapsed, along with the city. Scranton's growth declined, yet the population still grew to its peak at 137,900. Thirty thousand still worked in the coal industry. Twenty-eight thousand of them were immigrants.

In 1923, the Scranton Railway Company abandoned service from Scranton to Pittston. The long suburban lines of the Scranton Railway Company also cut back service in 1929, the year the coal industry reached its apex.

The textile industry began its decline as natural fibers were replaced by synthetics. Even with the development of other businesses, the area remained dependent on industries demanding muscle and sweat. The Great Depression of the 1930s reduced the local market, not only for expensive silk and lace, but for all other industries and services.

In 1932, Marcus and Leonard Frieder restructured Klots. They reopened their headquarters in Carbondale, with one mill there and one in Maryland. Every plant in the company had its own learning center with independent co-workers developing their own ideas for new manufacturing processes and products.

Prohibition had begun in 1920 and ended on April 7, 1933. Once again, the Hotel Casey and the Hotel Jermyn served bottled beer.

The Federal Works Programs Administration (WPA) employed the 3.3 million unemployed in the nation in 1938. A major local project was to line the banks of the Susquehanna River with stone walls. In the cities, they fixed streets, installed city sewers, and put out mine fires. On the East Mountain, they built the scenic overlook. In 1940, national unemployment was 14.6%, in Scranton it was 32%. Thousands of men left the city to serve in the war. Others left to get jobs in the war industry.

By 1941, Leonard Frieder had an excellent team of engineers at General Textile Mills designing advanced textile materials. They worked for the Bureau of Navy Weapons making high payload parachutes to drop mines.

To bring oil to the North during WWII, the War Emergency Pipelines were built to cover 1,200 miles from Texas to New Jersey. These double pipelines were essential for fighting the war. They put a final end to the anthracite coal industry.

Important questions remain for us to consider: Despite the major setbacks, why is Scranton so famous today? How have the diversified, supportive communities in the valley evolved from generation to generation? They built a quality of life to be proud of. They created loyalty to the communities.

The Twentieth Century

The National Stage

At the beginning of the 20th century, roughly 3.4 million people lived in New York City; 80% of them were immigrants. The poor of Europe had entered the world's largest metropolis. By 1907, another 1.2 million immigrants arrived from Europe. After being processed at Ellis Island, many moved to towns like Scranton to work in the mines.

In 1900, a contract was signed to construct the New York Subway. The goal was to connect all boroughs with a subway line that cost five cents no matter where you entered the system or how long you travelled. Seven thousand men, mostly Italians, began work in 1904. They cut twenty miles of subway tunnels to form the most modern transportation system in the world. It took just four years. They dug trenches, built walls, put in the ceilings, and lay streets above the subway. The express line was revolutionary! By 1916, one billion passengers travelled on the system per year.

Manhattan lies on granite bedrock. This enabled the engineers to anchor skyscrapers into the ground. In 1903, the twenty-one-story Flatirons Building became the first skyscraper. In 1908, the Simpson Building reached forty-two stories, the Metropolitan Life Building rose fifty stories, and the Woolworth Building towered sixty stories.

Ocean liners filled the wharves along the Hudson River. Penn Station was built in 1910 and Grand Central Station in 1913. Tunnels under the Hudson River and bridges over the river connected the city with New Jersey and the entire country to the west. Bridges over the East River connected the city with Connecticut and Long Island to the east.

There were roughly 30,000 factories in the city, with 612,000 workers who toiled eleven-hour days, six days a week. On March 25, 1911, teenage girls at the Triangle Shirtwaist Factory were collecting their pay when a fire broke out on the fourth floor. To prevent the fire from spreading, the doors were locked. There were no fire exits. The elevators were out of service. One hundred and forty-six girls died that day. This forced a factory commission to inspect the sweatshops in the city. There was child labor everywhere, no fire protection, and no disability compensation. Social welfare legislation was introduced to protect workers.

Segregation

Between 1890 and 1911, Blacks were eliminated from Southern politics and social life. The Jim Crow laws sanctioned segregation in churches, schools, housing, jobs, and restaurants. The ostracism extended to public transportation, sports, hospitals, orphanages, prisons, and cemeteries.

White supremacist groups violently opposed Black people's legal equality and suffrage. They disfranchised Blacks by creating barriers to voter registration.

In its 1896 decision Plessy v. Ferguson, the United States Supreme Court upheld the constitutionality of those state laws that required racial segregation in public facilities. They legitimized the "separate but equal" doctrine. Justice John Marshall Harlan was the only justice who dissented. He argued that in matters of law and civil rights there is no difference between races in the US Constitution.

WWI offered Blacks new hope. Three hundred and sixty thousand entered military service. Even more migrated to the Northern cities to work in the war industries. That hope was short lived. In 1919, twenty-five race riots broke out in American cities. Mobs burned, shot, and flogged Blacks who fought back. Housing tension and labor tension grew. Blacks were squeezed out of federal and private employment. The new Ku Klux Klan inflamed prejudice and race violence. Jim Crow laws were strengthened in the 1920s.

Yet the 1920s was a vibrant era for Black culture in the North. Jazz became popular. The Harlem Renaissance was formed by Black writers, musicians, poets, and critics in New York City. Jazz performers such as Fats Waller, Josephine Baker, Duke Ellington, and Louis Armstrong performed at the Cotton Club. Langston Hughes developed jazz poetry, wrote plays and short stories. W.E.B. Du Bois argued that Black leaders must fight for civil rights. Du Bois helped cofound the National Association for the Advancement of Colored People (NAACP). Marcus Garvey preached political separation from white America.

The Twentieth Century

Native Americans

In 1924, all Native Americans were made citizens of the United States. Attempts to annihilate their culture had failed. Starting in 1876, the government stole children from their homes and sent them to boarding schools. They were washed in kerosene. Their clothes, names, and hair were removed. Dressed as Americans, they were given one hour of hard labor as punishment for speaking their own language. Boys were taught trades and farming; girls were taught cooking and caring for farm animals. The goal was to provide cheap labor in American communities. Many children became ill, were abused, and were subjected to corporal punishment.

Meanwhile, their families lived in poverty on reservations. During the Depression, Native Americans were allowed to practice their ceremonies and arts. The Wheeler Howard Act of 1934 promoted self-government for Native Americans, but the damage had been devastating.

Electric Streetcars, Railways, or the New Motor Industry?

In 1900, there were only 8,000 cars in America. Streets were used as playgrounds. In the 1920s, the car took over. Streetcars were seen as obstructions to traffic. Streetcar systems and railways across the country, which would have been invaluable in the 21st century, were dismantled. Who was responsible? Local, state, and national governments eliminated electric transportation.

The Public Utility Holding Company Act of 1935 denied electric utility companies from supplying electricity and operating other businesses such as streetcar lines. Streetcar companies in America paid business and property taxes. They also provided street sweeping and snow clearance. In any country, urban and transcontinental transport systems must be subsidized by taxpayer money. In Norway today, cars pay a toll each time they enter city limits. That money goes to electronic public transportation services.

The big players on the oil, gas, and automotive stage—General Motors (GM), Firestone Tire, Mack Trucks, Standard Oil of California, and Philips Petroleum—also played a role in the decline of electric-powered public transportations systems.

Strive for Insight

After the stock market crashed in 1929, the Depression swept out of control. Morison writes, "Millions of investors lost their savings; thousands were forced into bankruptcy. Debts mounted, purchases declined, factories cut down production, workers were dismissed, wages and salaries slashed. Farmers, already hard hit, were unable to meet their obligations, and mortgages were foreclosed, often with losses to all concerned. Real estate sagged in value and tax collections dropped alarmingly."[2]

More than 5,000 banks closed between 1929 and 1932. According to the US Census Bureau, there were 3 million unemployed in 1930, and 13 million in 1933. Industries collapsed, people were evicted, and breadlines formed. Shanty towns were built in Central Park.

Mayer La Guardia led New York through the tragedy of 50% unemployment in 1933. He secured massive public programs for unemployment relief, healthcare, public housing, and labor reform. With New Deal money, La Guardia built highways, schools, hospitals, and an airport named for him.

To build public works, La Guardia turned to Robert Moses in 1924. He built highways to the Long Island parks, setting electric mass transit aside. At the 1939 World's Fair in Queens, General Electric exhibited a vision of the USA in the 1960s—highways and skyscrapers! Who would pay for the new landscape based on the automobile? The public, with their taxes!

In April 1935, the dust storm hit Oklahoma and Kansas. Three and a half million Americans became dust bowl refugees. Many migrated to California. Woody Guthrie told the story in his *Dust Bowl Ballads*. Guthrie was a singer and writer of folk and children's songs. In 1940, he wrote "This Land is Your Land." You will understand America better if you read his autobiography, *Bound For Glory*.

The World Stage

During World War I, the Russian Empire, the German Empire, the Austrian-Hungarian Empire, and the Ottoman Empire were demolished. The French Empire and the British Empire survived for only thirty more years.

The Twentieth Century

King George V of England, Kaiser Wilhelm II of Germany, and Czar Nicholas II of Russia were all first cousins through the Hanover family of Germany and England. Their grandmother was Queen Victoria. The cousins played together as children and teens in England while visiting their grandmother. As a boy, Kaiser Wilhelm was the odd man out, possibly due to his deformed left arm. On both fronts of World War I, the royal cousins would bleed the world for five years.

Before World War I, the European powers had been preparing for war for many years. Germany and England simultaneously built up their navies. Many history books proclaim the murder of Austria's Crown Prince Ferdinand on June 28, 1914, in Sarajevo as the start of World War I. It was more complicated than that.

On July 28, one month after the assassination, Austria declared war on Serbia. On July 31, Czar Nicholas II of Russia mobilized his army in response to German mobilization. Germany declared war on Russia on August 1. That same day, the Ottoman Empire's army was mobilized. On August 2, a secret treaty was signed between Germany and the Ottoman Empire to defend themselves against Russia.

Germany supported the Austrian-Hungarian ruler Franz Josef, a Habsburg Kaiser. Germany declared war on France on August 4. Great Britain declared war on Germany the same day. On August 5, Austria declared war on Russia.

Germany decided to attack France first. They wanted to take Paris within two months. Once France was on the defensive, Germany would attack Russia. Middle-class boys in Germany and England volunteered for their rulers, their country, and to experience the glory of war. They thought they would be home by Christmas. Instead, one million kids and young men were killed in the first three months.

Political leaders in London, Vienna, Berlin, Paris, and Moscow had chosen military escalation too soon. As in the previous centuries, the monarchs at war needed new soldiers to fill the ranks of those who were massacred. The machine gun was now perfected—it could fire 600 rounds in one minute. You only had to feed the bullets and keep the barrel cool.

Because England was a colonial power, the European war quickly became a World War. Soldiers came from the British Isles, Canada, India, and the African colonies to fight for the Empire.

The German Chief of Staff, General Helmuth von Moltke, was the symbol of German militarism. Excellent railways rapidly distributed soldiers in France.

The army moved so quickly that Moltke lost contact with them due to poor communication technology. They marched close to Paris.

The French commander, General Joseph Joffre, used the first wartime air reconnaissance to discover that the German front was about to break down. The French made a stand at the Marne River, holding back the Germans for seven days. Two million men fought over a distance of 300 miles.

After the battle, Moltke told the Kaiser that the war was lost. It was all over for the Germans, yet it would take four more years of bloodshed to end.

1915

Massive offences were planned for the spring of 1915. On the Eastern Front, the Austrians and Germans attacked the Russians at Galicia. Great Britain aimed their offensive at Istanbul. The Russians attacked the Ottomans in the Caucasus. On the Western Front, France decided to attack the Germans at Artois.

A new type of warfare evolved in Europe. Trenches were dug across 900 miles on the Western Front in France and Belgium and on the Eastern Front to Russia. The trenches became hell on earth. There, the inexperienced soldiers met water, mud, stench, diseases, rats, lice, and flies—not to mention bullets, grenades, and poisonous chemicals. The glory of war never appeared. By the end of 1915, over 3,150,000 men had been killed. They were all betrayed!

In 1915, Italy joined the war on the side of the Allies. Germany entered Poland. France and Great Britain entered Belgium. At Ypres, phosgene gas was used by the Germans on the French that December.

Beyond the war in Europe, the Ottoman Empire started the systematic mass murder of 1.5 million Armenians between 1915 and 1923. First, they arrested Armenians in Constantinople and Ankara. Men were massacred or forced into labor camps, where they died. Women, children, and the elderly were driven into the Syrian desert on death marches.

That same year, Japan declared war on Germany. They captured Chinese mines, railways, and harbors controlled by Germany.

1916

The war became bloodier and bloodier. All waring countries brought in millions of new soldiers. Families were torn apart.

Two major offensives in Verdun, France, took place in February and April 1916. The Germans gained control over the front line. The armies of Great Britain, Germany, and France bled to death that spring. Great Britain forced all men to join the military. On June 7, part of the French Army surrendered at Verdun.

At the Somme River, the battle began on July 1 and continued until November 18. In one day, 23,000 Englishmen were killed at Marmetz Wood. The military and their press lied to the people and spread more propaganda of an important victory for their men.

In 1916, the French and English decided how they would divide the Ottoman Empire into British and French areas of interest after WWI. Sykes-Picot was a secret agreement named for the British intelligence officer Mark Sykes and French diplomat Georges Picot. They drew a line in the sand to define British and French interests, not local, tribal, or religious interests. The French took Syria, Lebanon, Southeast Turkey, and Northern Iraq. The British took Palestine, Jordan, and Southern Iraq. The Kurdish people received nothing.

1917

A series of major events rapidly took place in Europe. Russia had advanced into Prussia on the Eastern Front. Four million Russian soldiers were killed by January 1917. The Russian advance helped Belgium, France, and England slow down the German war machine in the West.

In February, the war at sea was dominated by Germany. They threatened American supply ships with unrestricted submarine warfare.

Political revolution broke out in Russia on March 8. Czar Nicholas

II abdicated on March 12. Then the temporary Kerenski government took over.

On April 6, 1917, the USA declared war on Germany. President Wilson was given vast powers to build the American war machine.

The Germans wanted to end the war on their Eastern Front, so they allowed Lenin to leave Switzerland by train, arriving in Moscow on April 16. He worked for the Bolshevik Party in the revolution in Russia that created a communist government on October 24. This started a bloody civil war. A separate peace agreement between Russia and Germany was signed on December 22, 1917, at Brest-Litovsk, allowing the Germans to fight on one front.

On the Western Front, the French lost the Battle of Champagne on April 20th. French soldiers were desperate after four years of fighting, some decided to mutiny.

On June 26, the first of 2 million US troops arrived in France. General Pershing immediately asked for 4 million more. He did not get them. In Belgium, the third Battle of Ypres was fought from July to November under appalling conditions.

The British defeated the Ottoman Empire and captured Palestine on December 9, 1917. The Sykes-Picot agreement was implemented. Prime Minster Lloyd George wanted to give Palestine to the Jewish people. In his letter to the Zionist Baron Rothschild, Foreign Minister James Balfour declared that the British Empire considered a national Jewish state necessary for the Jewish people. This went into history as the Balfour Declaration of 1917. In Jerusalem, there were roughly 670,000 Muslims and 60,000 Jews. Both sides welcomed the British.

1918

On May 28, the US Third Division captured the southern part of Belleau Wood, only fifty-nine miles from Paris. A few days later, the marines fought at Château-Thierry, assisted by the French. They pushed the Germans back into the Belleau Wood. On June 5, they cleared the Germans out of the woods.

On July 15, the Second Battle of the Marne began. The Americans fought again at Château-Thierry on July 18. On August 8, the Germans

The Twentieth Century

were forced back to Armiens. The final offensives in the war were the Battles of the Meuse-Argonne.

The global influenza known as the Spanish flu was a factor in the battles of 1918. From 1918 to 1920, roughly 500 million people were infected.

On October 27, 1918, German General Ludendorff resigned. Shortly thereafter, Turkey and Austria-Hungary surrendered to the Allies at Compiegne.

On November 9, 1918, Kaiser Wilhelm II abdicated and moved to Holland, where he committed suicide. On November 10, the first German Republic was founded. On November 11 at 11 a.m., World War I was over.

In World War I, some 70 million soldiers served from one hundred countries on five continents. Thirty million were wounded and lamed. Eleven million soldiers were killed. An estimated 13 million civilians died. The European continent lay in ruins.

1919–1932

The first hearings of the Peace Conference began on January 18, 1919. England, France, Italy, and the United States made the big decisions. The defeated powers were not allowed to negotiate. Russia was not represented.

Who was to blame for the war: the British, the Germans, the Russians, the French, or all of the above? The victors decided to blame the losers for the war. The Germans were forced to pay reparations, placing the whole country in debt. This paved the way for Adolf Hitler, the Nazi Party, and World War II.

The conference lasted six months, and on June 28, the Germans signed the Treaty of Versailles. Morison summarizes: "It required Germany to admit her war guilt, stripped her of all colonies and commercial rights in Africa and the Far East, of Alsace-Lorraine, Posen, and parts of Schleswig and Silesia, rectified the Belgian boundary line, confiscated the coal mines of the Saar Basin, imposed military and naval disarmament upon her, saddled her with an immediate indemnity of $5 billion and a future reparation bill of indeterminate amount, and placed the whole of her economic system under temporary Allied control."[3]

Strive for Insight

One attempt to improve conditions in Germany and Europe was the founding of a new educational impulse on September 7, 1919. Lead by Rudolf Steiner, the Waldorf School in Stuttgart, Germany, was opened with pupils in eight grades, mostly from families of the factory for the Waldorf Astoria Cigarette Company. Steiner was an Austrian scientist, philosopher, and educator. He researched the human being for thirty-seven years before opening the school. Steiner used scientific principles to study the physical nature, soul nature, and spiritual nature of the human being. In over 200 lectures on education, Steiner taught the teachers how they could better understand children. Anthroposophy is the name of his spiritual science. It is built directly on the German Enlightenment.

In 1922, the Union of Soviet Socialist Republics (USSR) was formed as a one-party communist state. Its leader until 1924 was Vladimir Lenin of the Bolshevik Party, which won control of the Russia Empire after the October Revolution of 1917. After Lenin's death in 1924, Joseph Stalin became General Secretary of the Communist Party of the Soviet Union, based in Moscow.

The world empires continued to fall. In China, nationalists created a new government in Nanjing under Chiang Kai-shek in 1927. A civil war broke out. Zhou Enlai took control of the communists in March. Mao Zedong was captured by national troops but escaped to build the Red Army, supported by the farmers.

Military leaders in Japan wanted to control all 200 million people in Asia. They invaded Manchuria in 1931 to prepare for a full invasion of China, Southeast Asia, and Burma.

The French documentary *Decolonisation, du sang et des larmes*, by Pascal Blanchard and David Korn-Brzoza, portrays how the French Empire dissolved in twenty-five years. The empire included Ivory Coast, Vietnam, Madagascar, Syria, Lebanon, Morocco, Gabon, and Algeria. In the 1930s, new leaders and their people demanded respect, yet injustice and inequality ruled.

From 1919 to 1922, Gandhi led his noncooperation campaign. He was put in prison for two years, until 1924. There he read, prayed, and spun. In 1929, the Indian National Congress (INC) asked for full independence from the British Empire. They were refused.

From 1930 to 1931, Gandhi launched the civil disobedience and Salt Satyagraha campaign, using nonviolent methods to remove the British rule in India, which had started in 1757. The British had a monopoly on salt in India. Indians had to pay tax every time they bought it. The Salt March in March 1931 was an act of civil disobedience. Gandhi took some water and made his own salt from it. He had broken the Empire's Salt Law and was put in prison for eight months.

In 1931, Charlie Chaplin travelled 5,400 miles from Hollywood to London. At the same time, Gandhi travelled 4,400 miles from Bombay to London. While attending the Second India Round-Talk Conference to demand independence, Gandhi had asked if he could meet Chaplin, who was in the city for the premiere of his new film, *City Lights*. Two of the most famous people in the world met in a little house in the slum district off the East India Dock Road.

Gandhi stepped out of his taxi, dressed in a loin-cloth, and asked Chaplin to wave to the crowds with him. They went upstairs to a tiny room and sat on the couch. Gandhi had a big smile on his face. What should The Tramp say?

Chaplin wrote in his autobiography:

> "I felt all India was also waiting for my words. So I cleared my voice. 'Naturally I am in sympathy with India's aspirations and struggle for freedom,' I said. 'Nonetheless, I am somewhat confused by your abhorrence of machinery. After all, if machinery is used in the altruistic sense, it should help to release man from the bondage of slavery, and give him shorter hours of labour and time to improve his mind and enjoy life.'
>
> "Gandhi spoke calmly, 'I understand, but before India can achieve those aims, she must first rid herself of English rule. Machinery in the past has made us dependent on England, and the only way we can rid ourselves of that dependence is to boycott all goods made by machinery. That is why we have made it the patriotic duty

of every Indian to spin his own cotton and weave his own cloth. That is our form of attacking a very powerful nation like England.'"[4]

In that moment, Chaplin received the idea for his next film—*Modern Times*!

1933–1938

In 1933, Adolf Hitler was elected Prime Minister of Germany, giving the Nazi Party control over the country. Who made this possible? Hitler was the leader of the fascist National Socialist German Workers Party, abbreviated to NS. His co-workers were Ernst Rôhm, Rudolf Hess, Herman Goering, and Alfred Rosenberg. NS became a party of the people from all classes and locations. They were far-right, ultra-nationalistic, racist, and anti-democratic. Germans from the middle class, farmers, bureaucrats, workers, and even Catholics and Protestants supported them. Poor career opportunities brought young academicians to Hitler. As public jobs disappeared and the private sector shrank, the Nazis presented themselves both as revolutionaries and as conservatives who wanted to make Germany great again. They were the political party that denounced the Versailles Treaty and promised to save German industry and German farmers.

The party received many backers among the super-rich. Wealthy conservatives tried to use the Nazis to gain the support of the common people. They misunderstood Hitler. Among others, an older friend, Dietrich Eckart, introduced him to high society. At the end of 1922, Hitler appeared in Berlin at the National Club, whose elite members were businessmen, officers, professors, and bankers. The NS became accepted. Eckart also introduced Hítler to Henry Ford, the American industrialist who had written *The International Jew, A World Problem*. Ford sponsored Hitler with roughly $40,000 each year for mass rallies.

Wealthy women took Hitler to fancy hotels and parties. They gave him money, jewels, works of art, and brought him to music festivals. In July 1927, Elsa Bruckman introduced Hitler to the eighty-year-old Emil Kirdorf, a leader of heavy industry who hated unions and communists. Kirdorf joined the NS. Fritz Thyssen gave the Nazis loans and invited

Hitler to the Industry Club in Düsseldorf. Everyone wanted to hear what his plans were once he took power.

After the world financial crisis of 1929, many young Germans had no work, no money, and no future. Many fell into the hands of Hitler's Nazis. Hitler also won over many conservative parties.

In 1930, there were 2.5 million unemployed in German's Weimar Republic. In the elections that year, the Nazis gained 18% of the vote. A right-wing aristocrat, Kurt von Schleicher, wanted to use the Nazi Stormtroopers to control aristocrats and break the communists, social democrats, and labor movements.

On election day in 1933, the Nazis became the largest party in parliament, with 37% of the vote. Hitler's goal was to destroy democracy and become a dictator. Parliament was burned on February 27. The Nazis blamed it on the communists. President Hindenburg signed the Reichstag Fire decree, giving the Nazis emergency powers to imprison anyone and restrict civil liberties. Nazi segregation became official. Goering used the Stormtroopers, commanded by Ernst Röhm, to arrest 25,000 people in one week.

Parliament passed the Enabling Act to suspend parliament and restrict Jewish freedoms. Military build-up started secretly that year.

From Munich, Heinrich Himmler commanded the SS, a paramilitary group of fanatical Nazis that suppressed political opponents. Starting in 1933, hundreds of thousands were imprisoned in Dachau, outside Munich. It became a horrendous concentration camp where the Nazis gassed people.

Himmler controlled police forces in every state in Germany. Goering developed the Gestapo, a secret military police that removed gays, Jews, intellectuals, and anyone with anti-Nazi convictions.

Hitler also had the Storm Detachment (SA), a militia of 2 million young bullies commanded by Ernst Röhm, who also wanted control of the army's generals. Both Goering and Röhm wanted to be second-in-command to Hitler. Goering asked Himmler for help. They agreed that Goering would give Himmler the Gestapo if Goering used Himmler's SS force to take down Röhm and the SA. Hitler agreed to their plan, crushed the SA, and promoted Goering as his successor. The SS, under Himmler's command, became a separate power.

While the Nazis rearmed Germany to prepare for conquering the world, major revolutions were underway in India and China in 1933. Mohandas Gandhi started a three-week hunger strike in Yeravda Prison. He prayed for greater purification and watchfulness for the Harijan cause. On August 4, he was sentenced to one-year imprisonment. The fast caused serious health problems and he was brought to the Sassoon Hospital for treatment. That November, Gandhi started his 12,000-mile tour of India to protest social inequality. The Harijan cause strove to break inequality for the lowest caste, the untouchables, the people of God.

In China, the civil war raged between the communists, led by Mao Zedung and Zhou Enlai, and Chiang Kai Shek and the Kuomintang National Army. The Red Army suffered defeats in 1933 before carrying out the Long March from 1934 to October 1936. Only 60,000 men in the Red Army made it to Shaanxi Province to continue the revolution.

President Franklin Roosevelt was sworn in in 1933. He granted Saudi King Ibdal Said a concession to create the Arabian American Oil Company (Aramco) together with Standard Oil of California. The defense of Saudi Arabia was declared vital to American interests, making the USA dependent on Saudi oil.

Riots broke out in Palestine in October 1933, protesting the surge of Jewish immigrants fleeing Nazi Germany. The turmoil had begun at the end of World War I, when Britain and France carved up the lands of the defeated Ottoman Empire according to the Sykes-Picot agreement. In Mesopotamia, the British joined together three Ottoman provinces and named it Iraq. The southernmost of these provinces was dominated by Shiite Arabs, the central by Sunni Arabs, and the northernmost by non-Arab Kurds.

To the west of Iraq, the European powers took the opposite approach, carving Syria and Lebanon into small parcels under French rule. The British took Palestine and Transjordan, which would eventually become Israel and Jordan.

In the 1930s, hunger returned to the Ukraine and on the steppes north of the Caucasus. Josef Stalin led a government that systematically starved its own people to destroy the class of farmers who owned their own land, especially in the Ukraine and the Caucasus, where the best earth was. They resisted the Soviet collective agriculture programs. Massive arrests and punishment were normal. Cattle cars filled with prisoners were sent to Siberia. Crops were taken from the farmers. Grain disappeared. An estimated 3 to 7 million people died.

World War II, 1939–1944

The Nazis invaded Poland in 1939. One year later, they took Denmark and Norway, then France, Belgium, Luxembourg, and the Netherlands. The German Air Force set London on fire. The Royal Air Force forced the Germans into nighttime bombing. The Nazis invaded Greece and Yugoslavia, then the Soviet Union.

Goering instructed Heydrich to begin the Nazis' Final Solution Movement against the Jews in Germany. The Nazi goal was to remove the Jewish people from Europe and then the world. By 1946, 6 million Jews would be killed in the Holocaust. Other main targets were Roma, homosexuals, and political prisoners.

Two famous theoretical physicists born just after the turn of the century led their governments in developing the atomic bomb during WWII—Heisenberg for the Nazi Regime and Oppenheimer for the Allies.

Werner Heisenberg was a student of Max Born at the University of Göttingen. He had developed the idea of matrix formulation of quantum mechanics together with Born and Pascual Jordan. Heisenberg worked with Niels Bohr in Copenhagen in 1924 before he taught at Göttingen.

The Nazi nuclear weapons program was started by the military in September 1939. Heisenberg was made the head of the Nazi nuclear weapon project. In 1942, he gave a lecture for the Army Weapons Office entitled "The theoretical basis for energy generation from nuclear fission." That year, the army gave up control of the German nuclear weapons program. Only seventy scientists had worked for the program. The number of scientists working on applied nuclear fission diminished dramatically.

In 1939, Albert Einstein and other refugee scientists recommended to President Roosevelt that the USA start its own nuclear weapon

Strive for Insight

research to keep pace with the work being done by the Nazis. J. Robert Oppenheimer led the secret weapons laboratory at Los Alamos, New Mexico, after joining the Manhattan Project in 1942. His job was to develop a fast neutron chain reaction in an atomic bomb.

The Japanese military also wanted to conquer the world. A new government in Japan was created by General Hideki Tojo. They attacked the USA at Pearl Harbor on December 7, 1941. Two thousand five hundred soldiers were killed, half of them onboard the Battleship Arizona.

For close to a year, the Japanese were unstoppable. They took Guam and the Wake Islands. They attacked the Philippines, Burma, the Dutch East Indies, and the Malay Peninsula. A few months later, they captured Manila, Rangoon, Singapore, and Jakarta. By early 1942, Bataan and Corregidor in the Philippines were the only places that American forces held on for several months.

After the bombing of Pearl Harbor, the Japanese wanted to strike the fatal blow to the USA as quickly as possible. They outnumbered the Americans in aircraft carriers ten to three.

At the Battle of Midway on June 4, 1942, Douglass SBD Dauntless dive bombers left the USS Enterprise and the USS Yorktown to attack the Japanese fleet. The dive bombers aimed their aircraft in a vertical dive of sixty to eighty degrees at the target, dropped their bombs, and pulled up abruptly. Richard Halsey Best was a squadron commander on the USS Enterprise. He was the only pilot to successfully dive bomb and sink two aircraft carriers in one day. At Midway, the navy sank four aircraft carriers and two destroyers and acquired Midway Island for further attacks.

The next plan was to take the Solomon Islands, then the Philippines, then the island of Japan. Guadalcanal was the first Solomon Island attacked. In February 1943, the island fell after seven months. Then New Georgia fell in June.

On November 1, the invasion fleet was in position off Bougainville, the northernmost island. Crawling down the rope ladder along the side of the ship into the invasion boat at 6:45 a.m., Edward Steven Walker entered the world stage for the first time. He was a twenty-two-year-old native of Peckville, Pennsylvania. Walker was assigned to the 12th Marines in the Third Division. His landing boat motored through Empress Bay and landed at 7:40 along the beach. The marines advanced three miles inland along the Numanu trail. By November 15, they had gained one thousand yards. Jungle warfare was new to them. For the next four weeks, it was attack, counterattack, retreat, and advance.

At Peva Forks, Walker's battalion was sent to the high ground on the left flank under heavy enemy fire on November 19. They shot it out at point blank range, with the enemy often only ten yards away.

The next summer, in July 1944, the US Marines engaged 19,000 Japanese troops on the island of Guam. Walker landed with the Third Battalion on the northern beach above the peninsula. The Japanese collected 5,000 troops for an all-out counterattack. The marines from the north linked with marines from the south and cut them off. That midnight, the Japanese charged in hand-to-hand combat. The Americans held their ground, but 8,000 died in Guam. The island became a training base and a flight base for B29 bombers to attack mainland Japan.

1945

By the middle of February 1945, the 3rd Marine Division left Guam for participation in the Iwo Jima operation. Iwo Jima, a tiny volcanic island, had no water, no vegetation, no trees, merely volcanic ash beaches. The rest of the island was volcanic rock. To the south stood Mount Surabachi, to the north were the airfields the US wanted for bombing campaigns against the island of Japan.

The Japanese underground defense went five stories below the earth. They had a maze of volcanic caves and sixteen miles of underground tunnels. The enemy built 1,500 pillboxes, miles of sulfur tunnels, and placed thousands of artillery in the caves. They made the marines go in and get them.

On February 25, the marines launched an attack. Progress was very slow and casualties heavy during the first few days of fighting. The marines slowly pushed the enemy back and by March 3 had occupied positions overlooking the sea. At Kitano Point on 16 March, units of the 3rd Marine Division delivered the final attack of the Iwo Jima operation.

By mid-April 1945, the division was back in Guam preparing for the next operation. On August 3, 1945, they received plans for Operation Olympic—the attack on the island of Japan.

Edward Walker served his country for twenty-six months in three major campaigns. Like many other unknown heroes, he received no medals. When he returned to Scranton, he joined the state police at Blakely Barracks.

The War in Europe

In Europe, the Allied bombing of Dresden began on February 13. Within two minutes, 500 tons of explosives and 375 tons of firebombs were dropped on the city. Fire storms broke out with temperatures between 2,700 and 3,600 degrees Fahrenheit on the streets. Two days later, the bombing ended. At least 25,000 people were killed. Was civilian bombing necessary?

In April 1945, the Allied forces covered a 200-mile line from Bavaria in the south to Hanover in the north. They drove east to Berlin, only 150 miles away. This was the largest field command in American history, a total of 1.3 million soldiers under the command of General Omar Bradley.

In June 1944, Bradley had commanded the First Army in the landing on the beaches of Normandy. He commanded the Twelfth Army Group as they liberated France, successfully fought the Battle of the Bulge in the winter of 1945, and crossed the Rhine on March 22, led by General George Patton.

Under Generals Zhukov and Konev, the Red Army raced to Berlin from the east, with a force of 2.5 million men divided into 20 armies with 150 divisions. The Russians had 6,000 tanks, 7,500 aircraft, 40,000 artillery pieces, and close to 100,000 motor vehicles. Eisenhower asked Bradley for his advice on how to prevent these huge armies from colliding and fighting near Berlin.

Bradly wrote: "The obvious alternative to so hazardous a head-on meeting lay in a visible line of demarcation, a line on which both forces could be halted and held. Obviously, it would have to be some easily recognizable terrain feature. After studying the map Eisenhower and I agreed the Elbe River offered the likeliest bet."[5]

The Twentieth Century

On April 11, General Simpson's Ninth Army reached the river Elbe after racing 120 miles in ten days. Simpson could be in Berlin in twenty-four hours, but at what price? Bradley thought it would cost 100,000 men to take Berlin. These men were needed to attack the island of Japan later that fall. On April 14, Eisenhower brought the American troops to a halt at the Elbe.

Now American troops had to wait for Josef Stalin to take Berlin. They considered him as destructive as Hitler. In the great terror of the 1930s, Stalin had arrested 1.6 million people and executed 680,000 in the Soviet Union. Five million starved and 17 million were sent to Siberia.

On Victory in Europe Day, May 8, 1945, the Red Army held Berlin. The Battle of Berlin had cost 80,000 Soviet lives and 280,000 were injured.

In July, the Americans, British, and French troops took over their occupation zones in Berlin and Western Germany. At the Yalta Conference in February 1945, Roosevelt, Stalin, and Churchill had agreed on the details for dividing Germany. In the West, there was a French section, an English section, and an American section. In the East, there was a Soviet Union section. Berlin and Germany were divided in two.

By 1945, the Manhattan Project had 6,000 employees at Los Alamos. Oppenheimer directed the theoretical and experimental studies. The world's first atomic bomb exploded on July 16, 1945, at Alamogordo, New Mexico.

At 8:15 on the morning of August 6, 1945, the world's first deployed atomic bomb, nicknamed Little Boy, was dropped over Hiroshima, Japan. It exploded 2,000 feet over the city of 350,000 people, destroying 90% of the city and immediately killing 80,000 people.

What next?

CHAPTER 3

The Twentieth Century

1945-1999

The World Stage

What next?
Three days later, a larger plutonium atomic bomb, nicknamed Fat Man, exploded over Nagasaki. By the end of that day, August 9, 1945, the bomb had killed an estimated 75,000 Japanese civilians.

Emperor Hirohito announced Japan's surrender on August 15. The Americans cancelled their attack on mainland Japan. Foreign Minister Mamoru Shigemitsu signed the surrender agreement aboard the US Battleship Missouri on September 2, ending the Second World War.

The American Empire

The turning point for the American Empire came in 1945. The USA dotted the Earth with hundreds of armed bases, ready to intervene anywhere with its massive military. The American Empire was to save the world from communism and fight for democracy. America replaced the British Empire with a new capitalism by intervening in world affairs, especially in business. The US had 7% of the world's population but possessed 40% of global income, half the world's manufacturing output, and three-quarters of the world's gold reserves. Politicians called it a World Order rather than an Empire.

After World War II, the US backed the British, French, and Dutch attempts to regain their empires in Asia and Africa. None of them were successful. The Netherlands left Indonesia. Great Britain would leave Kenya, Ceylon, and Burma. On August 15, 1947, India finally gained independence. Religious violence broke out and Pakistan became a separate country.

The US feared that when the Europeans lost their colonies, the new countries may become communist allies of the Soviet Union. The West would lose important economic opportunities.

The initiatives of the American Empire from 1945 until today are important concepts for high school students to develop. What is the true nature of empire building in world history? What is the American version of empire? In this book, you will discover how the USA colonized itself. Millions of Native Americans were removed from their land to make way for the Europeans. We brought in Africans to work in slave colonies on our own soil. Rather than colonizing their own countries, France, England, Germany, and the Netherlands created colonies far away from home. When they left, there was no accountability for their actions. After the Civil War in America, the whites, immigrants, slaves, and Native people lived in the same states, valleys, and cities. Fear, anger, and hate continued to grow.

If you love someone, the love is in your heart. You choose to give it away unconditionally. If you hate someone, the hate sits in your brain and your instincts. The hate you carry within makes you dull. Your hate-filled mental images repeat themselves instinctively. Your concepts of hate become rigid for the rest of your life. You no longer notice the hate within you. This can lead to violence.

Universal Human Rights

After the destruction of WWII and the use of two atomic bombs against Japan, the world community was in shock. The need for genuine change was clear. One area of great importance was human rights. On December 10, 1948, the United Nations General Assembly approved the

The Twentieth Century

Universal Declaration of Human Rights. It states that "all human beings are born free and equal in dignity and rights regardless of race, color, sex, language, religion, political, or other opinion, national or social origin, property, birth, or other status. Everyone has the right to life, liberty and security of person."[6] There are thirty articles, which I have summarized below.

The declaration prohibits slavery, torture, degrading treatment, or punishment. Everyone has the right to recognition as a person before the law. There may be no arbitrary arrests or exile, no interfering with privacy, family, home, or correspondence.

Many countries have written the Universal Declaration of Human Rights into national law, making it legally binding for their citizens. If it is law in your country, your reputation may not be attacked. You are presumed innocent until proven guilty. You have the right to freedom of movement and residence within the borders of each state. You may leave and return to your country. You may seek asylum from persecution. You have the right to nationality, to marry, and to start a family. In marriage, you are entitled to equal rights. No one may be deprived of property, freedom of thought, conscience, and religion. You have the right to freedom of opinion, peaceful assembly, and association. You may take part in the government of your country. You have free choice of employment, protection against unemployment, and the right to equal pay for equal work.

You may form and join trade unions. Reasonable working hours and holidays with pay are also your right. In the event of unemployment, sickness, disability, old age, or other circumstances beyond your control, you have the right to security. In motherhood and childhood, you are entitled to special care.

All children should enjoy the same social protection. Elementary education should be free and compulsory. Parents have a prior right to choose the kind of education that shall be given to their children. You may participate in the cultural life of the community, enjoy the arts, and share in scientific advancement.

Strive for Insight

Postwar Europe

After WWII, for the second time that century, large parts of Europe lay in ruins. The continent was paralyzed. Would the real Europe ever come back? In 1948, the Marshall Plan was implemented to revive the economy of Western Europe. This time, the victors of WWII had learned not to seek war reparations, such as in the Treaty of Versailles twenty-five years earlier.

By 1950, Western Europe needed economic and political unions. The first step was taken in 1951, when France and West Germany formed the European Coal and Steel Community. On March 25, 1957, France, West Germany, Italy, The Netherlands, Belgium, and Luxembourg signed the Treaty of Rome, which established the European Economic Community (EEC) to improve trade between European countries.

Britain joined the EEC, along with Ireland and Denmark, in 1973. Greece joined in 1981, Portugal and Spain in 1986. In 1993, the European Union (EU) was formed through the Maastricht Treaty, which called for a common defense policy, a European Parliament, a Central European Bank, and the Euro.

Liberation of French Colonies

The 110 million people still under French rule in 1945 demanded respect, an end to injustice, and the removal of forced labor. Colonization was a civilization of betrayal. It would take twenty-five more years for the entire French Empire to dissolve.

First, Syria and Lebanon become independent of the French Empire in 1946. In the West Indies, Guadeloupe, Martinique, French Guiana, and the Antilles would become independent. In Africa, Algeria, Chad, Cameroon, Congo, Gabon, Senegal, Ivory Coast, Madagascar, Morocco, and Tunisia would become free.

Cambodia, Laos, and Vietnam were in full rebellion. French-Indochina was formed in 1887. During the Second World War, the Japanese ruled Vietnam. They allowed the communists to control the country. Communist leader Ho Chi Minh left China to fight for national independence in Vietnam.

The Twentieth Century

After the Japanese surrendered, the French Indochina War began on September 2, 1945, when Ho declared Vietnam a free country. The war raged for eight years. The final battle started on March 13, 1954. It lasted fifty-five days. The Asian nationalist army of Vietnam, with 300,000 soldiers, defeated France at Dien Bien Phu. Five thousand French were killed, eleven thousand captured. On July 20, 1954, France negotiated a ceasefire and retreated.

The American War in Vietnam, 1954–1975

In 1954, Vietnam was split above and below the 17th parallel. Ho Chi Minh controlled the North and Emperor Bao controlled the South. Ho had allies in South Vietnam called the Vietcong. In 1955, Ngo Dinh Diem removed Bao and set up the new Republic of South Vietnam. The goal for America was to create a non-communist South Vietnam, otherwise Southeast Asia—Laos, Cambodia, Burma, Thailand, Malaysia, and even the Philippines—could fall to communist control. This would threaten India to the west and Australia and New Zealand to the south. To the north, Taiwan, Korea, and Japan could also be endangered. They called this the Domino Theory—if one nation fell, all other nations would fall like bricks. Since 1944, the West had already lost Estonia, Latvia, Lithuania, Poland, Czechoslovakia, Hungary, China, and North Korea.

On April 29, 1961, President Kennedy sent a 400-man Special Forces team for training in Vietnam. One year later, Kennedy secretly increased the number of soldiers by 16,000 men.

In January 1964, the Joint Chiefs of Staff decided to expand the war and strike North Vietnam to slow down the Vietcong's invasion of South Vietnam.

Defense Secretary Robert McNamara knew that Ho Chi Minh's Vietcong controlled 90% of the provinces along the Mekong Delta, south of Saigon. On March 17, President Johnson asked the military to plan the bombing. During WWII, McNamara and Chief of Staff of the Air Force, General Curtis Lemay, had been involved in massive civil fire-bombing in Germany and Japan.

On August 2, 1964, the North Vietnamese attacked the USS Maddox.

Strive for Insight

President Johnson used the attack in the Gulf of Tonkin Resolution of August 7, 1964, in which Congress gave President Johnson the right to wage war without their approval. No longer did Congress have to declare war. This broke the balance of power in our Constitution. American Foreign Policy was changed forever.

While America bombed North Vietnam, the 250,000 Vietcong soldiers pushed farther south in their underground tunnels. No matter what losses the Vietcong suffered, they quickly regrouped and fought again. South Vietnam continued to collapse under its unpopular military dictatorship.

On November 3, 1964, Johnson was elected president and controlled Congress. A few weeks later, the question of massive bombing campaigns was taken up by General Curtis Le May of the Air Force, Admiral David McDonald of the Navy, and General Wally Green of the Marine Corps. They wanted heavy bombing campaigns and 600,000 more troops.

On February 13, 1965, the decision was made to launch Operation Rolling Thunder, massive B-52 bombing raids. Two thousand marines started ashore at Danang on March 8. The president sent in 22,000 more troops one month later. By June 15, the United States had 82,000 solders in Vietnam. The bombing was not succeeding. The president sent Pennsylvania Governor Scranton to evaluate the situation. When the governor returned, he told Johnson that the USA could never win the war in Vietnam. Johnson never spoke with Scranton again.

In May of 1965, the Vietcong began their Spring Offensive, systematically destroying South Vietnamese units. On June 7, General Westmoreland asked for 200,000 more American soldiers. Now what should President Johnson do? His civilian advisors—Walt Rostow, McGeorge Bundy, Robert McNamara, Dean Rusk, Earle Wheeler, and John McNaughton—urged him to escalate the war. The Joint Chiefs talked of sending one million more men into the war. Only the president could make that decision, not Congress. On July 28, Johnson decided to increase the number of men serving in Vietnam to 125,000. The South Vietnamese had 514,000 soldiers.

The Ho Chi Minh Trail was busy in 1966, though it was bombed every seven minutes. American coalition ground forces made little progress. In

June, the military began bombing North Vietnam oil storage at Hanoi and Haiphong.

On April 4, 1967, Martin Luther King Jr. spoke at Riverside Church in Upper Manhattan. He joined other leaders in attacking the government's conduct of the Vietnam War. King stated that racism went hand in hand with the evils of poverty and militarism that kept the country from living up to its ideals. He warned, "The image of America will never again be the image of revolution, freedom, and democracy, but the image of violence and militarism."[7] King called for the United States to halt all bombing.

In the same speech, King condemned the activities of the American Empire in South America. "During the past ten years we have seen emerge a pattern of suppression which now has justified the presence of military *advisors* in Venezuela. This need to maintain social stability for our investments accounts for the counter-revolutionary action of American forces in Guatemala. It tells why American helicopters are being used against guerrillas in Colombia and why American napalm and green beret forces have already been active against rebels in Peru."[8]

King's call was not heard. Six years later, on September 11, Nixon and Kissinger supported the military coup in Chile to remove the government of President Allende, who wanted to nationalize industries, especially copper.

By the summer of 1967, the United States had 470,000 troops in Vietnam; draft calls exceeded 30,000 a month. General Westmoreland wanted an increase of 680,000 mostly young people your age. The USA had already suffered 15,058 casualties and 109,527 wounded.

In October 1967, 35,000 Americans demonstrated against the Vietnam War in front of the Pentagon in Washington while the ground fighting in South Vietnam intensified. The North Vietnamese attacked near Saigon and in the Highlands.

Defense Secretary McNamara argued in a 1967 memo to the president that more troops and bombing would not win the war. He suggested that the United States declare victory and slowly withdraw. Nevertheless, Johnson increased the troop commitment to nearly 550,000. Before he was fired at the end of 1967, McNamara commissioned the Report of

Strive for Insight

the Office of the Secretary of Defense Vietnam Task Force, explaining the history of the United States' involvement in Vietnam from 1945 to 1967, known as the *Pentagon Papers*.

Sitting at home in front of their televisions, evening after evening, millions of Americans watched the Vietcong attack cities and towns with 70,000 soldiers between January and March 1968. This was the Tet Offensive. In May 1968, Johnson opened the Paris Peace Talks.

A network of connecting underground tunnels was located in the CùChi District of Saigon. In the tunnels, North Vietnamese soldiers were hiding. They used the tunnels for communication, supplies, hospitals, food, and weapons. The tunnels were the base for the Tet Offensive in 1968. B-52s, jet fighters, helicopters, and heavy artillery bombed the area above the CùChi tunnels. Then tanks and troops destroyed the land. Yet the Americans could not destroy the Vietcong bases or their war supplies. Something very wrong was happening.

Many Vietcong escaped in the 153-mile-long tunnel system. From 6 a.m. until 3 p.m. every day, the Vietcong avoided fighting.

In January 1969, Richard Nixon became president. Thirty-one thousand American soldiers had already died in Vietnam. Nixon promised to pull back 325,000 troops by 1971. His national security advisor, Henry Kissinger, wanted to attack the Vietcong in Cambodia while rebuilding the South Vietnamese Army to make them fully responsible for the war efforts. In April 1970, Nixon secretly authorized bombing campaigns and a ground invasion of neutral Cambodia. Forty thousand US troops were sent by Nixon into Cambodia. This prompted massive anti-war demonstrations across America.

On May 4, 1970, National Guard troops shot into a group of protesters at Kent State University, killing four students who were demonstrating against the invasion of Cambodia. On May 15, two college students were killed at Jackson State University in Mississippi. A total of 484 campuses were closed. The National Guard were called out in sixteen states.

Whistleblower Daniel Ellsberg leaked portions of the *Pentagon Papers* to the *New York Times*. On June 13, 1971, 7,000 pages were made public. On June 15, 1971, the Supreme Court voted 6–3 for the freedom of the press paragraph to allow the printing of the *Pentagon Papers*.

The Twentieth Century

Between 1961 and 1971, about 5 million Vietnamese and allied soldiers were exposed to dioxin, a toxic chemical sprayed in Agent Orange. Science has identified an association between exposure to Agent Orange and some forms of cancer, reproductive abnormalities, immune deficiencies, and nervous system damage. The Vietnam Red Cross recorded over 4.8 million deaths and 400,000 children born with birth defects due to Agent Orange.

In 1972, Nixon ordered Operation Linebacker, the bombing of the Ho Chi Minh trail. B-52 bombers dropped napalm bombs that caused severe burns all over the body. The substance was used from 1965 to 1972. Napalm was a mixture of plastic polystyrene, hydrocarbon benzene, and gasoline. It stuck to everything and melted the flesh. The only way to put the fire out was to smother it, causing even more pain. One of the most iconic photographs taken during the Vietnam War shows children fleeing from a napalm strike on June 8, 1972, on Highway 1. The little girl from the photograph, Kim Phuc, stated "Napalm is the most terrible pain you can imagine. Water boils at 212°F. Napalm generates temperatures of 1,500–2,200°F."[9] Kim Phuc sustained third degree burns to most of her body. She was one of the only survivors.

In May 1975, the Vietnam War ended. South Vietnam vanished.

The Cold War

In March 1946, in Fulton, Missouri, Winston Churchill gave his speech envisioning an Iron Curtain over Europe. The curtain consisted of political and military barriers created by the Soviets to prevent contact with European countries and non-communist regions. It was removed forty-five years later, in 1991.

On April 4, 1949, the North Atlantic Treaty was signed in Washington, D.C. The original members of NATO were the USA, Canada, Portugal, Italy, Norway, Denmark, and Iceland. The members agreed that an armed attack against any of them would be considered an attack against them all.

The Soviet Union countered in 1955 with the Warsaw Pact, joined by Hungary, Czechoslovakia, Poland, Bulgaria, Romania, and East Germany. Two sides in the Cold War were clearly established, NATO vs. the Warsaw Pact.

Strive for Insight

The Cold War turned into an arms race as well. By 1960, the USA had 25,000 atomic bombs, the Soviet Union had 2,500.

The Cuban Missile Crisis of October 1962 began when photographs of Soviet ballistic missiles in Cuba were made public. It ended on November 20 after President Kennedy agreed to remove NATO missiles from Italy and Turkey, while First Secretary Khrushchev removed Soviet missiles from Cuba.

After 2.5 million people had fled the country, East Germany built the Berlin Wall in 1961. For twenty-eight years, until November 9, 1989, it divided the city.

In 1991, Mikhail Gorbachev ended the Cold War, removed the totalitarian regime in Russia, permitted free voting, a free press, freedom of religion, and multiple political parties. East and West Germany were re-united. He followed the flow of history. On August 24, 1991, the Ukrainian Parliament declared itself independent of Russia.

Then Yugoslavia dissolved into separate states. The Bosnian war reached its terrible climax in July 1995 when the Dutch UN contingent abandoned Srebrenica and enabled the worst massacre of civilians on European soil since WWII. Eight thousand Bosnian Muslim boys and men were killed by Serbian military leaders between July 11 and 19. The UN Security Council authorized bombing by the USA. The Bosnian War ended with the Dayton Agreement.

The People's Republic of China Declared

On October 1, 1949, at Tiananmen Gate in Beijing, Mao Zedong declared the founding of the People's Republic of China. He slowly took over the entire nation. In December 1952, transition to Chinese socialism was adopted. The First Five-Year Plan was put into effect between 1953 and 1957.

The Great Leap Forward was a rapid industrialization project between 1958 and 1960. Widespread starvation and poverty spread as millions of people were moved out of the countryside to work in industry. Those who remained in the country were forced into new farms. Dutch-British historian Frank Dikötter is convinced that close to 45 million people died in the process. It was genocide without war.

The Twentieth Century

The Cultural Revolution was initiated by Mao Zedong to remove capitalist traitors in the Communist Party, military, and government. Countless Chinese were wrongly accused and mistreated between 1966 and 1976. The economy fell apart. Police took over schools. Foreign culture was eliminated. Today, the party considers it a calamity. New economic reforms and adjustments were made after the great setbacks of the Cultural Revolution. Both Zhou Enlai and Mao Zedong died in 1976.

On the night of June 3, 1989, People's Liberation Army troops entered Tiananmen Square to stop the student protests in Beijing from spreading across China. The students wanted a dialogue, not a revolution. They had protested since April. One day after the soldiers had fired into the crowd, the famous photograph of the unknown "Tank Man" was made public. He stood alone in front of a column of tanks, holding a shopping bag.

In 1990, stock exchanges were opened in Shenzhen and Shanghai. A modern corporate system was proposed in 1993, followed by China-Foreign trade reform. On July 1, 1997, the Hong Kong administrative region was founded in accordance with Great Britain.

The Middle East

Jerusalem is the Jews' most holy city, the Christians' second-most holy city after Rome, and the Muslims' third-most holy city after Mekka and Medina. Relations between these three religions in the region are essential for peace.

The State of Israel was proclaimed in 1948. By 1967, the population of Israel reached 2.7 million. That year, Egypt moved troops into the Sinai on May 15. They wanted to continue the blockade of Israeli shipping in the Straits of Tiran. On June 5, Israel responded with a surprise attack that put the Egyptian Air Force out of action. At the same time, the Israeli Army occupied most of the Gaza Strip. Facing an Arab coalition of Egypt, Jordan, and Syria, Israel entered the West Bank, which includes East Jerusalem. They displaced 325,000 Palestinians. Israel also entered the Golan Heights, displacing 100,000 Syrians. The occupation continues to this day.

Strive for Insight

In the Yom Kippur War of October 6 to 25, 1973, another Arab coalition invaded the Golan Heights and the Sinai Peninsula. After Israel entered Egypt along the Suez Canal, a ceasefire was negotiated by the UN. On March 26, 1979, a peace treaty was signed in Washington.

Israel officially annexed Palestinian East Jerusalem in 1980. In the Oslo agreement from 1993, Palestine was given limited self-government in parts of the West Bank and the Gaza Strip. Since then, Israel has illegally occupied and built homes on the West Bank. The negotiations for a two-state solution have stood still. Islamic extremists replaced the Palestine Liberation Organization, among them Hamas, which was formed in 1987.

Creating a Muslim Society

After a CIA-led coup in 1953, the Shah took over Iran to prevent the democratic government from nationalizing its rich oil reserves. The Shah ruled as a monarch until he was removed by the Iranian Revolution in 1979. On February 1, Ayatollah Khomeini became the leader of the Islamic Republic of Iran.

In 1979, Saddam Hussein became president of Iraq. Hussein invaded Iran, where a proxy war between Iraq and Iran raged from 1980 to 1988. The USA and Saudi Arabia supported Saddam Hussein; the Soviet Union supported Iran. Eight years of trench warfare, civilian bombing, and chemical weapons killed over half a million people.

The USA was dependent on the oil and gas from Saudi Arabia, who paid their oil transactions in dollars. During the 1980s and 1990s, the monarchy and clerics of Saudi Arabia are suspected of financing international jihad, supporting Muslim fighters in Afghanistan, Pakistan, Indonesia, the Philippines, Chechnya, Bosnia, Nigeria, and the West Bank and Gaza.

In his book of 1964, *Signposts on the Path*, the Egyptian scholar Sayyid Qutb declared the path to the creation of a truly Muslim society. "Those who accepted this program would form a vanguard of dedicated fighters, using every means, including *jihad*, which should not be undertaken until the fighters had achieved inner purity, but should then be pursued, if necessary, not for defense only, but to destroy all worship of false gods and remove all the obstacles which prevented men from accepting Islam. The struggle should aim at creating a universal Muslim society in which there were no distinctions of race, and one which was worldwide. The western age is finished: it could not provide the values which were needed to support the new material civilization. Only Islam offered hope to the world."[10]

Mujahidin freedom fighters defended Afghanistan from the Soviets in the 1980s. They were partners with the Saudis and the USA. Some of them formed Al Qaeda in 1988 together with Osama bin Laden. In 1994, Osama bin Laden was stripped of his citizenship in Saudi Arabia. From Afghanistan, he declared war on the USA and carried out attacks in Saudi Arabia. Yet the CIA continued to train his Mujahidin forces in Afghanistan. After the Soviets left Afghanistan, the Mujahidin remained. The Taliban controlled most of Afghanistan from 1996 to 2001. In Afghanistan, Al Qaeda prepared the 9/11 attack on the USA.

The National Stage

Changes on the national stage arose from the new roles of the American Empire. Government agencies and policies were adjusted to being a superpower. The National Security Act of 1947 moved the War and Navy Departments into a new Department of Defense. The National Security Council (NSC) at the White House and the Central Intelligence Agency (CIA) were formed.

That same year, unexpected messages appeared from Oraibi in the Arizona desert. The Hopi elders were deeply shocked by the explosion of two atomic bombs over Japan. As a contribution to world peace, they decided to make their ancient teachings public. In 1949, they invited Oswald White Bear Fredericks and Frank Waters to write down their creation stories. The stories tell of the Third World destroyed by floods. When the people entered this Fourth World, they landed on the shore of North America.

Sótuknang, the nephew of their Creator, spoke: "This is the World Complete. You will find out why. It is not all beautiful and easy like the previous ones. It has height and depth, heat and cold, beauty and barrenness. It has everything you want to choose from. What you choose will determine if this time you can carry out the plan of the Creation on it or whether it must in time be destroyed too."[11]

Anti-Communism

Since 1950, Senator Joseph McCarthy had terrorized the nation with charges in his Senate committee that nearly every branch of the government had been infiltrated by communists. He spread fear to destroy the careers of men and women in the military, State Department, Congress, and universities. He even accused the Democratic Party of treason. President Eisenhower decided not to confront him.

On March 9, 1954, Edward R. Murrow spoke out against McCarthy on his television program, *See It Now*. Murrow was a well-known WWII wartime correspondent. He criticized McCarthy's tactics of using demagogy, insinuations, half-truths, and utter falsehoods. That same night, the army released its report that resulted in the condemnation of McCarthy by the American public and the United States Senate. Three years later, McCarthy died of complications from acute alcoholism. Yet damage to the country was done.

From 1945 to 1975, the House of Representatives continued their House Committee on Un-American Activities. Hollywood stars, folk singer Pete Seeger, and many university students and faculty were blacklisted and accused of associations with communists. Fear of being a commie in America grew.

Segregation Confronted

Slavery had lasted in America for 256 years—from the day the first slaves went ashore in Virginia in 1619 until Congress proclaimed the Thirteenth Amendment on December 18, 1865. Though slavery was outlawed, segregation became firmly established, based on the Jim Crow laws in many states. The goal was to separate people and treat them differently. The US military was segregated. Education, professional sports, and entertainment were governed by Jim Crow laws. In train cars, steamboats, buses, hotels, restaurants, and prisons, the races were separated. It was an extension of American slavery and colonization.

Built into the separation was an artificial hierarchy of class. The white classes were considered superior, and the classes of Asians, Latinos, and Blacks were considered inferior. To this day, the class system gives power and wealth to the few and poverty to the rest.

Historian Isabel Wilkerson writes in her book, *Caste, The Origins of Our Discontent*, "As a means of assigning value to entire swaths of humankind, caste guides each of us often beyond the reaches of our awareness. It embeds into our bones an unconscious ranking of human characteristics and sets forth the rules, expectations, and stereotypes that have been used to justify brutalities against entire groups within our species. In the American caste system, the signal of rank is what we call race, the division of humans on the basis of their appearance."[12]

For eighty-eight years, between 1877 and 1965, the American version of segregation was considered normal by many people. In contrast, segregation under the Nazis in Germany lasted for twelve years, from 1933 to 1945.

We turn briefly to the world stage to better understand possibilities for reconciliation in America. In South Africa, segregation was called "apartheid," which meant "apart-ness." The Apartheid Laws lasted for forty-six years, from 1948 until 1994. What can Americans learn from the aftermath of segregation in South Africa? Nelson Mandela had been in prison for twenty-eight years before he became president of South Africa. Together with Archbishop Desmond Tutu, he founded the Truth and Reconciliation Commission (TRC) to create forgiveness, trust, and accountability among white and Black South Africans. Perpetrators received amnesty for meeting the families of victims and telling them what really happened to their loved ones.

In her book, *A Human Being Died That Night*, South African psychologist Pumla Gobodo-Madikizela tells how she helped Eugene de Kock admit to state murders. Nicknamed Prime Evil, de Kock was considered the most brutal of all police operatives during apartheid. He served twenty years in prison, where Gobodo-Madikizela interviewed him many times between 1997 and 2002. When people tell their stories of civil rights abuses and have learned to forgive, they bring a moral achievement towards ending generations of violence.

Gobodo-Madikizela writes:

> "The question is no longer whether victims can forgive 'evildoers' but whether we—our symbols, language, and politics, our legal, media, and academic institutions—are creating the conditions that encourage alternatives to revenge . . .
>
> Dialogue, of course, will not solve every problem faced by a society that has suffered sustained violence on a large scale. But dialogue does create avenues for broadening our models of justice and for healing deep fractures in a nation by unearthing, acknowledging, and recording what has been done. It humanizes the dehumanized and confronts perpetrators with their inhumanity. Through dialogue, victims as well as the greater society come to recognize perpetrators as human beings who failed morally, whether through coercion, the perverted convictions of a warped mind, or fear."
>
> "Far from relieving the pressure on them, recognizing the most serious criminals as human intensifies it, because society is thereby able to hold them to greater moral accountability. Indeed, demonizing, as monsters those who commit evil lets them off too easily. Managed carefully, dialogue condemns—but not too hastily, lest it foreshorten the accountability process and, perversely excuses the criminal by dismissing him into the category of the hopelessly, radically other. Sustained, engaged, ordered dialogue thus forces an offender to unearth what moral sensibilities he has buried under a façade of 'obedience to orders' or righteous 'duty to my country' and to face what he has done, not in the heady climate of the period of mayhem but in the sobering atmosphere of reflection on ordinary human lives now shattered."[13]

How would the criminal re-enter human community? Would he regain a sense of himself as a human being? She discovered that it was not enough to ignore a person who is in the abyss, even a former criminal.

The Twentieth Century

There must be a community with people to embrace the individual's remorse and humanity. This has been her work in South Africa. In America, serious work to create genuine reconciliation, accountability, and truth remains essential for all of us, now and in the future.

The Civil Rights Movement

There are important differences between civil liberties and civil rights. According to the Cornell Law School Legal Information Institute, our civil liberties are guaranteed in the Bill of Rights in the Constitution. Personal freedoms are civil liberties, such as the right to free speech in the First Amendment.

Civil Rights are not in the Bill of Rights. A civil right is a protection that may be in effect or may be ignored by local, state, or federal governments. One example is the right to vote. Although it is in the Constitution, some states interfered with it.

Charles Palmer writes: "In 1870, the 15th Amendment was ratified, which guaranteed the right to vote for all citizens, regardless of race or previous condition of servitude. However, in US v Reese in 1875, the Supreme Court stripped the Amendment of any real protection for African Americans by ruling that the Amendment did not deprive states and local governments of the power to make the right to vote conditioned on factors other than race, such as poll taxes, literacy tests, and knowledge tests to discriminate against black voters. Along with voter intimidation, lynching, and murder, black voter suppression laws eventually prevented the vast majority of Southern black men (and after 1920, black women) from being able to vote until passage of the Voting Rights Act of 1965. It has been estimated that by the late 1930s, less than 1% of blacks in the Deep South were registered to vote."[14]

If civil liberties are not protected, civil rights movements become necessary. Congress can pass legislation that protects our civil rights. In the spring of 1951, young Black students at Moton High School in Farmville, Virginia, protested their unequal status in the state's segregated educational system. Their strike was the beginning of the student civil rights movement. The NAACP challenged the US Supreme Court to make segregated schools illegal. On May 17, 1954, the court ruled in

Strive for Insight

Brown vs. Board of Education that segregation in public schools has a detrimental effect upon Black children. The court ruled that both Plessy v. Ferguson (1896), which made segregation in America legal, and Cumming v. Richmond County Board of Education (1899), which legalized segregation in schools, were unconstitutional.

On May 18, 1954, Greensboro, North Carolina, became the first city to abide by the court's decision and stop segregation policies. Other cities did not. Blacks demanded an end to segregation and racial injustice. Very often, high school students led the way.

In Arkansas, the National Guard was called in by Governor Orval Faubus to keep the students from entering the building on September 25, 1957. President Eisenhower countered by sending one thousand paratroopers from the 101st Airborne Division to Little Rock to protect nine Black students who were entering the segregated Central High School. Outside, white segregationists demonstrated.

In Montgomery, Alabama, buses were legally segregated. On one such bus, Rosa Parks refused to give up her seat to a white person and was put in jail in December 1955. The Southern Christian Leadership Conference (SCLC) led the Montgomery bus boycott for close to a year until the Supreme Court, in Browder v. Gayle (1956), desegregated buses in that city.

The March On Washington on August 28, 1964, was watched my millions on national TV. Over 250,000 attended. Activist Joan Baez sang "We Shall Overcome," Bob Dylan sang "Only A Pawn In Their Game." At the end, Martin Luther King Jr. delivered his most famous oration, "I Have a Dream."

Shortly thereafter, Congress passed the Civil Rights Act of 1964. It regulated interstate commerce. Discrimination based on "race, color, religion, or national origin" in public establishments that have a connection to interstate commerce or are supported by the state was prohibited. No longer could hotels, restaurants, gas stations, bars, and other places of commerce be segregated. The act ruled against segregation in public schools and colleges. Discrimination in federally funded programs was also prohibited. There was no reconciliation movement.

Environmentalism Awakens

From 1958 to 1962, both America and the Soviet Union allowed the testing of hundreds of atomic bombs in the atmosphere, from 16 to 250 miles above the Earth. Underground atomic testing was allowed in Nevada and on islands in the Pacific.

In 1962, Rachel Carson warned the public about the poisoning of air, earth, rivers, and seas with manmade chemicals since the end of WWII. In her book, *A Silent Spring*, she told us that the manipulation of the atom not only gave us the atomic bomb, but also "the production of synthetic pesticides in the United States that soared from 124 million pounds in 1947 to 637 million pounds in 1960."[15]

Carson, an aquatic biologist, asked a series of important questions to raise public consciousness on questions of life and death. She focused on the use of DDT and organic phosphates. Where did the chemicals designed to kill weeds, insects, and rodents end up in the food chain? How do they effect the ecology of the soil? How are birds and wildlife influenced? Do they cause cancer in human beings? Her work is inspirational to this day.

1968

In April 1968, the country was divided in many ways—racially, for and against the Vietnam War, and between the rich and the poor. There were 536,000 American soldiers serving their country in Vietnam. That year, 16,899 of them were killed, the most in any year of the war. The government was spending vast amounts of money on the war in Vietnam rather than investing in domestic infrastructure. The rich were receiving handouts in the form of subsidies to industry, deregulation, and tax loopholes. In the ghettos, parents were worried about the rats that crawled around their apartments at night. In the morning, they worried about lack of work.

It was a presidential election year, both Richard Nixon and Robert Kennedy were candidates. What the Hopi considered a "world complete" was on the verge of political revolutions.

The divisions among Americans were clearly visible from 1965 to

Strive for Insight

1967, when so many Americans demonstrated against segregation and the Vietnam War. Each summer, large cities in the nation were set on fire.

Once President Johnson started bombing Hanoi in 1965, demonstrations against the war broke out in America. The anti-war and civil rights movements were the real engines for new social justice.

In New York, civil rights activist Malcolm X was shot down on February 20, 1965. Violence continued that August when 34,000 people rioted in the Watts District of Los Angeles for four days. Fourteen thousand members of the California National Guard helped suppress the rioters. Thirty-four people were killed, 1,000 injured, and 4,000 arrested that week.

Anti-war and civil rights demonstrations continued in 1966. In Chicago, King demonstrated against racial segregation in housing, using the same tactics he had used in Mississippi and Alabama. It was unsuccessful. Northern racists responded with more hate than in the South. In March, demonstrations were held in seven cities. In the sizzling summer of 1966, riots broke out in the ghettos of New York, Chicago, Cleveland, San Francisco, Sunset Strip, and Atlanta.

In Mississippi, Stokely Carmichael was arrested for trying to set up tents at a Black school. Carmichael had already been in jail twenty-seven times. Now he was angry. At a SNCC rally, he said the only way to make progress was to take over. Black Power became his war cry! Roy Wilkens thought Black Power meant anti-white power separatism. King thought the slogan meant Black superiority, which he thought was as bad as white superiority. It also implied violence. Carmichael considered nonviolence irrelevant.

The Black Panthers was founded by Huey Newton and Bobby Seales in North Oakland on October 15, 1966. Their 2,000 members wore black leather clothes, dark glasses, and carried guns. Locally, they passed out food, provided jobs, and offered free learning for children and adults.

In 1967, civilian blanket bombing in Vietnam intensified. On March 2, Robert Kennedy spoke in the Senate, calling for a halt to the bombing and for peace negotiations. On June 1, Vietnam Veterans Against the War was formed. At a march in Chicago, Illinois, on March 25, 1967, Martin Luther King spoke against the war to over 5,000 protestors.

The Twentieth Century

In April, 50,000 young people in San Francisco protested the war. One week later, the heavyweight champion of the world, Muhammad Ali, refused to be drafted into the army. He declared himself a conscientious objector for religious reasons. Ali was banned from boxing for three years.

On October 21, 1967, some 100,000 anti-war protesters gathered at the Lincoln Memorial. Afterwards, they confronted soldiers and marshals at the Pentagon.

The Detroit Riots in July 1967 were some of the most violent in history. After five days, forty-three people were left dead, 340 injured, and close to 1,400 buildings were burned and looted. Five thousand were left homeless. Seven thousand National Guard and troops were called into the Virginia Park neighborhood, where low-income residents lived in tiny apartments.

At the same time, riots broke out in Newark, New Jersey. Black residents battled police for seven days, leaving twenty-six people dead. That summer, 120 other cities were set on fire in fourteen states.

King feared even worse riots in the summer of 1968. He decided on a new tactic to campaign against violence, hate, and poverty. His idea was to invite 3,000 poor people of all races to camp out in Washington, D.C. They would use massive civil disobedience to confront the federal government. Direct actions for three months would disrupt traffic and limit access to some federal buildings. He wanted Congress to act against poverty in the entire country. King called it the Washington Spring Project. It would be a class movement based on economic and social dissent. Thirty-five million Americans lived in poverty.

Many of his followers were sceptical. The press, radical Blacks, and liberal Whites did not want King to form a nonviolent, poor peoples' army. President Johnson had 23,000 National Guard troops he could bring to the capital at any time.

An economic bill of rights for America was King's goal. This would grant civil liberties under the Constitution. The whole economic structure would change. King was concerned that if the rioting continued it would strengthen the right wing of the country and destroy our democracy.

Strive for Insight

The civil rights bills had brought reform that did not cost America anything. Blacks could vote. They could share libraries, schools, restaurants, and hotels with white America. This was not enough. The country needed a campaign for jobs, housing for the poor, and better education for children. They wanted supplemental income for people below the poverty level, rent subsidies, welfare programs for children, and public health programs. Even boycotting companies that did not employ enough Blacks was prepared. The Constitution assured the right to vote, but there is no such assurance of the right to adequate housing and adequate income.

King selected ten cities and five rural areas from which to recruit the first 3,000 poor people to march on Washington. He expected to be joined by many others—churchmen, workers, students, and poor people—to pressure their congressmen.

It did not happen. He paid for his initiatives with his life. Martin Luther King Jr. was laid to rest on April 9, 1968, at the age of thirty-nine. One week later, his article, "Showdown for Nonviolence," was printed in *Look Magazine*.

King explained why he wanted the new protests:

> "We need an economic bill of rights. This would guarantee a job to all people who want to work and are able to work. It would also guarantee an income for all who are not able to work. Some people are too young, some are too old, some are physically disabled, and yet, in order to live, they need income. It would mean creating certain public service jobs, but that could be done in a few weeks. A program that would really deal with jobs could minimize—I don't say stop—the number of riots that could take place this summer."[16]

The riots did continue. Between April 4 and 11, riots exploded in Kansas City, Detroit, Chicago, Louisville, Pittsburgh, Boston, New York, Baltimore, Washington, D.C., Charlotte, Miami, and Berkeley.

One year later on October 15, 1969, the moratorium to end the war in Vietnam was conducted in New York City, Detroit, and Boston, where 100,000 marched. In Washington, D.C., 450,000 people marched.

The Twentieth Century

The follow up came on November 15, when half a million Americans demonstrated.

Native Americans Resist

President Eisenhower executed the Termination Act of 1953 to end all agreements with the tribes. The government urged Indians to leave the reservations and enter the cities, where they were to make it on their own. The 1956 Indian Relocation Act provided relocation transportation, money for the first four weeks, and job training in certain cities. Many suffered from homelessness and poverty.

New generations of Native Americans who were not subjected to government boarding schools created new schools. Started in 1966, the Rough Rock Indian School in Chinle, Arizona, is the oldest tribally operated school in the country.

In 1968, Dennis Banks, an Ojibway, Russel Means, a Lakota, and Clyde Bellecourt, an Ojibway, were three main leaders of the American Indian Movement (AIM). In truth, there were thousands of Native women who carried the new movement. Leonard Crow Dog taught Native American spirituality. They continued to fight for their land and their rights. In Minneapolis, they faced racism, police brutality, slum housing, and unemployment.

In the summer of 1972, the Trail of Broken Treaties began in Seattle and San Francisco. Two caravans converged in South Dakota on their way to Washington, D.C. When they arrived in the nation's capital, the Secretary of the Interior announced that no one in the government would accept their grievances. They had nowhere to sleep, so they occupied the building.

After four days inside, they left for Custer, South Dakota, where Bad Heat Bull had been murdered by police. Banks and Means were allowed into the courthouse to speak their grievances on police brutality, abuse, and murder. The officials would not sentence the police officer. Demonstrators burned down the building.

The next caravans were sent to Wounded Knee, South Dakota, to demand the rights to their land and water, as well as their rights to hunt, fish, and trap. Wounded Knee was the site of the 1890 Massacre of Chief

Bigfoot and his people. The occupation began on February 27, 1973. Hostages were taken as the federal marshals brought in planes. The AIM activists surrendered after seventy-one days. One of their demands was for the Senate Foreign Relations Committee to hold hearings on the broken treaties by the US government.

Two years later, a shootout took place at Pine Ridge, South Dakota. Two FBI agents were murdered. The prosecutor did not know who killed their agents, but Leonard Peltier was sentenced to two life sentences in 1976. In a song by Robbie Robertson, Peltier tells his story: "The sacrifice I have made when I really sit down to think about it, is nothing compared to what our people a couple hundred years ago, or fifty years ago, or twenty-five years ago have made. Some gave their lives. Some had to stand there and watch their children die in their arms. So, the sacrifice I have made is nothing compared to those. I've gone too far now to start backing down. I don't give up. Not 'til my people are free, will I give up. And if I have to sacrifice some more, then I sacrifice some more."[17]

Leonard Peltier stood up for his people's rights. After fifty years in federal confinement, he was pardoned by President Biden in 2025 and returned to Turtle Mountain, North Dakota.

NASA Space Programs

The culmination of the National Aeronautics and Space Administration (NASA) programs took place on July 20, 1969, when Apollo II Commander Neil Armstrong and pilot Buzz Aldrin successfully landed on the Sea of Tranquility on the Moon. The Apollo program involved nineteen missions before 1975. It was preceded by ten manned Gemini Missions, from 1962 to 1966. These were preceded by six manned orbital missions in NASA's Project Mercury-Atlas, from 1961 to 1962.

Other important space programs included Space Lab, the Venus 8 landing on Venus in 1972, the Viking 2 landing on Mars in 1976, and Voyager 1 passing Saturn in 1979.

The Hubble Space Telescope was launched on April 24, 1990, by the space shuttle Discovery. For thirty years, Hubble observed stars, galaxies, and the planets in our solar system. It was serviced five times by astronauts.

The Twentieth Century

The Woodstock Celebration

Michael Lang and Artie Kornfield took initiative for the music festival. In April 1969, Creedence Clearwater Revival signed a $10,000 contract with Woodstock Ventures to play at the festival in upstate New York. When word spread that Creedence was performing, thirty-one other bands and performers signed up.

After being forced off the first site, the festival moved to Bethel, New York, where Max Yasgur ran a dairy farm. They walked with him out on his property and discovered a large field in the shape of a natural amphitheater, dropping off to a pond to the north. Filippini Pond became a swimming hole for thousands.

Their working permit was granted on August 2, just two weeks before the event. This left them with two choices—either build ticket booths and fences but no stage or build the stage but no fences or ticket booths. Some kids had already bought $18 tickets for the festival at their local record shops. If the organizers did not have a stage, many young people would be very annoyed that no concert could be held. If they dropped the fences and ticket booths to build the stage, they would have no more income and soon go broke. Thousands of kids started camping out in the field the next day. The choice was easy—finish building the stage, the sound, and the lighting systems. The entire event was free of charge.

Bill Hanley set up speaker columns on the hills and had loudspeakers secured to platforms on top of seventy-foot towers. Three transformers were built behind the stage to power the amplification.

A massive traffic jam evolved on Thursday and Friday. It had rained, so roads and fields were wet. Poor sanitation, food shortages, and bad weather became major struggles. In the woods, Wavy Gravy set up the Hog Farm, where guests could rest, obtain food, or recover from bad LSD trips, illnesses, or exhaustion.

New York Governor Nelson Rockefeller declared Sullivan County a disaster area and sent in helicopters with medical supplies and forty-five doctors. When food supplies ran out on Saturday, local citizens provided food and Yasgur provided milk and yoghurt. The military at Stewart Air Force Base flew performers in and out on helicopters.

Most of the greatest bands and performers in America played for roughly one hour each between Richie Havens' opening on Friday evening and the final performance by Jimi Hendrix on Monday morning. More than 400,000 people spent the weekend at Woodstock.

New York City Redesigned

According to the 2003 Ric Burns documentary *New York*, the city was the unofficial capital of the world after WWII. It was no surprise that the United Nations Headquarters was built in Manhattan.

Between 1940 and 1970, close to 5 million Blacks and Hispanics migrated from poverty and segregation in the South to Northern cities. They settled in the over-crowded ghettos, only to find that the jobs were gone. The garment industry had left for North Carolina, the military industries for the South and the West. By 1960, the city was fighting for its existence. How could this happen?

In 1948, the federal government passed Title One, the Slum Clearance Bill. It should have provided affordable housing for the poor. That did not happen. Instead, the government paid for the city to confiscate land from slum owners, tear down the buildings, and give the land to private developers who were not even required to build housing. They wanted to build for middle-class Whites, not for poor people, Blacks, and Hispanics. It became a massive program for the removal of Blacks, Hispanics, and working-class Jews and Italians. Millions were relocated to massive housing projects segregated by race and class. Blacks and Hispanics were forced into overcrowded ghettos in Bedford-Stuyvesant and Harlem. Families broke apart, communities collapsed. The new districts were more segregated than before. City planners also decided to eliminate the streets, blocks, and life on the sidewalks. It was a massive betrayal of what makes a community in the city. Robert Moses chaired the city's slum clearance committee, commanding large sums of federal money.

Then Title Two enabled the federal government to underwrite the development of the suburbs rather than low-income housing in the cities. Feds told banks they would guarantee mortgages to people who moved to suburbs.

The Twentieth Century

The automobile industry was subsidized in the Federal Interstate Highway Act of 1956. The car became king in America, yet cars create traffic, and traffic always creates more traffic. City planners decided every city in America needed an expressway. Six new expressways were built across New York. The Cross Bronx Expressway tore apart the communities in fifteen different neighborhoods in 1955. Poverty increased. Then highways were built through Brooklyn, Queens, and Staten Island. The ports along the rivers disappeared. New York City declined as the flight to the suburbs accelerated. The tax base declined. Urban sprawl stretched from New York to Boston in the north and Philadelphia in the south.

Most shocking was the demolition of one of the most beautiful buildings in the USA. On October 28, 1963, the Pennsylvania Railroad began demolishing Penn Station. It was an industrial cathedral for mass transportation. Stunned citizens finally awoke to the meaning of their city, its people, and its buildings. Could they save the rest of New York? The new Penn Station was built below the earth, with Madison Square Garden above it.

Moses wanted to build three more expressways right through Manhattan—the Lower Manhattan, the Mid-Manhattan, and the Upper Manhattan Expressways. On December 11, 1962, the battle of the Lower Manhattan Expressway began. The ten-lane elevated highway was to go from Chinatown up through Greenwich Village. Moses would level fourteen blocks along Hudson Street.

Residents decided to stop the plans. They asked Jane Jacobs to lead the campaign. She had just published *The Death and Life of Great American Cities*, an attack on city planning that destroyed neighborhoods. Jacobs organized rallies, demonstrations, and formed coalitions of activists from all walks of life. They counter-planned urban renewal. The campaign exposed corruption. Jacobs was arrested. Moses fought them with all he had, but the people stopped the expressways.

New Yorkers realized their city provided strong connections in space and in time. New buildings, parks, and streets filled their space. In their experience of time, they enjoyed city history and legacies. They needed to take care of it. On April 19, 1965, Mayor Wagner adopted the

Strive for Insight

Landmarks Preservation Commission, preserving areas such as Greenwich Village, Soho, and Brooklyn Heights.

In the summer of 1964, riots broke out in Harlem and Bedford-Stuyvesant. A financial crisis hit. There were citywide strikes. The transit system stopped. Landlords in the South Bronx burned their own buildings to collect on insurance. Schools deteriorated. The city went $6 billion into debt.

Meanwhile, in Lower Manhattan, the Twin Towers were raised one quarter of a mile into the sky. One hundred and ten stories high, with 10 million square feet of office space, they opened in 1973. On the morning of August 7, 1974, passers-by looked up to see the high-wire artist Phillipe Petit walking on a wire between the North and South Towers. For forty-five minutes, he walked 1,300 feet above the city.

New generations created their own culture. From the burned-out South Bronx, colorful graffiti appeared. A lot of people were in jail. Afterschool music programs were shut down, but everyone had a record player at home. Black, Puerto Rican, and Jamaican youth created block parties with DJs using multiple turntables. Then rap appeared, with vocals with roots in street language, Black poetry, and Caribbean rhythm. Graffiti, mcing, rapping, and breakdancing evolved in the neighborhoods.

The city balanced its budget in 1981. Eventually, money returned to Wall Street. In the 1990s, talented people came to New York from all over the world and found work in the global economy.

Women's Liberation Activates

The National Organization for Women (NOW) called for a strike on August 26, 1970. Twenty thousand demonstrated in New York. Led by Betty Friedan, they wanted legal equality and new opportunities outside the house. That same year, Kate Millett published her book, *Sexual Politics*, to proclaim feminism and sexual freedom while exposing male domination in culture.

In politics, Barbara Charline Jordan was the first Black person elected as senator in Texas after Reconstruction and the first Black woman elected to Congress. She presented the opening address in the impeachment trial of Richard Nixon. Shirley Anita Chisholm served seven terms in Congress for New York. She ran for the Democratic presidential nomination in 1972. Bella Savitzky Abzug was a lawyer, activist, and member of Congress. She was one of the first to support gay rights. Gloria Steinem was an advocate for equal rights and co-founded *Ms. Magazine*.

The Equal Rights Amendment was passed by Congress in 1972. It guarantees protection against sexual discrimination for women by law. It was to provide legal equity of the sexes and prohibit discrimination. The law was sent to the states for ratification. It did not achieve the approval by thirty-eight states. It is still not in effect.

Gay Rights Emerge

The 1968 riot at the Stonewall Inn in New York launched a new era in gay rights activism. Each year, activism is commemorated with Gay Freedom Parades around the world. The parade in San Francisco in 1978 reached 375,000 people.

Founded in 1985, the National Gay and Lesbian Task Force has advocated for the civil rights of lesbian, gay, bisexual, and transgender (LGBT) people. They documented anti-gay violence and wanted gays to serve in the military. Since 2003, same sex sexual activity is legal. By 2015, LGBT Americans could marry.

In his college-level book *And The Band Played On, Politics, People And The AIDS Epidemic*, San Francisco journalist Randy Shilts defined the summer of 1985 as the turning point for the American public's awareness of Acquired Immune Deficiency Syndrome, AIDS. Mainstream movie star Rock Hudson went public with his diagnosis. "Suddenly there were children with AIDS who wanted to go to school, laborers with AIDS who wanted to work, and researchers who wanted funding, and there was a threat to the nation's public health that could no longer be ignored."[18]

The AIDS Coalition to Unleash Power (ACT UP!) was started in New York in 1987. To this day, they raise awareness using nonviolent protest and offering education programs around the world.

Neoconservatives Take Power

Along with large industry, the Republican conservatives moved south and west in the 1950s, where they attracted segregationists. With Barry Goldwater as their presidential candidate in 1964, neoconservatives abandoned civil rights.

In 1968, Richard Nixon decided to appeal to angry Southern Whites and frustrated Northern Whites without using racial language. The Nixon Administration had two enemies—the Blacks who demanded civil rights and the anti-Vietnam War demonstrators.

Ronald Reagan further developed the new right wing between 1981 and 1986. To this day, they are anti-government, anti-Washington, D.C., anti-welfare, anti-socialism, anti-abortion, anti-gay, and anti-regulation. Southern Black and White Evangelical and Protestant churches entered right-wing politics. Reactionary populism also went national through the media. Politics became entertainment.

On August 2, 1990, Saddam Hussein's Iraqi Army conquered Kuwait. The 1991 Persian Gulf War, involving 500,000 USA coalition soldiers in Operation Desert Storm, expelled the Iraqis and set up US military bases in the region. Neoconservatives backed the war efforts by President Bush.

From 1993 to 2001, President Bill Clinton gained support from Wall Street bankers and Hollywood stars. He repealed the Glass-Steagall regulation of US banks, setting up the housing bubble that led to the financial collapse of 2008. Clinton also liberalized global finances. Companies stopped paying taxes and hid their assets in tax shelters.

The Project for the New American Century (PNAC), a neoconservative think tank, was started in 1997. It included future Deputy Secretary of Defense Paul Wolfowitz, future Secretary of Defense Donald Rumsfeld, and future Vice President Dick Cheney. They advocated for the overthrow of Saddam Hussein, which came true during the next Bush administration in 2001. Republican globalization continued to be based on the military contract industry.

The Twentieth Century

The Local Stage

Victory in WWII meant more decline in Scranton, as military orders for silk parachutes, radar, shells, tanks, and the production of wings for bombers ended. Many soldiers returned home to no job. There were still jobs in the mines, but after many years at war, veterans chose not to work there.

Fortunately, ethnic diversity continued to grow. A large Irish Catholic population lived in Green Ridge, Welsh Methodists were in Hyde Park, German and Polish Catholic immigrants were on the South Side, German Jews lived in the Hill Section, and the Black population continued in the Lower Hill Section.

The Scranton Plan for Economic Development in Lackawanna County was implemented in 1945. Within ten years, seventy-five plant expansions and fifty-five new factories were added to the declining city.

On June 1, 1947, the Wilkes-Barre Scranton International Airport was dedicated, seven miles from Scranton and eight miles from Wilkes-Barre. On December 31, 1952, Laurel Line commuter service ended. Highways replaced electric-powered rails. When interstate highways linked the country in the 1960s, Scranton's location made it a warehousing distribution hub. Within 200 miles of Scranton, you could reach 50 million people.

The last regularly scheduled passenger train operated by the Erie-Lackawanna Railroad left Scranton Station in 1970. Passenger traffic was considered part of the past.

New industries entered the valley. The Daystrom Instrument Division built a $4 million plant to support the Korean war effort, making gunfire-control systems and radar dishes. By 1953, 3 million Trane convection heaters had been shipped from the Moosic plant. Under James Trane, the Trane Company opened a new plant at the Keystone Industrial Park in 1960. They produced heaters, air conditioners, steam valves, and unit ventilators.

The Rite-Aid discount drug store was founded in Scranton in 1962. The next year, Alex Grass opened five new stores.

Strive for Insight

After World War II, the US Navy asked General Textile Mills to produce a hard-shelled helmet for jet fighters. They produced helmets for the US Navy and the US Air Force. This was the beginning of their personal protection systems. In 1958, they became pioneers of advanced materials and changed their name to Gentex Corporation. In 1960, the company grew significantly, making seat belts for cars, life jackets for recreational use, helmets for ground troops, and more.

In 1972, Peter Frieder Jr. became president of Gentex at the age of twenty-nine. Frieder strengthened the company's engineering capabilities. He remained dedicated to the town of Carbondale, where flight helmets and infantry helmets were made. In the 1970s, NASA ordered pressure helmets for space shuttle missions. After acquiring Protection Incorporated in Sonoma, Gentex became a global leader in aircrew respiratory systems. They built communications headset solutions for ballistic helmets.

After working for his father at the American Record Company, Roy Marquart founded Specialty Records in 1950 in Olyphant. Roy's son, Richard Marquart, joined in 1960. In 1969, the firm won a contract to produce 45-rpm records for Atlantic Records, then Elektra Records. After the company entered the CD business, it was acquired by Warner Communications, Inc. in 1978.

Scrantonians on Many Stages

Many Scrantonians contributed on the national and world stages. One notable local resident was William W. Scranton, who served the commonwealth as Congressman of the 10th District before being elected Governor of Pennsylvania from 1963 to 1967. Scranton started the Community College System. He established strict strip-mining regulations, reduced unemployment, developed statewide banking codes, promoted major highway construction, welfare reform, and a new state constitution. Most importantly, he brought the commonwealth out of debt.

On the national and world stages, Scranton served as an aviator, ambassador, presidential candidate, presidential advisor, and chief financial officer. Locally, he was a lawyer, CEO, business developer, and trustee.

The Twentieth Century

In 1964, local athlete Timmy Mayer drove race cars on the world stage, while Cosmo Iacavazzi played football on the national stage. Iacavazzi was a 6-foot, 210-pound All-American fullback for Princeton University, and Mayer was a 6-foot, 145-pound Formula I driver for Cooper. Iacavazzi was from West Scranton. Mayer was from Dalton.

Scrantonian B.F. Skinner was a psychologist and behaviorist at Harvard from 1958 to 1974. He is famous for his 1971 book, *Beyond Freedom and Human Dignity*. Psychologist Howard Gardner pioneered the field of multiple intelligences in the early 1980s at Harvard. He defined eight intelligences: linguistic; logical-mathematical; spatial; bodily-kinesthetic; musical; interpersonal; intrapersonal; and naturalistic. Gardner defined intelligence as the ability to solve problems, to generate new problems, and to offer a service.

Next to Steamtown National Historic Site, many historic buildings on Lackawanna Avenue were converted into the Mall at Steamtown. Scrantonian Jane Jacobs, who led the campaign to stop expressways across Manhattan, wrote a letter in 1987 to protest bringing buildings from urban sprawl into the city, which otherwise was well protected in its original form.

The Lackawanna and Susquehanna Rivers Restored

Since the 1840s, waste from the iron, coal, textile, and other industries was emptied directly into the Lackawanna and Susquehanna Rivers. Domestic waste from cities and towns has also entered our rivers.

The Lackawanna River Conservation Association was formed in 1987 to restore and conserve the Lackawanna River and its watershed. From their website, LRCA.org, we learn that in 1866, the Lackawanna was condemned for public water drinking. One hundred years later, the river was still being used for sewer deposit. Drinking water was collected on the mountains at Lake Scranton, but in the valley, the river was dead from mine drainage, silt, sewage, garbage, and slaughterhouse waste. The city developed a sewer authority.

After the mines shut down in 1961, the river leaked into cracks and mines below. Iron, aluminum, manganese, and sulfur compounds

Strive for Insight

were dissolved into the mine water. When the polluted water under the city resurfaced, iron oxide and other heavy metals turned into an orange-colored sludge the miners called, yellowboy. Now there is a lake below Scranton the size of one of the Finger Lakes in New York.

PART TWO

Ancient History to the Nineteenth Century

CHAPTER 4

The Great Valley

Nestled between parallel ridges of the Allegheny Plateau to the west and the Pocono Plateau to the east, the Great Valley divides these long mountain ranges. The range to the west is called the Lackawanna Range. The range to the east is called the Moosic Mountains. When the ice of the Wisconsin Ice Age retreated roughly 15,000 years ago, it left the plateaus covered with lakes, ponds, and bogs.

These wetlands drain into the sixty-two-mile-long Lackawanna River. The eastern and western branches of the river meet just below Uniondale. From there, it flows through the northern anthracite coalfield to the Susquehanna River at Coxton, near Pittston, just opposite Scovill Island. The Lackawanna flows from its sources at roughly 2,000 feet above sea level, dropping thirty-nine feet per mile to an altitude of 500 feet at Coxton. From there, the waters flow 400 miles down the Susquehanna River until they empty into Chesapeake Bay and the Atlantic Ocean.

The wetlands on the Pocono Plateau to the east and on the Lackawanna Range to the west became filled with mountain laurel, high bush blueberry, and waterlily. Artic plants such as reindeer lichen, northern grasses, huckleberry, and sheep laurel lived on the plateau. The Moosic Range is the southern border of these plants, also found in the Adirondacks and Northern Quebec.

Strive for Insight

On the ridgetops and along the Pocono Plateau, scrub oak and pitch pine have thrived in the dry climate with rocky soils. Trees include tamarack, cherry, swamp oak, hemlock, and black spruce.

From the sky, the Great Valley resembles a gigantic canoe on its side, with the bottom placed against the Moosic Mountains to the east. The bow would be at Forest City in the north and the stern would be at Shickshinny in the south.

Geological Theory

As you know, small particles of carbon continually flow within our bodies. When we exhale, we breathe out the carbon as a gas, carbon dioxide, or CO_2. The plants transform our CO_2 into oxygen. When we inhale, we breathe in fresh oxygen. Every breath, the process of exhaling and inhaling, is a process of life and death. The CO_2 we breathe out is dead. The oxygen we breathe in is alive.

The carbon we find in our bodies takes a different form in nature. It is the main substance of plants. It is also found in minerals, especially coal. Hard coal is called anthracite and soft coal is called bituminous. Coal is non-transparent carbon, while diamonds are transparent carbon.

Now let us dive into the river of time that starts in the future, moves to the moment, and then widens our consciousness far back into the past. Experienced geologists do this every day. For us, it is a challenge. We leave the moment and go back in time to the Ordovician Period, when the Appalachian Mountains arose from the ocean floor about 450 million years ago. At that time, much of North America lay under oceans, where fish and sharks perpetually swam. Imagine the original Appalachians as tall as the Rocky Mountains today. Now they are old and low because they have been eroded by ice, wind, and temperature changes. In the early Mississippian geological era, between 359 and 323 million years ago, there is evidence of great swamps filled with coal on the plains between the mountains.

In the Pennsylvanian geological period, 323 to 299 million years ago, forests began to grow on these plains. As the conditions became more favorable for the dense forests to survive for hundreds of thousands of

The Great Valley

years, much of the dead plant material became preserved in areas with little oxygen. Tropical swamps were filled with vast deposits of fine coal.

The theory of plate tectonics assumes that at the end of the Permian Period, 252 million years ago, the continents were still compacted into one form. Since then, the continents have separated into plates with the shapes we know today. The Earth's outer shell was divided into seven rigid plates—the North American, African, Eurasian, Antarctic, Pacific, South American, and Australian plates. Originally, the North American Plate was near the equator, where a tropical climate existed with dense forests.

According to geological theory, 300 million years ago, anthracite coal deposits were re-pressurized during the continental shift after the African continent collided with the North American continent. When the continents withdrew, the Delaware River was formed and the land forming the state of New Jersey remained from the African continent. A thin slice of anthracite coal was folded like a piece of aluminum foil into the mountainside between Carbondale and Moosic Mountain, part of the northern or Wyoming field of anthracite. The other slices were called the middle field in Luzerne and Carbon Counties, as well as the southern field in Schuylkill County.

The water gaps are very distinct formations for you to discover in the Great Valley. They are remnants of an ancient fold-and-thrust belt that formed 325 to 260 million years ago. The layers of rock from vegetative matter had been folded westward. They were forced over massive faults where older rocks were pushed above younger rocks. In these areas, there was little heat, pressure, or chemical fluids that could change the structure of the rock. Nor was there volcanic activity. The ridges of a water gap are the edges of the layers of rock that resist erosion.

Geologists believe the Delaware River and the Susquehanna River are older than the mountains we see surrounding them today. Both rivers cut large water gaps. These water gaps run perpendicular to the hard, vertical ridges. Scientists believe the entire region wore down to a low level and the large rivers were flowing with water and sediments that were not influenced by the rock structure of the riverbed. The entire region was slowly lifted up and cut through the ridges we see today. The large rivers maintained their course while the water gaps formed.

Five major water gaps became the entrances and exits of the Great Valley. In the north, a gap was made where the Lackawanna River enters the valley near Forest City. In the south, a gap was made where the Susquehanna River leaves the valley at Nanticoke. Why not take your kayak and find these gaps?

Wyoming Gap is the longest. Beginning at Falls Township and ending at West Pittston, it covers twenty-two miles through Wyoming County. The ridge at the opening to the Wyoming Valley is known as Campbell's Ledge. Connecticut Yankee settlers called the ledge Dial Rock because they kept time by observing how the sun shone on the jaded rocks. If you are canoeing through the gap from the north and enter the opening to the Wyoming Valley, you need to look back over your left shoulder and then up to the 1,200-foot ridge!

The fourth gap is Cobb's Gap. It runs twenty-one miles along Roaring Brook Creek, beginning on the Pocono Plateau and flowing through the Moosic Mountains. Cobb's Gap enters the valley at Dunmore. Before reaching Scranton, the creek flows through a canyon called Nay Aug Gorge.

Thousands of years ago, Native Americans built a major path halfway up the East Mountain above Cobb's Gap to avoid flooding. The path became a wagon trail for Connecticut settlers in the 18th century and then the railroad extension to New York in the 19th century. It became part of the intercontinental highway Route 6 to Milford in the 20th century.

The fifth gap is officially named Liget's Gap, but is commonly known as the Notch. It runs nine miles from North Scranton uphill to Clarks Summit. Cobb's Gap and Liget's Gap are positioned directly east to west. The city of Scranton is in between. Both gaps were essential for the iron, steel, coal, locomotive, and railway industries in the Industrial Revolution of the 19th century.

As kids in the 60s, we would get up early on Saturday morning and ride our bicycles through Liget's Gap to the Spruce Record Shop in Scranton. The record shop was our cultural center, where we could learn about new music from the national and world stages. It was a cool ride.

The Great Valley

It took 150 million years for the Appalachian Mountains of this area to finally achieve the shapes seen today. Pressure and heat forced the mountains to rise. With the rise and fall of the mountains, along with changes in sea level, the coal deposits shifted many times. By the end of the Permian era, much of the continental plate collision had subsided; the mountain building continued. This pressure caused the vegetation to become peat, then lignite and coal.

All of the sediments deposited during the previous 30 million years became folded. The swamps had been covered by the ocean, leaving sediments deposited on the ocean floor. These became the shale and sandstone rock layers miners find between the coal veins. In the Lackawanna and Wyoming Valleys, the coal sits in older and harder white metamorphic rock compounded with quartz and sand.

The anthracite coal beds run in veins through the valley to Dunmore and Scranton and on the sides of the valley along the western ridge from Carbondale to Taylor before they cross the valley and twist up to the Moosic Mountain. Water reservoirs were built where these veins end along the hillsides, for example Lake Scranton on the East Mountain. The coal veins are between 30 and 700 feet below the surface. The deepest is at Dunmore, almost 800 feet below the surface.

Let us imagine we put on our hiking shoes and walk the entire Great Valley from Nanticoke in the south to Carbondale in the north. How wide are the coal deposits beneath our feet? The coal field below the Wyoming basin expands evenly until at the distance of about thirteen miles from Nanticoke, in the section near the town of Plymouth, it attains a width of four and a half miles. Near the city of Wilkes-Barre, which is about seventeen miles from Nanticoke, the width is near five miles. At the town of Pittston, the maximum width of five and a half miles is reached. Near the city of Scranton, thirty-four miles distant, the section will not measure over four miles. At Carbondale, the breadth of the coal field is no more than two miles.

The Susquehanna River through the Valley

The principal channels of drainage of the valley are the Lackawanna and the Susquehanna Rivers, together with their tributaries. The

Strive for Insight

Susquehanna flows through the entire length of the Wyoming Valley. By watershed area, it is the sixteenth largest river in the United States. It is 440 miles long and it drains 27,000 square miles of land.

The north branch of the Susquehanna begins at Lake Otsego in New York State. From there, it flows about 105 miles due west to a junction with the Chemung River called Tioga Point at Athens, Pennsylvania. This junction was a famous center of travel and commerce for the Iroquois people for thousands of years.

From Athens, the river flows south to Towanda, through Wyalusing, and then southeast to Pittston, where the Lackawanna River joins it. From Pittston, it turns southwest through the Wyoming Valley and flows through Wilkes-Barre down to Sunbury, where it meets the west branch.

The west branch of the Susquehanna River flows west to east, 228 miles within Pennsylvania from Cherry Tree in the Allegheny Mountains to its fork with the north branch at Sunbury. There is a vertical drop in the watershed of about 1,800 feet from its headwaters to the mouth. From Sunbury, the great river flows south before crossing into Maryland and emptying into Chesapeake Bay.

In colonial times, the west branch flowed through a northern hardwood forest of oak, maple, cherry, hemlock, and great white pine. Deer, bear, elk, birds, and trout were in abundance. The Susquehanna River Watershed is the largest tributary of the Chesapeake Bay ecosystem.

Countless tributaries are filled with rainfall, stored among the hills and in innumerable small lakes and underground veins that become springs of clear, pure, cold water. Springs and lakes are the fountainhead of many streams that make their way in every direction through the plains and banks of the Susquehanna.

Rattlesnake Country!

Had we walked through the valley or the hills one million years ago, we may have seen long-haired mammoths of the elephant species. In ancient times, we may have met mountain lions, moose, elk, or timber wolves.

Today we may see black bear, white-tail deer, fox, beaver, muskrat, skunk, opossum, and rabbits. In the sky, we may see eagles, red-winged hawks, great blue herons, grouse, owls, and kingfishers. The smaller

The Great Valley

birds you may see, but most probably hear, are robins, cardinals, Baltimore orioles, blue jays, sparrows, chickadees, mourning doves, bluebirds, or woodpeckers. In the creeks, rivers, and lakes, you may catch trout, shad, catfish, walleye, or bass.

Hiking in the rocky areas of the mountains, you may find salamanders, copperhead snakes, and five-foot timber rattlesnakes. Remember, this is rattlesnake country!

CHAPTER 5

The Native Americans and the First Europeans

More than 7,000 years ago, Manu led the ancient people to what is now the Taklamakan Basin, northwest of Tibet. There he was inspired by the Rishis to teach in Ancient China. Some of these teachings became the *Bhagavad Gita*, taught in Ancient India.

More than 5,000 years ago, Zarathustra taught in Ancient Persia, Gilgamesh in Ancient Mesopotamia, and Osiris in Ancient Egypt. Hermes taught in Egypt. Orpheus and Pythagoras taught in Ancient Greece.

Rama and Buddha taught in India 2,600 years ago. A century later, Moses freed the Israelites from Egypt.

The teachings of Aristotle, his thinking and his science, were spread by Alexander the Great for thirteen years, from 336 to 323 B.C. To spread Aristotle's teachings, he conquered civilizations from the Near East to Africa, Persia, and India.

During these millennia, the ancient people in the Great Valley remained devoted to the Great Spirit. There were no Middle Ages in the valley. No cities were built. No feudal system was established. There were no cathedrals built, no guilds for the craftsmen, no universities for the scholars were created. There was no Renaissance with new architecture, global banks, artworks, sculpture, and philosophy in the 15th century. The Native people retained their ancient ways. Then, starting in 1662, the English introduced land claims in Pennsylvania that would cause a series of civil wars one hundred years later.

The First Native People on the Local Stage

Two sites in the Upper Delaware Valley have changed our understanding of the ancient people. At the Shawnee Minisink site at today's Route 80 bridge over the Delaware Water Gap, charred hawthorn seeds, hickory nuts, carbonized grapes, plums, and fish bones were found in hearths. Now archeologists believe the Paleoindians in the east were foragers as well as hunters. They learned that the charcoal from other trees in the hearths indicate a combination of coniferous and deciduous trees not found in the world today. The hearths date as far back as 11,000 years. The site, called Minisink Flats, was found ten feet underground with three feet of flooded deposits. They found knives and scrapers to clean hides and make handles for tools.

The other site is on Minisink Island on the Delaware River below Milford, between Pennsylvania and New Jersey. Around 1900, Edward Dalrymple excavated European funeral objects—a copper kettle, a silver spoon, thimbles, a necklace of shell and glass beads, a bell, and copper bracelets. Later, the burial site of a European man, probably Nordic, was recovered. Trade between the Minisink and Europe has been proven, but there is much we do not know about the first Europeans in Northeastern Pennsylvania.

Long before the first Europeans came to North America, the Native people had land and water routes that connected distant communities. The paths were used for trade, relocation, and war. In the summer, the Minisink ran southeast to the Atlantic Ocean, where they fished. Their path to the east ran through Lake Hopatcong, Morristown, and Metuchen. It was three feet wide and well trodden.

Ten thousand years ago, the ancients travelled from their longhouses on Minisink Island. They ran across the Poconos through the Lackawanna Valley to their Wyoming friends, who lived on islands on the Susquehanna River outside of today's Pittston. The trail between the Delaware and Lackawanna Rivers was called the Shohola Minisink

The Native Americans and the First Europeans

Path. It traversed the bluffs at Indian Point, the Raymondskill Waterfalls, entered Lord's Valley, passed Blooming Grove to Paupack Church, Mt. Cobb, before it crossed Moosic Mountain, passed through Dunmore, and forded the Lackawanna River to Capoose Meadows, where Scranton High School and Memorial Stadium are presently located.

At Capoose, they ran north on the Lackawanna Path through Liggett's Gap and the Abington Wilderness to Oquaga (now Windsor), New York. Today, this ancient path follows Route 81 from the Clarks Summit exit to the Lenox exit! From there, the path runs north along Route 92.

The Minisink also picked up the Lackawanna Path at Capoose and ran south to the Wyomink, who lived on islands in the Susquehanna River near Wyoming. Maughwauwame was the Native name for Wyoming, meaning large plains. The Minisink and the Wyomink hunted elk, moose, deer, and bear for meat, skin, bones, and medicine. Wildfowl abounded—crows, grouse, turkey, and red-tailed hawk. The valley was filled with panthers, wolves, and foxes.

The Iroquois Rule the Valley

In Wyoming, the ancient paths turned north up the Susquehanna River to Athens, Pennsylvania. This was known for centuries as the Warrior's Path. The Iroquois warriors ran as many as one thousand miles along the river to control the tribes living in today's Carolinas. It was a war path and a path for transporting captives. It marked the western door of the longhouse. Wyoming was a crossroads for the Iroquois. Originating in central New York, Warrior's Path ran north to south through the middle of Pennsylvania along the Susquehanna River until it met the west branch of the river at Sunbury. From Sunbury, the path veered southwest through present-day Huntingdon and Bedford, Pennsylvania, before crossing the Potomac River near Cumberland, Maryland. The path continued into Virginia and the Carolinas along the eastern edge of the Appalachians.

The people of the longhouse are the Kanonsonnionwe. The French and Hurons called them Iroquois because they warned their enemies before they attacked. Iroquois means rattlesnakes. You can hear the hard rattle in the tip of the tail before the snake attacks. The Iroquois were an enterprising and warlike people. They knew themselves as the People of the Longhouse. Their goal was to never forget the Great Spirit.

The People of the Longhouse lived in villages with many rectangular longhouses. Corn, squash, and beans were grown between the stumps of cut down trees. They fished with hooks, nets, and spears. Birds, bear, and deer were hunted. Their clothing was leather breechcloths, leggings, and moccasins. Women wore skirts and jackets.

Religious ceremonies and healing rituals were carried out by a priesthood of three men and three women, each with their own dances, songs, masks, and rituals.

The Kanonsonnionwe traveled by foot or canoe. In winter they used snowshoes. At their height of power before the American Revolution, they sent war parties of more than 2,000 warriors as far away as Illinois and Northwestern Ontario.

Around 1570, the most powerful Mohawk tribe united five other tribes into the Six Nations Confederacy. From west to east, these nations were the Seneca, the Cayuga, the Onondaga, the Oneida, the Mohawk, and one hundred years later they added the Tuscarora. Women and children held the family fire. Each fire was part of a larger group of families traced through the mothers. Two or more large families became a clan. The clans within a tribe became the nation. Women held the authority of the clans. They named male delegates to represent them at the tribal councils. The peace sachems or chiefs, who ruled the council of the six nations, were also named by the women. The peace sachem ruled for life unless the older women decided to name a new chief. The Iroquois Confederacy made decisions after considering how they would impact the next seven generations.

Another body of leaders came from the warriors, the Pine Tree chiefs. Each summer, the league would meet in a village of the Onondagas. Rather than individuals voting, each tribe had one vote. In decisions of war, the separate tribes chose their own paths. Serious conflicts were resolved and there was a strong sense of unity. They held councils to pass down legends and traditions and to make decisions. Women contributed their opinion.

The Native Americans and the First Europeans

The Six Nations Confederacy claimed the Wyoming Valley. They needed the fishing and hunting grounds, but most importantly, the right to travel to other nations along the Susquehanna River. On the open plains, corn was grown. The Iroquois made various corn dishes to supplement the meat and fish they ate.

The Native people conquered other tribes with war and colonized them, but contrary to how they have been portrayed by Europeans, they were not violent. There was almost no murder among them. This came with the Europeans. They had unwritten laws of justice and human interaction. The parents taught their children. For amusement, they danced and sang.

The Great Valley was occupied by the Lenni Lenape, also called the Delaware people. Their name means original people. Many tribes considered them to be the great-grandfathers. They were peaceful and were easily controlled by the Iroquois. They had a village at Scranton as early as 1728. The Delaware had their council fire at Minisink Island on the Delaware River. Their hunting grounds extended from Easton, Pennsylvania, to the Atlantic Ocean.

The Delaware, Monsey, Shawanese, Nanticoke, Mohican, and Wanamese in the Wyoming Valley were controlled by the Iroquois to occupy the great highway along the Susquehanna River. They could not move without their master's approval.

The lower end of the Great Valley was occupied by the Nanticoke on the east side of the river and the Shawanese on the west side. Later, the Nanticoke were moved up the Susquehanna River.

The historic village of Shamokin was established in 1728. That year, the Oneida chief, Shikallamy, chief of the Turtle Clan of the Delaware, moved there, making it the capital of the province. Shikallamy was the vice-regent of the Iroquois Confederation. He had authority over the Shawnee.

Conrad Weiser was his interpreter when he travelled to Philadelphia with one hundred chiefs on behalf of the Six Nations. At the conference in 1733, the Iroquois sold all the land south and east of the Blue Mountains to the Colony of Pennsylvania.

Strive for Insight

In 1748, Shikallamy became vice-regent over all the tribes in Pennsylvania under Iroquois control. He died at Shamoken in December that year.

The First Europeans Enter the Valley

Before the Europeans arrived in North America, the Native people controlled the destiny of their own lives. Yet the Europeans considered them savages. In the Oxford Dictionary, savage means cruel, violent, vicious, not civilized, and primitive. Europeans considered themselves civilized and superior.

The first documented meeting between the Mohawks and a white man was with the French explorer Samuel de Champlain in 1609. He was exploring the St. Lawrence River for beaver trade. He demonstrated his firearms to the Algonquins in the area and agreed to get rid of the Mohawks. He met about 300 Mohawks by the lake that would be named for him. De Champlain fired some shots, killing three. From then on, the rule of firearms and the trade for beaver changed the course of life for the Iroquois.

Beaver felt provided the best quality and most expensive hats in European cities. It was originally supplied by the Russians, but in the 17th century, North America took over the fur trade. Beavers have two types of hair, the coarse outer guardhair, and the soft underfur, called beaver wool or duvet. North American trappers sold fur taken in the winter, when the course outer hair had fallen off. This fur required less processing before it was felted. When felted, the fibers shrank and could be more easily molded into hats.

The Dutch set up trade centers along the Hudson and Delaware Rivers. At Albany, they built Fort Orange in 1614. The Delaware Nation and the Susquehannock Nation could trade directly with the Dutch under the approval of the Iroquois. Yet beavers became over-trapped and the trade moved north to the Algonquins above Lake Ontario and west to the Hurons above Lake Erie.

The first known white man to sail down the Susquehanna River was Etienne Brule, the famous interpreter for Samuel de Champlain. Brule was a French fur-trader and explorer who lived much amongst the

Indians. While Champlain sailed back to Quebec, Brule explored Central Pennsylvania by sailing down the Susquehanna to Chesapeake Bay in 1615.

Between 1621 and 1623, Brule entered the land of the Hurons at Georgian Bay, the North Channel, and discovered the waters of the Sault Ste. Marie. He was the first white man to paddle along the shores of Lake Superior.

The Dutch began their genocidal warfare against the Mohawks in 1640. Along the Connecticut River, the Pequit and Narragansett Nations were submitted to slavery by the British.

In 1647, the Algonquin and the Susquehannock outnumbered the Iroquois and won victories. The Iroquois strengthened their confederacy and extended their power west to the Ohio River Valley and south to the Carolinas. Tensions between the nations grew. In 1660, the Iroquois sent a war party of one thousand warriors to the Long Sault below Lake Superior to conquer the Huron and remove the French Jesuit missionaries living there.

In 1661, the Susquehannock became allies with the British in Maryland. Warfare with the colonists continued for eleven years. In 1675, the Virginia and Maryland militia defeated the Susquehannock, killed their powerful chiefs, and left the rest of the nation to the Iroquois to assimilate in 1677.

By the early 1700s, the flat Wyoming Valley along the Susquehanna River was sparsely inhabited by Lenape, Shawnee, Mohican, and Nanticokes.

From the 1740s to the 1760s, the valley became the site of German Moravian missions led by David Zeisberger. The Moravians developed a community in 1741, which they named Bethlehem, Pennsylvania. Entering the Wyoming Valley meant establishing a missionary for the Indian tribes. The Germans never made land claims upon the Wyoming Valley.

King Charles II of England Sells the Valley Twice

In May 1661, Governor John Winthrop of Connecticut travelled to London to request a colonial charter from King Charles II. The Connecticut charter was issued in May 1662. It defined the boundaries to include the

Strive for Insight

New Haven Colony and a part of Rhode Island to the east, and a small slice of land westward to the Wyoming Valley and then all the way to the Pacific Ocean.

Nineteen years later, King Charles II sold the valley again. This time to William Penn in 1681. Why did the King of England sell the Wyoming Valley twice and cause three civil wars? Civil wars were nothing new for Charles II. His father, Charles I, was executed after the Second Civil War in England. In 1649, Charles II was proclaimed King of Great Britain and Ireland. Two years later, he lost the Third Civil War in 1651. While Charles II was in exile in France, protected by his first cousin, King Louis XIV, the English Commonwealth was led by the dictator Oliver Cromwell. When Cromwell died in 1658, Charles II returned to England and became its monarch. It is expensive for a royal family to lose three civil wars. It is also expensive for a king to live in exile. Therefore, Charles II granted the Wyoming Valley to the Connecticut Colony in 1662, and once more to William Penn in 1681.

William Penn's father, Admiral Sir Penn, was known for having captured Jamaica for the Atlantic Triangle slave trade in 1655. King Charles II had borrowed 16,000 pounds from the admiral. Rather than pay back the debt in 1681, the King approved William Penn's request for a charter to land in the New World.

The charter for William Penn included the land between the 39th and 42nd degrees of north latitude and from the Delaware River westward for five degrees of longitude. It was the territory north of Maryland and south of the province granted to the Duke of York. The charter assured the people the protection of English laws. William Penn created a democratic system of government, providing fair trials, elective representatives, and separation of powers between the governor, the assembly, and the courts.

William had shocked his family at the age of twenty-two by converting to the Society of Friends, or Quakers, a persecuted sect. Penn provided complete freedom of religion for everybody who believed in God. English, German, Welsh, and Dutch Quakers entered the Pennsylvania Colony. They were joined by the Amish, French Protestant Huguenots, Mennonites, and Lutherans from Catholic German states.

The Native Americans and the First Europeans

French and Indian War in the Valley

On October 16, 1755, the French and Indian War came to the Susquehanna River at Penn's Creek, where a massacre was committed south of Sunbury at present-day Selingsgrove. This inspired the Pennsylvanians to build Fort Augusta at Sunbury, at the fork of the Susquehanna River. It was the largest fort on the frontier, with sixteen cannons and up to 400 soldiers. It was never attacked. Pennsylvania used the county seats at Easton and Sunbury to control the Wyoming Valley.

The Iroquois Also Sell the Valley Twice

On July 11, 1754, the Mohawk King Hendrik and fourteen other chiefs sold the Wyoming Valley to the Susquehanna Company. The Connecticut Yankees secured a dubious deed to a large tract of land along the Susquehanna River, amounting to about one-third of Pennsylvania.

Indian raids continued along the western and northern branches of the Susquehanna. From May to July 1757, there were meetings between the Six Nations and the Colony of Pennsylvania at Easton. Teedyyuscung, King of the Eastern Delaware, wanted to settle at Wyoming. Two months later, 150 provincial troops from Philadelphia set out with the Delaware for Wyoming to build houses near present-day Wilkes-Barre. They were led by Captains Hughs and Pauling.

Between 1661 and 1762, no Europeans occupied the Wyoming Valley. In August 1762, about 200 Yankees arrived in Wyoming. One day later, 400 Iroquois appeared and ordered them to leave. The New Englanders remained. They built log cabins and planted wheat on the east bank of the Susquehanna at Mill Creek.

In the summer of 1763, the Connecticut settlers cleared the land along the big river flat. It was good soil from centuries of flooding. There were few rocks to remove and the earth was soft. Corn and wheat grew well. A blockhouse was built on the west bank, where livestock grazed by the river.

The new colonists chose to ignore the pleas of their governor in Connecticut to leave immediately as the Pontiac War moved eastward to the frontier in 1763. On October 15, it was too late. One hundred Iroquois warriors armed with muskets killed and captured most of the

Strive for Insight

Yankees. Others fled to the mountains. The buildings were burned to the ground. That day, a young man, Isaac Hollister, was working in the fields on the banks of the Susquehanna when Seneca warriors walked out of the woods and killed his father and brother. They captured him and hauled him 150 miles up the river to a town called Wethouooungque. About three months later, he escaped, only to be recaptured at the next village. Rather than killing him, the Natives decided to make him run the gauntlet.

Hollister wrote:

> "Next day I was brought forth, strip'd stark naked, and ordered to run; while the Indians, who were ranged in a row, at certain distances, in a most cruel and barbarous manner, belaboured me with their whips,—by which they sometimes laid me level with the ground, by their blows.—Thus they continued to lash me, until I had run about 40 rods, when I received a prodigious blow from one of them, which settled me to the ground as quick as if I had been shot through the heart. I was so stunned by the blow, that it seems I should never have recovered again, had not an old squaw run immediately to my relief, and helped me into her hut. By this time my whole body was covered with gore and blood. I tarried here after this about 14 days, and then they sent me up to the Senecas about 150 miles off."[19]

In the summer of 1765, Superintendent William Johnson granted the rights for the Pennsylvanians to build a large store at Mill Creek to trade with the Iroquois.

At a conference with the Governor of Pennsylvania, an Iroquois told of mining in Wyoming. The white people dug holes and filled their canoes with the stone later known as anthracite coal. When the Yankees in Connecticut heard of this, they again became interested in their claim for the valley.

In October 1768, a large council was held at Albany, New York. Three thousand Iroquois arrived. Governor Penn of Pennsylvania and the land speculator and scientist, Benjamin Franklin participated. The

The Native Americans and the First Europeans

Governor of New Jersey, the chief justices of many colonies, Colonel Eleazer Fitch, and a representative from the Susquehannah Company attended. Captain Ogden represented the Pennsylvanian settlement of Wyoming. Known as the Treaty of Fort Stanwix, on November 5, 1768, Pennsylvania purchased parts of Pennsylvania, West Virginia, New York, and Kentucky from the Six Nations of the Iroquois for 50,600 Spanish silver dollars.

That same day, the Wyoming Valley was bought by the government of Pennsylvania for 10,000 Spanish dollars, based on the 1682 Charter. With agents and a trading post in the valley, the Pennsylvanians surveyed their claims. The Wyoming Valley had been sold by the Iroquois twice—first to the Connecticut Yankees in 1754, then fourteen years later to the Pennsylvania Colony in 1768.

The Pennsylvanians, the Connecticut Yankees, and the Iroquois sought full control of the Wyoming Valley!

The First Civil War in the Valley

In January 1769, the first Yankee settlers returned to the valley, six years after the first Wyoming Massacre. It was a terrible winter. They travelled past Minisink Island down to the Delaware Water Gap and marched northwest to Wyoming. The Minisink warned the Pennsylvanians of the new settlers headed for the valley. The Yankees settled at Lackawanuck, present-day Pittston. There were forty pioneers. They erected a fort on the west side of the river and named it Forty Fort. Erecting a strong house and two cabins, they cleared land for settlers expected in the spring.

The Yankees called the Pennsylvanians, Pennamites. They considered them British loyalists or Tories. One hundred armed Pennamites under the command of Amos Ogden, Sheriff Jennings, and Captain Alexander Patterson arrested the Yankee settlers on March 13. They were brought under guard to Easton.

The Connecticut Yankees countered with a military expedition to the Wyoming Valley, with 146 men under Major John Durkee. In 1765, Durkee had formed the Sons of Liberty of Connecticut in his tavern in Norwich. The Sons of Liberty made Colonel Israel Putnam their leader. Ten years later, both Durkee and Putnam would become Revolutionary

Strive for Insight

War heroes. Durkee served in Putnam's Third Connecticut Regiment as a Lieutenant Colonel stationed in Cambridge as of May 1775. He fought with Putnam at Bunker Hill. In the American Revolution, John Durkee would command a regiment in the battles of Brooklyn, Harlem, White Plains, Trenton, Germantown, and Monmouth. He also fought in General John Sullivan's expedition against the Six Nations in 1779.

John Durkee and the soldiers settled and built Fort Durkee on the eastern bank of the river in today's Wilkes-Barre. Twenty log cabins were built with watchtowers at the corners. The Yankee settlement was named Wilkes-Barre after John Wilkes and Isaac Barre, two British members of Parliament who supported colonial America. Both were supporters of William Pitt the Elder, who led Britain during the French and Indian War and would oppose the British policies toward the American colonies in the 1770s. Barre coined the term "Sons of Liberty" for Americans who opposed British taxation of the colonies. Born in Dublin, Barre fought at Quebec in 1759, where he was shot in the cheek, losing his left eye. Though badly injured, he gathered with others around Major General James Wolfe, who died on the Plains of Abraham near Quebec at the moment of victory.

At the end of 1769, 200 Pennamites under the command of Sheriff Jennings and Ogden arrived at the gate of the Yankee Fort Durkee with a 400-pound cannon. The fort surrendered unconditionally, and Major Durkee was hauled off to Philadelphia as a prisoner. The Yankee families were expelled from the valley for the third time.

Ogden kept the Yankee livestock and the property for himself. The Pennamites then marched back to Fort Augusta. In January 1770, Ogden organized a new militia. He captured Forty Fort and build a new fort on Mill Creek. Then Ogden attacked Captain Lazarus Stewart at Fort Durkee, but Stewart escaped with thirty of his followers. The Pennamites renamed the fort Fort Wyoming.

In February 1770, Stewart led a group of farmers called the Paxtang Boys to Wilkes-Barre to retake the fort on behalf of the Yankees. They captured the famous 400-pound cannon at Mill Creek and moved it and the ammunition to Wilkes-Barre. Major Durkee mysteriously escaped from Philadelphia and returned to take over the Yankee military. Captain

The Native Americans and the First Europeans

Zebulon Butler and reinforcements from Connecticut were on their way. Hatred grew as the stakes increased.

In April, a mixed force of 150 men led by Butler and Captain Stewart sieged Fort Wyoming for twenty-six days. General Gage, commander-in-chief of His Majesty's forces in New York, refused to give Odgen assistance in the Wyoming Valley. The Pennamites were forced to leave the valley for the first time. The Mill Creek compound was burned to the ground.

After three months, the Pennsylvanians returned at night, with Odgen commanding 200 men. They easily took Fort Durkee. The only one not arrested was Stewart, who recaptured the fort on December 18, 1770.

When Ogden returned in January 1771 with one hundred men, he built a new fort in Wilkes-Barre, also called Fort Wyoming. The new fort was close to Fort Durkee, where Wilkes University is today. Stewart and his men escaped to Connecticut, making it the fourth time the Yankees were evicted from the valley. This time it was only six months before they returned.

Governor Penn decided to sell hundred-acre lots inexpensively before the next Yankee invasion. The invasion was not far off, as Captains Zebulon Butler and Lazarus Stewart were on their way back to Wyoming with seventy-four men. The Pennamites surrendered after sixteen days of fighting. The First Yankee-Pennamite War ended, a three-year war, from February 1769 to September 1771.

Between 1772 and 1773, new settlers from Connecticut poured into the valley. They were hardy people with ambition, seeking a better life in the wilderness. They came with oxen and carts carrying utensils and some furniture. Some brought their wives. Many came by foot with backpacks, a rifle, and an axe in their hands. They followed Native trails through the forests and swamps, climbing mountains and camping along the roads at night until they reached the valley.

They first built blockhouses at Forty Fort, Plymouth, and Hanover. Open holes were made in the houses to serve as windows. The chimney was open, and a rug was used as a door. Seeds were kept in a special place in the house until the wheat fields were plowed. As they worked hard, glass replaced greased paper in the windows. A wooden door replaced the rugs. Stables were made for the animals. Rail fences were built around the blockhouses. Corn, potatoes, pumpkin, and other vegetables grew rapidly. Flowers and fruit trees were planted. Beehives were established. Sugar maples trees were grown for syrup. School houses were built. Horses replaced the oxen. Cast iron plows were developed.

Beds were built in the houses on poles secured into the walls. Mattresses of hemlock were made. Simple chairs were made of basswood logs. Once the sawmill produced lumber, they could make shelves. Ironware included frying pans, dish kettles, and a bake kettle with legs that could be set into the fire.

The children wove thread for the family. They wore fawnskin vests, doeskin coats, and buckskin pants. To eat, they prepared hasty pudding, johnny cake, corn pones, and short cakes. Money was of no use, so they bartered. Hunting wild game and fishing were regular activities. They frequently switched jobs to build new skills. Loneliness was common. By 1774, Wyoming had approximately 1,900 citizens.

Following the Yankee victory in the First Yankee-Pennamite War, part of the Wyoming Valley territory became known as Westmoreland. It was part of Litchfield County, Connecticut, from 1771 to 1778. Zebulon Butler represented Westmoreland in the Connecticut General Assembly from 1774 to 1776, when he left to serve in the Continental Army as a general.

The land at Scranton and Dunmore was initially part of Providence Township, erected in 1770 as one of six townships granted to the Connecticut settlers. It was surveyed ten miles north of the mouth of the Lackawanna River at Pittston and five miles square. The boroughs of Scranton, Dunmore, Hyde Park, and Providence were later formed from Providence township.

The National Stage

Two hundred and sixty miles away, in the Colony of Massachusetts, the Boston Massacre took place on March 5, 1770. British Army troops stationed in Boston fired into a crowd, killing three people and wounding others. Two more later died of their wounds. There were uprisings in the colonies following the Stamp Act of 1765. King George III of England was in debt. England and France had fought a war for seven years. In North America, the war was called the French and Indian War. In Europe, it was called the Seven Years War. The King wanted the colony to pay taxes on stamps for their share of the costly war. American colonists did not like this. They had their own colonial governments and did not want to be treated as slaves by the British parliament. Their colonial autonomy was threatened, while the population was growing rapidly. In 1689, there were roughly 200,000 people in the American colonies. In 1770, there were close to 1.6 million people, the majority of whom wanted autonomy and fair treatment from the British parliament.

Along with Samuel Adams and other Sons of Liberty in Boston, Dr. Joseph Warren began organizing opposition to new rules and taxes imposed by the English parliament on the Massachusetts Colony. The Boston Tea Party, in December of 1773, was the tipping point on the national stage. When three shiploads of tea were dumped into the harbor, King George III ordered that Boston be punished. The British closed the Port of Boston. It would not be opened until the East India Company was compensated for its damaged cargo of tea. Trade halted and the town suffered immensely. Other colonies protested unfair British rule.

The separate colonies realized it was time to stand together. In September of 1774, the First Continental Congress met in Philadelphia. Boston was represented by Samuel Adams, John Adams, and Robert Treat Paine. Dr. Warren was asked to draw up a document stating the opinions of the people of Massachusetts. On behalf of delegates from every town represented at Suffolk, he wrote *The Suffolk Resolves* on September 6, 1774. In the introduction, he states their revolutionary concerns:

> "If we arrest the hand which would ransack our pockets, if we disarm the parricide which points the dagger to our bosoms, if we nobly defeat that fatal edict which proclaims a power to frame laws for us in all cases whatsoever, thereby entailing the endless and numberless curses of slavery upon us, our heirs and their heirs forever; if we successfully resist that unparalleled usurpation of unconstitutional power, whereby our capital is robbed of the means of life; whereby the streets of Boston are thronged with military

executioners; whereby our coasts are lined and harbors crowded with ships of war; whereby the charter of the colony, that sacred barrier against the encroachments of tyranny, is mutilated . . ."[20]

The introduction is followed by nineteen resolves, the gist of which includes: proclaiming the Coercive Acts to be unconstitutional and void; urging Massachusetts to establish a separate free state; suggesting that future tax collections be retained by the new Massachusetts government and not passed along to British officials; calling for a boycott of British goods and trade with Britain; advising the people of Massachusetts to appoint militia officers and commence arming their local forces; warning General Thomas Gage that officers who arrested citizens would be arrested, and that subjects no longer owed loyalty to a King who violated their rights.

Warren's good friend, Paul Revere, carried this message to Philadelphia by horseback in 1774. The Americans had stated their independence forcibly. So impressed was Patrick Henry of Virginia by the Resolves, that he said: "The distinctions between New Englanders and Virginians are no more. I am not a Virginian, but an American." The Congress voted to approve *The Suffolk Resolves* and send a copy to England.

CHAPTER 6

A Civil War Within The American Revolution

On April 19, 1775, "the shot heard round the world" was fired at British troops by Colonial Minutemen on the North Bridge at Concord, Massachusetts. This ignited the six-year American Revolutionary War.

At the end of that day, 1,700 Massachusetts militia marched back to the Charleston Peninsula, starting the siege of Boston. The next day, John Adams rode from his farm in Braintree to view the battlefield at Concord. At Mount Vernon, Virginia, George Washington received word of the military encounter.

Within a few weeks, militias from the other colonies joined Massachusetts troops in surrounding the British in Boston. Close to 20,000 colonists entered Boston to siege the British, armed and ready to fight for their liberties. The author of *The Suffolk Resolves*, Dr. Joseph Warren, president of the revolutionary Massachusetts Provincial Congress, was commissioned, but not yet approved, as major general of the militia on June 14. Soon thereafter, the British landed more troops in Boston.

Two days later, Israel Putnam was plowing his fields in Connecticut when he heard there would be a battle at Bunker Hill. Putnam rode all night and arrived in the early morning to join Captain John Durkee and other Connecticut men in the battle on June 17. They were all Sons of Liberty.

That morning, 2,500 British regulars fought the American militia on Bunker Hill. The Americans remained on the hill until the British made their final assault. To give time for the militia and many officers to escape, Warren continued to fight until he was identified by British soldiers, who then shot him from behind, killing him instantly.

At the end of June, Washington was made commander-in-chief of the Continental Army, which had been established by the Continental Congress on June 14, 1775. He arrived at Cambridge, outside of Boston, on July 22. The colonies retained their local militias and other troops. King George fortified Boston and replaced General Thomas Gage with General William Howe.

The Second Yankee-Pennamite War, 1775

Five months after Bunker Hill, in November of 1775, Governor John Penn decided to strike the Connecticut Yankees once more in Wyoming. At Sunbury, Governor Penn raised an army of 700 men under the command of William Plunkett. They marched to the west branch of the Susquehanna and quickly defeated one hundred Yankees. Their next move was to the village of Wilkes-Barre in the Wyoming Valley. They headed out in a blizzard, carrying two boats above the falls to Harveys Lake.

On Sunday the 24th, Christmas Eve, near Harveys Landing, Yankee Captain Stewart ambushed the Pennamites from rock ledges, forcing both enemy boats to go down the falls loaded with men. On Christmas Day, Colonel Butler and his 400 Yankees used the natural cover of Rampart Rocks to inflict nearly sixty casualties on the Pennamites. Among the casualties and survivors of the Second Pennamite War were members of the Continental Army, Yankees, and Pennsylvanians who should have been fighting the British, not an internal Civil War.

Our Founding Fathers in Philadelphia knew very well they had a civil war on their hands. They tried to stop it in 1776 by adding a provision to Article Six of the Articles of Confederation to prevent the states from conducting wars amongst themselves during a time of war. The Articles were not ratified until 1781. This left the states of Connecticut and

Pennsylvania at war in Wyoming, a fatal blow for the area, as the American revolutionaries needed all their men to fight the British.

July 4, 1776

The Declaration of Independence was declared in Philadelphia by the representatives of the United States of America on July 4, 1776. It dissolved the colonies' political bonds to England by declaring self-evident truths such as: all men are equal under their Creator, with unalienable rights to life, liberty, and the pursuit of happiness. In addition to proclaiming human rights, the declaration includes more than twenty-eight abuses of power that form the basis for separation from the tyrant, the King of Great Britain.

The Commonwealth of Pennsylvania Was Created

Less than two weeks later, Pennsylvania held its first constitutional convention, adopting A Declaration of Rights of the Inhabitants of the Commonwealth of Pennsylvania:

Section 1. All men are by nature free and have inherent rights within society. This entails the enjoyment of life, and liberty, the means of possessing property and pursuing safety and happiness.

Section 2. All men have the right to worship God according to their own consciousness and understanding.

Section 3. The people of the state have the right to govern the police of the state.

Section 4. The offices of magistrate, legislature or judge are not hereditary.

Section 5. The legislative and the executive powers of the state shall be separate and distinct from the judiciary.

Section 6. Free elections. All men have suffrage and may not be deprived of their property for public uses.

Section 7. Laws may not be suspended or executed by any authority without the consent of the people.

Section 8. In all capital and criminal prosecutions, a man hath a right to demand the cause and nature of his accusation and to a trial by an impartial jury without whose unanimous consent he cannot be found guilty. Nor can he be compelled to give evidence against himself.

Section 9. Cruel punishments may not be inflicted, bails may not be high and excessive fines may not be imposed.

Section 10. The House of the General Assembly may adjourn themselves respectively. The Governour shall not adjourn the Assembly during their sitting, nor dissolve them.

Section 11. A Privy Council, consisting of eight members, shall be chosen by both Houses of Assembly to assist the administration of the government. They shall annually choose from their ranks a president, who in the case of death, inability or absence, shall act as Lieutenant-Governour.

Section 12. The people have the right to freedom of speech, writing and publishing.

Section 13. Upon advice from the Privy Council the Governour shall appoint militia officers.

Section 14. The people have the right to uniform government. No government separate from or independent of the government of Pennsylvania ought to be erected within the limits thereof.

Section 15. All men have the natural right to emigrate from state to state or to form a new state in vacant countries or in such as they may purchase whenever they think that thereby they may promote their own happiness.

Section 16. The people have the right to assemble to consult their common good, to instruct their representatives and to apply for legislature. [21]

The first constitution of the Commonwealth of Pennsylvania took effect on September 28, 1776. It included the Bill of Rights and defined the form of government for freemen. Power was divided among the House of Representatives, the president with a council, and the Courts of Justice.

The new Commonwealth replaced all Penn family power, but they remained major landowners. In 1776, there were two John Penns, both grandsons of William Penn: John Penn of Stoke was sixteen years old and his older cousin, John Penn, was the last governor of colonial Pennsylvania. Both Penns were Tories who favored the British against the Americans in the war.

The Battle of Brooklyn

After defeating the British in the Siege of Boston in March 1776, Washington moved the Continental Army to Manhattan Island. That summer, the British sailed into New York Harbor on 150 ships with 20,000 soldiers onboard. Shortly thereafter, the Battle of Brooklyn was fought on August 27, 1776. The Americans had 6,000 troops. Washington placed Israel Putnam in command of the American forces. John Durkee led the 20th Connecticut Regiment of 500 soldiers that day.

After being surrounded near today's Prospect Park in Brooklyn, the Americans were ordered to retreat to Brooklyn Heights in the late afternoon. To protect them, Washington ordered Maryland riflemen to cover the rest of the depleted army. Known in history as the Maryland 400, they repeatedly charged the British forces of 2,000 men.

That night, Washington's army was trapped between the British and the East River. Very early the next morning, he noticed the fog rolling in. It was dense enough to hide the boats that rowed over from Manhattan to pick up the revolutionaries. Washington's army barely escaped to Manhattan across the East River, protected by the morning fog. In the

Battle of Brooklyn, 300 Americans were killed, 700 wounded, and 1,000 captured. It was the first major victory for the British.

On November 16, the British pursued Washington and routed the Americans once more in the catastrophic Battle of Fort Washington on upper Manhattan Island. The Continental Army lost another 2,800 soldiers, who were taken prisoner. Washington fled with his remaining troops to Morristown, New Jersey, and then to Pennsylvania. He badly needed a victory.

The Continental Army

In the American Revolution, a military company had roughly fifty men divided into two platoons of twenty-five men, each led by lieutenants. When the soldiers lined up to fire in a battle, one platoon would stand behind the other. A regiment, sometimes called a battalion, consisted of nine companies, or 450 men. A brigade consisted of three regiments, or roughly 1,350 men. A division had two to three brigades, or between 2,700 and 5,400 men.

The weapons for the Continental Army were English military muskets left over from the French and Indian War or muskets made for hunting. Some had bayonets. Later in the war, the army imported muskets from Mexico, France, and other European countries. Gunpowder, lead, and paper were scarce.

In 1776, the Wyoming Valley was the northernmost settlement along the western frontier of the colonies. The British and Iroquois controlled most of northern and western New York State. The northwest border at Wyoming was initially under the protection of a regiment commanded by Colonel William Cook at Easton. But the Continental Congress wanted a full regiment of 450 soldiers to protect the frontier, preferably inhabitants of Westmoreland stationed to defend the town. Westmoreland was the Connecticut name for Wilkes-Barre.

On August 26, 1776, Congress commissioned Robert Durkee of Wilkes-Barre and Samuel Ransom of Plymouth as captains for the companies attached to the Connecticut Line. Robert Durkee was the five-year-younger brother of the famous John Durkee. Captain Ransom enlisted his company along the west bank of the Susquehanna River. It was known as the Second Independent Company.

In September 1776, Congress sent recruiters into Wyoming to help enlist men to fight with Washington. From the local Wyoming stage, roughly one hundred men joined Washington's Connecticut Line under Zebulon Butler. On September 17, two Wyoming Companies were officially mustered into the Continental Army at Wilkes-Barre. Because of the civil war in the valley, the companies were considered independent of Pennsylvanian Colonel Cook's command at Easton.

On December 12, 1776, Congress resolved, "That the two companies raised in the town of Westmoreland be ordered to join Washington with all possible expedition."[22]

Before leaving, the men were promised they could return to protect their families at Wyoming as soon as the war was controlled. They would fight in the battles of Millstone, Bound Brook, Germantown, Fort Mifflin, Whitemarsh, and Monmouth.

The Crossing of the Delaware

On December 26, 1776, the famous surprise crossing of the Delaware River took place. Colonel John Durkee's regiment of 313 Connecticut men was under the command of General Hugh Mercer. They accompanied Washington in the river crossing, moving south to the town of Trenton, where they lined up on General Greene's right for the attack. The road was icy. Behind them rolled the cannons of General Knox. After the Continentals raided house to house in Trenton, one thousand Hessians surrendered and were sent to prisons in Pennsylvania.

British Commander Cornwallis marched immediately from New York with 6,000 men to Princeton and then to Trenton. Meanwhile, Washington moved his army just south of Trenton behind Assunpink Creek. Washington ordered 400 soldiers to make noise all night long while he escaped northeast towards Princeton. John Durkee and most of his men remained at Trenton.

Washington reached Stony Brook behind Sullivan's division, which was headed towards Princeton. After Sullivan entered the town of

Princeton, one of his gunners, Alexander Hamilton, shot at the college's famous Nassau Hall to force British officers on the run.

General Washington ordered his men to march to Morristown, New Jersey, where he made his winter camp. The British escaped to Trenton.

1777

On January 1, 1777, the Wyoming Companies, accompanied by Colonel Butler, marched one hundred miles from Wilkes-Barre along the lower road to the Delaware River to Wind Gap then to Easton to join General Washington at his winter headquarters at Morristown. The First Wyoming Company, under Captain Robert Durkee, joined Colonel John Durkee's Connecticut regiment.

On January 1, 1777, Colonel Zebulon Butler was made lieutenant colonel of the 3rd Connecticut Regiment, also commanding the garrison at Forty Fort. Colonel Nathan Denison remained with the 24th Regiment in Wyoming. His spies informed him of the notorious Tory, John Butler from Connecticut, who during a council at Fort Niagara was planning an attack on the northern frontier of Pennsylvania. Therefore, Congress sent arms to Wyoming in April 1777.

In May, both Westmoreland Independent Companies were attached to Colonel Butler's command from Litchfield County, Connecticut. On August 15, 1777, they were assigned to the 1st Connecticut Regiment under Colonel Josiah Starr. They marched to Neshaminy Creek, Bucks County, Pennsylvania—twenty miles north of Philadelphia. They marched another fifty miles to Wilmington, Delaware, as the British General Howe landed over 200 ships at Head of Elk, a small port at the northern tip of Chesapeake Bay, southwest of Philadelphia. Washington decided to prevent Howe from reaching the capital of the United States. He was not successful. The Americans lost the Battle of Brandywine on September 11, 1777. A chance at demolishing the British forces was lost. General Howe entered Philadelphia without opposition on September 26, 1777.

Howe camped the main British Army at Germantown. The Americans also lost the Battle of Germantown on October 4, 1777. It took the

A Civil War Within The American Revolution

British two more months to defeat American forts along the Delaware River and bring in supplies.

The Second Continental Congress moved west to York, Pennsylvania. As General Howe approached Philadelphia, Governor John Penn refused to sign a statement declaring he would do nothing to harm the revolution. He was arrested and exiled to New Jersey. Penn returned to Philadelphia in 1778 after the British evacuated Philadelphia. At that time, he took a loyalty oath to the Commonwealth of Pennsylvania.

In the fall of 1777, there were two important Battles of Saratoga. The British wanted to split the New England colonies from the Southern colonies. On September 19, 1777, British General John Burgoyne defeated the American revolutionaries under Horatio Gates and Benedict Arnold. When Burgoyne attacked again on October 7, he was defeated and forced to retreat. Burgoyne surrendered at Saratoga, New York, ten days later. This convinced the French that the Continental Army could win battles. They supported the Americans with ships, soldiers, weapons, supplies, and loans. French King Louis XVI entered a formal alliance with the Americans. Spain soon supported the French and the Americans against the British.

In October and November of 1777, the Westmoreland Independent Companies were posted at Woodbury, New Jersey. On November 12, 1777, a detachment of Samuel Ransom's Company was sent to Fort Mifflin, just south of Philadelphia along the Delaware River under Lieutenant Spaulding. The fort was sieged by the British from early October to November 15. Four hundred American soldiers prevented 2,000 British troops and 250 ships from sailing into Philadelphia. Two hundred and fifty of the four hundred and fifty men were killed. Ransom's company was reduced by casualties to sixty-two men. After losing the fort, they spent the winter at Valley Forge.

Congress had created a Committee of Inspection to find the traitors to the cause of liberty in the American Revolution. All British loyalists in the colonies were labeled Tories. There were many at all levels of society in Pennsylvania. Were there any Tories in or near Wyoming who wanted to attack or sabotage the Connecticut Yankees? Fear and suspicion spread in Wyoming. The local people found enemies everywhere. The Yankee forts at Wyoming were strengthened that winter.

The Winter at Valley Forge, 1777–1778

After the Battle of Germantown on October 4, 1777, the soldiers marched for two days to Valley Forge. Despite having lost one thousand more men, the camp was buoyant. Washington waited until night fell and the campfires blazed before he walked among his troops. The general could not hide his sorrow. He had lost 2,000 men, 20% of his army, in two consecutive defeats. There was no way he could remove the British from a comfortable winter in Philadelphia.

On December 4, 1777, the members of the Westmoreland Independent Companies were encamped at Whitemarsh. Normally fresh troops could march fifteen miles in one day. After the Battle of Whitemarsh, they marched thirteen miles in eight days to Valley Forge. Two weeks later, they were brigaded with the 4th and 8th Connecticut Regiments and the 1st and 2nd Rhode Island Regiments under the command of Brigadier General James Varnum. The companies were kept separate at Valley Forge in case they were needed that winter and spring eighty miles away in Wyoming.

Washington had placed the Continental Army eighteen miles from Philadelphia at Valley Forge. The exhausted soldiers were close enough to protect local farmers, but far enough away to make it difficult for the British to attack them. The soldiers were given tools. They built one thousand wooden structures in a two-mile-long camp. The cabins had no floors, and the thatched roofs were made of brush and mud. They leaked all winter.

From the start, men were starving. Food and supplies were not being transported from Boston and Baltimore to the men in the field. Washington was outraged and ordered Major General Greene to be quartermaster. Eleven thousand men were encamped that winter under terrible conditions. Some deserted, one-third were seriously ill with typhoid fever, dysentery, and pneumonia, another third were too sick to fight. The army hospital at Bethlehem was too far away. Two thousand died that winter at Valley Forge. Those who could work built defense lines and a bridge from which the army could escape under an attack. Each day, Washington walked through the camp.

Then the legendary German drillmaster, General Fredrick von Steuben, entered the camp at the end of February. He trained the men in Prussian military drills and bayonet warfare. Within three months, he built an 18th century army. This was invaluable experience for the next three years of war.

When spring came, mud filled with human waste and garbage was removed from around the cabins. By April, the supply wagons started arriving regularly. Cattle and horses grazed on the new grass. The men were ordered to bathe for five minutes each day in the Schuylkill River!

The Spring of 1778

In the winter of 1778, spies continued to report a significant build-up of Tories and Senecas at Fort Niagara, on the eastern bank of the Niagara River at its mouth on Lake Ontario.

Historian Jay L. Glickman explained the build-up at Fort Niagara: "In early June, 1778, while the five Seneca Chiefs were negotiating a bogus peace treaty to ensure Congressional inaction, the force of Rangers and Senecas moved southeast of Tioga Point. They were greeted by Queen Esther, who had earlier advised Butler of her loyalty to the Crown and of her interest in acquiring a portion of the looted property. Queen Esther herself recruited most of the population in the Tioga area to the expedition.

> "In command of the force of over 250 Rangers, 350 Seneca Warriors, and about 100 other Indians and Squaws from various tribes was Colonel John Butler, who was in no way related to Zebulon Butler."[23]

They were collecting their forces some 213 miles north of the Wyoming Valley. Congress, the Board of War, and Washington knew that the valley was a major target. In January of 1778, Colonel Thomas Hartley's regiment of Pennsylvanians had been designated to defend the Wyoming

Strive for Insight

Valley. Why should Pennsylvanians defend the Connecticut Yankees at Wyoming? Had the Board of War in Philadelphia forgotten about the civil war still being waged there?

On March 17, the Continental Congress ordered another company raised in Wyoming. One month later, Congress sent 175 rifles or muskets, 200 weight of powder, 800 weight of lead, and 500 flints to Westmoreland in care of newly promoted Colonel Denison of the 24th Regiment.

The British command replaced General Howe with General Clinton. Lord Cornwallis ordered Clinton to march the troops to New York. In the middle of June 1778, Howe's brother, Admiral Howe, spent a week ferrying 12,000 wagons and 5,000 horses across the Delaware River below Philadelphia. Ten thousand British troops started moving east on June 18, 1778.

Washington had 13,000 troops, many well trained and ready to march east to stop Clinton. He left Valley Forge on June 18 and crossed the Delaware at Coryell's Ferry on June 22.

Rather than sending the Connecticut Yankee regiments home to defend Wyoming together with the Pennsylvanians designated to defend Wyoming in January 1778, the War Department ordered Washington to keep the men to stop the British on their way to New York.

In an Act of Congress on June 23, 1778, two companies under command of Captain Spaulding were called the Consolidated Company in the 4th Connecticut under John Durkee. Spaulding and his men were sent sixty-six miles east to Monmouth, New Jersey, a total of ninety-six miles east of Wyoming. Hartley's regiment was also sent to Monmouth. The war records of these decisions have been removed from the National Archives.

Captains Ransom and Robert Durkee were sent to Reading, Pennsylvania, eighty-two miles west of Valley Forge and ninety-two miles south of Wyoming. They were to protect the ironworks and the prison camps filled with British and Hessian soldiers.

On June 24, the Continental Army marched through Hopewell, New Jersey, on their way to Princeton before heading south to Englishtown. They marched all night towards Monmouth Courthouse.

At Monmouth, John Durkee commanded General Varnum's division of Connecticut and Rhode Island troops. Colonel Hartley's men were with General Wayne's First Pennsylvania Brigade of one thousand troops. The Consolidated Company was commanded by Captain Spaulding. Butler was on leave in Wyoming. Ransom and Robert Durkee were in Reading, Pennsylvania.

The Battle at Monmouth Courthouse, June 28, 1778

At three in the morning, the Continental Army marched into Monmouth under the command of General Charles Lee. General Wayne advanced only to find the British in disarray. Washington was roughly three miles behind the army, but approaching slowly because of the extreme heat. As Generals Varnum and Wayne asked Lee for orders, they received none. Lee was a traitor—he had other plans.

Then twenty-year-old Major General Lafayette, who had been relieved of his command in favor of Lee that morning, rode off along the high ground to survey the battlefield. Lafayette rode up to Wayne, who shouted that the enemy was leaving the battlefield and all he needed was another regiment to defeat them before they could regroup. A victory would have ended the war. He asked where Varnum was. Lafayette shouted that there were no orders.

Wayne attacked the British, but he had too few men. General Knox had his artillery in line and started firing without any orders. General Lee was not commanding his brigades in the field, and then he ordered a retreat. Varnum was forced to counter-march. Durkee and his troops were exhausted that morning due to the heat and the all-night march, but they obeyed Lee and retreated.

Washington was outraged when he arrived to find his men retreating. He asked Lee to explain himself and then relieved him of his duty. Washington found Wayne and ordered him to hold ground while the new regiments were put in place. Wayne waited until the British cavalry were only forty yards away and then opened fire. Washington set up defensive positions with Greene to his right flank, Lafayette in the center, and Stirling to the left. Lafayette took command of Varnum's brigade. They fought off repeated assaults by Clinton's finest infantry. John Durkee was seriously injured. It was five o'clock in the afternoon, leaving two more hours to fight, but the British had fled.

Five hundred Americans were killed. Major General Charles Lee was court-marshalled the following day. Lee had been captured by the British at Morristown the previous December and released in May. While in captivity, he had given plans to the British on how to defeat the Americans. The plans were made public in 1857.

Just before the Battle of Monmouth, he took over Lafayette's command of 4,000 troops on the field. Washington was obliged to send 1,500 more men. That day, the American traitor commanded one half of Washington's army.

Monmouth was the first major victory in open battlefield against the British. The terrible winter in Valley Forge was revenged. The military training that spring by Steuben proved invaluable. Yet Clinton headed directly for the comfort of New York City.

The Battle at Wyoming, July 3, 1778

The Battle of Monmouth Courthouse was fought one week before the Battle of Wyoming. During the spring of 1778, the desperate Wyoming Yankees had repeatedly asked Washington, Congress, and the Board of War to send back two companies to Wyoming and protect the valley from the Iroquois, the Tories, and the British. Their pleas were ignored. Without the approval of Congress and the Board of War, Washington could not release the soldiers from Wyoming to defend their valley. The Continental Congress under President Henry Laurens refused to protect Wyoming. Laurens was a merchant, slave trader, and rice planter from South Carolina. President of the Board of War, Horatio Gates, a former British officer, also refused. Gates had abandoned his troops and left for Philadelphia the day before Washington's crossing of the Delaware in December 1776.

We know Hartley's Regiment was ordered to defend the western frontier. We know he was not at the Battle of Wyoming. We do not know who ordered him to be somewhere else during that first week of July.

On June 1, 1778, Colonel Butler rode to the Continental Congress

A Civil War Within The American Revolution

at York to ask for the return of the Consolidated Companies to protect Wyoming. They refused. On June 23, the commanders of the two original Wyoming Companies resigned their commissions in Reading. They were allowed to march to Wyoming to defend their families with merely twenty-five men.

On June 28, the Battle of Monmouth was over. The British force from Niagara landed their canoes in Wyoming on June 30. Spaulding and his men were finally released to march to Wyoming. They were expected to arrive on July 5. After marching 115 miles to defend the valley, they arrived too late.

Why were the Seneca with the British force? The Six Nations of Iroquois could not agree as to which side to take in the Revolutionary War. They let each nation decide for themselves. The Americans had broken the Treaty of Fort Stanwix and pushed them off their land. England promised the Iroquois land in Canada should the Americans win the war. They never kept their promise.

The Oneida and the Tuscarora decided to support the Americans. The Stockbridge, Delaware, Caughhnawaga, Tuscarora, and other tribes were in Washington's camp. The Onondaga remained neutral. Most of the Mohawk, Cayuga, and Seneca supported the British.

In late June, close to 1,500 warriors and soldiers moved south to Tioga to prepare for the attack on Wyoming. Queen Esther recruited many of the Seneca for the attack, and organized one hundred canoes for the war party down the Susquehanna River to Wyoming.

The Tory war party entered Fort Wintermoot near Pittston on June 30th, only five miles north of the Yankees at Forty Fort. According to local historian Charles Miner, four Yankees were killed in their fields. Four more were taken prisoner. The next day, a group of Yankees under Rosewell Franklin marched ten miles to the scene and found two Senecas there. Both were killed, one was the son of Queen Esther.

On July 2, a Pennsylvania militia with seventy-three soldiers, under Captain Clingman, were camped near Bloomsburg. George Dorrance asked them to come defend the Yankees at Wyoming, but they refused. The civil war was not over.

Colonel Zebulan Butler had only 400 militiamen to defend the entire

Strive for Insight

Wyoming Valley. Many of the men were grandfathers and teenagers. The patriots of Wyoming were badly outnumbered. Rather than waiting for Spaulding and his twenty-five soldiers to arrive, they decided to take the offensive and attack.

Captain Ransom reached Forty Fort on the morning of the Wyoming Massacre and reported to Colonel Butler. On a hot July 3, the British noticed the Yankees were gathering outside Forty Fort. They set Fort Wintermoot on fire.

The patriots left to confront the enemy, with Captain Ransom assigned to the extreme left, under the command of Colonels Denison and Dorrance. Marching single file in the late afternoon, they stayed close to the Susquehanna River as they headed north. The drums and fife played "St. Patrick's Day in the Morning."

Colonel Butler ordered the men to fire and advance in what is now Exeter Borough, where St. Cecilia's Church stands near Route 11. Denisen led his troops on the right flank and Butler kept the left flank while moving forward towards a wooden fence in the meadow. To his left lay a swamp with dense underbrush. For half an hour the gunfire was sustained, but the patriots were outnumbered. Samuel Ransom made a reconnaissance of the ground and was captured.

The Yankees fired a volley on the fence before them. Many green-coated Tories immediately stood up and retreated. The Yankees followed them directly into the Tory trap. As the Yankees advanced over the fence towards the north, the Iroquois let out their war whoops in the swamp and attacked from the left. Brandishing spears, tomahawks, and knives, they shut down the entire left flank of the patriots. Colonel Butler gave the order to stand their ground, but the Yankees retreated and lost their position.

The slaughter of 300 Yankee patriots began. Of the fifteen officers, eleven were slain. Every captain of the six companies, including Ransom and Durkee, was found dead at the front of the line. The place where they fell is about a mile above today's Lackawanna and Bloomsburg depot, at Wyoming Station. The only survivors had swum across the river or returned on horseback.

After the battle ended, the Wyoming Massacre began. Seeking revenge for past losses, the Seneca hunted down every survivor, scalped them, and dragged them to the corner of the field, where they were tortured. Queen Esther sought revenge for her son. From the fort at Pittston, the cries of Yankee captives being burned alive were heard long into the night.

The next day, Captain Ransom's body was found near Fort Wintermoot, with a musket shot through the thigh and his body scarred. It was identified by the shoe and knee buckles. He was buried with the other bodies near the site where the granite monument now stands, near the town of Wyoming on Highway 11. Ransom Township, in Lackawanna County, bordering the opposite side of the Susquehanna River, was named in his honor.

The suffering and outrages to which the survivors of the massacre and their families were subjected are beyond understanding. Samuel Ransom's house and buildings were burned, and his family fled with the other refugees.

On July 4, the Connecticut Tory John Butler ordered his dead to be buried, and then marched with the Seneca to secure Forty Fort. Butler claimed that his force had taken 227 scalps, burned one thousand houses, and driven off one thousand cattle plus many sheep and hogs.

Hundreds of women, children, and surviving men drove off their remaining cattle and marched towards Connecticut. Refugees took the road to the Lackawaxen and Mount Cobb over to the Shohola, while others marched to Easton and on to Connecticut. Some floated down the river to Sunbury.

New settlers would return from Connecticut at the end of July. The Pennsylvanians were not happy about this.

Zebulan Butler reached General Washington to report the battle. He also rode to Philadelphia to make the disaster known to the Board of War. Glickman found a gap in the records of correspondence in the Papers of the Continental Congress concerning Wyoming between February 2, 1778, and July 6, 1778. None of these documents are to be found in the National Archives. At the time, there were Pennamite members in the Congress and on the Board of War.

Strive for Insight

No doubt the events leading up to and during the Battle of Wyoming were heavily influenced by the civil war in the valley.

In September, Hartley's regiment arrived in the Wyoming Valley with 130 men. They were three months too late. In September 1778, elements of the regiment, Colonel Dennison, Captain George Bush, Simon Spaulding, and John Franklin ascended the east branch of the Susquehanna with 300 soldiers, destroying Indian villages as far as Tioga.

After the Battle of Monmouth, Washington moved his headquarters back to the Hudson Valley, where his army received good supplies from local farmers and the Continental Congress. That summer, he turned his attention to the Iroquois on the western frontier and the British at Newport, Rhode Island.

Iroquois attacks continued throughout the winter and spring. Settlers were captured and marched upriver. Families were scalped. The Tripp party was murdered along the creek in today's Clarks Green. The blockhouse at Kingston was raided, Fort Wyoming attacked. Zebulon Butler sent reports to the Board of War, but they were ignored.

At the age of five, Francis Slocum, the daughter of Jonathan and Ruth Tripp Slocum, was captured in Wilkes-Barre by Delaware Indians on November 2, 1778. Only weeks after her capture, her father was shot dead and her mother's father, Isaac Tripp, was tomahawked. Her brother escaped. Francis Slocum's family spent fifty-nine years looking for her. Then she was found in Indiana, the widow of a Miami chief with two daughters. She refused to return to Wyoming.

Sullivan's March, 1779

General Washington collected supplies and men to secure the northern frontier from the British and Iroquois. The Seneca People of Iroquois Confederacy in western New York built their villages on the Finger Lakes and the Genesee Valley surrounded by large gardens of squash, beans, corn, melons, and other vegetables. The shores of the lakes were covered with fruit trees. They produced most of the food for British forces in America.

Washington decided to launch an expedition from Wyoming to destroy Iroquois crops and livestock and thereby relieve the pressure on the northern frontier. Congress and the Board of War approved the expedition to completely destroy the Six Nations of the Iroquois. One third of the entire Continental Army was to march up the Susquehanna River to the Finger Lakes region of New York to punish the Six Nations. Total destruction of the crops and devastation of the land and people was Washington's goal. He wanted as many captives as possible, be they men, women, or children of any age.

Glickman quotes the original text of Washington's orders to Sullivan:

> "SIR, The expedition you are appointed to command is to be directed against the hostile tribes of the Six Nations of Indians, with their associates and adherents. The immediate object is their total destruction and devastation, and the capture of as many persons of every age and sex as possible. It will be essential to ruin their crops now in the ground and prevent their planting more."[24]

These orders mark the beginning of genocide of the Native Americans by military action. For the next hundred years, the United States military would be used to devastate our Native people.

After a six-day march, thirty-nine-year-old Major General John Sullivan arrived in the Wyoming Valley on June 23, 1779. There he was joined by Connecticut Yankees Captain Spaulding and Captain John Franklin.

Three thousand four hundred Continental soldiers under Sullivan's command set out on July 31. They had 214 flat-bottom riverboats that were poled against strong current and rapids up the Susquehanna River, carrying artillery, ammunition, and heavy supplies. Most men marched up the warrior trail in a long line of six miles. Twelve hundred packhorses carried the remaining supplies.

Before leaving the valley, the entire army stopped briefly at Monocanock Island to honor the victims of the Battle of Wyoming. The army moved slowly up the river to Wyalusing and Tioga Point. There they met American General Clinton with 1,600 men from the Mohawk Valley and Colonel Pawling with 200 men from the Hudson Valley. Every village they entered was completely destroyed. They salted the land to prevent future crops and cut down all fruit trees. A total of forty Iroquois villages in the region were destroyed. Sullivan's men left behind smallpox-infected clothing in the abandoned villages to spread the disease when the Iroquois returned.

Sullivan easily defeated approximately 1,500 Natives and 200 Tories at Newtown, New York, on the 29th of August, 1779. He pushed into Iroquois territory as far as the Genesee River, destroying everything alive to exterminate the Natives. The Iroquois took refuge at Fort Niagara.

On October 7, 1779, the Sullivan expedition returned down the Susquehanna River to the fort at Wilkes-Barre. The general and his army marched northeast to Washington's forces gathered along the Hudson River.

The War in the Carolinas, 1780

Lord Cornwalis sailed to South Carolina and sieged the city of Charleston during the months of April and May. Washington dug into the hills of New Jersey along the Hudson River with only 3,000 troops. He paraded them cleverly so spies would not discover how weak his forces were. In New York City, the British and the Hessians had close to 10,000 soldiers.

On August 16, former president of the Board of War, Horatio Gates, lost the Battle of Camden in North Carolina. Washington replaced him with General Nathaniel Greene. Greene arrived in Charlotte, North Carolina, on December 2, 1780, and began his harassment of the British armies. From Washington, he had learned how to stay close enough to the enemy to prevent them from tormenting local people, while far enough away to prevent them from attacking. Once Gates was gone, General Daniel Morgan agreed to rejoin the army.

British Surrender at Yorktown, 1781

Between January and October 1780, Cornwallis chased the American forces under Generals Greene and Morgan by marching over 700 miles. On January 17, 1781, Morgan won the Battle of Cowpens, South Carolina. After this key triumph for the Americans, Morgan and Greene marched their rebel armies north into North Carolina. Cornwallis pursued. At each river crossing, his men were forced to unload and load. The British became soaked crossing the rivers. Greene, however, transported his own boats, making the crossings quicker and drier. They had drawn Cornwallis far away from Charleston.

Then the British general chased Greene 160 miles from Cowpens to Guilford Court in North Carolina. On March 15, Greene chose to attack Cornwallis in the Battle of Guilford Courthouse. General Henry Lee's division of cavalry, together with General Francis Marion and General Andrew Pickens, were sent to harass the British cavalry under Tarleton. General Henry Lee of Virginia was not related to the Englishman General Charles Henry Lee, who had been court-martialed at Monmouth.

With Lee and his men placed at the front of the left flank, the North Carolina militia was in the middle and William Washington's cavalry on the right flank. The day ended with Greene retreating to Troublesome Creek, but as Lee told his commanding officer, he may have won the campaign. His son, Robert E. Lee, would become the commander of the Northern Virginian Army in the Civil War.

The British lost 600 soldiers and many officers. They were 286 miles from their base at Charleston, South Carolina. Cornwallis retreated ninety-eight miles south to Cross Creek. Greene followed the British, then headed north to Virginia. Cornwallis moved his army of 1,500 men north along the coast of North Carolina to Virginia.

The traitor Benedict Arnold attacked Virginia for the British, forcing Washington to send Lafayette to Virginia to capture him. In September, Anthony Wayne joined Lafayette with his Pennsylvania Cavalry at Green Spring, near Williamsburg. The French Admiral de Grasse arrived with his fleet and maneuvered inside Chesapeake Bay.

Then Washington made a daring move. He marched 6,000 men 382 miles from New Jersey to Williamsburg, Virginia, to support the newly arrived French Navy and soldiers. The siege of Yorktown was led by the German General von Steuben, the American General Knox, and the French General Rochambeau. It lasted two weeks. On October 19, 1781, Lord Cornwallis surrendered at Yorktown in Virginia. The Revolutionary War ended. America entered the world stage.

CHAPTER 7

Political Revolutions in the Eighteenth Century

The Local Stage

Two wars for land claims in the Wyoming Valley had already been fought between Pennsylvania and Connecticut, one before and one during the Revolutionary War. After the surrender of the British, a third war in Pennsylvania was imminent. Therefore, a convention was held in Trenton, New Jersey, to resolve the issue. On December 30, 1782, The Decree of Trenton gave the Wyoming region to the Commonwealth of Pennsylvania. The state declared that the Connecticut Yankees were not citizens of the Commonwealth, they could not vote, and they should give up their land claims to the Wyoming Valley.

In the hope of keeping their land, many Yankees swore an oath of allegiance to the Commonwealth of Pennsylvania. These hopes were lost in April 1783 when Captain Alexander Patterson arrived in Wilkes-Barre. Patterson gave the Connecticut settlers one year to move out of the valley. Pennsylvanian troops took over Fort Wyoming and changed its name to Fort Dickinson.

The Third Yankee-Pennamite War broke out in October when Patterson attacked the village of Shawnee. Yankee homes were confiscated.

Strive for Insight

That winter, huge snowfalls covered the valley. In the spring, the water of the Susquehanna rose twenty-five feet higher than ever before. The floods ruined homes, cattle, and food supplies. One thousand people requested help from the State Assembly. When the people tried to survive by fishing, Patterson set down a law not allowing fishnets. Soldiers randomly beat settlers. Terror reigned.

On May 12, 1784, Patterson ordered all Connecticut Yankees out of the valley. Soldiers forced them from their homes. This was their fourth expulsion from the valley. Zebulon Butler escaped to Sunbury and told President of Pennsylvania, John Dickinson of the order. To survive, the settlers hid in caves near Wilkes-Barre Mountain. Patterson then allowed the Yankees to return to the valley unarmed. At Forty Fort, they built Fort Defiance. Soon thereafter, Colonel John Franklin called the Connecticut Yankees to arms. The Yankees moved south to the village of Plymouth, where they fought Patterson's Pennamites along the road. Four hundred Pennsylvania militia under the command of Colonel Armstrong entered the Wyoming Valley. Armstrong attacked the Yankee fort at Kingston. The Yankees were taken prisoner and marched to Easton, where they were kept in chains. All of the men escaped from Easton; eleven were recaptured and sixteen made it back to Wyoming, where they burned down Patterson's house. In November 1784, the Third Yankee-Pennamite War ended. It lasted only one year. The Pennamites returned to Philadelphia.

Colonel Franklin travelled to Connecticut to gain support for their land claims from the famous General Ethan Allen of Vermont, who was a descendent of one of the original Susquehanna Company shareholders. Allen visited Wilkes-Barre in April 1786. He joined a group of Yankees who wanted to separate from Pennsylvania and create a new state called Westmoreland. He agreed to bring some Green Mountain Boys to support the Yankees in Wyoming.

The president of the Supreme Executive Council, Benjamin Franklin, and the Pennsylvania Assembly decided to create a new county in the Wyoming Valley. On September 23, 1786, they named it Luzerne County, for the French ambassador to the United States, Chevalier de la Luzerne. Colonel Timothy Pickering was sent to Wyoming to organize the new county. It was such a large area that in the following century it became divided into the counties of Lackawanna, Wyoming, Susquehanna, and part of Bradford County.

The Yankees still wanted their own state. They refused to vote in the new elections and to submit to Pennsylvania. A town meeting was held at Forty Fort on whether to obey the laws of Pennsylvania. John Franklin and Nathan Denison proposed that the Connecticut Yankees in the Wyoming Valley should retain their original claims and land. Benjamin Franklin read their petition but did not act on it. John Franklin returned to Wyoming and continued to agitate for the new state until Benjamin Franklin arrested him and brought him to Philadelphia.

Wyoming had an election in November 1787 to select a representative to the Constitutional Convention to ratify the new Constitution of the United States. Timothy Pickering was elected. No doubt the struggles in the valley had inspired such rights in the new constitution as the protection of home and property by due process, no forced quartering of troops in homes, and the right to a fair trial.

The Connecticut Yankees had their individual land claims honored by the State of Pennsylvania after it entered the Union on December 12, 1787.

The National Stage

The Revolutionary War began at a time when the colonies were not able to tax their own people. The Continental Congress in Philadelphia knew that even if they could tax the revolutionaries, there was little money to collect. Philadelphia had only 30,000 people, New York 22,000, Boston 16,000, Charleston 14,000, and Baltimore 6,000. Ninety percent of Americans lived on farms.

During the war, the only assets the Congress possessed were their will to win and their hope to succeed. The French were reluctant to loan money to the Congress, for they were not sure whether the revolutionaries would fight to the bitter end. If the British won, the Continental Congress would never pay back the loan.

Strive for Insight

When the Revolutionary War ended in 1783, the Union was in danger. The new states were in a financial depression and needed to boost their trade activities. On July 2, 1783, a decree had been passed in England stating that only British ships could be used to export from America to the West Indies. This included products such as tar, pitch, turpentine, hemp, masts, boards, shingles, and livestock. From the West Indies, products such as rum, sugar, molasses, ginger, coffee, and cocoa nuts were exported in British ships to America. In addition, American tobacco, indigo, potatoes, peas, beans, and grains were exported to Britain.

The French levied import duties on American whale oil, furs, hides, potash, lumber, turpentine, tar, and grains. The French exported firearms, jewelry, hardware, and woolen and cotton goods to America. French luxuries were popular in the American cities—brandies, linens, silk, and gloves. The Americans exported thousands of salted hog heads, fish, lumber, and tobacco to France.

The American ship, Empress of China, carried ginseng and otter furs from Vancouver to China and returned to New York with silk, ceramics, and tea.

The Pennsylvania Society for the Encouragement of Manufactures and Useful Arts was organized in 1787. They ordered two machines from England for carding and spinning cotton. One year later, a factory was built. Nails, gunpowder and guns, colors, and paintbrushes were manufactured in the state.

In New England, they made woolens, boats, and shoes. Buttons, thread, and cotton were produced in New Hampshire. Silkworms for silk production were reported in New Haven and in Pennsylvania. Paper mills supplied newspapers. Glass-making thrived. Americans also produced anchors, bricks, tiles, millstones, cabinet work, trunks, chairs, carriages, harnesses, saddlery, whips, hats, gloves, ploughs, linseed, soap, stoneware, and precious metals.

Some common professions of the new Americans included masons, butchers, carpenters, tobacconists, bolters, tanners, saddlers, skinners, brewers, plumbers, pewterers, silversmiths, bookbinders, tailors, coopers, blacksmiths, coach makers, stay makers, comb makers, rope makers, hairdressers, bakers, and stonecutters. The political revolution aimed at helping them achieve success.

The Bank of America was formed in 1781 by merchants, led by Robert Morris, superintendent of finance for the Continental Congress. It was a private bank that carried out transactions for the private and public sectors. Morris started the bank with gold and silver coins Congress borrowed from France. The bank was the first public offering in America. States were allowed to pay taxes to the Union by using certificates of the bank. The bank printed paper currency.

Alexander Hamilton founded the Bank of New York on June 9, 1784. As the second bank in the Union, it focused on international transactions.

The new country needed to pay for the war. The only option was for Congress to print more paper money. Between 1775 and 1779, Congress had already printed roughly $200 million in paper money called Continentals. Congress borrowed the money it printed and used it to pay merchants for the supplies used by the Continental Army. The quartermasters of the army often didn't have enough money to buy the necessary supplies for the soldiers. Congress also offered certificates, instead of money, for the supplies they secured.

The states had their own paper money in circulation. Each state tried to regulate their merchants, who were raising prices for imported goods. They tried to force them to accept paper money for the debts they were owed. The legislature in Pennsylvania asked their merchants to accept continental currency at a defined rate for their products. The merchants agreed and soon doubled the prices.

Most of the public debt was in Pennsylvania, which was the center of American finances during the war. Who were the public creditors who held the debt? They were the merchants and the military officers who received credit rather than money for their services, also the land speculators with claims on the western frontier, and many other investors. They owned the products, the shipping houses, the credit, the cash that was available, and the titles to the land.

Strive for Insight

The Constitutional Convention, 1787

In May 1787, the Continental Congress authorized a federal meeting in Philadelphia to address the weaknesses of the Confederation. Each state sent representatives who were to create a constitution for the population of 3.5 million people, including roughly 600,000 Black slaves. Virginia sent fifty-five-year-old George Washington, who became presiding officer.

The two major defects in the Articles of Confederation were the nation's finances and trade. The new country needed revenue and credit. The fair distribution of taxation among the states became a major issue. Trade policies were urgent. Naturalization, bankruptcy, education, inventions, and copyrights were matters requiring common procedures.

There were many questions. Who will handle the mail? Who will convict a person of treason? Will the country have a standing army? Who will govern the new western territories? How will new states enter the Union? Which states have the rights to the Delaware River, the Susquehanna River, and Chesapeake Bay? How will land be entitled? Who will build roads, canals, and bridges?

Where should the power lie—in the central government or in the state governments? What must be a federal task? What must remain a state task? What kind of executive power should be established? What type of legislature should levy taxes, create laws, and make treaties with foreign nations? How should trade be regulated by a navigation act? Who will print our money and pay our debt? Who should pay our Revolutionary War soldiers? Uniform federal policies were necessary. State rights were also necessary.

The Founding Fathers of American democracy were well versed in the philosophy of the Enlightenment in Europe. In *The Second Treatise of Government*, Englishman John Locke argued that sovereignty resides in the people. The treatise explained the nature of legitimate government in terms of natural rights and the social contract. His ideas of citizens' rights to life, liberty, health, and property had influenced the signers of the Declaration of Independence.

Frenchman Francoise-Marie Voltaire advocated for human rights, freedom of speech, freedom of religion, and the right to a fair trial. He denounced the injustices of the ancient regime in France.

The other French philosopher, Charles Montesquieu, declared the separation of power in three branches of government in his treatise on political theory, *The Spirit of Laws*. On May 20, Montesquieu's ideas were presented by Edmund Randolph in the Virginia Plan. It called for a separation of power in three branches of government—the legislative, executive, and judicial. A separate executive can take initiative when needed. It can handle foreign relations. It can have the power of appointment to key offices, and it can veto decisions taken by the legislature. These are some of the checks and balances of government. According to the Virginians, the president was to be chosen by the Congress for only one term, the judicial branch should determine matters relating to maritime issues, the collection of national revenue, and the impeachment of national officers. Congress should have two houses, one elected by the people of the state and one elected by the legislature of the state.

On June 15, the New Jersey Plan was presented. It differed from the Virginia Plan in the powers it gave Congress. The plan allowed Congress to raise revenue by import duties, stamp taxes, and postal charges, and to regulate trade and commerce. It also proposed having executives elected by Congress, but without the power to veto. The executive could appoint a supreme tribunal with power to regulate state courts in maritime issues, treaties, trade, and the collection of federal revenue.

On July 16, the compromise was reached that each state should have one vote in the Senate. Representation in the House was to be decided according to population, counting three-fifths of the slaves. At that time, a slave was considered only three-fifths of a human being.

The discussion moved to the appointment of the judiciary. Should the executive or the legislature appoint the Supreme Court Justices? Concerning the judiciary branch, our Founding Fathers thought cases should be tried in the state courts first and then brought to the federal courts. The jurisdiction of the federal court should include cases arising from the laws of the United States, the Constitution, treaties, and issues concerning national peace. Trials of criminal offenses should be by jury in the state in which the crime took place. The writ of habeas corpus should not be suspended unless in cases of rebellion or invasion. They did not mention the power for federal courts to declare laws null and void if they are inconsistent with the Constitution.

The convention then appointed a Committee of Detail, which presented a draft for debate between August 6 and September 10. A major question remained: How should the states be restricted in their activities? The committee of detail proposed prohibiting the states from coining money, entering into treaties, or granting titles of nobility. Nor should the states approve piracy against enemy vessels. The proposal prohibited the states, unless approved by Congress, from giving bills of credit, laying duties, keeping troops or ships of war, making agreements with other states, or engaging in war unless invaded.

The Committee of Detail proposed that if two-thirds of the state legislatures apply for an amendment to the Constitution, Congress should call a convention for that purpose.

Executive powers of the president were enlarged during the convention. The president executes the national laws and has the power to veto Congress. The president could be removed by impeachment in the House of Representatives. He was given the power to convene Congress, and to adjourn them if the Senate and the House are caught in disagreement. He became the commander-in-chief of the armed forces and he could grant pardons.

Two visions of the United States of America were present. One group called themselves the Federalists. Among those who advocated strong national government were Alexander Hamilton, Governor Morris, John Dickinsen, Elbridge Gerry, and Roger Sherman.

The other vision was held by the Republicans. They wanted the United States of America based on the people. They included Thomas Jefferson and James Madison from Virginia, James Wilson, Edmund Randolph, and George Mason. The Republicans wanted a model of government with agricultural sustainability, free trade, western expansion, and a federal government that is decentralized.

A compromise between both visions was agreed upon. The Constitution of the United States of America was signed on September 17, 1787.

Seven Articles of the Constitution of the United States

The First Article established legislative powers in the Congress of the United States of America, consisting of a Senate and a House of Representatives.

The Second Article vested the executive power in the president.

The Third Article vested the judicial power in one Supreme Court and in other inferior courts the Congress may establish from time to time.

The Fourth Article affirmed the rights of the separate states.

The Fifth Article provided the process for making Constitutional amendments.

The Sixth Article declared valid any debts or engagements in effect between the Articles of Confederation and the ratification of the Constitution.

The Seventh Article states that ratification by nine states is sufficient for the establishment of the Constitution.

In addition to the articles, the first ten amendments have been in force since November 1791. They are known as the Bill of Rights, and were introduced by James Madison. Without them, it would have been very hard for all states to agree to the new Constitution.

The First Amendment secured the right to speak, guaranteed the right to assemble, to petition the government, freedom of the press, and religious freedom.

The Second Amendment recognized a regulated militia, and gave citizens the right to keep and bear firearms.

The Third Amendment prevented soldiers from occupying citizens' houses during peace and allowed the military to do so in an orderly manner during war.

Strive for Insight

The Fourth Amendment eliminated random house searches, and required warrants for seizures of private property.

The Fifth Amendment removed punishment without law and due process. No one may be forced to witness against themselves. It guaranteed due process of law for everyone except for those in the military during war or public danger. Private property may not be taken without compensation.

The Sixth Amendment gave criminals the right to a speedy and public trial in the state where the crime took place. The accused has the right to find witnesses and to be assisted by counsel.

The Seventh Amendment preserved the right of trial by jury on common law.

The Eighth Amendment prevented excessive bail, fines, and cruel punishments.

The Ninth Amendment prevented the numerical listing of the rights in the Constitution from limiting the rights that are retained by the public.

The Tenth Amendment declared that any powers not delegated to the Unites States nor prohibited by the United States are reserved for the states or the people.

Since then, very important changes to the Constitution have been added. In January 1796, *the Eleventh Amendment* immunized states from suit for money damages or equitable relief from citizens of other states or citizens of any foreign state without their consent.

In September 1804, *the Twelfth Amendment* determined more specifically how the president will be elected by the electoral system.

In December 1865, *the Thirteenth Amendment* abolished slavery and involuntary servitude, except as a punishment for crime after due conviction.

In July 1868, *the Fourteenth Amendment* ensured that the rights of

Political Revolutions in the Eighteenth Century

every American citizen are protected from any trespasses by any state government. No one who previously engaged in insurrection or rebellion against the United States or any states may hold government office. The validity of public debt may not be questioned. Nor shall any state or the United States pay any debt to anyone who rebelled against the country. Any claim for the loss or emancipation of slaves, be they debts, claims, or obligations, are illegal and void.

In 1870, *the Fifteenth Amendment* secured the right to vote of all citizens of the United States. Neither states nor the United States may deny or abridge the right to vote on account of race, color, or previous condition of servitude. Congress can enforce this article by legislature.

In February 1913, *the Sixteenth Amendment* gave Congress the power to lay and collect taxes on income from whatever source derived, without approval by the states and without regard to any census or enumeration.

In May 1913, *the Seventeenth Amendment* determined that United States Senators are no longer elected by the state legislatures, but by popular vote. Vacancies are filled by the governor of that state.

What do these rights have to do with you? These are your civil liberties. It is very important to pay attention to them. They are easily abused by others. Let us take a simple example. Say you are sleeping next to the window on the bus from New York. I am across the aisle and notice your purse on the seat next to you. I take your purse and look through it. I find your phone and your wallet and begin checking them out. In just a few minutes, I have violated your rights and committed a couple of crimes. It is that easy to abuse your civil liberties!

The Second Amendment is perhaps the most controversial today. Why?

It recognized the need in 1791 for a regulated militia and it gave citizens the right to keep and bear firearms. The colonists were dependent on forming militias to win the Revolutionary War. After the Constitution was established, the USA used militias to claim land from the Native Americans. The federal government made the land claim official and then moved the Native Americans out. Until about 1845, most of the Southeast was taken to make cotton plantations east of the Mississippi River in Louisiana, Georgia, Alabama, and the state of Mississippi. Local militias suppressed the slaves and hunted down runaways. Militias were then used to take the land west of the Mississippi River.

Why should keeping and bearing arms be a civil liberty in America? Colonists and early Americans were armed all the time. They had to take loaded rifles to work their fields or be in the woods. Even when going to church or to the next town, they had to carry arms.

In 1794, the population of the USA was only 3.5 million people. Today we have roughly 340 million citizens and over 400 million private weapons. Therefore, major problems with firearms remain unresolved. We witness street violence and massive shootings in schools and churches. Forty-five states allow the right to carry a gun openly in private spaces. Five do not. Since 1993, we have federal gun-free school zones that make it illegal to carry a gun within one thousand feet of a school.

Although rights are given in the Constitution, the moral and social issues continue to challenge our everyday life.

The First Congress

Under the new Constitution, the First Congress convened in New York City on March 4, 1789. A federal mint was created and they levied federal taxes.

Alexander Hamilton became the first Treasury Secretary of the United States. He proposed a fiscal program to collect the debt from the war, the Confederation, and the states within one bank. He wanted the bank to issue securities based on the national debt. The government would guarantee the debt and pay the same interest to everyone. This would attract national and foreign investors, thereby promoting the economy on the international scene. Capital would be available to stabilize trade and promote the manufacturing and farming interests in the country. Hamilton wanted the central bank governed by private people, not by the elected officials of the United States of America.

The First Bank of the United States was chartered in Philadelphia on February 25, 1791. The charter lasted for twenty years. This was our first national bank. Congress chose to fund the national debt equally among speculators and the initial holders of debt. The country gained credibility in European cities—London, Paris, Amsterdam, and Hamburg.

Political Revolutions in the Eighteenth Century

Hamilton proposed selling stock in the new bank to the public, while the government would purchase one-fifth of the shares. The government at that time had no money, so Hamilton proposed the government could lend money from the bank to purchase its shares. The remaining four-fifths would be sold to American and foreign investors. Hamilton had devised a system of public credit, which was to be the main activity of the bank. On behalf of the federal government, it became the depository for collected taxes, a system for making loans to the government and for managing incoming and outgoing money. It was a private bank that could not purchase government bonds. Foreigners could own shares, but not vote.

To bring cash into the new central government, Alexander Hamilton proposed a duty on imported alcohol and a tax on whiskey produced in the USA. For many years, the farmers in the Appalachian Mountains of Western Pennsylvania, including the Wyoming Valley, had used the remains of their grain crops to produce whiskey. They did not want to be taxed by the federal government in New York. President Washington collected 13,000 militia and marched to Bedford, Pennsylvania, to settle the dispute. The new federal government stopped a local rebellion.

The differences between the Federalists and the Republicans continued. Alexander Hamilton, John Adams, and John Jay became leaders of the Federalists. As mentioned previously, they wanted a strong federal government with power over the states. Among them were the creditors who had made a fortune on the Revolutionary War. Their credit claims were settled in the 1790s.

Thomas Jefferson, James Madison, and James Monroe were leaders of the Republicans. They opposed the power of the central government, and they considered the Federal Bank unconstitutional. Republicans were against a bank governed by private bankers who would be able to print currency and make loans on behalf of the United States of America. They wanted an America based on freedom and land, not based on public debt, paper speculation, and banks. Jefferson, Madison, and Monroe saw Federalism as a step backwards into the monarchial order of the British. They feared the national government would become the tool of wealthy men and the states would lose their sovereignty.

Strive for Insight

The World Stage

The French Revolution, 1793

Military drums rolled as 80,000 soldiers marched from the prison at the Temple to the Place de la Concorde. The cavalry paraded with drawn sabers. Stores were closed. Streets were blocked off. A tense atmosphere filled the air. Thousands followed the soldiers by foot. A carriage humped along and passed over the bridge. In the carriage were three men. The first was a priest, the second was the executioner of Paris, and the third was King Louis XVI. The only sound was from the squeaking of the carriage wheels. Paris stood still.

The green carriage stopped at Place de la Revolution. The passengers stepped out. King Louis XVI noticed the statue of his grandfather at the center of the square. Near it stood the massive guillotine. All three men slowly climbed the scaffold. The King was dressed in gray knickers with white socks.

The executioner told him to be prepared. The King took off his jacket, wearing only a short-sleeved shirt. He hesitated to reach out his hands to be tied. Then he spoke with a high voice, "Frenchmen, I am not guilty of the crimes directed at me but I forgive my enemies."

The drums rolled again. The King was tied to a board and placed underneath the guillotine. The commander waved his hand and the enormous blade flew through the air and removed the head of the King of France. It was Monday morning, January 21, 1793.

How could this happen?

Five years earlier, in 1788, Louis XVI sat on the throne with his young wife from Austria, Marie Antoinette. He was a pious but weak person. The French treasury was empty, and state debt grew continually. Noblemen and churchmen never paid taxes, only the citizens and farmers. The grain harvest that fall was the worst in memory. At the royal court in Versailles, the parties for the noblemen continued as usual. No one expected a revolution.

Versailles was a gigantic castle built just outside of Paris by the King's grandfather. Louis XIV, known as the Sun King, expanded the buildings to 700 rooms, 2,000 windows, a hall of mirrors 240 feet long, and a facade 1,300 feet long. His royal bed was placed in the middle of the building. The Sun King had 7,000 servants. There were 25,000 royals and their servants living near the complex. In the summer, the park had 1,400 fountains and a grand canal three miles long.

Who was Louis XIV, the grandfather of the executed King? Much like an Egyptian Pharaoh, he ruled over New France in North America, the French slave colonies, and much of Europe for fifty years. The Sun King wanted to become the new Charlemagne and control the entire European continent. As sovereign king, he made the laws and was the supreme commander of the army and the French economy. New streets, canals, and armies were built. Harbors were improved, a merchant fleet expanded the slave trade, and the palace at Versailles was built to the envy of all Europe. To develop his kingdom, he levied severe taxes on the poor. Foreign-manufactured goods were taxed heavily. There was no freedom of religion—only Catholics were allowed. Protestant minorities, such as the 400,000 Huguenot craftsmen, left the country for England, Switzerland, and New France.

With a population of roughly 26 million people in France, only 300,000 were aristocrats and high clergy, who owned two-thirds of the land and paid no taxes. Eighty-six percent of the people paid the bills for the monarchists and their staff. You became a noble not on merit but on a recommendation from family or friends.

What problems had the grandson faced? On May 4, 1789, King Louis XVI was forced to allow the Consultative Chamber to meet for the first time since 1613. The chamber was divided in three parts, one for the noblemen, one for the churchmen, and one for the people, named the Consultative Chamber. Now they wanted equal representation. After six weeks of quarrelling over that possibility, the citizens decided to create a national assembly and not go home until they had a new constitution. When the King refused, the nobles and the churchmen left the chamber. The people remained sitting. When the King tried to remove them with his bodyguards, a man well known to Americans, Marquis de Lafayette, stood in the doorway and stopped the King's guards. Consequently, the citizens took over.

On July 11, 1789, Marquis de Lafayette proposed the Declaration of

Strive for Insight

the Rights of Man and of the Citizen to the French National Assembly. The declaration was drafted by Abbe Emmanuel Joseph Sieyes and Lafayette, who had consulted with Thomas Jefferson. It declared universal human rights for men, but not for slaves or women. All seventeen articles were approved, and it remains in the constitution of France.

Unrest broke out in the streets of Paris. On July 14, the Bastille prison was stormed. The next day, Lafayette was made Commander of the National Guard. His job was to protect everyone—something he managed for two more years. Lafayette added the color white to the red and blue of the soldiers' patches. All three colors were eventually placed in the new flag of France.

The revolution had begun. No one was spared. The deepest longing of the people for "Liberty, Equality, Fraternity" ran freely. The people's feelings swung from one extreme to the next. A whole parade of women marched to Versailles to dethrone the King. After Louis XVI calmed the crowd, the very same people enthusiastically escorted the entire family of the King to the city under the protection of Lafayette and the national guard!

On August 26, 1789, The National Constituent Assembly drew up a declaration of human rights, proclaiming, among other things, equal rights to all citizens, personal liberty, the right to own property, to be safe from oppression, freedom of profession, religion, and speech. They wanted noble titles abolished and the clergy to be public officials paid by the state. The peasants were to take over the large estates from the nobility and the clergy so they may be broken down into small parcels of land for the common people. Monasteries were to give their wealth to the state. Road tolls and forced labor were to be abolished. Society was to be based on Liberty, Equality, Fraternity!

In 1790, the revolution moved into its horrific phase. Revolutionary leaders, with Robespierre and Marat of the Jacobin club and Danton of the Coloniere club, fought for power in the new assembly. The revolution became a caricature of what it was intended to be. Thousands were sent to the guillotine.

Despite the violence, the new constitution was passed on September 3, 1791. The King took an oath to the state. A new National Legislative

Political Revolutions in the Eighteenth Century

Assembly was established. The constitution brought limited monarchy and equal rights for law and justice, regardless of social status. Taxes were to be equal among all of the people. The church became a state-church. In this phase of the revolution, there was still some idealism in the air. The National Assembly proclaimed: "Freedom—is the right to do everything that does not hurt other people."

Many of the nobles and the clergy left France. The royal family was preparing to escape to Pennsylvania, north of the Wyoming Valley at Towanda, where French nobles planned to build the Azilum for Marie Antoinette.

In 1792, neighboring countries moved troops to the frontier and eventually declared war. The new government was in the hands of fanatics. Lafayette had refused to support the violence known as the Reign of Terror. He was imprisoned as a traitor from 1792 to 1797.

The French Revolution sent its own leaders to the scaffold. Fear spread rapidly. On the posters in Paris, one could read: "Liberty, Equality, Fraternity—or death." The ideals became distorted. Hope vanished. Fear won!

Then, with the fall of the violent Jacobinian leader Robespierre, the revolution moved into the final phase: reaction. The masses wanted peace at any price. The answer came from a young general, who later said of himself: "I am the French Revolution!" France became one nation under the next emperor, Napoleon Bonaparte. He terrorized Europe for the next seven years. The great revolutionary pendulum was complete. The French Revolution was over.

While he was in jail in 1932, Jawaharlel Nehru wrote a series of letters to his thirteen-year-old daughter, Indira Priyadarshini. He described three revolutions at the end of the 18th century.

> "There were different types of revolutions—a political, an industrial and a social. The political revolution took place in America. The English colony revolted and created an independent republic. The Industrial Revolution began in England and spread to most European lands. It was a peaceful revolution, but it had severe consequences. It effected the world more than any other revolution in

history. The social revolution took place in France and ended the monarchy. Privileges were removed and new social classes came to power. We must observe these three revolutions separately and study the details.[25]

The Saint Dominque Revolution, 1804

Nehru did not mention the slave revolution in the wealthy sugar colony of Saint Dominque, which changed world trade significantly. The French Colonial government was expelled in 1804 after twelve years of revolutionary war. To this day, it has severe consequences in America.

The slave revolution began in 1791. Together with Jamaica, the island supplied most of the world's sugar production. Saint-Dominque produced almost 60% of the world's coffee and 40% of the sugar sold in France and England.

Thousands of slaves had been brought in from today's Nigeria, Benin, Congo, and Angola. There were 40,000 French colonists and 28,000 free people of color. In May 1791, the French granted citizenship to all wealthy free people of color. One hundred thousand slaves revolted in August 1791 in the northern part of today's Haiti. Four thousand whites were killed. Hundreds of plantations were burned to the ground. The Whites formed militias and killed close to 15,000 Blacks. Many runaway slaves hid in the mountains and attacked their masters. Hatred between the slaves and the French was extreme. The French sent 6,000 soldiers to the island.

In 1793, France declared war on Great Britain. Then Spain entered the war against France. Spain owned the eastern half of the island, today's Dominican Republic.

Toussaint Louverture was a free Black man who commanded the slave revolt. Unexpectedly, Louverture joined the French against the British and Spaniards. He was promised freedom for all slaves.

In 1795, Spain ceded Santo Domingo to the French. The British sent thirty thousand soldiers to destroy the French on the island. After the British withdrew in 1798, Louverture ruled as a dictator. In 1801, he wrote a constitution for the island based on human rights. This provoked

Political Revolutions in the Eighteenth Century

Emperor Napoleon, who sent a large force of warships in 1802. Louverture discovered Napoleon wanted to reinforce slavery all over his empire and took command of the slave revolt again. The Blacks used guerila tactics. When the rainy season returned in March, mosquitos hatched and spread yellow fever. By July, 10,000 French soldiers had died of the disease. Five thousand more were hospitalized. Louverture was sent to prison in France, where he died. The French began mass executions.

Jacques Dessalines was now the commander of the revolt. In October, a new French commander, Rochambeau, imported 15,000 dogs from Jamaica to kill the slaves. Napoleon sent 20,000 new soldiers. At the Battle of Vertières in November 1803, the slaves defeated the French. They created the first Black republic. Slavery was abolished in 1804. Dessalines changed the name to Haiti.

How did this effect America? In 1804, the merchants and rulers of the Atlantic Trade Triangle could no longer use slaves in Haiti. Instead, they agreed to move all cotton production to the USA, all coffee production to Brazil, and all sugar production to Cuba. This led to the complete removal of the Native Americans from the South. It also led to increased slavery on the new cotton plantations of Louisiana, Georgia, Mississippi, and Alabama.

Abandoning his enterprises in North America, Napoleon sold Louisiana to the USA for $15 million in 1803. With the Louisiana Purchase, President Jefferson had purchased 830,000 square miles of Native American land from the Mississippi River to the Rocky Mountains. In 1804, the Lewis and Clark Expedition was sent to explore the region.

In 1825, Haiti agreed to pay reparations for their independence to France. This and many exploitive dictators left the island impoverished to this day.

CHAPTER 8

Science and Colonization in the Seventeenth and Eighteenth Centuries

The World Stage

In the 17th century, scientific advances had been made, especially with instruments used in astronomy and biology. Key inventions such as telescopes, microscopes, alcohol thermometers, and mercury barometers were called mechanical arts. Scientific experiments with nature became more important than ancient, intuitive knowledge of the forces of nature in the stars, the animals, plants, fire, air, water, and earth. Modern science became a dominant way of thinking to this day.

A scientific revolution was proclaimed by the English philosopher Francis Bacon. It was based on empirical research in which you remove all other preconceived knowledge of nature and focus your observation on the experiment you carry out with instruments. Bacon demanded that all current theories, opinions, and notions should be brushed aside. The scientist should collect large amounts of facts about nature, and then carry out experiments that could be reproduced by others. From these facts, generalizations should be made and proven. Factors such as quantity, diversity, reliability, and weight could be measured. Bacon considered this a new induction.

Nature's own way of life would no longer be the source of knowledge. Bacon was convinced nature would reveal her secrets when controlled. This would benefit mankind. In 1620, he described his goals in a book called *Separation of Sciences and New Organon*. With new scientific methods, he promised to make nature our slave. To do this, we were to remove delusions from our minds, or idols, as he called them. Bacon considered his idols false concepts coming from past methods of understanding nature and thinking. He declared four types: idols of the tribe; idols of the cave; idols of the marketplace; and idols of the theater. What did he mean by this?

Idols of the tribe are in human nature due to our human senses. Without empirical experimentation, we let feelings influence our rational thinking.

Idols of the cave are a reference to the *Allegory of the Caves* by the Greek philosopher Plato. Every person has his private cave that colors the natural light he receives from nature. This is caused by our upbringing, education, or by authorities we worship.

Idols of the marketplace are given through language. The words betray us in two ways—the same word can mean two different things and humans tend to mix language with reality.

Idols of the theater are theological or philosophical systems Bacon thought gave people the wrong understanding of reality and a false consciousness. Today we call these idols ideologies or dogma. The *Categories* of Aristotle were to be removed from scientific work. The new scientific revolution would remove all religion and art from scientific experiments. Bacon no longer wanted science, art, and religion to build together the key relationships within knowledge.

The 17th century scientific revolution was highlighted by Newton's principles of motion, gravity, and scientific methodology. Among the major discoveries of the scientific revolution were Copernicus' heliocentric theory of the universe, Newton's three Laws of Planetary Motion, Harvey's understanding of the circulation of blood, then human anatomy, calculus, and mechanics.

The revolution presented new methods of research that promised universal, objective knowledge, methods that would act like a machine that guides the mind.

In 1661, Robert Boyle wrote a dialogue, *The Sceptical Chymist*, where he presented his hypothesis that matter consists of atoms and clusters of atoms in motion and that every phenomenon is the result of collisions of particles in motion. This marked the beginning of the chemistry revolution.

18th Century Scientific Revolutions

The English had established the Royal Society of London for Improving Natural Knowledge in 1662, when King Charles II granted incorporation. Sir Isaac Newton was president from 1703 to 1727. Scientists surveyed ecology and climate. They improved natural knowledge, navigation, shipping, and the construction of machines. England's mercantile power increased. Slave colonies were developed.

In 1743, Benjamin Franklin became the first president of the American Philosophical Society. Like the Royal Society in London, the American Philosophical Society in Philadelphia has promoted the advancement of science and the humanities ever since.

The work with gasses and chemistry led to a better understanding of electricity. Franklin's famous experiment with the key tied to a kite was published by the Royal Society in 1752. Franklin asked Priestley to write a history of electricity. Priestley moved to Leeds and continued his electrical and chemical experiments. He received plenty of carbon dioxide from the local brewery. He worked with electrical discharges and the conductivity of charcoals.

Many great scientists and inventors were born between 1700 and 1750!

Luigi Galvani was an Italian physicist who researched electricity in animals. He discovered electrical patterns from tissues in the nerves and muscles. This is known as bioelectricity.

Allesandro Volta repeated the experiments of Galvani. He was a physicist who worked with chemistry, electricity, and batteries.

John Dalton was an English physicist, chemist, and meteorologist.

Strive for Insight

He introduced the atomic theory to chemistry and published a table of atomic weights. He worked with mixed gasses, steam pressure, vacuum, and vapor.

Sir Humphry Davy used a series of elements such as potassium and sodium with electricity and became the founder of electrochemistry. He discovered laughing gas and developed a safety lamp for use in the coal mines.

Joseph Priestley toured Europe in 1774. In Paris, he replicated his experiments with air for Antoine Lavoisier. When he returned to England, The Royal Society published an article about his discovery of sulphur dioxide, SO_2. His famous experiment focused the sun's rays on a sample of mercuric oxide. The mice he trapped in the air survived. He declared that air was better than normal air in the atmosphere. He had discovered oxygen gas, O_2. This was published in 1776. Priestley suggested oxygen played an important role in respiration and the blood system. Lavoisier continued where Priestley left off and developed modern chemistry. He found that water was a compound of oxygen and hydrogen.

Michael Faraday studied electromagnetism and electrochemistry. He discovered electromagnetic induction and the laws of electrolysis. As a young man, Faraday was a laboratory steward for Davy and would go on to succeed him as president of the Royal Society in 1829. He discovered the conditions for building an electric motor and the principles of an electric transformer.

Johann Wolfgang von Goethe was a German scientist, poet, and playwright. He wrote treatises on botany, geology, anatomy, and color. In 1788, he returned from a tour of Italy and published his first major scientific work, *Metamorphosis of Plants*. In 1810, he published his *Theory of Colors*, which differed from Newton's theory. Though it was rejected by the Royal Society, many philosophers, physicists, and artists have worked with his way of observing and experiencing color and nature.

Scientific instrument makers became experts in forming metals. The use of coal led to progress in modern metallurgy, which led to the construction of elaborate machines that changed the textile industry and led to the development of steam engines to propel furnaces, ships, and locomotives. Called applied science, it became the backbone of the early Industrial Revolution, starting around 1760.

Science and Colonization

Colonization during the Scientific Revolution

There is an important connection between Bacon's scientific revolution and the growth of colonization from 1620 to 1949. Bacon's way of experimenting only with empirical methods demanded no interference by religion or art. The fact-based research had no moral responsibility. In all walks of life, people learned to consider nature man's slave. The Native people of the world were considered savages or part of nature, and therefore could be rightfully enslaved along with all of the world's natural resources. This was racism put into social systems.

New machines were made based on the applied sciences. Colonies were developed based on applied racism. Machines and colonization were mutually important for the empires.

The Virginia Colony gave male colonists a local representative government and human rights. They also created slave colonies with no human rights. Did it make a moral difference whether or not you were a slaveholder? Slave traders and slaveholders felt no moral responsibility for their actions. Owning humans as property was normal for them. They felt justified in their racist actions. British racism was based on their attitude that they were the superior race and all other races were inferior. If nature was to be made man's slave, then members of other races could be enslaved to meet the needs of British civilization.

How did racism enter the world stage through slavery? Was it a logical result of Bacon's scientific revolution in which nature is to be enslaved? How could the British, French, Dutch, and other Europeans consider Africans, Asians, and other white men inferior savages, merely a human extension to nature? Why did the new scientific methods and applied science become the basis for slavery and colonization? These are good questions for you to consider.

To better understand world slavery, we need to look even further back to the year 641. Daniel Cattier's excellent French documentary *Slavery Route*[26] describes African slave routes from the 7th century to modern days.

Slavery was illegal in the Arab world because Muslims could not be made slaves. But to expand their empire, they needed cheap labor. Arab rulers wanted to transform the desert to soil. They had to remove the salt and irrigate. In 641, the Arab Army came to Egypt to capture slaves. They established Nusfat, the first Arab city in Egypt.

In the year 900, Cairo became the center of the Arab world in Africa. For the next 400 years, there was a huge demand for domestic slaves in Cairo. Slave women were treated as luxury items confined to the masters' houses.

In 1375, African slave routes were moved to Southern Europe. Slaves were transported from the Sub-Sahara to ports along the Mediterranean Sea, Algiers, Tunis, Tripoli, and Cairo. They entered Europe at Venice, Genoa, Marseille, and Granada. Some were sent by ship to Japan and China.

These slave routes are still used today. These days, hundreds of thousands of Africans cross the Sahara to the Mediterranean to escape violence and poverty. None of these people are shown respect as human beings. At the ports, they meet human traffickers. How much do they pay for a place on a boat across the Mediterranean Sea to Italy, Turkey, or Greece?

In 1550, Portugal controlled the seas between Europe and the East. Portugal filled the islands off the western coast of Africa with slaves from the Congo. For sugarcane plantations in the 16th century, the Portuguese chose Säo Tromè, an uninhabited volcanic island in the Gulf of Guinea. On this tropical island, the Portuguese combined slavery with the production of sugar. Four thousand new slaves arrived each year from the Congo. The sugar was sent to Europe.

In 1515, sugar production was moved to Brazil. A new slave trade route was established from equatorial Africa to Brazil. An estimated 300,000 African captives were sent to the Brazilian slave colony on the island of Sao Vincente.

Europeans Control the Seas

Columbus sailed to the West Indies in 1492, on the first of four journeys for Spain. The Aztec Empire in Mexico was soon conquered by the Spanish Conquistadors in 1521. The Inca Empire in Peru was conquered in 1532.

Spain controlled the West Indies and Central and South America. Great wealth came into Spain from the stolen gold and the silver mines of South America. Wealthy Spanish popes appeared in Rome and the Spanish Armada grew strong. If you controlled the seas, you controlled the sea trade and the colonies.

How could the little island of England conquer North America, Africa, India, and China? China was a land nation, in contrast to the island of England, which became a sea nation. All resources were focused on ruling the seas. England became a maritime superpower, a global trading empire with its financial center in London.

The turning point for England came in 1588 when the Spanish Armada was beaten by the British. During Queen Elizabeth's reign, England's domination of the seas laid the foundation for an empire that would last until 1945, almost 350 years.

In December 1600, 218 merchants founded the East India Company (EIC). They were given a huge monopoly by Queen Elizabeth I. Wherever they traded, the company ruled over the British Army. They had the right to wage war and produce their own money. The EIC became the largest company in the world—a state and a commercial company in one. The founding of the company marks the beginning of the British Empire.

The company realized they could not compete with the Dutch and the Portuguese, who controlled the spice market throughout the region. Instead, the British decided to conquer India. The EIC secured the ports of Bombay, Madras, and Calcutta. At first, cotton, indigo, salt, tea, opium, and saltpeter were exported. The value of the products was weighed in gold and silver. Later, textiles were bartered with Chinese tea, and thereby protected their reserves of gold and silver. In the 1600s, India was a world leader in textile production and trade. England was a poor farming country fighting a civil war. India had 25% of world industrial production, while England had just 3%. Within the next 250 years, England would be the most powerful and wealthy country in the world, while India would be destroyed.

King Charles II granted the charter for The Royal African Company (RAC) in 1660 in London. It was a private company founded by the British royal family, the Stuarts. King Charles II started the mercantile trading company for gold, silver, ivory, and humans along the coast of

Western Africa. The RAC shipped more slaves to the Americas than any other company in history. Under the Navigation Acts, Britain decided to take over the slave trade to the West Indies from the Dutch. Ships sailed from Bristol, Liverpool, and London.

Another major trading company was established for the British Empire in North America. The Hudson's Bay Company received its royal charter in 1670. It is one of the oldest companies in the world that is still active today. The company ruled large parts of North America until it sold the entire Hudson Bay drainage basin to Canada in 1869. The fur trade was its main source of income. Their headquarters was at York Factory by Hudson's Bay. From there, they expanded their trade stations throughout the country.

On the west coast of Africa, Europeans set up fortresses for slave trading. Local tribes stole Africans inland. They set up six new forts on the Gold Coast and one farther east at Ouidah, which became the center of the slave trade. They built new factories, maintained troops, and ruled over the entire territory.

The brother of King Charles, the Duke of York, ran the company. He would later become King James II. The city of New York was named after him. Every slave sold to the East Indies to produce sugar or to grow tobacco in Virginia was branded with the initials of the Duke of York, DoY.

By 1620, Holland, France, and England had colonized the Caribbean. The Dutch took Curacao, Saint Eustatius, and Saint Martin. The Spanish took Cuba and Puerto Rico. The French took Saint Dominique, Guadeloupe, Martinique, and Grenada. The British took the Bahamas, Jamaica, Antigua, Barbados, and Domenica. Europeans were addicted to sugar. Bankers helped finance the expeditions for shipowners and merchants. Pirates took their piece of the action.

For two centuries, the main slave ports in France were at Nantes, Bordeaux, and Le Havre. Slavery money flowed up the rivers to inland cities, where wine, flour, and metal tools were produced and sold abroad. To win the sugar war, Louis XIV built 500 naval ships with seventy-four cannons on each. A French fortress was built for the slave trade in 1684 in Senegal.

Science and Colonization

In 1655, a British expedition under Admiral Sir William Penn and General Robert Venables captured Jamaica and expelled the Spanish. Slave traffic and European immigration increased and the island's population grew to about 18,000 in the 1680s, with slaves accounting for more than half of the total. African slaves soon outnumbered Europeans five to one. Jamaica became one of Britain's most valuable colonies in terms of agricultural production, with dozens of processing centers for sugar, indigo, and cacao.

New France

In 1534, the French navigator and explorer Jacques Cartier entered the Gulf of St. Lawrence and took possession of New France. The City of Quebec was founded in 1608 by Samuel de Champlain. He then explored the state of New York, the Ottawa River, and the eastern Great Lakes.

The Sun King, Louis XIV, established French colonies in the Americas, Africa, and Asia. From 1534 to 1763, the colony known as New France stretched from Newfoundland in the east to Lake Superior in the west, from Hudson Bay in the north to the Gulf of Mexico in the south. At the outset of the Seven Years War in 1756, there were an estimated 55,000 colonists in New France.

Louis XIV centralized authority and formed a professional bureaucracy and military in an absolute monarchy. He kept his nobles busy with social functions at his court at Versailles so they could not interfere in state affairs. In 1673, Louis Jolliet and Jacques Marquette explored the Mississippi River. In 1682, Sieur de La Salle followed the Mississippi to the Gulf of Mexico and claimed the vast Mississippi basin in Louis' name, calling it Louisiane.

Louis XIV published the Colonial Ordinance of 1685, best known as the Black Code. The Code's sixty articles regulated the life, death, purchase, religion, and treatment of millions of men, women, and children by their slave masters in all French colonies. Slaves were to be baptized and educated in the Catholic faith. It required that slaves be clothed and fed and taken care of when sick. It prohibited slaves from owning property and stated that they had no legal capacity. It also governed their marriages, their burials, their punishments, and the necessary conditions to gain their freedom.

Voltaire wrote that Louis XIV had no ideas regarding human rights. The Sun King's Black Code was a crime against humanity, a masterpiece of tyranny. The Black Code remained in force for 163 years.

French trading posts were also established in India and in the Indian Ocean. By 1750, the French East India Company was conducting a trade war with England in India. After the Seven Years War in 1763, the British EIC took all of India.

Colonization of Ireland

The ancient Celts never recorded their history. We first learn about them from Greek and Roman historians. Given their combative nature, their enemies certainly noticed them. The Romans fought many times, but never conquered the Celts. Nor did the Celts ever organize as a dynasty and conquer other people.

As a tribe, the Celts migrated from east to west. Where they came from originally, we do not know. They had close contact with the Ancient Greeks. They lived outside Delphi, where the famous oracle was located. Some tribes lived in Asia Minor, now called Turkey.

The Celts were renowned for their cart-wrighting, their festivals, their music, and their art. They loved ornaments. They painted their bodies and lavished in jewelry. Near their villages, the warriors had warlike games to practice their skills with swords.

As early as 800 BC, they worked with iron and bronze. Then they mastered gold, silver, pottery, glass, enamel, ivory, and amber. They were excellent weavers and wooden cabinetmakers. Their artists loved geometry. They made coins, helmets, shields, and weapons.

Druids were a privileged class of scholars and priests. Bards composed songs and told the history and legends of the Celts in verse.

The Celts bordered the Romans in Europe for 300 years and were considered the true fathers of European culture. In the year 500, St. Patrick evangelized the entire island of Ireland. By 590, Celtic monks were christianizing Europe—St. Columbanus in France, St. Gallus in Switzerland, and many more in Germany. Irish literature is dated near 600.

Science and Colonization

By 1300 BC, the tribes moved west to Germany, Switzerland, and Northern Italy, where some of the greatest archeological finds have been made, especially of burial cities where kings and queens were prepared for their journeys after death.

King Henry VIII conquered Ireland in 1536 and removed the Fitzgerald dynasty from power. The King declared the new Kingdom of Ireland in 1541. In the Nine Years War, from 1594 to 1603, Hugh O'Neill and Hugh O'Donnell of Ulster led the rebellion. In 1603, they surrendered to King James I. For the next century, England would colonize the Irish by making plantations. The largest plantation was at Ulster in Northern Ireland, with 80,000 Scottish and English Protestants as the colonists in 1641. The British made a half million acres available for Protestant settlement in the north. Traditional Irish culture and society were repressed. Clans were exterminated. Penal laws were set up for all religions other than the Anglican Church of Ireland.

From 1649 to 1653, Oliver Cromwell committed atrocities at the siege of Drogheda. War prisoners were sold as slaves in the West Indies. The British scorched the earth, causing famine. All Irish Catholics' land was stolen by the British. The Catholic Jacobites surrendered at Limerick in 1691, conceding to British Protestant dominance. In the 1720s, many English Protestants and Lowland Scots came to Ulster.

Scots-Irish is the name for Ulster Scots, who immigrated to Canada and the American colonies. Between 1717 and 1775, an estimated 200,000 Ulster Scots migrated to America. Another 40,000 men and women prisoners were sent from England and Ireland to the colonies in North America to work as white slaves on the plantations.

The Scots-Irish fought for the Continentals in the American Revolution. Many were generals and officers. Most of the other Scots who came to America remained on the British side as Tories. The Scots-Irish moved westward after the revolution into Ohio, West Virginia, Tennessee, and Kentucky. The immigrants would farm, work the mines, dig canals, lumber the forests, man the textile mills, or build railroads in the 19th century. In the South, they grew rice and cotton.

Strive for Insight

The Atlantic Trade Triangle

From the 16th century to the 19th century, the Atlantic Trade Triangle flourished. The British, French, Portuguese, Dutch, Danes, Spaniards, and Americans drove the trade of manufactured goods, cheap labor from slavery, and crops.

On the first side of the Atlantic Trade Triangle, European textiles, rum, weapons, and other manufactured goods were sold to Africa. The slave trade and the Atlantic Triangle were of critical national interest for England, Holland, and France, whose farmers were turned into soldiers. The countries built military fortresses along the coast of Africa from Senegal to the Niger delta.

The second side of the triangle was formed in Africa when the British RAC transported slaves from West Africa to the West Indies and North America. The French, Portuguese, Dutch, and Danes also sold slaves to South America, North America, and the West Indies. Slaves were sold to sugar, rice, and tobacco plantations. This was called the Middle Passage. Governments financed the ships. Companies, merchants, or private investors paid for the slave cargo and the insurance. Depending on weather conditions, the crossing of the Atlantic could take between one and four months.

In Africa, kings, warlords, or professional kidnappers came into villages and stole people. In five minutes, it was all over. Imagine someone coming to your front door and stealing you and your family. You would never see them again. You were marched in chains to the European coastal forts and sold.

On the slave ships, you were chained in pairs, crammed underdeck. Can you imagine lying on the wooden floor of a ship with 200 other people for one month? Once a day, you got some food and water. Sometimes you could stand up and move around. You were becoming a slave. Diseases such as dysentery and scurvy often broke out. Starvation was also a major killer.

Many Europeans considered the captive Africans to be less than human; they were seen as cargo or goods to be transported for trade. Whipping was common. Everyone knew the ships were oceangoing torture chambers.

Science and Colonization

The third side of the triangle included raw products not produced in Europe—tobacco, rice, cotton, and sugar in the form of molasses. These were exported back to England and other parts of Europe. In England, the cotton was spun and woven, made into clothes or fabric that were exported back to Africa, where new slaves were captured and sold. Cotton clothes and fabric were also sent to India. Between 1750 and 1769, cotton export reportedly grew ten times. From 1633 to 1807, when England outlawed slavery, experts estimate that 2,750,830 Africans were transported by the English alone.

Eight million Africans were transported as slaves on the triangle by 1789. All total, nearly 12 million Africans were sent to South and North America.

The East India Company

In 1720, the British parliament banned Asian textile imports to increase domestic production. This made India dependent on British textiles and clothing!

It opened a huge market for the EIC that would continue until Gandhi led the revolution that ended British rule in 1949. He taught the people to weave and make their own clothes as a major part of their nonviolent resistance.

At first, the EIC was interested in spices from India. The trade in tea grew as it became the national drink of England. To make trade safe, the company became a territorial colonial power. It had its own army in India. The soldiers in the EIC Army were Muslims and Hindus. The company created a feudal infrastructure in India to conduct trade. England took over the administration of the entire sub-continent and demanded taxes. The EIC owned all British trade between both continents.

Trading monopolies were set up in Hong Kong, Singapore, Ceylon, and Malaysia. Until then, there had been silk road trade routes by land to China and India, but now sea routes provided a tremendous increase in contacts.

In 1743, Robert Clive became the ruler of Bengal at the age of eighteen. Sixteen years later, in the Seven Years War, Clive defeated local rebels who were supported by the French off the coast of Bengal at Plassey.

Bengal was the last province of India with productive agriculture and a textile industry. The province was annexed into the company. The company's army of 150,000 men cost more money than the company earned. They increased taxes to cover their costs. Roads and water canals were built.

In 1770, the EIC entered the commodity market. They bought tons of rice and placed it in their forts until the price went up, when they sold it for profit. Though millions of Bengalis died of hunger that year, the colonial Brits transferred a million pounds to their accounts in London.

In the Tea Act of 1773, parliament approved the export of cheap Chinese tea to the colonies in America under the protection of the British Army. Cheap tea in Boston was unfair for the America tea merchants. The famous Boston Tea Party in 1773 was an act of rebellion against these trade policies.

After losing the American colonies, England moved the focus of its empire to the Indian subcontinent. In 1783, Charles Cornwallis, who surrendered to the Americans at Yorktown, was made governor in Calcutta. There, he learned how to govern people of a foreign civilization using colonial rule as absolute conqueror.

The East India Company Enters China

The East India Company sent the first English ships to China in 1637. The charter of the EIC gave them monopoly over all British trade in the East. In 1713, the English secured trading rights to sell opium from Sumatra to China so the EIC could pay for the spices they bought in the East Indies. Opium was a good product for the British to trade because it was addictive.

In 1729, the Imperial government in Beijing banned the importation of opium except under license as a medicine. The penalty for dealing drugs was to wear a wooden collar and be whipped with the bamboo one hundred times. The official trade agents of the EIC in Canton were afraid that if they were discovered importing opium to China they would lose their trading rights.

Changes in the company's activities in India in 1756 would profoundly affect their activities in China. A new Nawab of Bengal, Surajah

Science and Colonization

Dowlah, seized the EIC headquarters in Calcutta. Robert Clive won the battle at Plassey, putting an end to the Mogul Empire in India. Opium trade increased.

Through Bengal, the Ganges flows in hundreds of channels into the sea. Vast plains of rich soil were used to grow rice, spices, sugar, and oils. To control the fields of Bengal, the EIC found cheap labor and lowered prices. Patna became the center of British opium production in Bengal. Rather than spend British silver in China to buy porcelain, tea, and silk, the EIC decided to develop a product that would replace the silver exchange, namely opium from Bengal. Cotton plantations in Bengal were declared illegal for cotton production. Instead, they were used to produce opium.

By 1779, nearly one thousand chests of opium were illegally imported each year into China by the British. One chest weighed 180 pounds. The EIC would hold the trade monopoly to China's 300 million people for sixty more years.

The Asian Trade Triangle

The Atlantic Trade Triangle is well known; the second trade triangle in Asia is not. The first side of the Asian Triangle began in England, bringing cargo to India. The second side brought cargo from India to China. The third side brought cargo from China back to England. What do you think all three cargoes consisted of?

The EIC prevented millions of people in India from growing cotton and manufacturing their own clothes. Cotton textiles and clothes were the cargo on the first leg from England to India. The cotton came from America to England in the Atlantic Trade Triangle. Demand for cotton grew as the population of India grew.

The second side of the Asian Trade Triangle was based on opium that the EIC produced in Bengal and Afghanistan and sold in China! The British commanded the seas and they could force illegal trade upon foreign lands. Britain forced the Chinese to import opium even though it was illegal in their country. Opium is the same drug as heroin but a little less potent. It is addictive and poisonous. In China, opium was smoked, not eaten or chewed as in India. The British loaded their ships with the drugs in Calcutta and sailed to the coast outside Canton. There, Chinese sailors approached the ships to take on smaller loads of the drug. The British Royal Navy protected the drug trade and dictated the doctrine of free trade to the empire's advantage. Jobs were created at home in England. In Africa, India, and China, millions of people were exploited. The third side of the Asian Triangle included the sale of jade, silk, tea, and porcelain back to England's high society.

The European nations owned the sailing ships on both triangles. Merchants invested in the cargo. In the Americas and in Europe, merchants knew the value of the various cargoes at different times. They could choose the cargo and when to invest in it. They could invest in weapons and alcohol from England to Africa, slaves from Africa to the Americas, sugar, tobacco, rice, indigo, or cotton from the Americas to England and Europe. They could invest in British textiles to India, opium from India to China, or Chinese silk, spices, tea, and porcelain back to England.

Envision two trade triangles in constant motion, one over the Atlantic Ocean and one over the Indian Ocean to China. This is a picture of the world trade that propelled the British Empire as well as the traders in America. From these trade triangles, we find the origin of the Cotton Exchange in Lower Manhattan and banking on Wall Street.

You will remember figure-eight curves, called lemniscates, from your geometry lessons. They look like the number eight lying on its side. Lemniscate is from the Greek, meaning ribbons. It is used as the symbol of infinity! Both trade triangles flowed into each other, with England at the point of intersection. World trade should be never-ending! The next question must be: Where do we find these ribbons in world trade today?

The National Stage

In the Public Broadcasting Service's documentary *New York*, Ric Burns[27] gives an excellent introduction to the history of the city from New Amsterdam to the 21st century. Burns tells us that the first African slaves from Angola arrived in Manhattan in 1626. They cleared the land and

Science and Colonization

built Fort Amsterdam. The Dutch West India Company hired Peter Stuyvesant to run the colony with an iron hand. Streets were built. Slave trading was the source of income. Anyone could move to the colony if they were willing to work.

On August 27, 1664, four English frigates sailed into New Amsterdam's harbor and demanded New Netherland's surrender. Peter Stuyvesant ceded. A war broke out between England and the Dutch Republic, but in June 1665, New Amsterdam was named New York City for the Duke of York. The conquest was finalized in July 1673.

The British quickly destroyed the Native American population on the island. The Atlantic Trade Triangle was established in New York. By 1740, 700 ships left the port each year. Local producers of food, barrels, and ships were on the world market. The slave market was at Wall Street.

The French and Indian War of 1756 was celebrated by British merchants. By 1758, there were 25,000 British troops in New York until the war ended in 1763. In 1765, the colonists were subjected to the Stamp Act. On November 1, 1765, a mob gathered on the Commons to march to Bowling Green to demand that King George II repeal the Stamp Act. The British Parliament put new acts in place.

In June 1773, Alexander Hamilton emigrated from the British West Indies. One year later, he was a sophomore at King's College. Hamilton would help New York become a center of commerce and manufacturing. In 1792, he helped turn the slave market at Wall Street into a banking capital.

Colonizing Native Americans

The colonizer has a language, technology, training, education, and money he imposes on the colonized to meet his own purposes. There are many stages of European colonialization: conquest; dehumanization; expropriation; and violence.

We need to reach even further back in history than the slave trades of 650 in Africa mentioned previously in this chapter. Let us imagine life 4,500 years ago, in the year 2500 BC on the coast of South Carolina. From that period, undecorated pottery built of grass and vegetable fiber

Strive for Insight

mixed with clay has been found in the swamps along the Savanna River. Imagine how these people lived near the Atlantic.

At the same time, across the ocean in Africa, we find the zenith of Ancient Egyptian pyramid building—the Great Pyramid built for Pharaoh Kufu, known as Cheops, at Giza outside Cairo. This was a golden age for Egypt, with a stable central government and important military raids in Libya and Nubia. The Sun God, Ra, was the center of their worship.

Two thousand years after the Cheops pyramid, the forefathers of the Cherokee people were part of the Mississippian culture that spread to the Southeast by 566 BC. This was when Prince Siddhartha Gautama was born in Northeast India, roughly 2,500 years ago. The prince would become the great teacher and enlightened being, Buddha.

By the time the first Europeans came to the Carolinas, the Cherokee were still building temples in round mounds. They had been doing so for the past 5,000 years. Historian Alvin M. Josephy, Jr. writes, "The Cherokee, occupying generally the hill and mountains country of western North Carolina and eastern Tennessee, was the largest tribe in the Southeast, with some 20,000 people living in sixty towns."[28]

Five nations joined together in colonial times as the Five Civilized Tribes—the Cherokee, Chicksaw, Choctaw, Creek, and Seminole. Like the Iroquois in the North, the tribes were a matrilineal society, where the family was based on the female line. They shared government, military, and agricultural interests. The Cherokee raised animals, worked large farms, and built houses much like the Europeans. They developed a written language and adopted a constitution.

In 1754, at the start of the French and Indian War, 700 Cherokee fought with the British against the French. As colonials took Cherokee land, the people went to war against the British from 1758 to 1761. Twenty-nine chiefs were taken by the militia to Fort Prince George. In February, the Cherokee attacked the fort. The chiefs were massacred. The Cherokee attacked Fort Dobbs in North Carolina and raided smaller settlements. The British sent an army of one thousand men and were severely defeated. In 1761, an army of 2,600 Brits levelled fifteen Cherokee towns and burned their crops. A treaty was signed with South Carolina in 1762. Life would never be the same for the Cherokee.

Science and Colonization

The next major colonial campaign against our Native people began in 1790 in western Pennsylvania and Ohio. Major General Arthur St. Clair had been named first Governor of the Northwest Territories in 1788. These territories included today's Ohio, Indiana, Illinois, and Michigan, plus parts of Wisconsin and Minnesota. His goal was to clear the way for white settlers. On November 4, 1791, St. Clair's army and militia met forces under the Miami Chief Little Turtle and the Shawnee Chief Blue Jacket near the headwaters of the Wabash River. More than 600 soldiers and militia were killed at The Battle of One Thousand Slain. Losses also included many Native women and children.

After multiple defeats, the Legion of the United States was put under command of the Revolutionary War hero General Anthony Wayne. In the Battle of Fallen Timbers on August 20, 1794, at Maumee, Ohio, Wayne's 2,000 soldiers and the Kentucky militia defeated 1,500 Shawnee, Delaware, Wyandot, Ojibway, Odawa, Mingo, Mohawk, and Canadians dressed as Natives.

Two major treaties were signed after the Battle of Fallen Timbers. First, in New York, the Iroquois signed the Treaty of Canandaigua on November 11, 1794. All Native American title to land within Pennsylvania's modern borders was extinguished. The people migrated north into Canada or west to Ohio Territory.

The second treaty was signed one year later. Josephy writes, "And by the Treaty of Greenville (1795) Wayne forced a group of chastened chiefs to cede almost two thirds of the present state of Ohio, part of Indiana, and various strategic sites in other parts of the Northwest Territories. The treaty set a pattern for the westward movement of Americans."[29]

The treaty was signed by President Washington and ratified by the US Senate in December 1795. Thirty million Native Americans were colonized.

CHAPTER 9

The Industrial Revolution in England

The World Stage

In 1763, the British Empire had just won the Seven Years War in North America, Europe, and India. France lost the war and many of her colonies along with it. Most of North America and India became colonized by the British. Spain, Portugal, and France still had colonies in South America, Africa, and Asia, but were no longer major competitors in trade. Britannia ruled the seas.

The banks, insurance companies, and merchants connected with the British Empire and the Double Trade triangles made fortunes. They lived on all continents. The sale of human beings to the cotton plantations in America, cotton textiles to India, and opium to China would grow tremendously. To make the cotton products, the textile industry needed machines. The machines needed iron. To mold iron, producers needed coal. These factors were dependent on improved transportation systems—railroads and ships that were driven on steel infrastructure.

Industry revolutionized England when mechanical power created new products more effectively. As the tempo of revolution increased, the modern factory evolved. As large industry grew, so did huge social problems. Greater prosperity for some brought greater poverty for others. Nature and human beings would become even more enslaved.

Where did the Industrial Revolution start? England. Global trade was her moneymaker when she became revolutionized by industry in 1764. Great Britain had great scientists, practical craftsmen, access to the necessary fresh water, coal, lumber, and iron. There were large amounts of capital available. Her farms could produce an abundance of food for the people living in the cities. Improved transportation systems secured more revenue. English patent laws were effective.

In 1712, Thomas Newcomen had already constructed a steam engine that was used to pump water from the coal mines. His machines used a lot of coal because the wheel of the pump was driven by cooling off the cylinder.

The factory, run by a steam engine, did not need waterpower from a river to produce energy. It could be built anywhere, and the coal could be brought to any location. This was revolutionary.

At the same time, the agricultural revolution in England modernized farming during the second half of the 18th century. Jethro Tull had a farm in Berkshire, where he devised a new way to sow seeds. Tull scratched a long groove in the ground and sprinkled in a thin line of seed. Soon machines were doing this.

Lord Townsend discovered that limey clay from the marshes could be added to the soil. He grew turnips and grasses. Soon his cows became fat.

For many centuries, farming was a communal effort in the local village. Each village had open fields, meadows for animals, and woods or heaths. These areas were divided by fences. Many owners had strips of open fields that were ploughed, sown, and reaped by the villagers as a group. Ploughmen had teams of four to eight horses pulling wooden ploughs. The owner then took his share of the produce. When the hay had been cut, those who owned cattle could graze them on the fields. In the meadows and woods, the villagers kept livestock. Farmers barely produced enough to eat. Much of the land was not used. Diseases spread rapidly.

Arthur Young proposed a redistribution of the land that would improve food production. The Enclosure Movement, from 1795 to 1815, rearranged village lands in lots, where the new methods could be used more effectively. Parliament favored the wealthy landowners and passed the Private Acts, which forced other landowners to rearrange their farmland. Not only arable land, but woods, meadows, and heath were rearranged. But many people lost their land, and their self-respect. Tenant farmers were charged high rents. The young left the villages for the cities to work in factories. Others entered the military.

Key Inventors and Inventions in Industry

Parallel with the changes in agriculture and steam engines, the textile industry advanced when John Kay invented the flying shuttle in 1733. Wider material could be woven at twice the speed. The demand for textiles grew. Nine spinners would work overtime to meet the needs of one weaver.

In 1751, The Royal Society of London created a prize for the best one-man machine that could simultaneously spin six threads of cotton, flax, or hemp. Not until 1764 did James Hargreave create such a machine. Soon thereafter, Richard Arkwright discovered the initial spinning machine, which spun cotton into thread. His idea was to have increasingly rapid movement of the spinning wheels so the cotton was continuously stretched and spun evenly. Initially, he used four rollers, one clothed in leather and the other three with grooves. Each roller moved progressively faster, thus stretching the cotton evenly, twisting it and winding it on spindles. He labored for many months to make a full-size model of his spinning machine. Once completed, he asked Mr. Smalley, a man with capital, to manufacture and market the machines. Arkwright convinced Smalley that he had a machine that could produce strong yarn, stronger than linen, and at a rate one thousand times faster than a spinning wheel. Arkwright formed a partnership with two stocking makers. Together they bought a mill driven by water in the valley near the River Derwent. For twenty years, they made stockings on their water frames, and by 1774 they made cloth entirely of cotton.

The weaver, James Hargreaves, had constructed a spinning machine known as the Spinning Jenny. In 1779, the mechanic Samuel Crompton combined Arkwright's and Hargreaves' machine into a mule stool that not only improved the quality of the products but also centralized the location of production near the water sources for the mills.

Edmund Cartwright, a priest at Oxford University, created the power loom, a mechanical weaving machine, in 1786. Now Englishmen could transform cotton and create products that were as good as those they had previously imported. In 1781, England imported roughly 5.5 million pounds of raw cotton wool. In 1810, the country imported 120 million pounds worth of cotton from America. Therefore, more slaves were needed in America.

The cotton was woven in England and then exported as clothing products to India. By 1830, more than 80% of the weaving in the world was located in Manchester. To India alone, export grew thirteen times between 1820 and 1840. In 1840, British firms exported 484 million meters of cotton cloth to her colonies and 183 million meters to other parts of the world.

In May 1765, James Watt, a twenty-one-year-old student at the University of Edinburgh, was asked to repair one of Newcomen's steam engines. Watt discovered the idea of cooling off the cylinder in a separate condenser. In 1769, he was given a patent for his idea. Two new steam engines were in use by 1776. Watt was a simple mechanic who needed a partner with money to produce the new machines. He found Mathew Boulton in Soho, near Birmingham. They built stable and precise cylinders and pistons.

Once John Wilkinson discovered a new technique for boring cannons from solid castings in 1774, the production of the real steam engines could begin. He built a boring lathe that enabled Watt and Boulton to bore cylinders for steam engines. They produced 496 machines, some of which worked for 129 years.

The first working railway in England was completed by Richard Trevethick in 1804 in South Wales. The first commercial railway was built in Leeds in 1812.

In 1825, George Stephenson and his son, Robert, built the locomotive for the first steam railway in the world. In 1829, they produced The Rocket. This was true innovation. They used a simple pair of driving wheels, multiple boiler fire-tubes, blastpipes, and cylinders that were directly connected to the driving wheels and were almost horizontal to the ground. They also had separate fuel injection. One of their apprentices on the project was James Dickson, who later immigrated to Nova Scotia, then moved to Carbondale, Pennsylvania, where he taught his three sons how to produce locomotives.

The Liverpool and Manchester Railway opened in 1830. It was the world's first intercity passenger railway.

Factories, Family Life, and Child Labor

Before factories arose, the family worked in their house and on their farm. In towns, children worked in the shipyards, as sellers in the street, domestic servants, rat catchers, hat makers, pickpockets, errand boys, chimney sweeps, or as potterers. The average age for starting work was eleven and a half years old.

Chimney sweeps were as young as three years old. The tiny kids could crawl into the narrow smokestacks and down chimneys. Kids were underfed so they were thin enough to go down the chimneys. Falling down and getting stuck was their greatest fear. At the age of nine, they were too big. In 1788, England passed a law to prevent children under eight from working as chimney sweeps.

Both girls and boys were in demand in the coal mines of England. They were much smaller, could move in tight spaces, and they demanded a lot less pay for twelve- to eighteen-hour days. In the mines, children usually started by minding the trap doors, picking out coals at the pit mouth, or by carrying picks for the miners. Employment underground of boys under the age of ten and all girls became forbidden. No one under the age of fifteen was to run machinery.

To work in the factories, families came from poverty in Wales and Scotland, and from Ireland, where people were starving due to the English landlord rule. Spinning offered higher wages than other jobs. Shoemakers and tailors left their jobs. The cotton mills were based on cheap child labor. Sometimes parents were given a job if their children also worked. They were called free-labor children. In the mills, children worked as piecers, joining pieces of thread together which had been broken in the machines. Four- or five-year-old children picked up cotton waste on the floor.

In 1776, there were eighty workhouses in London with roughly 16,000 poor men, women, and children. In the workhouses, they slept, were fed, and put to work. The workhouses for the poor existed for two centuries. When the factories appeared, children and the poor were sent to the cotton mills at Liverpool and Manchester.

By 1839, the commissioners reported that 42,000, or half of the workhouse population, were children. If a man was sent to the workhouse, his whole family was also put in. They were spilt up into the various sections of the house. Many children in the workhouse were orphans, deserted children, bastards, or children of cripples.

There were strict rules for corporal punishment. A child under twelve was not to be locked in a dark room. They were forbidden to use corporal punishment on females. Only the master could inflict corporal punishment on boys below the age of fourteen. Punishment could only be inflicted with a rod.

In 1847, the five-year-old orphan John Rowlands became an inmate of the St. Asaph Workhouse for the Poor in Wales. In later life, Rowlands became famous as Sir Henry Morton Stanley. At the end of his dramatic life, he was the most famous Welshman in the world. In his book, *The Autobiography of Sir Henry Morton Stanley*, Stanley described the workhouse as a "house of torture." The boy finally left the workhouse in 1856 after a violent showdown with the one-handed schoolmaster. He got on a boat for America.

The German Enlightenment

An enlightenment brings new ways of thinking to mankind. The verb "enlighten" means to give greater knowledge or understanding. Knowledge can free you from prejudices and help you act productively. The British Enlightenment (Bacon, Newton, Locke) brought new scientific methods. The French Enlightenment (Montesquieu, Voltaire, Lafayette) brought new ideas for social life and government. The German

Enlightenment brought a new way to experience nature, increase consciousness, and develop humanity.

At the beginning of the Industrial Revolution, there were many important German scientists, composers, philosophers, dramatists, and historians. How to understand children and the world of nature and how to live together as different people were their common themes. We will look at nine men.

Gotthold Ephriam Lessing wrote a play, *Nathan the Wise*, in 1779 in which he developed the idea of religious tolerance. The play takes place in 1129 in Jerusalem during the Third Crusade, when Islam, Judaism, and Christianity were conflicted with each other. How could people of the different religions live together?

Lessing's final work is entitled *The Education of the Human Race*. Here, Lessing referred to the Jewish People, who had discovered that revelation can guide your reason. They were aware of the doctrine of immortality as they had lived among the ancient Chaldeans and Persians. Immortality was also taught in the schools of the Greek philosophers in Egypt. Lessing stated that the doctrine of immortality, "Our soul does not die," has been preached to believers rather than taught with human reason. With reason, we think and understand. We form judgments and opinions. Lessing thought immortality should be taught with reason.

Lessing asked many important questions: Will we come back to Earth in the future? Has every individual existed more than once upon this world? Why has the idea of immortality disappeared from our consciousness?

Lessing called immortality a hypothesis, an idea that is based on facts and that is used for reasoning and further investigation. His questions continued. Why should I not come back as often as I am able, to acquire fresh knowledge, fresh expertness? Do I bring away so much from one lifetime that there is nothing to make it worth the trouble of coming back?

Wolfgang Amadeus Mozart composed over 600 classical works of opera, symphonies, piano concerts, string quartets, violin sonatas, and sacral music. In 1791, Mozart set the Egyptian Osiris-Isis myth to extraordinary music in his opera *The Magic Flute*. In Act II, Sarastro, the leader of the Egyptian Sun Temple, meets with his council. They decide Tamino and Pamina should be married and that Tamino should succeed Sarastro as leader of the temple. First, they must go through many trials to prove their worth. To obtain enlightenment, there are trials of silence, fear, fire, and water. Soon thereafter, the Queen of the Night and Monostatos storm the Sun Temple, but the Sun cannot be conquered. The stage becomes a gigantic Sun. Sarastro stands quietly. Tamino and Pamina are now wearing priestly robes. Egyptian priests surround them. Teenagers all over the world are inspired by this opera.

While a professor of history and philosophy at Jena, Friedrich Schiller published *The Esthetic Education of Mankind* in 1794. He described how the human soul may be awakened to moral character by experiencing beauty. There are three drives in all people: the sensory drive; the form drive; and the drive to play. In each person, there are conflicts between the material sensory world and the world of reason. The drive to play is the same as beauty and life. The sensuous drive of the material world is conflicted with the form drive, where our reason is active. By way of the drive to play, Schiller seeks a new union between the material world and reason. This union will awaken the human being in us.

Between 1822 and 1824, Ludwig van Beethoven wrote his *Symphony No. 9* while totally deaf. The symphony includes a full chorus and soloists singing the text of Schiller's poem "Ode to Joy," which was published in 1785. The poem appeals to unity and freedom of humanity. Joy unites what is divided. All people shall become brothers. Millions will be embraced. We can sense the Creator beyond the stars. The artistic experience and the message of the symphony continue to inspire people all over the world.

In 1830, Goethe was finishing the two-part play that would become one of the most important pieces of German literature, *Faust*. The play shows how spiritual beings affect men on Earth. During the play, we follow Faust in the world of the spirit, the soul world, and the physical world on Earth.

Part One begins in heaven, where the Lord makes a bet with the devil that Faust may not be led astray by evil. On Earth, Faust feels useless and considers suicide. He is sitting in his studio when suddenly a poodle turns into Mephistopheles, the devil. Faust is desperate for more knowledge and signs a pact with the devil sealed in a drop of blood. The deal is that Mephistopheles will do whatever Faust wants while he is alive, but after death Faust must serve the devil in hell.

In Part Two, Faust awakens in the world of elementary beings. He experiences the Carnival in Florence, the printing of money, an artificial human being, a palace in Ancient Sparta, a mountaintop, the ocean, and a war. At the end, he is an old man living in a castle, and becomes blind and dies. The devil thinks he has won the bet with the Lord and will use Faust in hell. Angels take the soul of Faust to heaven, where he is reborn. The play closes with Faust being initiated into the mysteries by Isis, the goddess and mother of nature.

Johann Herder argued that all peoples have a unique identity, expressed in culture, language, and science. The German identity was expressed in its enlightenment. Three great philosophers—Kant, Fichte, and Hegel—stand out.

Immanuel Kant wanted to bring religious belief, individual freedom, political authority, and rationalism into a meaningful relationship. In 1770, he published an 800-page book called *Critique of Pure Reason*, where he declared human understanding limited and that men can never attain knowledge of God or the soul. He wanted people to be free to use their own intellect.

Johann Gottlieb Fichte was a founding figure of German idealism. He argued that self-consciousness developed by the self with moral force, revealed the phenomena of the world we observe with our senses. Self-awareness is called out of the unconsciousness into awareness and freedom. We need the self-consciousness of others to bring forth more of our own consciousness. This is mutual recognition in a community of people developing their consciousness.

Georg Wilhelm Friedrich Hegel defined idealism by showing how thinkers can overcome the dualism of mind and nature or subject and object. He developed a philosophy of the spirit. Hegel built upon Aristotle's categories in his work *Science of Logic*, especially the category of being. Englishman Francis Bacon had warned scientists against that in 1620.

Hegel, Fichte, Kant, Goethe, Schiller, and Lessing are college-level studies.

The National Stage

In 1794, Eli Whitney patented the cotton gin, a machine that revolutionized the production of cotton by greatly speeding up the process of removing seeds from cotton fiber. Cotton fibers allowed it to be stored for a long time. The seeds were difficult to separate from the plants. Most farmers grew short-staple cotton that was picked by hand, one plant at a time. It took one slave one day to remove the seeds from a pound of cotton on the plantations of North America. Whitney created a well-functioning cotton gin that could remove the seeds from fifty pounds of cotton in one day. Gin meant "engine." The new machine worked something like a strainer. A wooden drum with a series of hooks inside caught the cotton fibers and dragged them through a mesh. The hooks easily pulled the fibers through, while the mesh did not let the seeds through. Workers cranked smaller gins by hand. Larger gins were cranked by horses and, later, a steam engine.

Now cotton could be produced cheaply. It became America's leading export to England and to the textile mills of New England. Slavery became more and more important because planters wanted larger fields to gain more profit. In 1791, 190,000 cotton bales were produced. By 1803, the production of cotton bails rose to 41 million in one year. As the population in India grew, England needed more cotton from America to export clothes and cloth. By 1860, 4 million people were slaves, or one of seven people in the United States.

The era of the steamboat had begun in America in 1787, when inventor John Fitch completed the first successful trial of a steamboat on the Delaware River below Philadelphia. His competitor, James Rumsey, received money from President Washington, while Fitch built a steam engine based on Watt's and Newcomen's design with money from private

The Industrial Revolution in England

investors. On August 26, 1791, Fitch was granted a United States patent for the steamboat. After Fitch died, Robert Fulton from Pennsylvania set up a steam ferry system from New York to Brooklyn.

New machines were made for the fields. In 1831, Cyrus McCormick demonstrated a horse-drawn mechanical reaper. His father had worked unsuccessfully on the design for twenty-six years. A slave on their plantation, Jo Anderson, helped him with a design that was pulled by horses and cut the grain to one side of the team. His machines spread from Virginia to all of Europe.

Three men in New York City are notable for their initiatives before the Industrial Revolution broke out in America: John Jacob Astor; Dewitt Clinton; and Benjamin Wright.

Benjamin Wright was the chief engineer on the Erie Canal. Starting in 1817 near the Hudson River at Rome, New York, the Erie Canal was dug 363 miles long. It opened in May 1821, and was completed near Buffalo in October 1825. Now it took only seven days to get from Buffalo to New York City.

Products from all over the world could be shipped to New York and transported up the Hudson River to Rome, where they could be shipped on the canal through thirty-six locks to the Great Lakes. Products from the Great Lakes could then be shipped east to New York City and sold all over the world. By 1825, more than 40,000 passengers travelled the canal yearly—tourists, businessmen, and settlers. The canal ensured the Port of New York as the multiregional commerce center of the United States. New York City now connected Europe and Asia with the Middle West. The Atlantic Trade Triangle grew larger. The State of New York became the Empire State.

Money followed the trade to the capital center of the world. Due to the Erie Canal, the harbor, and the Double Trade Triangles, New York City was more important than Boston, Baltimore, Philadelphia, and Pittsburgh combined. Merchants in New York had excess capital and they began colonizing the iron and coal deposits of Pennsylvania and Ohio. After 1840, New York had such powerful banking and insurance businesses that most railroad and mining businesses had offices there.

John Jacob Astor was a merchant, real estate mogul, and investor.

He made a fortune from his fur trading empire, which extended from the Great Lakes and Canada to the Pacific Coast. In 1816, he became an opium smuggler. Astor's American Fur Company purchased ten tons of Turkish opium, then shipped it to Canton on the packet ship Macedonian. In 1825, he stopped smuggling opium into China and sold the drug to England.

In 1822, Aster set up his headquarters on Mackinac Island and traded furs in Canton, China, Paris, and London. He left the fur trade in 1830, and invested the profits in real estate in New York City. At the time of his death in 1848, he was the richest man in America.

Dewitt Clinton was the most important person in New York in 1807. He commissioned a great eight-foot map to plan the grid of avenues and streets, imposing geometry on the island. Manhattan would become a manmade artificial island. They levelled the hills and made twelve avenues running north-south, crossed by 155 streets running east-west. The city was 11,000 acres placed into 2,000 blocks. At that time, there were 100,000 people in the city, and they expected one million more.

The Local Stage in the Wyoming Valley

The Connecticut Yankees of the 1770s became the elites of Wilkes-Barre in the 1800s. Family relations became the basis for the growth of the city as Butlers, Denisons, Hollenbacks, and Stewarts became the founding families.

By 1802, Mathias Hollenback became the leading entrepreneur, owning 10% of the land in Wilkes-Barre. He started with dry goods and hardware, then he ran a gristmill and a sawmill while developing fur trading.

In 1806, Wilkes-Barre was already a borough with 700 people living there. Dairy barns, horse barns, chickeries, icehouses, and homes filled the landscape. The Wyoming Valley was a rural paradise. Clean, pure, cold water ran from springs, lakes, and streams into the Susquehanna River as it coiled through the hills. Rainfall and natural water storage enabled fresh nutritious grass in the region, providing abundant pastures. The soil varied from sandy loam to red shale and clay loam. Peaches, grapes, plums, cherries, apples, and pears thrived. Blackberries and raspberries grew wild.

The Industrial Revolution in England

In 1808, there were still dangerous animals roaming the valley. Luzerne County paid $1,800 for the scalp of a panther and $2,800 for the scalp of a wolf. In 1810, one post office at Wilkes-Barre and one at Kingston were established. The mail came once a week from Easton.

The Susquehanna River arks floated down the river loaded with grain, hay, apples, potatoes, coal, and many other items. They were built of rough timber at the start of the shipment and dismantled and sold at the destination further down the river. The river arks were eighty to ninety feet long, forty feet wide, and four feet deep. This was the main means of transportation of coal.

In 1824, the State of Pennsylvania raised $40 million to build the North Branch Canal along the Susquehanna River to New York State. Construction began in 1829. The first boats were The Wyoming and The Luzerne. By 1833, boats floated wealth from the valley down the Susquehanna River to Philadelphia. In 1834, the canal reached north to the Lackawanna River.

By 1856, the canal was finished north of Elmira, New York, where it connected with the New York Canal. Coal was shipped to Elmira, then to Buffalo, and by steamboat to Cleveland, Ohio. Two years later, the canal was sold to the Sunbury & Erie Railroad Company. This was the end of the canal technology.

Meanwhile, the Lehigh Valley Railroad had been incorporated in 1846, with Asa Packer acquiring most of the stock. By 1855, trains were running from Mauch Chunk to Easton. By 1869, the line extended to White Haven, Wilkes-Barre, Tunkhannock, and the New York State line.

The Local Stage in the Lackawanna Valley

In the northern half of the valley, coal mining had been attempted in Carbondale, where a new village sprang up in 1813. New York City needed the coal to fire steam engines, iron furnaces, heat homes, and make fuel for the gas lamps. To bring the coal to New York, investments were made in Carbondale.

Once the Erie Canal had been built, New York shippers cornered the trade for Southern cotton by centralizing British-American trade in

Strive for Insight

Liverpool and New York City. New York City became an empire that expanded with new merchants while the population grew.

In 1823, the Delaware and Hudson Canal Company was chartered in New York and the Commonwealth of Pennsylvania. This enabled the Philadelphia merchants Maurice and William Wurts to construct the canal. Benjamin Wright was hired to survey and decide the route. He had just completed building the Erie Canal. At the start in 1825, the new D&H Canal posed difficult problems due to the 600-foot elevation difference from the Hudson River at Rondout, near Kingston, New York, up to the Delaware River at Lackawaxen, Pennsylvania.

To haul the coal from the valley at Carbondale up to Honesdale, the H&D Canal company built the Delaware and Hudson Gravity Railroad in 1826. The canal started in Honesdale, Pennsylvania, and ended in Kingston. The canal was 108 miles long, including 109 locks, 15 aqueducts, and 14 boat basins. John Roebling, who later built the Brooklyn Bridge, built four suspension aqueducts, one of which still stands. Barges carried coal and lumber from 1828 to 1899!

In May 1829, the D&H Canal Company bought the nine-ton locomotive, Stourbridge Lion, in England. From New York, it was transported by canal to Honesdale. On August 9, 1829, it became the first steam locomotive to run on a track in the United States. The locomotive proved too weak to pull the cars and too heavy for the new track. It was quickly retired.

At first, coal was produced by a few original settlers. In 1830, 7,000 tons of coal were sent to market, mainly by Theodore Von Storch. He was one of the few original settlers who did not sell their land before the coal became so valuable. He mined and then leased the rights for large sums of money.

In 1836, Lackawanna Township included portions of Providence and Pittston. It was fifteen square miles. Two-thirds of the township was cleared for wheat, rye, corn, oats, and buckwheat. They had five sawmills, one gristmill, one powder mill, three churches, an equal number of taverns, four coal openings, and thirty dwellings.

The Industrial Revolution in England

We have seen how the heavy industries of the Industrial Revolution started in England with the production of coal, iron, railroads, and textiles. It was only a matter of time before these industries started in the United States. Where did the Industrial Revolution in America originally break out? Scranton, Pennsylvania.

CHAPTER 10

The Industrial Revolution In America

The Local Stage

One spring morning in 1846, William Earle Dodge sat uncomfortably in his office on Lower Broadway, New York. He was stunned by the news from an English captain that the empty ship was docked in the Battery. The British would not deliver the 12,000 tons of T-rails Mr. Dodge had ordered for the New York and Erie Railroad. Six months previously, the New York State Legislature had passed a bill donating to the railroad the sum of $3 million for purchase of rail to finish the line along the Delaware River between Port Jervis and Binghamton, passing through Susquehanna, Pennsylvania. The rails had to be laid in eighteen months—one third of the time had already passed. Would the state forfeit $3 million?

Dodge spoke with his father-in-law, Mr. Anson Phelps, also a director of the Erie Railroad. Phelps mentioned the Scranton brothers in the Pennsylvania coal region, who had been experimenting with the production of T-rails. Two weeks later, George and Selden Scranton sat in the office of Phelps, Dodge, and Company. George told the New Yorkers that they had a stockpile of T-rails. He offered to start shipping over the

Strive for Insight

Delaware and Hudson Canal and down the Delaware River. They could start building a second furnace right away.

The London price for rails was $80 per ton. The Scrantons offered a price of $46 per ton. At the time, the brothers were flat broke. They needed an advance from the New Yorkers. Director Phelps made an offer to buy 2,000 tons of rails at $46 a ton, for $92,000. He gave them a check for $100,000 from the Erie Board. The deal was made and the race was on!

If construction was completed before January 1, 1849, the railroad would not have to repay the loan of $3 million to the State of New York.

Joseph H. Scranton became a partner in the business. Joseph Curtis Platt became general purchasing agent, and they named the firm Scrantons and Platt. The new company listed capital stock at $230,000. The firm owned 5,000 acres of land, 1,200 of which were underlain with anthracite coal.

The risk takers had two years to deliver 4,000 tons of fifty-eight pound T-rail in wagons drawn by four horses over the mountains to the Erie Railroad bed along the Delaware River. William E. Dodge ordered another 12,000 tons of rails. The company enlisted 800 employees.

The Scrantons found experts in T-rail production in Wales. They built two rolling mills and delivered their final goods on December 27, 1848, merely four days before the deadline! The loan from the State of New York was released and many new orders of rails followed. Historian Patrick Brown formulated this historical event into one sentence: "Scranton was the first city in the nation to produce the iron necessary to expand the nation's railways, and it mined the anthracite coal and forged the steel that drove America's industrial revolution."[30]

After the first wave of Welsh, Irish, and German immigrants had reached the Lackawanna Valley in 1840, the population settled at 1,169. For many years, cheap labor came from Europe. The Scrantons built houses for their workers near the furnaces. They named it Shanty Town. Laborers received about $17 per month and carpenters made $22 per month. Contract miners who excavated coal and iron ore were paid $1.09 to $1.68 per carload.

In 1853, Scrantons and Platt incorporated under the name Lackawanna Iron & Coal Company. Some 8,000 shares were issued, and the firm's capital rose to $800,000. Joseph H. Scranton managed the company until 1858, when he was elected president, and continued until his death in 1872. Company assets in Scranton included three furnaces, the rolling and puddling mill, a foundry, two blacksmith shops, a car shop, two carpenter shops, a sawmill, a gristmill, an office, a company store, 200 houses and dwellings, a boarding house, officers' houses, ore and coal mines, a tavern, and a hotel.

A puddling mill was new to the Wyoming Valley, but not new to the world. In the Han Dynasty of the 1st century AD, high-grade iron was made more than 1,700 years before the Scranton Brothers.

By 1784, Henry Cort had developed and patented the technology they used in Scranton to refine cast iron. Heat was applied from above. This oxidation lowered the carbon content of the cast iron while the puddler extracted the mass of iron from the furnace using an iron bar. The ball of metal was shingled by a hammer and then rolled in the mill. Puddled iron was used in bridges, and then later in the Eiffel Tower in Paris and in the framework of the Statue of Liberty.

Joseph H. Scranton privately owned 3,750 acres of land on the southern end of Moosic Mountain. Bought for $11,250 in 1841, the area was filled with pure mountain lakes that became the source of water for the Scranton Gas & Water Company. The company built a water main on Lackawanna Avenue with a reservoir in the Hill Section. Water was pumped from the Lackawanna River, enabling the fire company to throw streams of water over any house in the city. In 1857, the company obtained a capital value of $250,000.

Let us return to the geography of the gaps in the valley from Chapter 4. In Wyoming, the Susquehanna River flows through the gap into the lower valley to Wilkes-Barre. Along the river, Asa Packer built the Lehigh Valley Railroad in 1853. It ran in a north-south direction between New York State and Philadelphia.

Eventually, the Great Valley was commercially spilt into two separate valleys, the Lackawanna Valley and the Wyoming Valley. The Lehigh

Valley Railroad served the Wyoming Valley to Philadelphia and the Lackawanna Railroad served Scranton and the Lackawanna Valley to New York City. In finance, trade, and culture, Scranton was oriented to New York. Wilkes-Barre was oriented to Philadelphia.

The Ligget's Gap Railroad Became the Lackawanna and Western Railroad

George Scranton formed a partnership with William Dodge to link the anthracite coal resources of Northeastern Pennsylvania from Buffalo in the north to New York City in the east. To do this, they built a new railroad that entered the Lackawanna Valley from the west at Ligget's Gap, crossed the valley to Dunmore, and exited the valley to the east through Cobb's Gap. They named it the Liggett's Gap Railroad.

In the midst of building the railroad, an Irish War broke out in May 1850. The gang wars in Northern Ireland and New York City also played out in Scranton. Such Irish gang wars are vividly depicted in Martin Scorsese's 2002 film, *Gangs of New York*.

Colonel Hitchcock writes: "The grading of the Liggett's Gap Railroad was commenced early in May, but before the month closed there was an Irish War in Liggett's Gap between the Corkonians and Far-downers, as they called each other. Each side was determined to drive the other off the road, but both parties were, if possible, more hostile to the Germans, and as determined to oust them. The Germans armed themselves and continued at their work. A battle was fought on the 28th, one person being killed instantly and a number wounded, all of whom were said to be Corkonians. Two bodies were found in the woods nearby the following month bearing marks of having been shot. On the 30th, the Counought men to the number of some 200 returned to drive the Corkonians further. On their way, they came to the Dutch shanty and demanded the fire arms but failed to get them."[31]

Halfway through construction, the railroad was renamed the Lackawanna and Western Railroad. On October 15, 1851, the first train from Great Bend to Scranton was drawn by a twenty-nine-ton steam engine with Stephenson link motion. The first ton of coal shipped on the

Liggett's Gap Railroad was personally mined by John Jermyn, a future large mine operator, real estate developer, and hotel owner.

The Lackawanna and Western Railroad climbed westward from Scranton through the notch below the Abingtons, and headed north to Great Bend, where there was a connection with the Erie Railroad. At Great Bend, there was also a connection to Ithaca, New York, where the coal could be transported over Lake Cayuga to northern New York and the Erie Canal. Now the Great Lakes and the western wildernesses were connected by rail from Buffalo to the markets at New York Harbor.

Local coal was also transported to New York markets by the Pennsylvania Gravity Railroad. Built in 1850, it ran for forty-seven miles from Pittston over the East Mountain in Scranton to Hawley. Steam engines pulled the cars on cables up eleven planes. The cars descended by the force of gravity and were switched back to the cable system to be pulled up the next plane. The Pennsylvania Coal Company transported anthracite coal on its gravity railroad until 1885.

The Lackawanna and Western Railroad became the Delaware, Lackawanna, and Western Railroad

Blair, Phelps, and Dodge also wanted a route from Scranton to the eastern seaboard market at New York. John Blair left his chain stores, flour mills, and cotton factories to family members and dedicated all his time to the new railroad, the Delaware and Cobb's Gap Railroad Company, starting at the Delaware Water Gap in New Jersey and climbing westward over the Pocono Mountains to Cobb's Gap south of Scranton. In 1853, the new railroad was named the Delaware, Lackawanna, and Western Railroad Company (D.L.&W.) It stretched from Buffalo, New York, to Scranton and on to Hoboken, New Jersey, a distance of 395 miles.

Before the southern division was completed, two mortgages were placed on the D.L.&W. line, the first for $1.5 million and the second for $2.6 million. These deals were engineered by Moses Taylor of the D.L.&W. board and the National City Bank of New York.

The year 1854 was a turning point for the Lackawanna Valley as 20,000 Irish immigrants entered the USA and about 5,000 of them came to Scranton, vastly outnumbering other citizens. To this day, Scranton is home to the Irish. Every year, New York City policemen spend the St. Patrick's Day weekend in Scranton and march in the parade.

In 1855, Thomas Dickson, with his brothers, John and George, founded an engineering company named Dickson & Company in Carbondale, Pennsylvania. A year later, it was moved to Scranton at the request of George Scranton. Their first major contract was to supply locomotives for a new railroad constructed by the Delaware and Hudson Canal Company. In the first years of the Dickson Manufacturing Company, five or six locomotives were built each year.

The California Gold Rush of 1849 had brought gold and money in greater supply, but afterwards, far less gold was mined. Panic hit in 1857, when there was too little gold in New York and Great Britain. The crisis hit many American entrepreneurs, who were overextended. The Scranton brothers sold their interest in the Scranton Coal Company. Seldon resigned as president of the Lackawanna Iron and Coal Company and returned to Oxford, New Jersey. George remained in Scranton and was elected to the United States House of Representatives in 1860. The railroad barons wanted railway men in Congress to protect their interests, provide subsidies, and limit government control!

Terrence Powderly was apprenticed to the machinist trade in the D.& H. company shops. He worked for James Dickson, who immigrated from England in 1832 and moved to Carbondale in 1836. In those days, an apprenticed machinist had to learn how to forge and temper the tools he worked with. He was taught how to operate lathes, planning, slotting, and other such machines. He fitted the parts at the bench and then assembled them as one complete whole, whether locomotive or stationary engine.

In Powderly's words: "I became the subject matter of a legal instrument in which my father and the master mechanic were the parties. In that document I promised to be a good boy and due diligence exercise, in consideration of which James Dickson, the master mechanic, obligated himself to initiate me into *the arts and mysteries* of the machinist trade. By James Dickson I was duly and truly prepared to travel in foreign countries and earn journeyman's wages. Dickson had served his time in the old country as an apprentice under George Stephenson, the inventor and builder of the first locomotive, and worked on its construction. Stephenson gave to Dickson, when his term expired, a number of machinist tools of his own make. Among these was a pair of four-inch calipers. Dickson loaned these to me, I used them during my apprenticeship, and on its expiration, he presented them to me with a blessing. Through the hands of James Dickson, they passed from George Stephenson to me so you needn't wonder why I prize them so highly. A kinder man or a better mechanic I never met than James Dickson."[32]

The apprentice was a future lawyer, mayor of Scranton, and Grand Master Workman of the Knights of Labor.

The National Stage

Before the Civil War, merchants were the most powerful businessmen in the North and the South. They sold rice, cotton, indigo, sugar, and tobacco to Europe, and imported manufactured goods from Europe. Markets were accessed via ports such as New York, Boston, Providence, Philadelphia, Charleston, Savannah, and Norfolk. They had access to capital through banks in London, Liverpool, Rotterdam, Hamburg, and Le Havre.

The trade routes were part of the Double Trade Triangle. As the population of China grew, the demand for more opium from the English grew. As the population in India grew, the demand for more cotton textiles from England grew. This greatly increased the demand for slaves as cheap labor in the American slave colonies. Adam Rothman writes, "Cotton production in the United States increased from about 50 million pounds in 1800 to 180 million pounds in 1820 and 650 million pounds in 1840. In 1860 the US cotton crop exceeded 1.6 billion pounds—about two-thirds of the world's cotton."[33] Cotton production was based in three states—Mississippi, Alabama, and Louisiana. Britain's textile manufacturers in Manchester and Liverpool bought their cotton from the United States.

Some merchants became merchant bankers. They loaned money

to farmers, shippers, and manufacturers. Exporting cotton secured the USA credit on the European money markets. This kept the banks running. Merchant bankers also sold insurance on the products they transported abroad.

Others invested in manufacturing rails, steam engines, weapons, and tools. In the 1830s, a new group of artisans became manufacturers. They obtained capital from the merchants and developed new skills as entrepreneurs. In Boston, merchants invested heavily in New England's textile mills. The merchant Moses Brown, in Providence, hired Samuel Slater to set up the first cotton spinning mill. Peter Cooper made a fortune selling glue in New York City and later moved into iron manufacturing. The Steinways built pianos. Isaac Singer made sewing machines. The Scranton brothers manufactured rails and built railroads. The Dicksons built locomotives. There were many more.

Each city had skilled workers who were tailors, printers, coopers, firemen, coal passers, carvers, painters, box makers, cigar makers, coachmen, and many more. They were often immigrants from Europe who soon organized their labor and demanded public acknowledgment and power. From the workers, a new class arose in local and state politics. They created unions and carried out strikes.

Who were the merchants who invested in the Lackawanna Valley? Four merchant-financiers made investments from New York—Phelps, Dodge, Blair, and Taylor. Two merchants moved to the valley—Joseph Platt and Joseph Scranton.

Anson Phelps imported iron, tin, and brass from England. He exported cotton to England and New England. His son-in-law, William Dodge, ran their office in Liverpool. He ran railroads before developing copper mines in Arizona and coal mines in New Mexico. Phelps Dodge Corporation became one of the largest mining companies in the USA.

At the age of twenty-six, in 1832, Moses Taylor was an exporter and an importer with his own firm at 55 South Street on Manhattan. Taylor dealt mostly with commodities in the Caribbean trade—coffee, fruit, and sugar. Then he specialized in sugar. The Drake Brothers of Havana were Cuba's biggest shippers, two-thirds of the sugar shipped from Cuba to the USA passed through their hands. Taylor became their agent in New York, investing millions of dollars for them.

Taylor was known in the business community for his honesty. As a director of the Manhattan Gas Light Company, the price of coal was important to him. The lamps in Manhattan were powered by coal. Transportation of the coal to the city was part of the price. In 1852, Taylor bought 800 acres of coal fields in the Lackawanna Valley and created the Scranton Coal Company one year later. Decision making in the Lackawanna Valley was transferred to New York City based merchant-financiers. In 1855, he became president of the City Bank of New York.

In February 1856, the coal committee of the D.L.&W. Railroad included Moses Taylor, William Dodge, and John Phelps. They decided the price of coal in New England. These merchants established a coal yard on Manhattan and hired a shipping agent to run the coal operations of the D.L.&W. in New York. During the panic of 1857, Taylor bought large amounts of D.L.&W. stock at five dollars a share and became the main owner of the railroad. By January 1865, he had 20,000 shares.

The other outside investor, John I. Blair, built the Warren Railroad Company to fill the 18-mile gap between the Central New Jersey Railroad and the D.L.&W. In the 19th century, he owned the most railroad mileage in the world. As president of sixteen railroad companies, Blair travelled 40,000 miles a year in his private railcar.

Two merchants settled in the Lackawanna Valley. In his early twenties, Joseph H. Scranton had moved to Augusta, Georgia, to work for his wealthy relative, Daniel Hand. Mercantile houses in Augusta offered credit, export, and import. They exported coffee, tobacco, indigo, cotton, and rice. They imported slaves and sugar. From England, they imported tools. Within ten years, Joseph Scranton made a fortune in the mercantile business. In 1847, he sold his enterprises in Georgia and moved to Scranton after having invested money in his cousins' iron forgery. He became a commissioner of the Union Pacific Railroad. In 1857, Scranton became president of the Lackawanna Iron and Coal Company. In 1861, the Civil War quickly accelerated the demand for rails from the valley.

Joseph Curtis Platt was a merchant of Fairhaven, Connecticut. One of the founders of the city of Scranton, he came to the Lackawanna Valley in 1845 at the invitation of his brother-in-law, Joseph Hand Scranton. Platt became a pioneer coal operator and railroad organizer, director of the Lackawanna Iron and Coal Company, then director and treasurer of Dickson Manufacturing Company.

The Financial Panic of 1857

Five hundred thousand people lived north of 14th Street in New York City when the Financial Panic of 1857 struck. The mayor, Ferdinand Wood, and the city bought vast tracts of land to build Central Park. A writer, Frederick Law Olmsted, won the contest to design the park together with Calvin Vaux. Olmsted believed that the common green space must always be equally accessible to all citizens. It should be defended against private encroachment. They designed the park with social consciousness.

By the spring of 1858, German gardeners, Italian stone cutters, and Irish day laborers earned less than one dollar a day building the park. Blacks and women were excluded. The rocky and swampy landscape was blasted into shape. Topsoil was brought in from Long Island and New Jersey.

Meanwhile, the fighting continued between pro- and anti-slavery militia along the borders of Kansas and Missouri. In October 1859, radical abolitionist John Brown led a raid on the federal armory at Harpers Ferry, Virginia. He was captured by Robert E. Lee, tried, and hanged on December 2, 1859.

In February 1860, a strange lawyer from Illinois walked into the reception at the Astor House Hotel on Manhattan wearing a beaver hat. His name was Abraham Lincoln. Before 1,500 people at Cooper Union, Lincoln gave the speech many believe secured him the nomination as Republican candidate for president. It was a short speech in which he gave his views on slavery and why he did not want slavery extended to the Western territories. The 1860 presidential election threatened to break up the Atlantic Triangle as the Republican Party supported taxes and the end of slavery.

The American Enlightenment

Let us turn our attention away from the merchants, bankers, entrepreneurs, and master mechanics of the Industrial Revolution. I mentioned in earlier chapters that countries and peoples make a significant and unique contribution to all mankind, as in England, France, and Germany. Our Founding Fathers of the American Revolution gave us their version of the English Enlightenment and the French Enlightenment. What are the goals of the true American Enlightenment? Can we identify a number of the major contributors so far? I would look to Henry D. Thoreau, Ralph W. Emerson, Sarah Margaret Fuller, Walt Whitman, Frederick Douglass, Black Elk, Ralph Bunche, Rachel Carson, and Martin Luther King Jr. There are many more and even more coming in the future.

Before the Civil War, one of the most influential people in America was Henry David Thoreau. In 1848, he gave lectures at the Lyceum in Concord, Massachusetts, entitled "The Rights and Duties of the Individual in Relation to Government." Thoreau collected his thoughts in a short essay published a year later, "Resistance to Civil Government." It was published by Elizabeth Peabody in an anthology called *Æsthetic Papers*. Thoreau compared bad government to a machine. If the government creates injustice, it is the duty of the people to stop the machine.

> "The government does not keep the country free. It does not settle the West. It does not educate. The character in the American people has done all that has been accomplished; and it would have done somewhat more, if the government had not sometimes got in its way."[34]

Thoreau appealed to the development of conscience. He asked whether a citizen must ever resign his conscience to a legislator. If the majority must always rule, why does every individual have a conscience? Why should people become agents of injustice?

The government was not only his government, but a slave's government as well. This disgraced him. He saw 100,000 merchants and farmers in Massachusetts who were more interested in commerce than

Strive for Insight

humanity. Thoreau defined revolution as the right to refuse allegiance to or resist the government. For him, action based on principle was most important, most revolutionary, though it divided relations between states, churches, families, and even the relationship between the diabolical and the divine in each individual.

> "A minority is powerless while it conforms to the majority; it is not even a minority then; but it is irresistible when it clogs by its whole weight. If the alternative is to keep all just men in prison, or give up war or slavery, the State will not hesitate which to choose. If a thousand men were not to pay their tax-bills this year, that would not be a violent and bloody measure, as it would be to pay them, and enable the State to commit violence and shed innocent blood. This is, in fact, the definition of a peaceable revolution, if any such is possible."[35]

Many leaders throughout the world have built their campaigns for change upon Thoreau's ideas of civil disobedience. There is a golden thread from Thoreau to Tolstoy to Gandhi to King and to many more. They share the conviction and practical use of nonviolent resistance.

Leo Tolstoy was a Russian count who became one of the most famous writers in world history. He had Thoreau's essay published in Russia. In 1894, Tolstoy wrote *The Kingdom of God is Within You*, where he shared his ideas on nonviolent resistance over the previous thirty years. Tolstoy and Gandhi sent letters to each other discussing how to use love as a practical, nonviolent weapon to overthrow the colonial British Empire.

In 1907, Gandhi was carrying out his first satyagraha campaign in South Africa. To fight racial discrimination, he published a newspaper, *Indian Opinion*. Gandhi considered Thoreau's ideas relevant to the Indians in Transvaal.

> "He was one of the greatest and most moral men America has produced. At the time of the abolition of slavery movement, he wrote his famous essay *On the Duty of Civil Disobedience*. He went to jail for the sake of his principles and suffering humanity. His essay

has, therefore, been sanctified by suffering. Moreover, it is written for all time."[36]

Martin Luther King Jr. built the ideas of his civil rights campaign on Gandhi and Thoreau. At the age of fifteen, King discovered Thoreau's essay at Morehouse College.

> "During my student days I read Henry David Thoreau's essay *On Civil Disobedience* for the first time. Here, in this courageous New Englander's refusal to pay his taxes and his choice of jail rather than support a war that would spread slavery's territory into Mexico, I made my first contact with the theory of nonviolent resistance. Fascinated by the idea of refusing to cooperate with an evil system, I was so deeply moved that I reread the work several times. I became convinced that noncooperation with evil is as much a moral obligation as is cooperation with good. No other person has been more eloquent and passionate in getting this idea across than Henry David Thoreau. As a result of his writings and personal witness, we are the heirs of a legacy of creative protest. The teachings of Thoreau came alive in our civil rights movement; indeed, they are more alive than ever before."[37]

Many women in America strove for justice during the Industrial Revolution. Sarah Margaret Fuller was a journalist, critic, and the first female war correspondent. In 1840, Fuller edited *Dial*, a journal for the Transcendentalist Movement. She wrote America's first major feminist book in 1845, *Women in the Nineteenth Century*. Fuller and Elizabeth Peabody organized meetings in the women's rights movement, which also included Maria Lowell, Elizabeth Oates Smith, and Caroline Sturgis.

Ralph Waldo Emerson is still considered America's essayist and philosopher. He believed every human being had an over-soul, a supreme mind that gives us direct experience and intuition. Emerson taught Americans to trust their experiences and intuitions. In his famous essay, "Self-Reliance," published in *Essays, the First Series* in 1841, he challenged his reader to look at the relationship between God and Nature and to trust his own judgment. How six great men have influenced society is the theme of his seven lectures published in 1850 as *Representative Men*. Emerson was an abolitionist, a man against slavery.

> "A man who steals another man's labor steals away his own faculties; his integrity, his humanity is flowing away from him. The habit of oppression cuts out the moral eyes, and, though the intellect goes on simulating the moral as before, its sanity is gradually destroyed."[38]

When Walt Whitman published *Leaves of Grass* in 1855, he was thirty-five years old and living in Brooklyn. The poem gives a picture of the diversity and power of the people of New York. Whitman decided to write about new things to appeal to the reader's imagination and help him connect with his own destiny. He wanted it to be an American poem, with American character, democracy, and the essential life of the New World. He wanted to express the spirit of America, its greatness, its genius, the people, and their strivings.

Also living in New York was Frederick Douglass, a leader and speaker in the abolitionist movement, which sought to end slavery. He wrote five autobiographies and published a newsletter, *North Star*. Douglass strongly advocated for women's rights. He was the only Black to attend the Seneca Falls Convention, a gathering of women's rights activists in New York in 1848. In his famous 4th of July speech of 1852, the former slave questioned what independence meant to America's slaves.

Those who inspire our enlightenment bring specific American impulses to us. As a young person in your particular generation, who would you consider? This is a very important question to keep alive in our hearts.

The World Stage

As the guests of Graf Clemens von Metternich from November 1814 to June 1815, most European monarchs attended the Congress of Vienna to create a new world order and prevent revolutions in their own countries.

The Industrial Revolution In America

After the defeat of Napoleon, they wanted to rebalance European power. Austria, Prussia, Russia, and Great Britain were most responsible for Napoleon's defeat, therefore they wanted to decide over all other countries. New borders in the Alps and Italy were formed. Austria received Lombardy, Venice, and most of Tirol. Denmark gave up their 500-year-old occupation of Norway.

Thirty-three years later, in 1848, revolutions broke out against the new world order in Paris, Italy, Germany, Austria, and Prague. In Germany and Austria, the revolutionaries wanted to unify the people under one democratic republic that guaranteed human rights, freedom of speech, freedom of the press, and freedom of learning at the universities. They wanted the lessons from the German Enlightenment to inspire everyday life, rather than an out-of-date authoritarian regime that repressed the masses. They demanded change!

In Germany, the revolutionaries considered the Holy Roman Empire of the German Nation (911–1806) out of date! Nor did they want the future empires that would appear in Germany—the Second German Empire under Kaiser Wilhelm II (1871–1918) or the Third German Empire under the Nazis (1933–1945)!

A new German parliament was started in the Paulus Church in Frankfurt. Their constitution demanded a constitutional monarch, but the King of Prussia refused. Instead, he sent troops to demolish their initiative in July 1849.

Many revolutionary German democrats moved to American cities—Galveston, Cincinnati, Milwaukee, and New York. In America, they were called the 48ers.

One remarkable 48er was Carl Schurz, a student during the revolution in Germany. He took to arms against the King. When the Prussian Army entered the Fort at Rastatt, Schurz escaped through a canal and became a wanted man until 1852, when he arrived at the harbour in New York. Schurz moved to Milwaukee, where he became a lawyer. His wife, Margarethe Schurz, became a founder of the kindergarten movement in America. In 1861, President Lincoln sent Schurz to Spain as minister to convince them not to support the South. In April 1862, he became a brigadier general of Union volunteers.

Strive for Insight

Strongly against slavery, thousands of 48ers fought for the North in the Civil War. After the war, they worked as educators, artists, musicians, journalists, writers, publishers, doctors, architects, engineers, scientists, businessmen, investment bankers, and political activists. They are known for developing the wine and beer industries in our country.

CHAPTER 11

The American Civil War

"Never did a day open more beautiful. We were astir at the first streak of dawn. We had slept, and soundly too, just where nightfall found us under the shelter of the hill near Keedysville. No revile call this morning. Too close to the enemy. Nor was this needed to arouse us. A simple call of a sergeant or corporal and every man was instantly awake and alert. All realized there was ugly business and plenty of it just ahead. This was plainly visible in the faces as well as in the nervous, subdued demeanor of all. The absence of all joking and play and the almost painful sobriety of action, where jollity had been the rule, was particularly noticeable . . .

"We were on the march about six o'clock and moved, as I thought, rather leisurely for upwards of two miles, crossing Antietam Creek, which our men waded nearly waist deep, emerging, of course, soaked through, our first experience of this kind. It was a hot morning and therefore, the only ill effects of the wading, was the discomfort to the men marching with soaked feet. It was now quite evident that a great battle was in progress. A deafening pandemonium of cannonading, with shrieking and bursting shells, filled the air beyond us, towards which we were marching. An occasional shell whizzed by and over, reminding us that we were rapidly approaching the *debatable ground*. Soon we began to hear a most

Strive for Insight

ominous sound which we had never heard before, except in the far distance at South Mountain, namely, the rattle of musketry. It had none of the deafening bluster of the cannonading so terrifying to new troops, but to those who had once experienced its effect, it was infinitely more to be dreaded.

"About eight o'clock we were formed into line of battle and moved forward through a grove of trees called East Woods, but before actually coming under musketry fire of the enemy we were moved back again, and swung nearly a mile to the left to the base of a circular knoll to the left of the Roulette farmhouse and the road which leads up to the Sharpsburg pike, near the Dunkard Church. The famous *sunken road*—a road which had been cut through the other side of this knoll—extended from the Roulette Lane directly in front of our line towards Sharpsburg . . .

"Reaching the top of the knoll we were met by a terrific volley from the rebels in the sunken road down the other side, not more than one hundred yards away, and also from another rebel line in a cornfield just beyond. We were ordered to lie down just under the top of the hill and crawl forward and fire over, each man crawling back, reloading his piece in this prone position and again crawling forward and firing. These tactics undoubtedly saved us many lives, for the fire of the two lines in front of us was terrific. The air was full of whizzing, singing, buzzing bullets. Once down on the ground undercover of the hill, it required very strong resolution to get up where these missiles of death were flying so thickly, yet that was the duty of us officers, especially us of the field and staff. My duty kept me constantly moving up and down that whole line."[39]

These are the words of Colonel Richard Hitchcock in his book *War From The Inside, The Story of the 132nd Regiment Pennsylvania Volunteers*. He had promised to write his memoirs for his children in Scranton. It was the first day of battle for more than 200 volunteers from Luzerne County in Companies I and K of the 132nd Pennsylvania Volunteers. They had been under fire for four hours.

The American Civil War

This was the Battle at Antietam Creek on September 17, 1862. Hitchcock later learned that his brigade had borne the brunt of a long and persistent effort by General Robert E. Lee to break the Union line at this point, and that his regiment made up half of the brigade. The regiment was in General William French's Third Division of the Second Army Corps in the 1st Brigade under General Nathan Kimball.

Three days later, after Lee had hauled off, the men were allowed to walk the battlefield. Together with his friend Captain Archbald, Hitchcock walked along the position of his line and down to the sunken road where the Confederate soldiers still lay dead. They were the 6th Georgian.

Lee and the Confederacy did not have enough men or weapons to win a significant battle. His men had been marching for ten weeks and had not rested for three days. They were hungry, poorly dressed, fatigued, and many of their best leaders were dead. In the first five hours of the battle, 8,000 men on both sides within a 700-yard radius were killed on the cornfield. Within the first seven hours, 18,000 men were dead or wounded. The battle lasted seven more hours and 5,000 more died. It was the bloodiest day in American history.

The Union had repelled the first Confederate invasion of the North. That week, pictures of the battlefield were published in most newspapers, making the American people aware of the devastation of the war. Due to the victory at Antietam, the midterm election of November 1862 resulted in Lincoln's Republican Party gaining seats in the Senate while maintaining a majority in the House. President Lincoln could continue the war efforts and deliver the Emancipation Proclamation one month later:

> "That on the first day of January, in the year of our Lord one thousand eight hundred and sixty-three, all persons held as slaves within any State or designated part of a State, the people whereof shall then be in rebellion against the United States, shall be then, thenceforward, and forever free; and the Executive Government of the United States, including the military and naval authority thereof, will recognize and maintain the freedom of such persons,

and will do no act or acts to repress such persons, or any of them, in any efforts they may make for their actual freedom."

In the Emancipation Proclamation, Lincoln warned that in all states still in rebellion on January 1, 1863, he would declare their slaves free. The proclamation committed the government and armed forces of the United States to liberate the slaves in rebel states. It exempted the border slave states and all or parts of three Confederate states controlled by the Union Army on the grounds that these areas were not in rebellion against the United States.

The proclamation also authorized the recruitment of freed slaves and free Blacks as Union soldiers. During the next two and a half years, 180,000 Blacks fought in the Union Army and 10,000 in the Navy, making a vital contribution to Union victory as well as their own freedom.

Which events led to the terrible destruction at Antietam Creek? By the time of the battle, the American Civil War had been waged for a little over a year. There were 21 million men in the North and 9 million men in the South, of which 4 million were slaves. The need for slavery was increasing due to the Double Trade Triangles. The mills of Manchester and Liverpool, England, needed more cotton to supply their empire with textiles and drive the opium trade from England to China.

In 1860, first South Carolina, then Mississippi, Florida, Alabama, Georgia, and Louisiana proclaimed independence from the USA. They withdrew their allegiance to the Union to form the Confederate States of America. Lincoln denied the states the right to secede. War broke out on April 12, 1861, at Fort Sumter, Charleston, South Carolina. That year, Virginia, North Carolina, Tennessee, Arkansas, and Kentucky also joined the Confederacy.

Three million Americans would fight in the Civil War. Six hundred thousand Americans would be killed. This was 2% of the total population of 30 million people.

On April 15, Lincoln called for 75,000 volunteers. He had decided to save the Union by declaring war on the Confederacy. Robert E. Lee was offered command of the Union Army. He could not fight against his home state of Virginia and therefore resigned from the Union Army.

The American Civil War

On July 21, 1861, just two months after the attack on Fort Sumter, the first battle of Manassas was fought. Only twenty-five miles from Washington, D.C., Confederate General Thomas Jackson held firm in the battles and received the name Stonewall Jackson. More Southern troops arrived by train. The battle ended with 5,000 Union casualties. Many more were injured. The North was in shock.

The Blue Ridge Mountains of Virginia send their water east over the Piedmont plains down a series of rivers and into the Chesapeake Bay. Each river expands as it approaches the bay, creating large peninsulas between them. The Potomac River flows past Washington, D.C. before widening into the bay. South of the Potomac flows the Rappahannock River, creating the Northern Neck Peninsula between them. The city of Fredericksburg lies along the Rappahannock just before it widens. To the south of the Rappahannock River flows the York River, with the famous city of Yorktown just before the bay. This is called the Middle Peninsula.

South of the York River flows the James River, first through Richmond, then past Williamsburg, and at its mouth past Norfolk, Virginia. Between the York River and the James River stands the Virginia Peninsula.

On March 17, 1862, General George B. McClellan's army sailed from Alexandria to invade the Virginia Peninsula. Ninety thousand troops landed at Fort Monroe. Their goal was to take Richmond, roughly seventy-five miles north.

Before the Army of the Potomac landed on the peninsula in southeastern Virginia, the Confederacy attacked again north of Washington, D.C. at the entrance to the Shenandoah Valley, near Harpers Ferry. With 16,000 men, Stonewall Jackson successfully attacked General McDowell's 70,000 troops and prevented the Union forces from meeting each other near Richmond.

With the largest Union Army of the war, McClellan then marched up the Virginia peninsula, fighting many battles between March and July 1862. He reached the gates of Richmond but was stuck in a swampy area on the Chickahominy River, giving Robert E. Lee time to reassemble his forces and save the Confederate capital. McClellan retreated to the safety of the cannons of the Union Navy at Fort Monroe, thus prolonging the war for three more years.

McClellan was a pro-slavery Union General. When McClellan returned to Washington, President Lincoln replaced him with General Pope. A few months later, McClellan was given another command to defend the US capital.

In the Civil War, most men enlisted by county and state. In Pennsylvania, some were mixed in state regiments, while others were in companies from their own county. A company consisted of roughly one hundred men. A regiment usually had ten companies, or 1,000 men. Regiments were put into brigades of 5,000 men, and three brigades formed a division of roughly 16,000 men. A corps had three divisions, or 48,000 men. According to historian Bruce Catton, the State of Pennsylvania sent 360,000 soldiers into the Civil War.

There is always a local side to a terrible war. Men and women leave their homes to fight on the national or world stages. Eighteen companies were recruited from Scranton, close to 2,000 men. Among them were 200 commissioned officers. The city of Scranton had 9,223 residents in 1860. Two thousand men in the Civil War was roughly 21% of the population serving for five years.

In August 1862, Lincoln had called for nine-month volunteers. Company I of the 132nd Pennsylvania Volunteers was recruited from the Delaware, Lackawanna & Western Railroad; they were nicknamed the Railroad Guards. Company K was recruited from the local militia and called the Scranton Guards. Many were from Hyde Park.

The Battle of Fredericksburg, Virginia

We return to October 1862. As General Lee pulled out of Antietam, the Union Commander McClellan refused to march after the Confederate Army. This greatly angered President Lincoln. On November 5, McClellan was again relieved of his command of the Army of the Potomac. General Ambrose Burnside replaced him. Burnside moved his troops rapidly south to try to reach Richmond before Lee could return from Maryland. At Fredericksburg, he chose his battleground. His plan was to cross the Rappahannock River on pontoon bridges and follow the railroad south to Richmond. One of the homes of George Washington lay on Stafford Heights, overlooking the town. Burnside made it his headquarters. One hundred and thirty thousand men started digging in. They placed their cannons on the heights to the east to prevent the Confederates from defending the town.

Lee arrived at Fredericksburg a day later and immediately set up Lieutenant General Longstreet's cannons on the hills to the west called Marye's Heights, giving them control of any Northern advance through the town. He now controlled the open plain below, which the Union soldiers would have to cross to attack. The open plain included some fences, railroad tracks, and a deep canal that would slow down attacking forces. In addition, the Confederate infantry were set up behind a long stone wall just beyond a sunken road. This would be the open field the 132nd Regiment would be sent across under the barrage of Longstreet's cannons. They would have to eat the artillery fire as they crossed the half-mile-long opening. But first they waited two long weeks for the bridges to arrive. Longstreet had 40,000 men in these hills, and Lieutenant General Stonewall Jackson was 150 miles away with another 35,000 men.

The people of Fredericksburg abandoned the town on December 11. Sixteen hundred Confederate sharpshooters entered town to pick off the Union soldiers assembling the bridges that had finally arrived. On December 12, a brigade from Couch's corps was dispatched across the Rappahannock to sweep the Confederates from Fredericksburg.

The Scranton company, 132nd Pennsylvania Volunteers, was moved into town along with Sumner's Second Corps. They huddled near the buildings and made no fires all night long. The wind was freezing cold. The next day there would surely be an advance. Midday, December 13, Couch's troops were readied for the attack under General French across the open plain between the town of Fredericksburg and Marye's Heights.

Once again, Hitchcock tells the story from the Northern perspective:

> "About ten o'clock the command *Forward* was sounded and our brigade moved out towards Marye's Heights. The rebel batteries, numbering at least one hundred guns, were massed on these heights, and covered not only every street leading out from the city, but every square foot of ground of the plain below. A third of the

Strive for Insight

way down the terrace was an earthwork filled with infantry, whilst at its foot ran the famous stone wall, extending southward from the cemetery above the city. Behind this stone wall was massed a double line of Confederate infantry. To enter either street leading out to those heights was to face the concentrated fire of that mass of artillery and the deadly work of those three lines of infantry. Yet that was just what we had before us . . .

"Our division, General French's, led the assault. Our regiment brought up the rear of our brigade column. As each regiment turned into the street leading out, it took up the run to cover this exposed ground as quickly as possible. Lieutenant-Colonel Albright was leading our regiment and I was by his side. We passed rapidly up the street, already covered with the dead and wounded which had fallen from the regiments that preceded us, until we reached the railroad, which was nearly parallel with the enemy's works. A temporary halt was made here preparatory to moving forward in line of battle."[40]

In his memoirs, Lieutenant General James Longstreet described the battle from the Confederate command on Marye's Heights:

"The opening against the Confederate left was led by French's division of the Second Corps about 10:30 A.M. On Marye's Hill, back and above, was the Washington Artillery, with nine guns, Ransom's and Cooke's North Carolina brigade in open field, the guns were under partial cover, pitted. Other batteries on Taylor's and Lee's Hills posted to this defense as many as twenty guns, holding under range by direct and crossfire the avenues of approach and the open field along Cobb's front . . .

"French's division came in gallant style, but somewhat hurried. He gathered his ranks behind the swell of ground near the canal and moved to the assault. An intervening plank fence gave the troops some trouble in crossing under fire, so that his ranks were not firm after passing it to the attack. This advance was handsomely maintained, but galling fire, they encountered, forced them to open fire.

Under this delay their ranks were cut up as rapidly as they had collected at the canal, and when within a hundred yards of the stonewall they were so thinned that they could do nothing but surrender, even if they could leap to the roadbed."[41]

The 132nd Pennsylvania Volunteers were one of fifteen brigades that charged the Confederates at Marye's Heights that day. None of them reached the stonewall. Each division of the Second Corps was repelled in turn and the corps sustained over 4,000 casualties, cut down before the deadly wall that day. After the war, they nicknamed the battlefield "the slaughter pen."[42]

The Battle of Chancellorsville, Virginia

That winter of 1863, Burnside was replaced by Union Major General Joseph Hooker. General Lee remained on the heights above Fredericksburg all winter. He sent Longstreet to secure supplies from North Carolina, and Generals Pickett and Hood south to defend the Virginia Peninsula against the Federals. Jackson remained with Lee. They waited for the hard ground of spring before they could move north for a decisive battle or the occupation of large cities such as Harrisburg, Scranton, or Philadelphia to force the Union to accept defeat.

The 132nd Pennsylvania Volunteers' third major battle started on April 27, when Union forces crossed the Rappahannock River. Knowing he was severely outnumbered, Lee bravely split the Confederate forces into two armies, one with Jackson to attack the Union west of the city and the other to meet the Union General Sedgwick near Fredericksburg.

On April 28, the Scranton company joined the column northward to circle around to Chancellorsville, only ten miles directly west of Fredericksburg. Two days later, they reached the abandoned Chancellorsville House, the new headquarters of the Union Army. The ominous sound of musket fire in the distance and the constant flow of wounded soldiers into the hospitals nearby made the men exhausted and nervous. On the morning of May 1, Hooker made a statement to the army that victory was surely near. Sedgwick was successfully embattling Lee near

Fredericksburg, but Hooker left his army of 70,000 men inactive in the thick forest all day. Why were there no orders from the commander of the Army of the Potomac?

On the evening of May 2, 28,000 Confederate troops carried out a surprise attack in the dense forest. This was Jackson's famous attack. Eight thousand demoralized Union soldiers fled in despair. The Union Army was forced to retreat again, leaving Lee and Jackson with another major victory on Virginian soil. Seventeen thousand Union soldiers were killed at Chancellorsville. Thirteen thousand Confederate soldiers breathed their last.

Lee suffered a devastating blow on May 2 when General Stonewall Jackson, operating in the darkness of the early evening, was hit in the shoulder by a bullet from his own troops. On May 10, Lee's greatest general died of the wounds. No other leader displayed the bold leadership of Jackson on the battlefield. Only he could inspire the troops so powerfully.

During the month of May 1863, most of the 132nd Pennsylvania Volunteers mustered out of the Union Army after three major battles.

The Invasion of Pennsylvania

The Battle for Chancellorsville left many Northerners afraid Lee would directly attack Washington, D.C. and the war would be over. The South was running out of officers, soldiers, and supplies. Lincoln was running out of political support. In June 1863, the federal army moved closer to Washington while Lee moved quickly north to Pennsylvania. His army had never been beaten and they knew it. The final blow was near.

Lincoln moved quickly as well. He placed a Pennsylvanian, George Gorden Meade, in command of the Army of the Potomac. When they learned of Lee's invasion of the North, they moved quickly each day to catch up with him.

In his invasion of Pennsylvania, Lee used defensive tactics as he advanced into enemy country. They marched north, down solid roads through the Shenandoah Valley protected by the Blue Ridge Mountains and the South Mountains.

The American Civil War

Longstreet's Second Corps drove off all federal forces in the Shenandoah Valley and collected supplies for the march into Pennsylvania. The thirteen-mile-long trains of soldiers marched north along the west of the ridge behind the mountains. Stuart's cavalry held watch between the First Corps and the Union Army.

When Hooker discovered that the Confederate forces were thinned out near Fredericksburg, he crossed the Rappahannock. On the 23rd of June, the Confederate Third Corps and the First Corps crossed the Potomac River. They met at Hagerstown, Maryland, and marched north until the 27th of June, resting two days at Chambersburg, Pennsylvania. The first target was Harrisburg, a city of 14,000 people, a major Northern rail hub.

On the evening of June 28, General Robert E. Lee was encamped on the eastern edge of Chambersburg. That night, one of General James Longstreet's spies reported to him that the Union Army of the Potomac was approaching Frederick, Maryland. This startling news forced General Lee to abandon his plans to capture Harrisburg. Instead, he needed to recall Ewell's scattered corps and concentrate the army in one spot. The same night, he gave counter-orders to force the enemy eastward. His troops marched on the 29th from Cashtown towards Gettysburg. General Ewell was ordered to march east through Gettysburg.

Stuart's cavalry was circling between Carlisle and York. He had no contact with the rest of the Confederate Army. His cavalry was caught between the Army of the Potomac, which was moving too fast, and the Army of Northern Virginia, forcing Lee to advance without scouting reports.

Gettysburg was a strategic point, with roads running to Baltimore, Washington, and north to Harrisburg. The roads converge from the mountain passes with roads that border the Potomac and the Susquehanna Rivers.

On June 30, 1863, Major General John Buford entered the town of Gettysburg with 4,000 cavalry, including Company K of the 17th Pennsylvania Volunteers. In autumn 1862, Company K, with 150 men, was recruited in Luzerne County. They were unusually skilled horsemen with no military experience. Most of them were farmers, lumbermen, or mechanics. The captain of Company K was Richard Fitzgerald from Scranton. Company K took part in more than fifty-one battles.

Buford noticed that the high ground about the city was the hills to the south of the town. His task was to delay the Confederates so the Union could take the high ground known as Cemetery Ridge. Buford posted his troopers on Seminary Ridge, a low ridge to the west and north of town, to buy time for the Army of the Potomac.

Gettysburg, July 1

The next morning, Buford's cavalry fought for four hours, holding off almost one-third of the Confederate Army. Confederate General Hill had stumbled into two brigades of Union Cavalry two miles north of Gettysburg.

The Northern cavalry had Spencer breech-loading carbines that gave them the advantage in those skirmishes. The cavalry also had Smith carbines with a break-action mechanism much like a double-barrel shotgun. They pulled the barrel downwards to remove the spent cartridge and load a new one.

The 17th Cavalry fought alongside the rest of the Second Brigade in a two-mile-long skirmish line until Major General Oliver O. Howard reinforced them with his Eleventh Corps. The commander of the Eleventh Corps was Major General Carl Schurz, the German Revolutionary of 1848. He was ordered by General Howard to take the First and Third Divisions of the Eleventh Corps through the town and to place them on the right of the First Corps. About 12:30, the head of the column of the Eleventh Corps arrived. But the deployment could not be made as designed. Meanwhile, a strong Confederate force had arrived on the battlefield.

Here are Schurz's reminiscences of the day: "I saw the enemy emerging from the belt of woods to my right with one battery after another and one column of infantry after another. The enemy was advancing the whole force of at least two army corps—A.P. Hill's and Ewell's against us, that is to say 40,000 men, of whom at least 30,000 were there before us.

The American Civil War

Less than 14,000 men we had at that moment in the open field without the slightest advantage of position . . .

> "Regiment stood against regiment in the open fields, near enough almost to see the white in one another's eyes, firing literally in one another's faces. The slaughter on both sides was awful. A few minutes later, while this butchery was still going on an order was reached me from General Howard directing me to withdraw to the south side of town and to occupy a position near or on Cemetery Hill."[43]

Lee arrived in Gettysburg in the afternoon. Jeb Stuart still did not show up with the Confederate cavalry, leaving Lee desperate to know where the strengths and weaknesses of the Union forces lay. He did not know what was in front of him. Lee won a major victory that day. But that afternoon, General Early declined to attack the Northern troops on Cemetery Ridge and Culp's Hill.

Gettysburg, July 2

Union reinforcements arrived on Cemetery Ridge. Lee and Longstreet disagreed on the battle strategy. Lee wanted to attack the Union, split them apart, and win the war. Longstreet wanted to take a defensive position until Stuart returned with knowledge of how the Union positions were set up.

Without orders, Union General Sickles, with the Third Corps, moved to a new position between the Peach Orchard and Devil's Den. A bloodbath occurred. The Union forces retreated.

There were two hills above called Little Round Top and Big Round Top. At four in the afternoon, 20,000 Confederates under Longstreet attacked. Colonel Joshua Chamberlain, who was commanding the 20th Maine, successfully defended the left flank of the Union Army for two hours. Two-thirds of his men were killed, the rest ran out of bullets. Chamberlain ordered his men to fix bayonets and attack in a charge. The Union kept Little Round Top.

Strive for Insight

General Lee did not know the Union positions to make a final attack. Time was running out. If he was to break the Union Army and attack Harrisburg or Philadelphia, the North would lose the war and seek a truce. That was his only hope for saving the Confederacy. Lee decided to attack Cemetery Ridge the next day by crossing the field unprotected for three-quarters of a mile.

Gettysburg, July 3

That morning, Stuart attacked the rear of the Union line, but they were held to a standstill. Longstreet, who was second-in-command, bombarded the Union forces on Cemetery Ridge for a couple of hours.

Longstreet did not agree with Lee's decision to attack that day. Against his own free will, he had to give the order to charge! Generals George Picket and A.P. Hill charged across the field with 15,000 men at three o'clock. It turned into a massacre. Only a few Confederate soldiers reached the Union line and broke into it. Then they retreated. This was the high tide of the Army of Northern Virginia. Lee admitted it was all his fault. The campaign in the North was over. Lee had been at the gates of Harrisburg and Philadelphia.

On November 19, the president took the train to Gettysburg to honor the fallen soldiers who were buried on Cemetery Ridge. He held his famous two-minute speech known as The Gettysburg Address.

Sherman's March to Atlanta

By April 1864, 500,000 American men had already been killed or wounded in the Civil War. Illness and disease killed many more. There was poor sanitation in the camps, with contaminated water. Southern supply problems led to starvation for the Confederates. Food was scarce in a modern industrial war.

After his victories at Vicksburg and Chattanooga, General Ulysses S. Grant was appointed Lieutenant-General Commanding the Armies of the United States. In a letter on April 4, 1864, Grant ordered William Tecumseh Sherman to break up Johnston's army and penetrate the interior of the enemy's country as far as possible. He was to damage Confederate

The American Civil War

war resources, including the civilian population—homes, farms, crops, food supplies, factories, and cities.

Sherman decided to move on Atlanta, Georgia, a city with one million citizens. It was a major manufacturing center for munitions. To supply his army, Sherman redirected all rail lines to bring in his supplies from Chattanooga.

Confederate General Johnston had roughly 60,000 men. He was convinced Sherman wanted a battle to solve the campaign. Instead, Sherman avoided battles but allowed wanton destruction of the houses and barns along his march. Private property was destroyed as the soldiers foraged for food.

For the next three weeks, Sherman advanced over eighty miles, leaving only twenty-five more miles to Atlanta. In July, it rained torrentially. Grant wanted Sherman to prevent Johnston from sending troops north to support Lee in Virginia.

Meanwhile, battles continued back in Virginia. In May, Grant was stalemated in the Battle of the Wilderness, at Spottsylvania, and Cold Harbor. Later in June, Grant sidestepped the Confederate Army south to a point below Richmond, but Lee once again blocked him at Petersburg.

Back in Georgia, Sherman committed atrocities not only against his enemies. He also decided to bypass the horrendous Confederate prisoner-of-war camp at Andersonville on his march to Atlanta in July 1864. Rather than liberate the Union prisoners, he left them there to starve for another year. Would their freedom have delayed his campaign to Atlanta?

The city of Atlanta lay on a plateau with the Chattahoochee River to the north. South of the city were streams that would have to be crossed. Sherman chose to attack from the north and destroy the railroad running east to Charleston, South Carolina. At five o'clock in the morning on the 20th of July, the advance began.

Within four days, his men repaired the Chattahoochee Bridge. The railroad now supplied Northern troops. On July 28, Sherman ordered guns to bombard the city. The Confederate Army in Atlanta suffered from lack of supplies and ammunition. By the evening of the 31st,

Strive for Insight

General Hood realized he could not hold Atlanta. The Confederate Army retreated to the west.

Sherman threatened to empty Atlanta of all its inhabitants. In one day, Sherman set fire to all buildings in the city that could help the Southern war effort—machine shops, mills, warehouses, stores of every kind.

On November 6, Sherman marched out of Atlanta with 60,000 men. He had destroyed an area 200 miles long and sixty miles wide through the farmland of Georgia. Corn, cotton, cattle, horses, mules, and 265 miles of railroad were destroyed. All cotton he found in storage was sent to New York for sale. Sherman accused his enemy, Jefferson Davis, the president of the Confederacy, of being responsible for all the destruction. The next goal was the railroad to Macon, Georgia.

On December 22, Sherman captured Savannah, Georgia. When financial war speculators arrived from New York, he threatened to arrest them if they did not return immediately.

Grant allowed Sherman to remain in the South and operate however he liked. Should Sherman allow his army to destroy South Carolina, the symbol of secession? He marched north. On the 17th of January, the Union forces marched into Columbia, the capital of South Carolina. Fires broke out at 8 p.m. and left half the city in ashes. Thousands were left homeless.

His troops began their 400-mile march north on February 1. The Confederate Generals Beauregard, Hardee, and D.H. Hill led about 33,000 troops to stop the Northerners. Sherman continued to burn crops and buildings as he moved.

Jefferson Davis was afraid General Johnston would be deprived of essential supplies from eastern North Carolina. This would make it impossible for the South to continue operations in North Carolina and Virginia. Johnston chose to give battle at Bentonville, North Carolina. The fighting began at two o'clock in the morning of March 20th. The battle was indecisive. The terrible march was over.

Another march of destruction had been executed by General Grant in the Shenandoah Valley in September 1864. First he sent Philip Sheridan and his cavalry, including the 17th from Pennsylvania, on a mission to make the Shenandoah Valley a "barren waste." In September, Sheridan's

The American Civil War

35,000-man cavalry and infantry troops burned the entire valley to the ground. Sheridan reported to Grant on October 7, 1864, that he had destroyed barns filled with wheat and hay, mills with flour and wheat, and had driven off cattle. Railroads and factories were destroyed. Over 400 square miles of the valley became uninhabitable, from Winchester to Staunton, Virginia. President Lincoln personally thanked him.

In October, however, Jubal Early caught Sheridan off-guard. Early launched a surprise attack at Cedar Creek on the 19th. Sheridan was ten miles away in Winchester, Virginia. Upon hearing the sound of artillery fire, Sheridan rallied his troops. For his actions at Cedar Creek, Sheridan was promoted to Major General in the regular army. The Union victories in the Shenandoah Valley came just in time for Abraham Lincoln and helped the Republicans defeat Democratic candidate George B. McClellan in the election of 1864.

A twenty-nine-year-old Scranton lawyer, E.N. Willard, volunteered in the late summer of 1864 and served as Captain of Company C from Scranton and Luzerne County, of the 127th Regiment United States Colored Troops (USCT). Their regiment was the last to leave Camp William Penn. Some 11,000 free Blacks and escaped slaves had been trained there. Because of racism, the Black troops were not treated equally. Many soldiers complained of harsh treatment. Confederate soldiers hated commanders of Black regiments and shot them on the spot.

The 127th Regiment USCT was ordered to City Point, Virginia, in September 1864, and there attached to the Tenth Corps. They fought battles at Chaffin's Farm, New Market Heights, Fort Harrison, Darbytown, and the Battle of Fair Oaks before serving duty in the trenches outside Richmond until March 1865.

Grant's army fought for eight months in trenches around Petersburg. Sheridan's cavalry trapped Early's army in March. In April, General Lee was forced to evacuate Petersburg when Sheridan cut off his lines of support at Five Forks. At Sayler's Creek, the Union captured almost one quarter of Lee's army.

From March to April 9, the 127th Regiment fought in the Appomattox Campaign, including Hatcher's Run March, the Fall of Petersburg, the pursuit of Lee, and his surrender at Appomattox Courthouse. After the surrender, they accompanied President Lincoln back to Richmond and then occupied the capital.

On April 9th, Lee was forced to surrender the Army of Northern Virginia at Appomattox. They gathered in the Wilmer McLean house for the surrender.

Major General Joshua Chamberlain wrote: "Grant approached slouch hat without cord, common soldier's blouse unbuttoned, high boots, mud splashed to the top, trousers tucked in. No sword, sword hand deep in his pocket . . . When Lee appeared he startled them. He was dressed in a suit of new uniform, sword and sash, a handsomely embroidered belt, shining boots and a pair of gold spurs. Mounted on Traveler, the big handsome iron-grey horse with black points that had carried him safely through battles since 1862 . . . Seeing the surprise on their faces Lee stated quietly 'I'll probably have to be General Grant's prisoner and I thought I must make my best appearance.'

"At the signing Grant welcomed Lee with a warm handshake. They talked about old times and their families. After the signing Grant asked Lee if it would be acceptable for some of his officers to visit friends in the Confederate ranks. Lee was only too pleased to oblige."[44]

The American Civil War was over.

CHAPTER 12

Reconstruction and the American West

The National Stage

War always creates more problems than it solves. In five years, the Union Army lost an estimated 306,000 soldiers, the Confederacy another 260,000. There were at least another million wounded and lamed soldiers. Hunger, malnutrition, disease, and broken families caused suffering throughout the country. War debt for the North was estimated at $3 billion, with $2.8 billion in interest due. Most states were in debt. The South had loans of over $2 billion they defaulted on. The total debt for the North and the South was estimated at $20 billion.

Before the Civil War, America had a Federal Union of thirty-four states in the United States of America. After the war, that type of Union was gone. It was replaced with one federal state based in Washington, D.C., which removed much of the sovereignty and political power from the original states. This change began with five years of the Civil War; then the common-wealth of the United States and of the separate states were weakened in favor of federal and corporate power.

The war ended the slave labor system. Slavery was gone, but it was quickly replaced by severe segregation and poverty. Democracy, our government by the people and for the people, was set aside for ten years in the South, during which time their right to self-government was denied.

The Atlantic Triangle was broken. The Southern planters temporarily lost their political power. During the Civil War, the North took over the cotton trade. The US Treasury bought cotton for use in the Northern textile mills and to ship to Europe. Southern plantation owners needed the cash and Northern buyers made huge profits. Lincoln decided to continue the cotton trade to keep Great Britain satisfied. If they lacked cotton, they might enter the war on the side of the South. The sale of cotton also provided a source of gold for the US Treasury.

After the war, America's participation in the worldwide Double Trade Triangle was overshadowed by railroads built across America. The railroads were granted huge tracts of public land and run by modern-styled corporations. Capital was put in the hands of the few. The Industrial Revolution continued full speed.

Reconstruction in the South

Not until the end of World War I would the South recover from the physical devastation of the Civil War. Cities were destroyed. Battlefields in Virginia, Tennessee, South Carolina, Georgia, Alabama, and Arkansas scarred the countryside. Guerilla bands pillaged neighborhoods. Civil government and administration disappeared. There was no money, no industry, no work. There were no sheriffs, police, or judges. No bank or insurance company was solvent. Private property was ruined or confiscated. Bridges had been destroyed, roads torn apart. Railroad tracks had been bombed. Steamboats were docked. Four million former slaves needed land and work.

Frederick Douglass depicts the status of Blacks: "They were free from the individual master, but the slaves of society. They had neither property, money, nor friends. They were free from the old plantation, but they had nothing but the dusty road under their feet. They were free from the old quarter that once gave them shelter, but slaves to the rains of summer and the frosts of winter. They were in a word, literally turned loose, naked, hungry, and destitute to the open sky. The first feeling towards them by the old master classes, was full of bitterness and wrath. They resented their emancipation as an act of hostility towards themselves, and since they could not punish the emancipator, they felt like punishing the objects which that act had emancipated. Hence, they drove them off the old plantation, and told them they were no longer wanted there. They not only hated them because they had been freed as a punishment to them, but because they felt that they had been robbed of their labour. An element of still greater bitterness came into their hearts: the freedmen had been the friends of the Government, and many of them had borne arms against their masters during the war."[45]

During the war, President Lincoln installed military governors in the South as early as 1862. He authorized martial law in Louisiana, Arkansas, North Carolina, Kentucky, and Texas. In Tennessee, he installed a war democrat, Senator Andrew Johnson, as military governor, with the rank of brigadier general. Johnson would later become his vice president and succeeded him as president after the war.

For the coastal region of South Carolina, the new military governor was Major General Sherman, who had just burned a large part of the South on his campaign. There were 18,000 Blacks living along the southeast coast. In January 1865, before the war had ended, Sherman enacted Special Field Order 15 from Savannah, Georgia. He set aside 4 million acres of land along the Atlantic Coast for thousands of freedmen. Nine months later, in September 1865, President Johnson rescinded Sherman's order and restored the land to the Confederate owners.

Some radical Republicans wanted more reconstruction. Congressman Thaddeus Stevens, chairman of the House Ways and Means Committee, unsuccessfully fought for the confiscation of 400 million acres of Confederate land to give to the freedmen. In 1866, the radicals took control of reconstruction in the South.

Major General Oliver Howard took charge of the Freedmen's Bureau in 1865. He had 900 employees who helped former slaves gain decent lives in the South. The Freedmen's Bureau required freed Blacks to work the land of former plantations, with salaries determined by the Bureau. Howard was supported by the radical Republicans in Congress, but not by President Johnson.

Strive for Insight

Johnson hated the planter aristocracy and Northern abolitionists. Nor did he tolerate Blacks. He pardoned many Confederate officials and wanted the Southern states to quickly re-enter the Union. There were no war crime trials or military tribunals for treason. Most former Confederate soldiers were granted amnesty by President Johnson. The rebel states elected new governments. In South Carolina and Mississippi, Blacks were in the majority; in Louisiana, they were equal to the Whites.

General Grant was elected president in 1868. Seven Confederate states had returned to the Union. Mississippi, Texas, and Virginia followed in 1870.

White Southerners were back in charge of local government. The Deep South states quickly enacted Black Codes, or laws, controlling every aspect of the freedmen's public lives. As an example, the Louisiana Black Codes reads:

Section 1. . . . No negro or freedman shall be allowed to come within the city limits . . . without special permission.

Section 2. . . . Every negro freedman who shall be found on the streets after 10 o'clock without a written pass . . . shall be imprisoned and compelled to work five days on the streets.

Section 5. No public meetings . . . of negroes shall be allowed. . . .

Section 6. No negro shall be permitted to preach, exhort or otherwise disclaim to congregations of colored people without special permission of the police.

Section 7. No freedman who is not in the military service shall be allowed to carry firearms. . . .

White racist militias allied with Southern Democrats to intimidate the Blacks. The most infamous group was known as the Ku Klux Klan (KKK). The Klan was formed in Pulaski, Tennessee, by Confederate veterans. They used lynchings, assassinations, and the destruction of houses to terrorize Whites and Blacks. The members of the KKK wore white sheets over their heads to appear "as ghosts of the Confederate dead." The Ku Klux Klan Act of 1871 was passed at the request of President Grant to weaken their power.

The National Compromise of 1877 is considered the great betrayal of Blacks because the federal government withdrew its military forces from the South. After the war, the federal army never counted more than 30,000 men across the entire South. After Northern troops pulled out of the South and turned government over to white locals, the reign of terror continued. Between 1890 and 1910, Southern states changed their state constitutions to prevent Blacks from voting. This is called disenfranchisement. It continued for Blacks until the federal government enforced the Fourteenth and Fifteenth Amendments.

Now that the planter class was back in charge, a new type of slavery was introduced: segregation and disenfranchisement. Not until the Voting Rights Act of 1965 did the federal government enforce voting rights for Blacks.

Reconstruction in the North

The North won the war, and with it came the power to develop corporate industry. During the war, population and wealth had increased tremendously in the North. Factories supplied armies with food, clothing, and weapons. Protected by tariffs against England, the wool, iron, and steel industries were profitable. At the end of the war, the USA had 35,000 miles of railroad track. By 1875, there were 74,000 miles. Railroads and continental commerce became the new moneymakers. They replaced the old slave-labor plantation system of the Double Trade Triangles.

During reconstruction, Silver Barons in the West increased the value of silver production from $150,000 to $38 million. Coal production tripled and iron ore production along Lake Superior increased ten-fold. The woolen industry, cotton industry, iron, lumber, meat, and milling industries prospered.

During the war, some 800,000 immigrants entered the United States. By 1875, another 3.25 million immigrants entered the cities and farms of the North and West.

Strive for Insight

During the Civil War, legislation was pushed through Congress that changed America forever. The Morrill Tariff increased the taxation of imports from foreign countries to the USA by an average of 35%, and a series of war tariffs met the needs of Northern businessmen.

The National Banking Acts of 1863 and 1864 provided a national treasury system more attractive for private business. It instituted federal control over the banking system and reduced the state banking systems. A system of national banks was created to make a uniform national currency and a new market for treasury bonds to help pay for the Civil War. The federal state had no control over banks chartered by the states. The national banks were chartered by the federal state and could therefore be regulated and controlled at the federal level.

One currency was developed for national banks. By 1865, there were 1,500 national banks, about 800 of which had converted from state banking charters. The rest were new banks, like the First National Bank of Scranton. State banking was reduced even further by a 10% tax on all state banknotes. State banks developed checking accounts as a substitute for banknotes.

Secretary of the Treasury Salmon P. Chase had used the national banks to finance the war. Each national bank was required to carry Treasury securities or war bonds. The amount of currency or national bank notes the bank could put into circulation was defined by the market value of the Treasury securities or war bonds the bank had in reserve. If the bank wanted to increase the amount of loans to private citizens or companies, it had to increase its reserve of war bonds.

In 1864, Congress allowed contract labor to be imported from other countries. Telegraph wires and cable lines were paid for by the federal government. They granted millions of acres of lands from the public domain to railroad companies and financiers.

Richard Heffner gives a clear picture: "Though businessmen spent large sums to purchase vulnerable politicians, their investments in political power paid lush dividends in governmental assistance to industry's unrestrained expansion. Railroad interests alone received from friendly federal and state governments land grants and subsidies that attained staggering proportions. These land grants equaled in size the state of

Texas, and their value, together with direct money grants made to the railroads, totaled almost three-quarters of a billion dollars!"[46]

Three Reconstruction Amendments

During the war, Lincoln's Emancipation Proclamation of 1862 freed slaves in the Confederate States. The Thirteenth Amendment of 1865 abolished slavery from places not covered by the Emancipation Proclamation. Section 1 of the amendment states: "Neither slavery nor involuntary servitude, except as a punishment for crime whereof the party shall have been duly convicted, shall exist within the United States, or any place subject to their jurisdiction."

The Fourteenth Amendment was ratified in 1868. It guaranteed United States citizenship to all persons born or naturalized in the United States and granted them federal civil rights. Section 1 of the amendment states: "All persons born or naturalized in the United States, and subject to the jurisdiction thereof, are citizens of the United States and of the state wherein they reside. No state shall make or enforce any law which shall abridge the privileges or immunities of citizens of the United States; nor shall any state deprive any person of life, liberty, or property, without due process of law; nor deny to any person within its jurisdiction the equal protection of the laws."

The Fourteenth Amendment stated that no state could deprive any person of life, liberty, or property, without due process of law. This protected business interests from state interference. Businesses were to be protected by the federal government. Corporations were treated with individual rights and were no longer responsible to state governance. The Fourteenth Amendment gave federal protection to the personal and property rights of the freed Blacks, but it stopped short of giving them the vote. Nor did women in America receive the right to vote.

In 1870, the Fifteenth Amendment gave Blacks the right to vote. Section 1 of the amendment states: "The right of citizens of the United States to vote shall not be denied or abridged by the United States or by any state on account of race, color, or previous condition of servitude."

To this day, states can determine voter registration and electoral laws.

Reconstruction in the American West

From the Louisiana Purchase of 1803 and the Oregon Treaty with Great Britain of 1846, the US government obtained large tracts of land in the West. The 1862 Homestead Act opened the public domain lands for free. Individuals were granted 160 acres of land, as long as they cultivated it.

Miners, Cattlemen, and Farmers

The famous 49ers in California were miners who found gold and created local towns in 1849. They also developed agriculture in their regions. The same process took place in the 1860s in Colorado, Nevada, Arizona, Idaho, Montana, and Wyoming. After the mines were emptied, farmers and cattlemen moved in. The railroads and the government created permanent territories. California had entered the Union in 1850. The other mountain states followed—Nevada in 1864, Colorado in 1877, Montana in 1889, and Idaho in 1890. Wyoming entered the Union in 1890. It was named after the Wyoming Valley in Pennsylvania. Utah entered in 1896.

Hundreds of thousands of people moved onto the Native American land on the Great Plains and into the mountain valleys. The westward movement was already underway during the Civil War. Morison states: "During the war years, the population of nine western states and territories increased by over 300,000, while the agricultural states of Illinois, Wisconsin, Minnesota, Iowa, Kansas and Nebraska received 843,000 immigrants from Europe and the East."[47]

He describes the population after the war: "In the twenty-year period from 1870 to 1890 the population of California doubled, that of Minnesota and of Texas trebled, that of Kansas increased four-fold, of Nebraska eight-fold, of Washington fourteen-fold, and of Dakota Territory forty-fold. Altogether the population of the trans-Mississippi West rose from 6,877,000 in 1870 to 16,775,000 in 1890."[48]

Gold was discovered in 1860 on the Nez Perce reservation in eastern Washington. The mines in Wyoming along the Sweetwater River were closed by 1865. Gold was found in 1869 at Pikes Peak, Colorado. The Comstock Silver Lode was found at Virginia City, Nevada, near Lake

Tahoe. Last Chance Gulch and Bannock City in Montana provided $100 million in precious metals. Then gold was discovered in the Black Hills and made available to miners in 1874.

Cattlemen invaded the Great Plains and replaced the buffalo with millions of Texas Longhorns, Herefords, Wyoming steers, and Montana steers. Long drives with up to 35,000 Longhorns moved up the Chisholm Trail to Abilene, Kansas. Dodge City and Newton were other famous cattle towns. Cattlemen took Native American land and public land. They wrote the laws of the territories. They controlled the grasslands and pushed out the farmers. American cowboy culture evolved.

By 1875, the refrigerator cars on the transcontinental railroads carried meat to the slaughterhouses and packing centers in Chicago and on to worldwide markets.

The cattle boom reached its climax in 1885. Lands were over-grazed. Barbed-wire fences protected the homesteads. Two extremely cold winters from 1885 to 1887 reduced the herds. To survive, cowboys created smaller dude ranches.

Killing off the North American buffalo was part of Reconstruction in the American West. In ancient times, North American buffalo ranged from the Alleghenies in the East to the Rocky Mountains. This included the Mississippi Valley from the frozen lakes in Minnesota south to Mexico. They migrated together in herds on the Great Plains. Buffalo weighed between one to two tons. They were essential for the Native American nations, who used every part of them for food, clothing, tools, storage vessels, and shelter. Destroying the buffalo meant destroying Native Americans. Between 1800 and 1890, the Native American population dropped from around 600,000 to just 228,000.

The army encouraged soldiers and civilians to kill about 50 million buffalo for sport, fur, and food during the Reconstruction of the West. By 1873, buffalo were nearly extinct.

The Expedition on the Colorado River

Born in 1834, John Wesley Powell loved exploring rivers. At the age of twenty-two, he rowed down the Mississippi from Minnesota to the sea.

Strive for Insight

One year later, he rowed down the Ohio River from Pittsburgh to the Mississippi River, then rowed north to reach St. Louis. In 1858, he rowed down the Illinois River, then up the Mississippi and the Des Moines River to Iowa.

At the Battle of Shiloh, Powell lost most of his right arm. He continued in the army for three more years and commanded an artillery brigade with the 17th Army Corps in the Atlanta Campaign.

In 1867, Major Powell led a series of expeditions into the Rocky Mountains along the Green River and the Colorado River. In 1869, the *Chicago Tribune* financed Powell's major expedition, with nine men in four boats for four months. Powell bought round-bottomed Whitehall rowboats. Three boats were built of heavy oak, twenty-one feet long and four feet wide. Powell's boat was sixteen feet long and built of pine. He could clutch a strap with his left hand and keep his balance while standing in the boat. Powell shipped the boats directly from Chicago on the transcontinental railroad that had been completed in Utah Territory just two weeks earlier.

The expedition set out from Green River Station, Wyoming, on May 24, 1869. Passing through dangerous rapids, the group moved down the Green River to where it meets the Colorado River near present-day Moab, Utah. The members of the expedition were Powell and his brother, four Civil War veterans and trappers, an editor, an Englishman, and a Scotsman. None of them had whitewater experience.

At Lodore Canyon, Utah, one of the boats sank in the rapids. They lost one-fourth of their provisions and valuable barometers used to measure the elevation of the cliffs. The altitude was essential for producing good maps, and it allowed Powell to estimate how much vertical drop remained before the journey's endpoint, which had a known elevation.

When they travelled through the Utah canyons of the Colorado River, he wrote in his diary: " . . . wonderful features—carved walls, royal arches, glens, alcove gulches, mounds and monuments. From which of these features shall we select a name? We decide to call it Glen Canyon."[49] Powell measured Glen Canyon at 149 miles long.

After a long day on the river, the one-armed Powell regularly climbed the cliffs of Glen Canyon to measure elevation. On August 12, Powell spent two hours climbing among the shelves of rock and passed through a long slope to the foot of a cliff. He tried to reach the top but was cut off by an amphitheater. "Then I wander a way up a little gulch until I reach an altitude of 2,000 feet and can get no higher. From this point I can look off to the west, up to side canyons of the Colorado, and see the edge of a great plateau, from which streams run down into the Colorado, and deep gulches in the encampment which faces us, continued by canyons, ragged and flaring and set with cliffs and towering crags, down to the river. I can see far up Marble Canyon to long chocolate-colored cliffs, and above these the Vermillion Cliffs."[50]

Powell measured that canyon at sixty-five miles long. At its head, it is 200 feet deep and steadily increases to where its walls are 3,500 feet high. He described the limestone rocks as a polished, beautiful marble of many colors—white, gray, pink, and purple, with saffron tints. No wonder he named it Marble Canyon.

After traversing almost 930 miles, Powell reached the mouth of the Virgin River on August 30. The voyage produced the first detailed descriptions of much of the unexplored canyon country of the Colorado Plateau. It was one of the most inspiring events in scientific research during the reconstruction period.

Powell returned to the East and became a key figure in the founding of the National Geographic Society in 1888.

New York City

Back on the East Coast, New York had the greatest wealth and the greatest poverty in America. There were new ways of making money with the telegraph, cheap steel, oil, coal, and railroads. The goal was to dominate the machines and the natural products that drove them. The city became a clearinghouse for money, which rushed in and out of Broad Street and Wall Street. There were few rules on the stock exchange. Pure speculation was normal. You were expected to invest beyond your means. Some speculators made fake stock certificates in their basements.

J.P. Morgan became the mastermind of the economy. He loved rules and he loved making people play by the rules. In his spare time, he played a lot of solitaire. With headquarters at 23 Wall Street, Morgan bought up railroads and forced other railroads to stop undercutting each other.

As a member of the Treasury Note Commission during the war, Moses Taylor worked with other Eastern industrialists to raise a $150 million loan for the war effort. He also helped to expand the Union Navy and to support the Secretary of the Treasury, Salmon P. Chase. In 1864, Taylor was appointed chairman of the campaign committee of the Union Republican Party to win Lincoln's re-election.

Three years later, to everyone's surprise, the East River froze on January 23, 1867. This natural event would cause great changes for the city of New York. The idea of a bridge across the river became even more obvious. John Robling envisioned one great arch across the East River, 275 feet tall with a 1,600 foot span. Two years later, work began on the Brooklyn Bridge.

New immigrants poured into the Lower East Side—Irish, Chinese, and Blacks. They moved into the cheap tenements owned by Astor and run by the Tammany political machine. The Civil Rights Act of 1875 guaranteed equal access to public conveyances, accommodations, recreation, and juries.

Major issues that Americans still face today have their roots in Reconstruction: immigration; race; white supremacy; voter rights; corporate power; and the scope of federal versus state power.

The Local Stage

There are two very famous oil paintings of the valleys from the 19th century. One is entitled *The Valley of Wyoming*, by the American painter Jasper Francis Cropsey. Completed in 1865, this work is now on display in the American Wing of the Metropolitan Museum of Art in New York.

The other painting, entitled *The Lackawanna Valley*, is at the National Gallery of Art in Washington, D.C. It was painted by George Inness in 1855. The painting shows a steam engine leaving the first roundhouse of the D.L.&W. at Scranton and heading north to the Gap.

Reconstruction and the American West

American rail producers increased their capacity from 205,000 tons yearly in 1860 to 735,000 tons in 1865. This was mostly Civil War investment in infrastructure. Rails were the moneymakers in Scranton. During the 1860s, the Lackawanna Works at Scranton was the largest iron enterprise in the US, with the exception of Cambria Iron Works in Johnston, Pennsylvania.

During the Civil War, the D.L.& W. operated two divisions. The southern division connected to New York City tidewater at Elizabethport, New Jersey. It crossed the Pocono Mountains from Scranton to the Delaware Water Gap. From the Delaware River to Hampton, New Jersey, they used the Warren Railroad, which connected with the Central Railroad of New Jersey to Elizabethport.

The western division connected with the Erie Railroad at Great Bend, Pennsylvania. From Great Bend, they leased the Cayuga and Susquehanna Railroad, which gave them rail access to Lake Cayuga and the Erie Canal. This connected Scranton with the huge Western and Canadian markets.

During the Civil War, Taylor made good money on his investments in the valley. In 1862, the Lackawanna Iron and Coal Company paid a dividend to Taylor of $38,000 on $183,000 of stock. In 1863, he received $138,500 on $230,900 worth of stock, and in 1864, $115,450 on the same shares.

In 1854, Moses Taylor bought a strip of valuable land along the Hudson River across from New York. He made a railroad transfer point at Hoboken, New Jersey. In 1864, he built piers and docks. The D.L.&W. purchased a parcel of his shoreline.

Taylor was the largest shareholder of the Manhattan Gas Light Company. By 1865, he also owned 2,000 shares of his rival, the New York Gas Light Company. He wanted to reduce the price of coal for both companies. The companies supplied gas to public lamps, factories, schools, and private buildings.

In 1866, Scranton was prospering from the sale of rails, coal, and locomotives. Industry was powered by four smelting furnaces, one rolling mill, one planning mill, four foundries, machines shops, and many stationary steam engines!

Strive for Insight

In 1866, Taylor had possession of the Scrantons' original equity in the Scranton Coal Company. Then he gained ownership and control of the Union Iron and Coal Company and merged it into the D.L.&W. Railroad. Taylor acted as a salesman and approved expansion in the Scranton iron mills. During the war, he sold rails to New York, Pennsylvania, and New Jersey.

On December 10, 1868, the D.L.&W. Railroad leased the Morris and Essex Railroad main line from Hoboken to the Delaware River. Now the D.L.&W. had complete access to the tidewater at New York Harbor.

In February 1869, the D.L.&W. gained control of the Syracuse, Binghamton, and New York Railroad, which was the closest link between Canada, the Great Lakes, New York, and Philadelphia. The Lackawanna and Bloomsburg Railroad was extended from Scranton to Wilkes-Barre and to Bloomsburg.

By 1870, the population of Scranton reached 35,000 when Polish, Russian, Lithuanian, Hungarian, and Italian immigrants found work in the mines. In 1880, the population reached 45,000, and in the early 1900s, the addition of 17,000 Slavs pushed the population of Scranton over 100,000.

In 1872, Joseph H. Scranton died at the age of fifty-nine. His son, William Walker Scranton, the superintendent of the iron mills since 1867, took over for his father. The family business empire included the iron and steel mills, a bank, coal and iron mines, and the City of Scranton's gas and water works.

Since 1855, the Bessemer technology reduced fuel costs and the amount of time it took to make steel. W.W. Scranton secretly went to Germany and England to learn the secrets of these technological innovations. The process sent oxygen under pressure through the bottom of large egg-shaped vessels filled with several tons of molten pig iron. This burned off excess carbon. Then a controlled amount of carbon was added to the pure iron.

Moses Taylor wanted the Lackawanna Iron and Coal Company to adopt the Bessemer process. Together with W.W. Scranton, he convinced the company's other investors to adopt the Bessemer process in 1875. The first Bessemer steel rolled in the mill on December 29, 1875.

Reconstruction and the American West

Labor disputes began as early as 1870, when the Lackawanna Iron and Coal Company cut wages in the coal mines by 10%. The company also cut wages in the mills. In January 1871, the mine-workers union went on strike. W.W. Scranton personally led strikebreaking miners of immigrants from other countries to and from the mines. One afternoon, he was attacked by a mob and two striking miners were killed. The State Militia protected the strike breakers and reopened the mine.

The financial depression of 1873, known as Jay Cooke's Panic, spread throughout the USA. Workers were discharged everywhere. Terrence Powderly at the Dickson Manufacturing Company was one of them. Powderly became a tramp in Canada in the dead of winter: "Only the man who stands utterly alone, friendless, moneyless, ill clad, shelterless, and hungry, looking at the sun sinking red in a mid-winter snow, can know what it is to be a real tramp."[51]

After returning from Canada, Powderly was helped by W.W. Scranton to secure a new job at the Cliff Locomotive Works of the Dickson Manufacturing Company in 1874. That year, Powderly became a Knight of Labor in Philadelphia.

"One day in 1874 I was delegated to attend an anti-monopoly convention in Philadelphia and while there met a number of men prominent in the labor movement, among them one William Fennimore of that city. One evening he invited me to his room, locked the door, and told me to kneel down. I thought he wanted me to join him in prayer, and refused to kneel until he captured me with a little soft solder by saying I was just the kind of young man he was looking for. He had sounded me, liked my sentiments—such as they were—and desired that I join an order that had for its object the recognition of the rights of all who toiled, etc. I knelt and then took an oath to foster, cherish, and further the Knights of Labor."[52]

The first local assembly of the Knights of Labor was organized in 1869. In 1870, the coal companies cut workers' wages by 15%. Terrence V. Powderly began organizing workers for the Knights of Labor in Scranton. In 1877, Powderly quit his job to focus on union activities full time. The difference between the Knights of Labor and a trade union was that men could be members no matter what trade they practiced. In 1881, they granted women the right to membership.

Strive for Insight

Every time local lawyers in Carbondale and Scranton needed to check land deeds, they rode horses to the courthouse at Wilkes-Barre. They grew tired of this and decided to create a county of their own. On August 13, 1878, Lackawanna County, the last county in the State of Pennsylvania, was formed.

One memorable local spot was the City Hotel on Penn Avenue, owned by Richard Fitzgerald, the captain of Company K in the 17th Cavalry. They called him Old Fitz. Two local officers who were under his command in Company K for thirty-six engagements, John and James Auglun, worked for him at the hotel. At the bar, Old Fitz told stories to his guests. They say his place was very popular.

CHAPTER 13

Colonial Empires in the Nineteenth Century

The World Stage—The British Empire Expands

By the year 1800, the British Empire was already 245 years old. Five years later, Vice Admiral Nelson won a victory over the French and Spanish fleets at the Battle of Trafalgar, securing for Great Britain one hundred more years to rule the seas.

Captain Cook had claimed the continent we now call Australia for the Empire in 1770. He named it New South Wales. After losing their colonies in North America, the British turned to New South Wales to create a penal colony in 1788. Convicts of petty crimes in England were transported to the other side of the world. By 1848, some 150,000 convicts had been sent to the colony. Martial law was used to control the Europeans and the Aboriginals. Two years later, Britain took over the entire Australian continent. In the early 1850s, gold was discovered, bringing new colonists from the whole world, especially the USA, China, and Europe. The Commonwealth of Australia was established in 1901, making Australia a sovereign state and a dominion within the British Empire.

There are important differences between the Commonwealth of Pennsylvania and the Commonwealth of Australia. The words do not have a common meaning. As you read in Chapter 6, the Commonwealth of Pennsylvania was created in 1776 to establish the rights of the citizens in the State of Pennsylvania when they left the British Empire. The Constitution of Pennsylvania is based on the Bill of Rights. The Commonwealth of Australia gave the country limited independence from the British Empire except in foreign trade and the defense industry.

With the Constitution Act of 1791, the British divided Quebec into two separate colonies, upper Canada was mostly British and lower Canada was mostly French. In 1848, French was permitted to be spoken in the Canadian Parliament. A governing model was formed in Canada that would later be used in other colonies. The colony was given freedom to govern itself in a parliamentary system, while foreign affairs and trade were decided in London.

The British North America Act created the dominion of Canada in 1867. It solidified Ontario, Quebec, Nova Scotia, and New Brunswick as the four provinces of the Canadian Confederation. The dominion had a full-fledged military, though Canada remained a British colony.

Although Britain removed herself from the slave trade as early as 1807, the conquest of foreign lands continued. The Charter Act of 1813 renewed the charter of the EIC and declared Crown sovereignty over all territories acquired by the EIC. The private army of the EIC and the Royal Navy cooperated outside of India. By 1842, the East India Company had taken over Egypt, Java, Singapore, Burma, Hong Kong, and New Zealand.

Starting in 1843, a new type of dry rot in Ireland destroyed most of the potato harvest for the next four years. The Great Famine broke out, in which roughly one million Irish died of hunger and illness. The British did not help. Those who made it to the harbors and over to America were fortunate. Thousands of Irish worked as cheap labor in America.

Charles Darwin and Natural Selection

From 1831 to 1835, Charles Darwin sailed around the world. During the voyage, he wrote a 770-page diary, made 1,750 pages of notes, and created twelve catalogs of his 5,436 skins, bones, and carcasses from jungles, forests, islands, and mainland. Darwin amassed this data to support his idea of why some species survive while others die off. Darwin called his idea natural selection—a competition between species, some win and some lose. Some live and others die. From this idea, he created a scientific theory of evolution and published it in 1859, entitled *On the Origin of Species*. The book revolutionized 19th century biology.

Darwin took his convictions a step beyond biological evolution to explain his new theory of the evolution of human races and civilization. In 1871, he published *The Descent of Man, and Selection in Relation to Sex*, where he suggested that animals and humans share a common origin among African monkeys. If animals practiced selection, Darwin thought human beings did too. He proposed that the origin of human races began in primitive societies with different preferences for beauty.

Many people thought Darwin had explained human evolution. He did not. In his theory, man is a higher-level animal. Life has no meaning; it is reduced to survival at the level of biology.

Sociologists and anthropologists investigated the differences between races, peoples, genders, and classes. The differences were explained logically using Darwin's modern theory of evolution. Science created a dogma stating that natural selection had created an elite race and elite classes. Hard competition and war had created the rightful winners. Savages did not have the same right to life as the British. The theory of natural selection supported 19th century colonialism.

On June 22, 1897, almost one-fourth of the population of the world, 400 million people, went on holiday to celebrate Queen Victoria's sixty years on the throne. Soldiers from the whole world marched through London. Princes, lords, and ambassadors from around the world attended. The British Empire was the largest ever. They had conquered 178 countries and ruled the seas with a global network.

The British Empire in India

Raising the Indian people to the level of the Christian-Liberal British civilization was the mission Britain used to legitimize their colony. They used absolute monarchy and racism to rule their feudal system in India. Pax Britannica followed the Pax Romana principle of *divide et imperi*, divide and conquer! In addition, the religious division between the

Strive for Insight

Muslims and the Hindus, as well as the social divisions among 2,300 castes in India, kept the people of India divided.

From their trade offices in London, the merchants and the Crown controlled the subcontinent. Historian Brian Inglis wrote: "Bengal cotton, cheap by comparison with British, had long enjoyed a good sale in Britain, as well as at home. Towards the end of the 18th century the Manchester manufacturers had petitioned parliament to ban imports on the ground that the low standard of living of the Indians enabled their employers to undercut British prices. When the growing use of child labor enabled the British manufacturers to reverse the process, they abandoned this line; instead, they called for, and obtained, the right to have their goods sold in India duty free, their argument now being that they wanted to provide the mass of the people of India with 'the means of putting on the appearance of respectability by being decently clad at a small cost.' They also secured a ban on the export of any machinery which might enable Indian entrepreneurs to compete. As a result, the trade in Indian cotton goods collapsed, eliminating their competition in Britain, but also eliminating the Bengal incomes which might have been used to buy British manufactured goods."[53]

The Charter Act of 1833 established the Council of India, with four members elected by the EIC directors. Then both bodies ruled the whole country. To save face, the Council proclaimed, "The East India Company, which required a revenue sufficient to meet the running costs of governing India, as well as profit for its shareholders, relied no less on the sale of the drug. The British government at home, needing tea from China to maintain its revenues, and consequently needing some commodity which would sell in sufficient quantity in China to maintain the balance of trade, was equally involved. As it held the controlling interest parliament, in a sense, had become the chief shareholder in the opium business."[54]

In 1858, the British government dissolved the EIC and took control over India using the Government India Act. The British Raj ruled from 1858 to 1947. One thousand British civil servants controlled the country.

The Suez Canal was opened in 1869, making India and England 5,000 miles closer. Now the sea crossing lasted only one month. Retaining the colonies in Asia became easier. In 1876, Queen Victoria was crowned Empress of India.

Taxes in India were twice as high as taxes in Great Britain. They needed money to pay for the British Army stationed from Afghanistan in the west through India to Burma in the east. British companies exploited the Crown colony. They imported indigo, jute, tea, rice, wheat, and other products. At its height in 1884, the British sold 81,000 chests of opium from Bengal to China. One chest weighed 180 pounds. The profits were invested in London.

The British built an artificial irrigation system that compensated somewhat for the monsoon season. They also built 25,000 miles of railroads to bring products to market quickly. At the turn of the 20th century, the Viceroy of India, Lord Curzon, ruled over 300 million people in India, mostly Hindus and one-third Muslims.

The British Empire in China

Starting in 1779, the EIC illegally imported one thousand chests of opium into China each year. The British managed the world's largest drug cartel. Opium is only one level below heroin in strength. The illegal Chinese distributors even put the substance in the beer people drank.

The center of trade was the city of Guangzhou, which the British called Canton. There were thirteen offices of the merchant guild Howqua along the Pearl River near the royal harbor. China was closed to foreigners.

Opium, Slavery, and Cotton Production from 1800 to 1917

The number of opium chests sold illegally in China by the EIC grew from 4,000 per year in 1800 to 70,000 per year in 1858. The number of slaves in American slave colonies grew from 700,000 in 1800 to 4 million in 1858. This enabled the increase of cotton production. Sales of cotton to New England and England increased from 720,000 tons in 1830 to 5 million tons in 1858. Increased cotton production increased the sales of textiles to India, which then enabled the increased production of illegal opium. The Double Trade Triangles were in full production. Huge fortunes were made.

Strive for Insight

By 1838, there were roughly 2 million opium addicts in China among a population of 416 million people. In March 1839, Imperial Commissioner Lin Zexu was sent by Emperor Daguang to Quangzhou, where he arrested 1,700 opium dealers in two months. Lin demanded that Charles Elliot, the British Superintendent of Trade, turn over the supply of opium he had in the warehouses. Using police force, Lin Zexu destroyed some 20,000 chests of opium owned by the British. For twenty-two days, 500 workers labored to destroy the opium by mixing it with lime and salt before dumping it in the ocean.

Then Lin prepared for war. In June 1840, the British returned to Quangzhou with sixteen war ships, four steam-powered gunboats, and 4,000 marines to start the First Opium War. By 1842, the British had conquered the coast of China, plus the Pearl River and the Yangtze River. In the Treaty of Nanjing, China was forced to pay the British 21 million silver dollars in war reparations. Five harbor towns, among them Shanghai, were signed over to the British. Hong Kong as well. The EIC pumped even more opium into China.

In September, the Emperor made Lin a scapegoat for the war. He was exiled to Li in Xinjiang. Then one of the bloodiest civil wars in mankind's history broke out in Taiping. It lasted fourteen years and cost 30 million people their lives. Lin died in 1850 on the way to help put down the Taiping Rebellion.

On October 8, 1856, Qing officials went onboard The Arrow, a British Chinese vessel, and arrested thirteen Chinese sailors while searching the ship for contraband. The British used this event to declare war and start the Second Opium War in Canton. The Qing Dynasty was already fighting the Taiping Rebellion.

This time, Britain was joined by France, Russia, and the USA. For four years, they bombed Chinese cities from their ships. The Westerners wanted to open China to merchants, remove taxes on foreign imports, suppress piracy, and sell more opium legally. In 1857, the British Army, led by Lord Elgin, and the French Army attacked Quangzhou and controlled it for four years.

In the summer of 1860, 10,000 British troops and 6,700 French troops with 173 ships sailed from Hong Kong. They captured Dalian and

Colonial Empires in the Nineteenth Century

Yantai to close off the Bohai Gulf. On September 21, at the Battle of Palikao, 10,000 Chinese troops and Mongolian cavalry were destroyed by the Anglo-French troops.

The troops entered Beijing on October 6. The French looted both summer palaces and the gardens before Lord Elgin destroyed both palaces. The Second Opium War ended on October 18, 1860, with the Convention of Peking on the condition that China paid the French and the British 8 million silver dollars each. England acquired Kowloon and the opium trade was further legalized.

In 1864, the Taiping Rebellion was crushed at the Third Battle of Nanking. The Qin government built military arsenals in Shanghai, Fuzhou, and Tianjin. They developed military weapons with French and British advisors and learned Western scientific knowledge. The Steam Navigation Company in Shanghai, the Kaiping Coal Board, the Tianjin Telegraph Company, and other iron and textile plants were created. The Chinese Navy was developed.

In the 1880s, close to 120 million of a population of 369 million Chinese, or half the male population, were opium addicts. Foreign aggression continued. Tibet was invaded by the British and the Gurkhas from Nepal.

Then the Japanese waged war on China in 1894. The Beijing fleet was defeated. China owed Japan indemnity of 200 million silver dollars. Western nations carved up China. Britain demanded a monopoly over Chinese railway development. They wanted more open ports to establish naval bases. Germany took Shandong and Japan took the coastal province of Fujian.

During the one hundred days of reform in 1898, the Emperor made 200 decrees, with drastic changes in government, economy, education, and the military. Among them were Peking University, newspapers, allowing people to study abroad, central and provincial bureaus to create commerce, and a modern army.

Then Empress Dowager Cixi put the Emperor under arrest and carried out a military coup. In 1899, the USA prevented further foreign occupation of China with its Open Door Policy, which demanded equal access to commercial activity in China. The Chinese economy collapsed.

In 1900, the Boxer Rebellion broke out, an anti-foreigner movement in Northern China. It was called Boxer because members thought they had a way of boxing that was not vulnerable to Western weapons. Empress Cixi supported the Boxer's advance on Beijing. She ordered them into militias and declared war on all foreigners. The eight-nation alliance—Britain, Japan, Italy, Germany, France, Austria, Hungary, and Russia—invaded China on August 14. China lost the Boxer Rebellion in 1901. Again, foreigners plundered Beijing. In 1910, after 130 years of failed attempts to rid the country of illegal opium, the Chinese convinced the British to dismantle the India-China opium trade. The illegal trade had begun in 1730. Not until 1917 was China free from native-grown and illegal foreign opium.

The Ottoman Empire in the Middle East

Historian Albert Hourani defined the Ottoman Empire: "Its origin was similar to that of the two other great states which rose at roughly the same time, those of the Safavids in Iran and the Mughals in India. All three drew their strength in the beginning from areas inhabited by Turkish tribesmen, and all owed their military success to their adoption of weapons using gunpowder, which had been coming into use in the western half of the world. All succeeded in creating stable and lasting policies, militarily powerful, centralized and bureaucratically organized, able to collect taxes and maintain law and order over a wide area for a long time."[55]

Starting in 1413, the Ottoman Empire held together lands with different religions, ethnic groups, and traditions for over 500 years. The ruler stood above everyone. The family, the House of Osmani, was the authority, not the individual family members. Second-in-command to the ruler was the Grand Vizier. He and his vice-viziers controlled the army, the local governments, and the civil service. They collected taxes. Christians and Jews were taxed personally, but not Muslims.

The Ottoman Empire colonized the Middle East, Northern Africa, Eastern Europe, and Southern Spain for 400 years. By 1800, the European merchants and shipowners gained control of most of the trade. At the Port of Moche on the Red Sea coast of Yemen, English merchants sold spices from Asia and bought coffee. Cheap cotton, woollen cloth, and metal goods from England and France could compete with the local Middle East products. Moche coffee could not compete in Cairo and Istanbul with coffee imported from Cuba, Jamaica, and other islands of the Antilles. Sugar from the Antilles was refined in Marseille to compete with Egyptian sugar. French textiles were sold in Istanbul. Europeans bought silk from Lebanon and cotton from Palestine, plus grain from Algeria and Tunisia. Russia occupied the Crimea, a peninsula at the northern coast of the Black Sea.

The Ottoman Empire slowly dismantled as European countries conquered its colonies. Between 1830 and 1860, regular steamship lines were established between Liverpool, Marseille, and Trieste with Mediterranean ports. Ottoman grain continued to be exported, as well as Tunisian olive oil to make soap in France. Lebanese silk was exported to Lyon and Egyptian cotton to Manchester.

In 1856, the Ottoman Empire, together with France and Great Britain, won the Crimean War against the Russian Empire. The Europeans wanted the Ottomans to build their empire in line with the Western colonial model. Not until World War I would the Ottoman Empire fall to the British Empire.

Since the 1880s, a new kind of Jewish community was growing in Palestine. These were not the established oriental Jews, but Jews from Europe who came to Palestine to restore a Jewish nation in the land. The first Zionist Congress was held in 1897 to call for a home for the Jewish people in Palestine. Only twenty years later, Israel was carved out of the Middle East as a separate state.

The German Empire in Africa

Bismarck's new German Empire needed an international bank to compete with J.P. Morgan and the Bank of England. On March 10, 1870, the Deutsche Bank was started. Shortly thereafter, the Commerzbank and the Dresdner Bank were created. In 1872, the banks created branches in Shanghai, China, in Yokohama, Japan, and in New York. In 1873, the London branch opened.

Strive for Insight

The German Empire turned to Africa. Thirty-two-year-old Carl Peters represented the empire on December 4, 1884, when the land of the Sultan Muinin, called Sagara, became a German colony. This included today's countries of Tanzania, Burundi, and Rwanda. Also in West Africa, the German Empire controlled Togo and Kamerun. In South Africa, they had Namibia with its gold mines. The Railway for German East Africa built a line from Dar es Salam to Lake Tanganyika to transport goods from their plantations out of the countries.

To conquer colonies and protect them, the Germans built cruisers, fast and well-armed heavy metal ships. To do this, Emperor William II became commander of the army and the navy.

The Belgian Empire in the Congo

I mentioned John Rowlands in a workhouse in Wales. In 1859, he left for New Orleans, where he took the name Henry Morton Stanley. After serving on both sides in the American Civil War, he worked as a sailor and journalist.

In 1867, Stanley became special correspondent for the *New York Herald*. Two years later, he was commissioned to Africa to search for the Scottish missionary and explorer David Livingstone, who had set off to search for the source of the Nile in 1866. Stanley reached Zanzibar in January 1871 and proceeded to Lake Tanganyika. There, in November 1871, he found the sick explorer, greeting him with the famous words, "Dr. Livingstone, I presume."

In 1873, Stanley explored vast areas of central Africa and travelled down the length of the Lualaba and Congo Rivers, reaching the Atlantic Ocean in August 1877.

Failing to gain British support for his plans to develop the Congo region, Stanley contacted King Leopold II of Belgium, who was eager to tap Africa's wealth. In 1879, Stanley returned to Africa, where he constructed roads to open the lower Congo to commerce. He used brutal forced labor. Peasant communities were placed under military control. Slaves were captured by Tippu Tip and sold by Henry Stanley to plantations. Armies paid by Belgium terrorized villagers.

Competition with French interests in the region helped bring about the Berlin Conference of 1885, in which European powers sorted out colonial claims in Africa. The Congo Free State became privately owned by King Leopold II.

French Colonialism in Vietnam

In the 1880s, the French Empire spanned into the islands in the Caribbean and the Pacific. The French proclaimed that colonies were needed to introduce modern political ideas, social reforms, and new technologies, otherwise these lands would remain uncivilised and poor. The real motive was economic exploitation. They wanted opium, rice, rubber, and cheap labor.

To manage Indochina, France divided local communities and religious groups into those who were for and those who were against France. Vietnam was carved into three separate provinces: Tonkin in the north; Annam along the central coast; and the colony of Cochinchina in the south. There was no national identity or authority. It was illegal to use the name Vietnam.

Millions of Vietnamese were no longer self-sufficient on their farms and in their villages. The French stole land from the Vietnamese and turned it into large plantations. The farmers had to choose between remaining as laborers on these plantations or moving elsewhere. Rice and rubber were the main cash crops. The French also constructed factories and built mines to tap into Vietnam's deposits of coal, tin, and zinc. Most of these resources were exported.

The workers on plantations worked thirteen hours a day and were paid in rice rather than money. Bosses beat workers. Malnutrition, dysentery, and malaria were rife on plantations, especially on those producing rubber for French cars.

In 1901, the French required male peasants to complete thirteen days of unpaid work on government buildings, roads, and dams. The state developed monopolies on rice, wine, and salt. French colonists also grew, sold, and exported opium.

The American Empire Abroad

John Jacob Aster came to America from Waldorf, Germany, in 1783, at the age of twenty with twenty-five dollars and some wooden flutes in his leggings. In New York, he became a street sweeper to support the music store he opened. Later, Aster cornered the fur market in Canada. He traded in Japan, China, Hawaii, and Paris. Aster had a license to all harbors of the EIC for his trade, including opium from the Ottomans in Turkey. He invested profits in real estate in Manhattan, owning a large part of the tenement buildings on the Lower East Side.

After the Native Americans were reduced from roughly 4 million to half a million people, the American Empire sought new territories abroad. Colonies were won in the Spanish-American War of 1898. Cuba was taken, then Puerto Rico, the Philippines, Guam, and Hawaii within nine months.

To create colonies and carry out military interventions, President Theodore Roosevelt made large investments overseas, calling it his "big stick policy." The American Sugar Refining Company in Brooklyn, with the world's largest refinery, gained access to Cuban sugar plantations. Formed in 1899, the United Fruit Company, now Chiquita Brands International, entered South America. Phelps Dodge established copper mining in Peru and in the Congo. The Amalgamated Copper Company from New Jersey developed large mines in Chuquicamata, Chile, and Cananea, Mexico, as of 1899. Roosevelt seized the Panama Canal in 1902.

The National Stage

Colonies are designed to prevent Native people from developing their own technology, religion, and modern culture. Colonists want cheap labor. The British did not establish colonies on their own island, nor did the French establish colonies in their country. The US established slave colonies with 4 million Africans east of the Mississippi and Indian colonies west of the Mississippi. This created the peculiar form of American racism we still face today.

In school, you are taught that it was our "manifest destiny" to conquer the West. The idea is that we were predestined to expand our territory over all of North America. Nothing should stop us. The idea of manifest destiny is also used to justify the war and racism we committed. Indian affairs were placed under the War Department. All trade was controlled through government stores.

The Colonies East of the Mississippi

At the turn of the 19th century, Ohio was considered the Northwest Territory of the United States. In 1811, when the Shawnee Chief Tecumseh made a stand, William Henry Harrison marched to Tippecanoe River and burned down Tecumseh's village. The tribes of the Northwest Territory agreed to move to reservations in eastern Kansas. After losing the Black Hawk War in 1838 at Bad Axe, Wisconsin, the Sauks, Fox, and Kickapoos were sent to Iowa.

To establish slave colonies, the government decided to remove the Native Americans from Florida, Georgia, Mississippi, and Alabama. They declared war on all tribes and marched them out to Oklahoma. Millions of slaves from Africa were brought to the cotton plantations over the next fifty years. Great wealth was produced for the merchants and the plantation owners.

On August 30, 1813, Creeks killed 300 settlers at Fort Mims, Alabama. Andrew Jackson successfully forced the Creeks to cede over two-thirds of their territory in Alabama and Georgia to the USA. The states of Georgia, Alabama, and Mississippi outlawed all tribal governments and placed the Native people under state law. In Florida, the Seminole Wars were fought from 1817 to 1842. Hundreds of thousands of acres of land from Indian nations were transferred to white farmers.

On March 28, 1830, President Jackson signed the Indian Removal Act, which gave the federal government the power to create an Indian colonization zone west of the Mississippi in Oklahoma. The president had power to exchange land west of the Mississippi River for land owned by the Southeast tribes. In the winter of 1831, under threat of invasion by the army, the Choctaw became the first nation to be expelled from its land altogether.

Native Americans were not protected by the Supreme Court. In a case presented in 1831, entitled Cherokee Nation vs. Georgia, the Cherokee claimed that the State of Georgia, where they had lived for thousands of years, had created laws that would annihilate their existence. The court debated whether the Cherokee Nation was a foreign state as defined in the Constitution. The judges decided that the Constitution defined Indian tribes and their human rights to be inferior to those of the foreign states. The tribes were considered "domestic dependent nations" with the government as their guardian. The next year, in 1832, in Worcester v. Georgia, the Supreme Court defined the Cherokee Nation as sovereign, meaning the state could not enforce state laws in their territory.

In 1836, the federal government drove the 15,000 Creeks from their land. Three thousand five hundred of them did not survive the long walk to Oklahoma. The distance from Georgia to Oklahoma is 750 miles as the crows fly.

The next president, Martin Van Buren, carried out the removal policy to the extreme. In the summer of 1838, he sent 7,000 troops to evict the remaining Cherokee. Fifteen thousand Cherokee were forced to walk to Oklahoma. Four thousand Cherokee women, children, and elders died of exposure, starvation, and disease along the way. An estimated 80,000 Native people were forced to march on The Trail of Tears from North Carolina across the Mississippi River to Oklahoma.

The Mohawk Nation was exposed to extermination for more than 400 years by the Dutch, the French, the British, the Canadians, and the Americans. In New York State, Mohawk land has never been ceded to the USA. They never signed the Fort Stanwix Treaty in 1768. In 1838, just as the USA moved people from the Southeast to Oklahoma, New York wanted to remove the Hotinonsonni to Kansas. Seneca lands were reduced around the city of Buffalo in 1842. Some Oneidas and Mohawk were moved to Green Bay, Wisconsin. Many Mohawks refused to be moved and remained at Akwesasne. The Whipple Report of 1888 recommended that New York State exterminate the tribe. The Hotinonsonni government was abolished in Canada but not in New York State.

The Colonies West of the Mississippi

American settlement had taken 200 years to reach the Missouri River—from 1621 to 1821. After the Civil War, the transcontinental railroad enabled settlements to sweep over the rest of the continent in just twenty-five years—from 1865 to 1890.

During Reconstruction, the government decided to use the military to remove our Native Americans. This was war on civilians. You remember that General Philip Sheridan led a six-week "scorched earth" campaign through the Shenandoah Valley one month before William T. Sherman began his 300-mile scorched earth campaign through Atlanta to North Carolina. War, according to Sheridan, was not simply men against men in battle. It was far worse. It was deprivation and suffering for private citizens.

In June 1865, Sherman was sent to St. Louis by General Grant to set up headquarters for the Military Division of the Mississippi River. This vast area extended 1,000 miles from Canada to Mexico and 1,700 miles from the Mississippi to the Pacific Ocean. The great Missouri River lay to the north. Its headwaters began in Montana. The river flowed down into Dakota, along the eastern edge of Nebraska, touching Kansas, through the state of Missouri and into the Mississippi River just north of St. Louis. It served as the gateway to the mining activities in Montana.

In addition, overland routes led to the West. The Overland Trail extended up the Platte River Valley. On this trail, the Mormons, the Oregon settlers, and the 49ers had moved westward. Now it was filled with wagon trains transporting goods for the mining camps in Montana. In Nebraska, the road forked into Colorado for stagecoach travel and wagon trains. South of the Overland Trail ran the Smoky Hill route that led to the mines in Colorado. Further south was the old Santa Fe Trail leading into New Mexico and Arizona.

A new road, known as the Bozeman Trail, branched northward from the Overland Trail. Upon it, immigrants poured into Montana. Just beyond Fort Laramie in Wyoming, the trail passed into Montana near the northern spur of the Big Horn Mountains. This was the heart of buffalo country.

Before the Civil War, Native people were forced west by American colonizers. By the end of the war, miners were moving east from California into Idaho, Montana, and Colorado. Two great railways were prioritized by President Lincoln to facilitate the doctrine of manifest destiny.

Strive for Insight

Sherman sent troops to protect intercontinental railroad workers from Indians. He set up military outposts under federal authority. His tactics were to kill off the buffalo in the vast region, destroy the tribes' food stores and horses, and attack Native Americans in their winter camps. He believed in the extermination of Native American men, women, and children.

The initial wars on the Great Plains were the Comanche Wars from 1836 to 1877. The Ute Wars in Colorado lasted even longer, from 1850 to 1923. The Lakota Wars, from 1854 to 1890, lasted thirty-six years. In 1864, the Cheyenne were banished from their hunting grounds on the Northern Plains and sent to the desert in southeastern Colorado. The Utes were removed from their large tracts of land in Colorado. The Crow and Blackfeet lost their reservations in Montana. Promises were broken.

The nations not yet conquered in the Northwest included the Sioux, Lakota, Blackfeet, Cheyenne, Arapahoe, Modoc, and Crow. In the South, the Commanche, Kiowa, Ute, Apache, and the South Cheyenne were not conquered.

There were still roughly 300,000 Native Americans who could become hostile to the immigrants and the railroads. In his *Memoirs,* General Sherman wrote that the Indian Peace Commission of 1867–68 was formed to remove Indians "from the vicinity of the two great railroads then in rapid construction, and be localized on one or other of the two great reservations south of Kansas and north of Nebraska; that agreements not treaties, should be made for their liberal maintenance as to food, clothing, schools, and farming implements for ten years, during which time we believed that these Indians should become self-supporting."[56]

Once the Native people were removed to reservations, they were to be ruled by military officers who organized "the two great reservations into regular territorial governments, with governor, council, courts, and civil officers."[57] Sherman considered the Native Americans brave men fighting against their destiny.

In the Winter Campaign of 1868–69, Sheridan attacked the Cheyenne, Kiowa, and Commanche in their winter quarters. At the Battle of Washita River, Lieutenant Colonel George Armstrong Custer's 7th

Cavalry attacked the Southern Cheyenne, taking their supplies and livestock and killing those who resisted.

In the Indian Appropriations Act of 1871, US Congress stated that the United States could no longer make treaties with the Native American Nations, who were no longer considered sovereign. Native Americans were made wards of the federal government. The idea was to assimilate them in white culture.

The Lakota did not give in. Many consider Crazy Horse the greatest warrior who ever lived on American soil. Small of size and slender of body, with eyes that saw right through you, Crazy Horse had a great vision as a boy. His cousin, Black Elk, tells us that as a teenager Crazy Horse received a vision where he entered the world of spirit, the real world beyond this one. The vision showed him riding a horse that danced in queer movements while the trees, grass, and rocks floated continually. In battle, he could think of his vision and he would not be hurt.

Black Elk described the famous warrior's way of being: "Now and then he would notice me and speak to me; and sometimes he would have the crier call me into his tepee to eat with him. Then he would say things to tease me, but I would not say anything back, because I think I was a little afraid of him. I was not afraid that he would hurt me; I was just afraid. Everybody felt that way about him, for he was a queer man and would go about the village without noticing people or saying anything. In his own tepee he would joke, and when he was on the warpath with a small party, he would joke to make his warriors feel good. But around the village he hardly ever noticed anybody, except little children. All the Lakotas like to dance and sing; but he never joined a dance, and they say nobody ever heard him sing. But everybody liked him, and they would do anything he wanted or go anywhere he said. He never wanted to have many things for himself, and he did not have many ponies like a chief. They say when game was scarce and people were hungry, he would not eat at all. Maybe he was always part way into that world of his vision. He was a very great man and I think if the *Wasichus* had not murdered him down there, maybe we should still have the Black Hills and be happy."[58]

At the Battle of the Rosebud on June 17, 1876, Crazy Horse led about 1,500 Lakota and Cheyenne against Brigadier General George Crook,

Strive for Insight

with one thousand cavalry and infantry plus 300 Crow and Shoshone warriors. The battle delayed Crook from joining the 7th Cavalry under George A. Custer. A week later, at 3 p.m. on June 25, 1876, Custer's 7th Cavalry attacked a large encampment of Cheyenne, Arapahoe, and Lakota bands along the Little Bighorn River. Hunkpapa warriors led the main attack under Chief Gall. Custer and his troops were defeated.

On January 8, 1877, Crazy Horse's warriors fought their last major battle at Wolf Mountain in Montana. All winter, his people struggled with hunger until Crazy Horse decided to surrender at Fort Robinson in Nebraska.

In 1877, the United States government removed the Nez Perce from the Wallowa Valley of northeastern Oregon. They were forced into Idaho along the Salmon River. That summer, another American gold rush started in Idaho. There were so many violent encounters with the whites that the Nez Perce, together with a band of Palouse people, left for Canada. They wanted political asylum. Seven hundred men, women, and children were led by Chief Joseph. They fought for their freedom. General Oliver Howard pursued them in a 1,200-mile escape known as the Nez Perce War. Troops pursued them into Yellowstone Park, Montana, and to the border of Canada. Just forty miles from Canada, they were cornered and forced to surrender. The people never returned to Wallowa.

In the American Southwest, a series of Chiricahua Wars were fought between 1860 and 1886. Victorio's War lasted two years, from 1879 to 1880. The famous Geronimo War raged from 1881 to 1886.

The Dawes Act of 1886 stripped Native nations of all their land and transferred millions of acres to Americans. Collectively owned Indian reservations were broken into individual lots. Now that tribal sovereignty was nullified in the Appropriations Act, Congress assumed the right to legislate on all matters concerning Indian affairs as it saw fit.

In 1890, a Paiute holy man preached a new nonviolent religion. He developed a slow "Ghost Dance." The belief reached the Sioux tribe and spread quickly. A dance was to be held in the Badlands of South Dakota. The police decided to arrest Sitting Bull. There was a battle, and the great chief was killed.

Colonial Empires in the Nineteenth Century

Then the 7th Cavalrymen surrounded the band headed to the dance along Wounded Knee Creek. One hundred and forty-six Indians were killed, including sixty-two women and children. It was a massacre that signaled the final act of the colonization of our Native Americans in the 19th century. Therefore Dee Brown's important book, *Bury My Heart At Wounded Knee.*

The elimination of indigenous sovereignty was completed in 1898 with the Curtis Act. Congress declared all previous treaties invalid. All Native American governments were abolished. Tribal lands were sold off.

War on civilians was practiced throughout World War II, with civilian bombing in England and Germany, plus the use of two atomic bombs. The same total warfare was used in Vietnam from 1954 to 1975.

In 1977, the Geneva Conventions approved Article 14, which provides:

> "It is prohibited to attack, destroy, remove, or render useless objects indispensable to the survival of the civilian population, such as foodstuffs, agricultural areas for the production of foodstuffs, crops, livestock, drinking water installations and supplies, and irrigation works, for the specific purpose of denying them for their sustenance value to the civilian population or to the adverse Party, whatever the motive, whether in order to starve out civilians, to cause them to move away, or for any other motive."

The idea of Article 14 of the Geneva Conventions is an ideal for everyone to live up to.

PART THREE

History Powered by Electricity to This Day

CHAPTER 14

The Commerce Revolutions

The National Stage

Commerce is simply the buying and selling of goods. In the commerce revolutions, everyday needs and services are mass-produced then bought and sold. Your toothbrush, toothpaste, t-shirt, T-bone steak, and most everything else is mass-produced on the national or world stages for you to buy locally.

Who controls commerce? Before the Constitution was adopted in 1789, the federal government had no power over commerce. In the Commerce Clause of the Constitution, Congress received the power to regulate commerce with foreign nations, the states, and with Indian tribes.

Some experts argue that the clause refers simply to trade or exchange, while others claim it describes commerce and communication between citizens of different states. Did Congress have the right to control economic matters between the states? This is an important dividing line between federal and state power.

To this day, towns and cities develop along transportation lines, be they railways, highways, or airports. Hospitals, stores, housing, restaurants, colleges, and much more arise in the cities and towns along transportation lines. The railroad system for commerce involved federal and state funding, enormous land grants, the removal of Native Americans, cheap labor, western migration, the iron and steel industry, the coal industry, agriculture, and high finance.

The need to regulate the monopolies of the railroad industry is expressed in the Interstate Commerce Act of 1887. Farmers, small businesses, and passengers were charged unfair rates. The railroad tycoons, called robber barons, fixed the prices and gave their patrons rebates for shipping across the country. They milked the public. There was discrimination against small markets. The Act of 1887 forbade these unfair practices. Companies were forced to make their prices public. The Interstate Commerce Commission was created to enforce regulation and investigate fraud and discrimination. This regulation was reserved only for the federal government, not the states.

Three years later, in 1890, the Sherman Antitrust Act prohibited activities that restrict interstate commerce and competition in the marketplace. Section 1 states that "every contract combination in the form of trust or otherwise, or conspiracy, in restraint of trade or commerce among the several States, or with foreign nations, is declared to be illegal."[59] It prohibits attempts at monopolizing interstate trade or commerce and makes such actions a felony. The Antitrust Act was used to break up cartels, improve competition, prevent price fixing, and keep markets for industries open. The Sherman Act was used in 1911 to break up Standard Oil into eight smaller companies. That same year, the American Tobacco Company was broken into several competing firms.

The Electric Grid Was Fired Up

In August 1878, Thomas Edison visited the state of Wyoming to observe a total eclipse of the sun. During that journey, Edison stood on a ledge overlooking the North Platte River. Below, he saw men drilling iron ore by hand. He wondered why the power of the river could not be transmitted to the men by electricity. Edison would have to wait before his idea could become reality. First came the electric lamp, then electric heat, and afterwards the electric tools and trolleys.

The Commerce Revolutions

On September 14, 1878, Edison spoke about a safe, clean indoor electric light—the incandescent bulb—but no one knew how to make one burn for a long time. There were also no sockets to put the bulb in, no generators, no power stations, and no grids. One year later, he made an incandescent bulb that burned for thirteen hours.

Edison moved to New York City in 1881 and started the Edison Electric Light Company. He designed the first power grid in the world. The inventor was also an aggressive entrepreneur. He took out patents on the electric light and power grid in Austria, Belgium, France, Germany, Italy, Russia, and Spain.

Back in New York City, two buildings were purchased on Pearl Street in Lower Manhattan. There, Edison set up six steam engines weighing thirty tons each, with switchboards for 80,000 feet of copper conductors. All this to light up one square mile of Manhattan. The engine boilers were fueled with eight tons of anthracite coal per day. Two thousand cubic feet of water were heated, building up 120 pounds of pressure per square inch to drive the shaft linking each dynamo and non-condensing steam engine together. It took three months to work out the bugs. Edison placed the electric cables underground.

The commerce revolution was launched on September 4, 1882! That evening, the master switch to the electric grid was thrown. The Pearl Street Station generated electricity for 400 lamps and 82 customers. The first electronically lit house in Manhattan was owned by J.P. Morgan on Madison Avenue. His office at 28 Wall Street became the first office to use electricity from Edison's generating station at Pearl Street.

By 1884, the Pearl Street Station had 500 customers with 10,000 lamps. New engines were installed to drive the dynamos for the electric grid. The extra steam produced was sold to local manufacturers and households for heat.

Competition was just around the corner. The technical wonder boy of the military, George Westinghouse, entered the stage. He had made a fortune selling air-pressure brakes to the railroads.

The Serbian scientist Nikola Tesla had arrived in New York in 1864 with four cents in his pocket and a recommendation from Thomas

Strive for Insight

Edison for work he had done in Paris. Like many other foreigners, Tesla was rejected at first. To survive, he dug ditches for two dollars a day. Tesla had no family and no friends in the USA, but in the spring of 1886, two investors gave him a laboratory to further develop his idea of alternative current (AC). Tesla built a brushless AC induction motor and took out patents for his new type of electric power distribution. It could retain the high voltage lines over longer distances without losing power. Yet the high voltage was dangerous.

In 1885, Westinghouse imported transformers and a Siemens-produced AC generator from Germany for experiments in Pittsburgh. Westinghouse bought the patent for the new motor from Tesla for $75,000. He built a ventilator into the Tesla motor and made a fortune! Tesla used the profit to start his own company.

One year later, Westinghouse installed a multiple-voltage AC power system in Great Barrington, Massachusetts. They could reduce the current to one hundred volts and light up incandescent bulbs. A transformer increased the voltage for distribution in the grid and another transformer reduced the voltage for consumer use. Huge power plants could supply electricity over long distances to cities. Edison's direct current (DC) systems had limited range with low voltage.

By the end of 1887, Westinghouse had 68 AC-based stations and Edison had 120 DC stations. This was called "the war of the currents."

In 1891, the first long-distance transmission of industrial-grade AC was made in Ophir, Colorado, to supply hydroelectric power to the Gold King Mine three and a half miles away. Edison's vision above the Platte River in 1878 came true. The "current war" ended when J.P. Morgan forced Edison to use AC current for greater range and higher voltage.

In 1892, Edison's company was merged with the Thomson-Houston Electric Company in Massachusetts to form General Electric. At Niagara Falls in 1895, Westinghouse built a two-phase AC generating system, while General Electric built a three-phase system for the same project.

During the next century, Nikola Tesla would devise a system for wireless communications, fax machines, radar, radio-guided missiles, and aircraft.

The Commerce Revolutions

Modern Transportation and Conveniences

The original revolutions in commerce were driven by electricity. Electric lights slowly replaced gas-lit lights powered by anthracite coal in New York and Boston. America has been electrified since 1882. By 1890, 760 electric railways were running in the USA and Germany.

In New York, the streetcar was elevated above the streets. As we have learned, electric subways were built underground in 1907. Both were based on the dynamo. They accelerated the growth of the cities. Electric elevators were used as the skyscrapers grew taller.

What would happen if the grid failed, the lights went out, and the elevators got stuck? No one wanted to be stuck in an elevator in a skyscraper or underground in the subway! Their fear was justified, but not until 1965 and 1977 would the power grid suffer major blackouts in New England.

At the 1905 Electrical Show at Madison Square Garden, electric stoves, ovens, tea pots, and laundry irons were exhibited. One highlight of the show was an electric-driven refrigerating cabinet for the home.

The age of electrical appliances began. Apartment buildings had centralized heating, hot and cold running water, and steam laundries in the basement. Designers shaped the new conveniences for practical and esthetic purposes. The typewriter appeared in offices in 1867, the adding machine in 1888, and the cash register in 1897. Edison and the Columbia Phonograph Company presented the dictaphone for businesses. George Eastman perfected motion picture film and Edison the camera.

Today, nuclear energy provides about 20% of total electricity. Lights burn all night long in empty buildings and along the suburban roads. When you fly over the country at night, the landscape looks like a flashing dragon winding in all directions.

Corporate Innovation

During the commerce revolution, companies used innovation to continue to meet the daily needs of more and more citizens. America became a country of consumers in the 20th century.

One way for you to follow the flow of products is to go to the website of a major company and find their history link. At GE.com, the site for General Electric, they have timelines for four categories of GE innovation: transportation; power; devices; and environment. I name a few innovations to give you a feeling:

Transportation
2018 Commercial Supersonic Engine, 1975 Gas turbines for US Naval destroyers

1955 Gas turbines for electric locomotives, 1941 First US jet engine

Power
2018 Cypress wind turbines, 2007 Industrial internet-distance protection of the grid

1957 Shippingport Atomic Power Station along the Ohio River near Pittsburgh

1936 Hoover Dam on the Colorado River, 1930 Moldable plastic products

Devices
2019 Deep Learning Image Reconstruction, 2016 Mammography system

2000 4D high resolution ultrasound system, 1983 Magnetic Resonance Imaging (MRI), 1929 Magnetic compass for aviation

Environment
2016 Digital Hydro Plant technology with data-driven automation

2012 Consortium in China built Three Gorges Dam spanning the Yangtze River

GE powered the grid for the car industry, the weapons industry, the airplane industry, and many more.

The Commerce Revolutions

In the 20th century, highways, roads, and parking lots slowly covered the entire country. William Durant financed the General Motors Company in 1906. He merged it with the car operations of Ransom Olds, David Buick, and Cadillac. Henry Ford introduced the assembly line in his Highland Park Plant. In 1914, he declared a five-dollar, eight-hour day for his workers. Ford produced 500,000 Model Ts annually.

The weapons industry increased dramatically on land, at sea, and in the air during World War I and again in World War II. Every city in America built an airport. Today, the highways in the sky are filled with roughly one million passengers flying thousands of feet in the air at any time of the day or night.

The Culture of Advertisement

Commerce in America led to standardized products and a more standardized social life. Massive consumption was promoted through advertisements that made people want, what you wanted to sell them. New York City advertisers became the factory for popular culture. Consumer capitalism boomed. Magazines promoted standardized ideas, lifestyles, needs, and tastes.

From advertising companies, the image of the modern housewife evolved—with an ice box, oven, iron, and washing machine. Radios were common by 1925. The Hoover Model 541 vacuum cleaner entered the market in the 1930s, toasters with built-in timers appeared, along with the Beatty "Model F" washing machine.

Notice how your lifestyle, needs, and tastes are influenced by advertising on social media and the internet today. Artificial Intelligence tells you what you need and want. Their goal is to make you happy and keep your attention. Are they succeeding with you and your friends?

eCommerce

Now commerce is even more electrified. Much of it takes place on the computer and in the electronic clouds. In 2013, eCommerce sales topped $1 trillion worldwide. Can you imagine how you might explain that to your ancestors at the beginning of the 20th century? The internet has colonized businesses. Electricity has colonized our senses. We are online.

In 2019, eCommerce revenue was $280 billion. In 2020, the eCommerce giant Amazon reached $96.1 billion in third-quarter sales. Online shopping surged during the Covid-19 pandemic. Amazon was founded in 1998 by Jeff Bezos. In 2020, they had one million employees.

Now Amazon sells clothes, electric appliances, books, music, film, office equipment, and much more. The company also owns Amazon Prime, a streaming provider of exclusive shopping and entertainment. AMZN Cloud is a social media company. The company recently rolled out a cloud-based healthcare service called Amazon HealthLake. Amazon Web Services is their cloud provider, and offers computer, container, storage, and security services. Amazon retains a dominant position in the cloud market, competing with Microsoft, Google, and Alibaba.

The World Stage

We return briefly to the 19th century to understand the commerce revolution in Germany. Germany grew quickly as a world power due to German ingenuity, work ethic, the new empire created by Bismarck, using reparation money from the war with France, and the power of electricity.

In 1869, General Carl Schurz returned to Germany as a reporter. When he visited Berlin, he contacted Chancellor Otto von Bismarck. They were sitting in his palace office smoking Cuban cigars when Bismarck suddenly turned to Schurz and said, "I do not think he (Louis Napoleon) is personally eager for war, but the precariousness of his situation will drive him to it. My calculation is that the crisis will come in about two years. We have to be ready, of course, and we are. We shall win, and the result will be just the contrary of what Napoleon aims at—the total unification of Germany outside of Austria, and probably Napoleon's downfall."[60]

Bismarck's prediction came true. Two years later, Prussia defeated France, and the downfall of Napoleon III was complete. The Second

The Commerce Revolutions

German Empire was declared on January 18, 1871, in Versailles, when the German Emperor William I was crowned in the Hall of Mirrors. The Germans would return to the Hall of Mirrors forty-seven years later, this time as the losers of World War I.

Between 1860 and 1900, almost 25,000 miles of railway were built in Germany. The need for coal grew from 12.3 million tons in 1860 to 129 million tons per year in 1900. Tunnels, bridges, locomotives, and railway wagons were built. The Gotthard Tunnel and Railway opened between Switzerland and Italy in 1882. Oskar von Miller built the first electric powerline in 1891. Now inexpensive electricity could be sent to factories and shops.

The population in Berlin grew to almost 2 million in 1900. Back then, almost no one had electric lights in their homes in Germany. They had flowing water, an oven, and a stove, but no central heating, bathtubs, or telephones.

Prussia had coal, iron, and industry, and Berlin was the transportation center. The rest of Germany was very weak. The railroads, telegraph, and telephone became modern communication systems. Electric lights, electric streetcars, subways, and canals for water were put in place effectively. Bankers and businessmen worked nationally. Hamburg, Munich, and Berlin grew rapidly.

Wheat came from Canada and Argentina. Tobacco, cacao, sugar, and plant oils came from the USA and the Caribbean. Germany sold industrial products to Siberia, the Midwest in America, Canada, and South America.

The four-stroke internal combustion engine was developed by Karl Benz and Nicolaus Otto in the late 1870s. Benz fit his engine to a coach in 1887, marking the beginning of modern cars. Ford Motor Company came to Germany in 1925. Daimler-Benz started producing cars called Mercedes-Benz in 1926. BMW started car production in 1928. General Motors bought up Opel in 1929.

The Germans have retained their position of producing high-class cars, selling 3.7 million in 2020. That year, the USA sold 8 million cars, while the Chinese built and sold 25 million cars.

During the commerce revolutions, many theoretical physicists and mathematicians in the West broke with the thinking determined by Sir Isaac Newton and the British Enlightenment. They shared research, collaborated on projects, and mentored each other. They taught thousands of students in Germany, Denmark, England, Canada, and America. This led to new products, new industries, new weapons, and new sources of energy.

Max Planck became a professor at the Friedrich-Wilhelms-Universität in Berlin in 1892. There he wrote his *Thesis on Thermodynamics* in 1897. Planck was concerned with entropy, which is a degree of disorder in a system that makes thermal energy unavailable. He studied thermal electromagnetic radiation at equilibrium within a body, called black-body radiation. He wondered how the intensity of the radiation depended on the frequency of the radiation and the temperature of the body.

In 1900, Planck postulated that electromagnetic energy could only be released in quantized form, energy was a multiple of an elementary unit. Planck discovered energy quanta and formulated the quantum theory to understand atomic processes. This was considered the birth of quantum physics, which broke with the classical physics of Newton.

Meanwhile, J.J. Thomson had discovered the electron at Cambridge in 1897. That same year in Montreal, the New Zealander Ernest Rutherford was working on the conductive effects of x-rays on gases. He discovered two types of x-rays, the alpha ray and the beta ray. Rutherford then worked on Marie Curie's research in Paris, where she was convinced that radioactivity was an atomic phenomenon.

In 1904, Max Born entered the University of Göttingen. There he met three extraordinary mathematicians: Felix Klein; David Hilbert; and Hermann Minkowski. They helped theoretical physicists express their ideas in mathematic formulas. Born researched special relativity together with Minkowski.

In 1905, Albert Einstein published *On the Electrodynamics of Moving Bodies*. Einstein's special theory of relativity is the relationship between time, speed, and space. Planck recognized Einstein's work. Born and Hermann Minkowski researched it. During this time, Born improved his matrix algebra to work with four-dimensional Minkowski space matrixes.

The Commerce Revolutions

In 1910, the abnormal behavior of specific heat at low temperatures could not be explained by classical physics. Einstein pointed out how heat at constant low temperatures displayed abnormal behavior.

At a conference in Brussels in 1911, Max Planck met Albert Einstein. In 1914, he gave Einstein a professorship in Berlin. They became very good friends and often played music together. Planck played the organ, cello, and violin. Einstein played the violin. Many evenings, they played sonatas from Mozart and Beethoven in Planck's apartment. In 1914, Planck invited Born to the University of Berlin. Born attended their chamber concerts and became a lifelong friend of Einstein.

By 1915, Einstein's *General Theory of Relativity* was complete. He used the theory to calculate deflections from the planet Mercury. During the solar eclipse on May 29, 1919, his calculations were proven correct by Sir Arthur Eddington. Einstein became world famous. He had broken with Newton's laws of the universe. Einstein discovered that the laws of physics are the same no matter how you are moving. Even light bends downward and time slows because of gravitation. Gravity works in geometric laws so that space-time keeps the planets in orbit. Space-time is elastic relative to gravitation and light. This changed our understanding of space, time, and matter.

After WWI, Born returned to the University of Göttingen as director of the Physics Institute. Werner Heisenberg moved to Göttingen to study under Born for two years. In 1925, Born and Heisenberg researched matrix mechanics so it could represent quantum physics.

The New Yorker J. Robert Oppenheimer wrote his thesis on the quantum theory of molecular band spectra in 1927 under Max Born at the University of Göttingen. He calculated the photoelectric effect for hydrogen and x-rays.

Meanwhile, Edwin Hubble, an American astronomer, discovered that clouds of dust and gas in the night sky are galaxies beyond our Milky Way. Nebulae outside of our galaxy were then classified according to their distance from the Earth. He developed laws to show that the universe is expanding. Edwin Hubble worked with the telescope on Mount Wilson near Los Angeles, California, from 1919 to 1953. He discovered that most stars moved away from the others. Hubble's work inspired Einstein to change his theory of the universe in 1929.

Niles Bohr, a Danish physicist, collaborated with Ernest Rutherford to create the Bohr-model of the atom, which you will probably learn in high school. They used Rutherford's nuclear structure with Max Planck's quantum theory to develop the popular model. To understand the concepts of quantum theory and relativity, you will probably need to study mathematics and physics in college.

In 1933, Einstein renounced his German citizenship in protest of the Nazi regime. He moved to the USA and took a position at the Institute for Advanced Study at Princeton University. His theory of general relativity became essential to modern astrophysics.

The Local Stage

Historian Burton Folsom compares the leadership of Wilkes-Barre and Scranton in 1880. Wilkes-Barre had forty-five economic leaders with two or more directorships. "They totally controlled the First and Second National Banks, the Wyoming Valley Coal Company, the Wilkes-Barre Coal and Iron Company, and the Delaware, Lehigh, and Wyoming Railroad. In fact, they held almost 90% of all positions on boards of directors in Wilkes-Barre."[61]

No kinship group dominated the companies in Scranton. Scranton's forty economic leaders held 60% of the local boards of directors. Immigrants and unskilled laborers won elections in local politics in Scranton as they outnumbered the local capitalists. Irish Catholics took the risk of democracy and ran the city. They expanded city limits, bringing bordering townships into the city—among others, Providence and Hyde Park.

Paved streets, electric lights, and the first successful streetcar system were the main advances in cities in the 1880s. But starting in 1880, the national transportation networks broke down the protection of local markets. The commerce revolution replaced local ownership and companies with large corporations, national chain stores, and multiregional banks. Cheaper goods arrived from the national economy. Professional training became more specialized in a national system.

In 1880, Charles S. Woolworth set up a five-and-ten-cent store in Scranton. The idea caught on, though sales were modest the first year—$9,000. In the 1890s, Woolworth started branch stores in New York and Maine. By 1920, it had become a major national corporation.

Moses Taylor died in 1882. His estate was estimated at between $40 million and $45 million. Taylor was an important capitalist but not a philanthropist. The only gift he made was for free lifetime healthcare for the employees of the D.L.& W. Railroad and the Lackawanna Iron and Coal Company and their families. A few years before he died, Taylor gifted $270,000 to build The Moses Taylor Hospital in Scranton.

By 1890, five railroads served the valley: the Delaware and Hudson Railway; the Delaware, Lackawanna and Western Railroad; the Erie Railroad; the Central Railroad of New Jersey; and the New York, Ontario, and Western Railroad. These railways also controlled 96% of the coalfields in the Scranton area. The mines covered 650 miles of road under the earth. There were twenty-two mines under the city and eleven coal breakers above ground. Anthracite production jumped from 15.6 million tons in 1870 to 46 million tons in 1890.

Companies in Scranton mass-produced steel, coal, mine pumps, and coal mining machines. Smaller products included stoves, incandescent lamps, bolts, nuts, textbooks, mattresses, beds, tiles, and cigars. The Scranton Electric Construction Company built electrical apparatus for use in the mines—mechanical drills, locomotive hoists, and mining pumps.

The Scranton brothers, William and Walter, formed Scranton Steel, located along the Lackawanna River. By May 1883, two six-ton Bessemer converters were producing 250,000 tons of ingots. Ingots are semi-finished steel products that need to be cut or rolled into useful products. These were rolled into steel rails.

In 1891, Scranton Steel merged with the Lackawanna Iron and Coal Company to form the Lackawanna Iron and Steel Company. By 1894, the new company manufactured one-sixth of the total national output.

By 1898, only two of the Scranton furnaces were still active. They also operated furnaces in Lebanon County, Pennsylvania, and one at Franklin, New Jersey. The Bessemer pig iron was shipped to Scranton and made into steel rail.

Heavy Industry Leaves Scranton

Because the markets for steel were moving west, the Lackawanna Iron and Steel Company struggled to compete with US Steel. The majority of the board of directors were now from New York City, with no local loyalty to Scranton, where 5,000 men were close to losing their jobs in the furnaces, mills, mines, and shops. Despite labor activity in Scranton and the cost of shipping iron ore from out of state, the steel mills were making a profit in the year they were moved out of state.

In 1899, the board of directors decided to move the Lackawanna Iron and Steel Company to Buffalo, New York, on the shore of Lake Erie. This would position them to access the iron ore deposits at Marquette on the Upper Peninsula of Michigan. They would also be able to ship products west by boat on the Great Lakes.

On 24 June, 1901, the Dickson Manufacturing Company's locomotive division was merged with seven other manufacturing firms to form American Locomotive Company (ALCO). Locomotive production ceased in Scranton in 1909. The rest of the Dickson Manufacturing Company became part of Allis-Chalmers.

Local Entrepreneurs

From 1880 to 1920, the Sauquoit Silk Manufacturing Company and the Klots Throwing Company made Scranton number one in silk cloth production in the country, with a total of twenty-five plants. Fifteen of them were throwing mills and ten were weaving mills. By 1890, Sauquoit had 1,500 employees.

On November 30, 1886, the Scranton Suburban Railway Company opened a new electric car system. That evening, the famous African explorer Sir Henry Stanley held a lecture at the Academy of Music, opposite St. Luke's Church on Wyoming Avenue. Scranton was the focal point of the Welsh in America. Stanley was the most famous Welshman in the world. That night, he spoke about his discovery of Mr. David Livingstone in Africa, who was searching for the source of the Nile. After the lecture, the electric car moved people from St. Luke's Church to Green Ridge for five cents a ride. It was the first electric trolley system in the country.

William Connell was successful in coal operations before launching Lackawanna Knitting Mills Company and the Scranton Button Manufacturing Company in 1887. Henry Belin Jr. was successful in manufacturing gunpowder before he organized the Scranton Lace Company in 1890.

New Immigration to the Valley

Employment in the mines grew from 11,300 men and boys in 1875 to 23,400 in 1890 after massive waves of immigrants arrived from Southern and Eastern Europe. They had left devastating poverty in their homelands. From 1880 to 1900, Scranton's population grew from 45,000 to 102,000. It became the third largest city in Pennsylvania. In 1941, the population peaked at 140,393.

Erin Nissley of the *Times Tribune* described the life of Michael Bosak, a Slovakian immigrant who brought entrepreneurial skills to the valley. At the age of seventeen, Bosak arrived at Ellis Island in 1886. He took the train out to Hazelton, where he worked picking slate. Bosak moved to Olyphant in 1893, where he opened a bar and distributed liquor wholesale. He then exchanged foreign currency and sold steamship tickets. Shortly thereafter, he went into banking, organizing the Citizens Bank of Olyphant in 1902, the Slavonic Deposit Bank in Wilkes-Barre in 1912, and the Bosak State Bank in Scranton in 1915.

New Business, Culture, and Entertainment Established

From 1850 to 1880, most of Scranton's doctors, lawyers, and businessmen were trained in apprenticeships, not at universities. Engineers and chemists were trained on the job. The valley was self-sufficient.

The Diocese of Scranton founded St. Thomas College in 1888. It was named for Saint Thomas Aquinas, the famous Dominican philosopher and theologian of the Scholastic school of thought from 1245 to 1274. The college became the University of Scranton in 1938.

John Jermyn opened his world-class hotel on Spruce Street in 1895. The Hotel Jermyn had 350 rooms, steam heat, hot and cold water, and one hundred private baths. The Board of Trade Building on Linden Street, later called the Scranton Electric Building, was built the same year.

The state passed the Mine Safety Act of 1885, requiring a mine foreman to pass exams on coal mining procedures and regulations. Thomas J. Foster of Scranton wrote *The Colliery Engineer*, describing the Pennsylvania mining code. He had many requests. Foster began a correspondence school in Scranton. He taught the technicalities of mining to engineers all over the world. The International Correspondence School became incorporated as the International Textbook Company. By 1920, the company was capitalized at $10 million and they had educated 3 million people by mail. The company had 3,200 employees.

The *Times Tribune* tells us that, in 1907, Sylvester Z. Poli of New Haven, Connecticut, built the Poli Theater on Wyoming Avenue for $250,000. It held 2,000 guests and was considered one of the finest showhouses in the country. Shows cost ten cents. Poli built another theater in Wilkes-Barre. Both theaters in the valley were part of his chain of eighteen showhouses in New England.

Poli came to the USA in 1881, at the age of twenty-three. He was an apprentice in show business at the Eden Muse in New York City. Why would an immigrant operate a house for vaudeville in Scranton until 1925? What did he know about the market for such an enterprise? He knew the artists needed to prove their skills on the big-time circuit. The people of Scranton were not easy to please artistically. If the artists succeeded in Scranton, the bookers would bring them to the big city. Early stars included Lillian Russell, John Philip Sousa, and Buffalo Bill Cody. Huge names included Mae West, W.C. Fields, Houdini, Will Rogers, the Marx Brothers, and Buster Keaton. Later, Jack Benny and Fred Astaire performed. The Big Bands of Glen Miller, Guy Lombardo, Duke Ellington, and Count Basie all played Scranton.

At the Scranton Catholic Youth Center, Sammy Davis Jr. performed in 1965, the Grateful Dead in 1971, and Johnny Cash in 1982. At Montage Mountain, Traffic, the Allman Brothers Band, Fleetwood Mac, Aerosmith, Lynard Skynard, and hundreds more have performed.

The Commerce Revolutions

The Keystone State

Transportation revolutionized commerce in the valley. The Grand Army of the Republic Highway covered 3,198 miles, connecting Long Beach, California, with Provincetown, Massachusetts, in 1936. They called it US Route 6, now an interstate scenic highway. Four hundred miles of it passed through Northern Pennsylvania along Native American paths through the Endless Mountains.

Another transcontinental highway is US Route 11. The 1,645-mile-long highway crosses the eastern United States. It begins east of New Orleans, Louisiana, and winds through nine states before it enters Canada.

Route 11 follows the Susquehanna River into the Great Valley at Wilkes-Barre. At Pittston, it breaks east from the river and winds north to Scranton. North of downtown it becomes the North Scranton Expressway, which leads through Liggett's Gap a few miles until it crosses Route 6 at Clarks Summit. It joins Route 6 westward to Factoryville, where both intercontinental routes separate; Route 6 winds westward while Route 11 treks north to the New York border. The country's transcontinental highways cross in the Keystone State in the Lackawanna Valley!

Before World War II, commerce was severely reduced when the steel mills left, the anthracite coal market disappeared, the Great Depression hit, the textile mills shut down, and the public trolley system was removed. Malls replaced downtown as centers of buying and selling.

Airline commerce was established at the Scranton Wilkes-Barre Airport in 1947, and one year later the first TVs entered the valley. In the 1950s, we had 140 churches, twenty-two theaters, ten parks, four airlines, six railroad carriers, and a natural water reserve of 8 billion gallons.

CHAPTER 15

Land, Labor, Capital, and the Great Anthracite Strike of 1902

Land

Soon after Terrence Powderly took office as Mayor of Scranton in 1878, a meeting of the best people in Scranton was called, excluding him. All the best people were wealthy. Powderly wrote, "It was decided at the meeting that property was not safe in Scranton with a mayor of communistic tendencies in the chair."[62]

Powderly was not a communist, but a labor mayor. As an Irishman in America, he had raised money for the Irish Land League to remove famine and enable the Irish peasant to own the soil he cultivated in the home country. The English Crown and the landlords had robbed the land from the Irish people. The best people in Scranton were aware of this.

Powderly proposed a radical tax system for the city. The idea was that natural resources are the shared inheritance of all people, not just the wealthy who buy the land. The wealthy should share their profits with the people by paying taxes.

Strive for Insight

In 1887, the Scranton City Council voted down a proposal from the mayor to buy land in the valley to obtain revenue for the city from coal. They also refused to build a cooperative boot and shoe factory he proposed. He wanted labor and the people to have their share of wealth in America.

The European relationship to land is private ownership. It came from the Roman Empire 2,000 years ago. This relationship evolved into the Doctrine of Discovery, which stated that European explorers who discovered land immediately acquired ownership rights. It was used by Pope Alexander VI in 1493 to divide the Americas between Spain and Portugal. The British Crown used it when establishing their thirteen colonies in North America. Not until 1823 was it made into United States law by the Supreme Court decision of Johnson vs. McIntosh.

In America, we are taught to believe in private property as the only solution to ownership. Is it? Who should own the land? Today, individuals hold titles to the land. If you do not pay your taxes, you can be evicted. The taxes are paid for the common good—streets, sidewalks, police protection, firefighting, the military, public transportation, public health, and education. This is important because the common-wealth of a country must be continually improved and increased to prevent the decline of infrastructure, healthcare, and education. To this day, Congress has not prevented the increase of poverty in America.

Nor have they used taxpayers' money to increase the common-wealth by giving states, cities, and local government land grants for future income. As we learned, during Reconstruction, Congress gave land grants, the size of Texas, to privately-owned railroads. Millions of acres were held by land speculators who enjoyed absolute dominion over the land.

Powderly wrote about the resistance to changing the ownership of land in America: "In any event, the day is here for an overhauling of the way land is held from use. Our whole system of land tenure needs to be inquired into with a view to making the land serve the greatest number for the greatest good. Socialism, anarchy, Bolshevism, and radicalism will be manufactured out of thin air to shout at the man who undertakes in earnest, to readjust land-holding to the needs of the many.[63]

Land, Labor, Capital, and the Great Anthracite Strike

In his book *Progress and Poverty*, published in 1879, Henry George argued that landowners in the free-market economy kept a large portion of the wealth created by social and technological advances. They kept the wealth by charging rents. He considered this unearned wealth the cause of poverty. Why should private people and companies own the land and restrict access to our natural resources? Why should productive work be heavily taxed? He proposed a land value tax in which governments could tax the value of the land but allow the investors to keep the value of their improvements to the land. In other words, George believed the capitalists should own the value they produce from the land, but the value of the land and its resources above and below ground should be shared equally among all members of society. He sold 3 million copies of the popular book.

The very same idea was put into practice by the Norwegian government when they discovered a huge quantity of oil and gas in the North Sea. In May 1963, the government proclaimed sovereignty over the Norwegian Continental Shelf underneath the North Sea. They passed new regulations giving the state ownership of any natural resources on the shelf. Only the government was authorized to award licenses for exploration and production.

The Norwegians sat down with leaders of the large oil companies and invited them to explore for oil and gas in Norway, knowing they would have to pay 60% of their income to Norway each year. The companies agreed. They knew they would still make a fortune. Exxon Mobil became the largest taxpayer in Norwegian history.

Norway has a population of 5 million people, less than half the size of Pennsylvania. Since production started in the early 1970s, petroleum activities have contributed to Norway's gross domestic product by more than $1,846 billion. It is called the Government Pension Fund. In 2020, the surplus fund had returns of $127 billion. It is invested in over 9,000 companies in seventy-four countries. At the end of 2022, the fund was worth $1.25 trillion. During the Covid-19 pandemic, some of this common-wealth surplus was used to bail out industries, companies, and citizens.

Can you imagine if the state of Pennsylvania had a surplus fund worth $1.25 trillion today? The state, local governments, and schools could be helped, for example, by sufficiently taxing the export of millions of gallons of liquefied natural gas that is transported through Pennsylvania each day. Instead, Pennsylvania was dealing with a budget deficit of near $5 billion in 2021.

What would the other states say? Would Pennsylvania be criticized for socialistic or communistic activities? Would people try to privatize the fund and put Pennsylvania back into debt? Or would it be a successful revolution?

The idea behind the Norwegian model makes sense. Had Pennsylvania taxed energy companies 60% for the past thirty years, the state would have a surplus to spend on infrastructure and common-wealth today.

Labor in the Valley in the 19th Century

An unknown reporter from *Harper's New Monthly Magazine* published an article entitled "The Scranton Miner" in November 1877.

> "The miners are almost all of foreign birth, the Irish being the most numerous, next the Welsh, then the Germans, and lastly the English and Scotch. Among the miners there are some Pennsylvania Germans. With the exception of these, there is scarcely to be found at Scranton a native of this country working under-ground, either as miner or laborer . . .
>
> "Gaelic is extensively spoken by the Irish here. The Welsh language is more extensively employed. There are seven churches of which the services are in that language, a Welsh newspaper, and a literary society. The Welsh claim that they were never subjugated by England. They are Republicans almost to a man, and equally Protestant; lovers of liberty, stubborn and enduring, not fickle . . .
>
> "The Welshman is the miner, who blasts and takes down the coal, while the Irishman loads it upon the cars, a certain number of carloads forming his daily income . . .
>
> "The Irish are more volatile. They do not practice much domestic economy; their motto is more, *Come day, go day*. On a long strike they have generally nothing laid by for the emergency. It must be accounted one of his hardships that he has not regular employment.

Land, Labor, Capital, and the Great Anthracite Strike

At the time of my visit more than half the mines were not working at all, and the rest only on half time.

"The Irish are fond of singing, dancing, and carousing. The saloons on Lackawanna Avenue have two rooms, the front one for drinking, and the back room for dancing and general amusement. On the contrary, dancing is generally considered a heinous sin among the Welsh. Says a friend, the ministers denounce balls and dancing parties as they would manslaughter or murder . . .

"The German is fond of hunting. He has a gun and dog, and on a Sunday or other holiday, or when there is a breakdown in the mine, he goes hunting on the mountain, and brings home partridges, rabbits, or per chance a deer. Their picnics and musical festivals generally begin on Saturday afternoon and conclude on Sunday evening."[64]

Work in the Mines

A colliery is a coalmine with its connected roads and buildings. It includes the mine shaft, a breaker, steam engines, roads for hauling coal, and the company housing. Roughly one-third of the men worked above ground, where they sharpened tools, transported coal, ran the steam engines, or were members of the first-aid team.

Anthracite coal was broken down into even sizes to burn easily. The coal was crushed and sorted in buildings called breakers. Coal breakers were huge wooden structures. Many were nine stories high. They were the skyscrapers of their day. The first breakers were built in 1850. Louis Poliniak tells us that by 1913 there were approximately 300 coal breakers in Northeastern Pennsylvania. They were still being built in 1936, when child labor in them was forbidden.

Coal cars were hauled on a steel wire at a forty-degree angle to the top of the breaker, known as the tipple, because they tipped the coal cars filled with coal, slate, rock, and wood. The contents let out a roar as they crashed down iron chutes onto the vibrating bull shaker, which moved back and forth sending coal to picking tables.

At the bottom of the chutes, on wooden boards, sat the young

Strive for Insight

"breaker boys," between the ages of eight and fourteen. With their bare hands, they sorted the chunks of coal from the rock for eight hours a day. This was a peculiar form of child labor. They chewed tobacco to keep their mouths filled with saliva, otherwise the dust from the coal would have dried out their throats and entered their stomachs. The children were covered with black dust all day long. Lung damage was common. They urinated on their fingers to harden the skin. Noise from the steam engines in the breaker made it impossible to hear. The boys developed their own sign language to handle the breaker boss, who stood over them with his ever-present stick.

In the Lackawanna Valley, many kids between the ages of five and ten dragged themselves out of bed by five-thirty in the morning. Often, they were the only male breadwinners in the family.

During the lunch breaks, they would play football on the hard ground next to the breaker. When the miners enjoyed picnics on Sundays or Saturdays, they would have with them an odd-shaped ball they could carry, throw, and kick. One of the great secrets of American History is who designed the American football?

The men and boys who worked underground entered the mines through shafts, tunnels, drifts, or slopes. The vertical shafts gave the workers direct access to the coal seams. Some shafts went down 1,200 feet. They rode the mine cage down to total darkness. At this depth, stables for the mules were carved out of rock. The gangways were timbered so coal wagons could transport the coal.

The anthracite miner did not use a pick and shovel to loosen the coal. He blasted it with explosives! First, he drilled holes six feet into the coal wall, where he placed the explosives before covering the hole with dirt. Then he fired the shot.

Rectangular chambers were five to ten feet wide. Some were 600 yards long. At the end of the corridor was a main door that small boys opened when they heard the coal wagon approaching. After the car arrived, they quickly closed the door to maintain air currents in the corridor, keeping gasses out of the tunnels. The boys were called nippers, the youngest down in the mines. The nippers sat all day alone in the dark with a little candle on their headlamps burning whale oil. The rats smelled the food in their lunch pails. When the rats ran down the chambers, everyone knew they needed to get out of there. Animals sense the earth moving before humans.

To slow down the wagon pulled by mules, very athletic boys ran alongside the coal car. They held wooden sprags they would set in the spokes of the wheels to slow it down. This was very dangerous. They ran all day in the dark between a stone wall and a moving wagon. The spraggers often worked in pairs and dealt with up to eight moving cars at a time. As they ran, they had to be careful not to hit the walls or ceilings. They also had to stay away from the mules that sometimes pushed them against the walls. If a car jumped off the track, they were in serious danger!

Mule drivers were usually boys in their early teens. They learned how to drive six mules at a time. The driver sat on the front car and used his voice to drive the beast. He yelled commands and cracked his snake whip. The boys picked up full cars and dropped off empty cars. The driver would give his mule sugar, apples, or dates. Mules had good memories. If they were angry, they kicked the boys' legs.

Child Labor in the Valley

Child labor was very important for the anthracite region for close to eighty years. We do not know how many children were involved, as the Pennsylvania State Labor Statistics for this period are missing. Child labor was common not only for boys in the mines but for girls in the textile mills. The factory workers employed children as young as seven for ten-hour days. It was extremely cheap labor. The children worked to avoid going hungry. Orphans were treated worst, sometimes not even paid, and were more likely to be beaten.

In the valley, eleven-year-old girls worked as bobbin hands or lacers. For a ten-hour day in 1907, unskilled women earned $0.53, a skilled woman $1.08.

In 1885, Pennsylvania made a law making it illegal to hire children under the age of twelve in a coal breaker. Parents who needed the income broke the law and allowed their children to enter the mines. Reformers argued the children were deprived of their education and exposed to health issues the rest of their lives.

Organized Labor Arrives

Religious hate was common between Protestants from Wales and England and Catholics from Ireland, Poland, and Italy. In addition, the Irish, Poles, Slovaks, and Italians distrusted each other. Most of them spoke their own language and did not yet speak English. This division allowed the corporations to further repress the miners. Miners and unskilled laborers needed to organize their demands for improvement.

How long was a working day? In the 1860s, steel workers had twelve-hour days, seven days a week. This lasted until 1923. In the textile industry, workers had eighty-four-hour weeks. On the railroads, workers had seventy-hour weeks.

How could organized labor confront the corporations? Labor needed bargaining power to make their opinions heard. In 1866, the National Labor Union was organized, initially by iron molders in Baltimore. The union included women's suffrage leagues, farmers, plus national and local unions from many trades. At their height, they had 600,000 members. They convinced the government to give government workers eight-hour days.

The unions could strike or boycott. The corporations could lock out workers, blacklist them, engage company police, detectives, local militia, or ask for the national guard. They also used court orders to stop a strike or boycott.

In 1867, the Knights of St. Crispin were organized, initially by shoemakers in Milwaukee. They had 50,000 members. They wanted to keep the old apprentice system and not allow shoe machines.

The Noble Order of the Knights of Labor was organized in 1869 by Uriah S. Stephens, a tailor in Philadelphia. You heard about them when Terrence Powderly joined in Philadelphia. They wanted to unite all workers in America. Membership was open to all workers—men and women, skilled or unskilled, Blacks, laborers or capitalists, farmers or merchants.

Land, Labor, Capital, and the Great Anthracite Strike

The members promised not to drink alcohol. Liquor dealers, gamblers, lawyers, and bankers were not included!

They strove to "secure to the toilers a proper share of the wealth that they create; more of the leisure that rightfully belongs to them; more societary advantage; more of the benefits, privileges, and enrollments of the world; in a word, all those rights and privileges necessary to make them capable of enjoying, appreciating, defending, and perpetuating the blessings of good government."[65]

The Order used cooperation and arbitration to achieve its goals. They were strongly against child labor. They wanted an eight-hour day, social reform, and economic reform secured by state and federal laws. In 1878, Terence Powderly became Grand Master. The Order became very powerful by winning a railroad strike in the Southwest in 1884. New York financier Jay Gould met with the union and agreed to their terms. In 1885, the Knights had 700,000 members. By 1890, the Knights had dwindled to 100,000 members. It was hard to keep skilled and unskilled labor in one union.

In 1886, a strike against the McCormick Harvester Company in Chicago ended in a riot in which the police killed six people. The next day, someone threw a bomb into the crowd on Haymarket Square. In the trial, eight anarchists were found guilty of murder and seven of them were put to death.

The American Federation of Labor worked within the system. They lost the Great Homestead Strike against the Carnegie Steel Corporation in 1892 and the Pullman Strike in 1894. In 1900, they had 500,000 members.

The First Strikes in Anthracite Fields

Let us return to the 1870s. On Tuesday, January 10, 1871, the Workmen's Benevolent Association (W.B.A.) called for a general strike for the anthracite fields. For the first time in the history of anthracite mining, every mine was idle. This weakened local business. Stored coal kept railroads moving for the next month.

Early in May, the Lackawanna Iron and Coal Company opened its

Briggs' Shaft in Hyde Park and started the mine with upwards of fifty miners and laborers. A squad of militia was posted to guard the breaker and the men from attack. On May 17th, a squad of thirty laborers on their way home from the shaft, with Mr. W.W. Scranton at their head, was set upon by a mob of 200 men and women. One of the guards fired a shot in defense, killing two of the rioters. The mob dispersed.

Mr. Scranton was arrested and sent to the county jail at Wilkes-Barre. A special train was provided for the prisoner and his counsel. Two companies of soldiers escorted the party. He was acquitted. On May 22, the strike was ended.

A very important event in the labor history of Scranton was the strike of August 1, 1877. It was part of a nationwide railroad strike that paralyzed the whole country. On July 25, the employees of the Lackawanna Iron and Coal Company went on strike. A meeting took place near the steel mills with close to 3,000 men. Their leaders lost control and a mob marched up Washington Avenue. They were armed with clubs, pistols, and stones. They attacked workers at the machine shops, at the car shops of the Lackawanna Railroad Company, and at the blast furnaces.

The mayor had a militia of one hundred Civil War veterans. They arrived with Remington rifles stored at the Iron Company. The mayor was attacked on Lackawanna Avenue. Sergeant Bartholomew was in command with Colonel Hitchcock second-in-command. With thirty-eight men, they marched towards the mob, with Mr. Scranton at the head and W.W. Patterson at his side. When they met the mob, a few pistol shots were fired, wounding the superintendent of the blast furnaces. The militia answered with three volleys. Twenty-five men were wounded and several died. Another volley was fired and the mob dispersed.

What is Capital?

This important question always leads to more complicated questions. If you own a coal mine and a colliery, where is your capital? Is it in the deed that proves you own the land? Is it in the buildings and equipment you own? Is it in the breaker boy who flicks his wrist to move the coal into the right bin? Or is it in the final sale of a coal car at the Port of New York?

Land, Labor, Capital, and the Great Anthracite Strike

At work, the breaker boy never builds capital of his own, yet the owner sitting in his office continually builds his capital.

The Oxford Dictionary defines capital as wealth or property that can be used to make more wealth. Capital assets are the wealth a person or company owns. Capital gains are the profits made from sales of the assets. Capitalism is an economic system in which the country's industry and trade are controlled by private owners for profit rather than being owned by the state.

Leaders of capital and academia used the theory of Social Darwinism to justify their advantages. The theory gave companies and states the right to take advantage of the workers or the poor, who were not the fittest in society.

William Graham Sumner, professor of sociology at Yale University, became a proponent of Social Darwinism. He thought all social behavior conformed to natural laws. There were two sides of the struggle. First, the biological struggle between the human being and nature to even exist. The second was the social struggle between man and man to survive. Sumner opposed government interference in social and economic life. He was against the welfare state.

The welfare state, which is part of the common-wealth, has nothing to do with communism. In 1848, the ideas of communism were formulated in the *Communist Manifesto* by co-authors Karl Marx and Friedrich Engels. In 1867, Marx published, in German, *Capital, a Critique of Political Economy*. It appeared in English in 1887. His works inspired communists in the Russian Revolution and the Chinese Revolution.

There are important distinctions between individuals and corporations. A person is always responsible for his actions in his own conscience. A corporation is only responsible to its stockholders. The directors of a corporation do not act as individuals from their own conscience. They act to make payments to the stockholders. If a person lies, he lies according to his own conscience. If a corporation lies, the individuals have no responsibility for the lies.

Corporations want access to better markets and cheaper resources. To save money, they want to lower wages. Huge corporations are impersonal and complex employers. They control production and rate their workers' activities.

In the Commerce Revolution, industry and transportation grew into nationwide corporations. Work became standardized. Corporations could reduce wages in their companies all over the nation. Some regarded strikes as treason. Labor rights were considered conspiracy. The government was to protect and help businesses.

From the government, merchants wanted lower tariffs to reduce competition with products from abroad. Manufacturers wanted high tariffs to increase competition and protection at home. Farmers wanted tariffs on the wheat they sold, but not on manufactured goods they bought.

In Congress, the industrial owners wanted to regulate railroad prices. In a speech for the state legislature in Harrisburg in 1889, Andrew Carnegie attacked the Pennsylvania Railroad for charging Pittsburg manufacturers twice as much as Chicago manufacturers to have their products transported by rail.

The Anthracite Combine was a formidable cartel in the railroad and coal industries. Sales managers from rival companies would meet each month to set prices and determine the rate of production that best supported those prices. The railroads were allocated the amount of tonnage to ship to the tidewater ports.

The cartel between competing companies was set up to prevent other coal and railroad companies from entering the anthracite coalfields. In Scranton, seven railways made contracts based on a percentage of the price when the coal reached the tidewater ports to be sold. Small coal companies paid the percentage decided upon by the members of the cartel. The federal government used the Sherman Antitrust Act and the Interstate Commerce Act to dismantle the cartel.

The Great Anthracite Strike of 1902

In 1899, John Mitchell became president of the United Mine Workers Association (UMWA). At the age of twenty-eight, he led the most powerful union of the period. Mitchell wanted a centralized union with national power.

Land, Labor, Capital, and the Great Anthracite Strike

John Mitchell arrived in Northeastern Pennsylvania understanding he had little chance at convincing the coal barons to reward employees. His first hurdle was to communicate with miners who spoke little English. Mitchell and his organizers learned several languages.

Mitchell tried to bargain with the coal barons for better wages, working hours, and living conditions for miners. The coal barons told the thirty-three-year-old former breaker boy to go home to Illinois.

On September 17, 1900, Mitchell called 8,000 anthracite mine workers on strike. After thirty-three days, the chairman of the Republican Party, Senator Mark Hanna from Ohio, convinced the mine operators to give the workmen a 10% pay increase. The mines reopened.

According to testimony at the Proceedings of the Anthracite Coal Strike in 1902, the average daily wage for men in the mines of Lackawanna County was $5.04, in Luzerne it was $4.93; this did not include boy laborers. Miners earned $903 a year, working 300 days a year at a colliery. Boys who picked slate in the breakers earned $188 a year.

After the strike, George F. Baer testified to the commissioners at the County Courthouse in Scranton that the company needed to keep the price of a ton of coal at New York Harbor to $4.50 or they would have losses on their operations. Wages cost about $1.50 on a ton of coal. The supplies that go into the cost of the coal amount to forty-five cents. Coal roundly cost about $2 to put on the car.

In March 1902, the anthracite laborers had five demands: first and foremost, recognition of the UMWA as a union; a 20% increase in wages; a reduction from ten to eight hours in a workday; a new system of weighing coal; and a new system for paying by the ton rather than paying by the cartload. Mark Hanna called the representatives of both parties to meet with him in New York. Mitchell presented the miners' requests. He was interested in arbitration but the coal operators' representative, George F. Baer, refused.

The strike was ordered by the UMWA on the 12th of May, 1902. Eighty percent of the 140,000 anthracite mine workers joined the strike. They created the longest and largest labor strike in mining history. Anthracite coal mining was practically suspended. The strike lasted for six

Strive for Insight

months, and winter was on its way. The northeastern United States, including New York and Boston, depended on anthracite coal for their heating systems. The governors of Massachusetts and New York warned of great suffering if coal was not delivered in November.

Local Catholic leader Father Curan travelled to Philadelphia to meet George F. Baer and to New York to meet J.P. Morgan to ask them to meet in arbitration. The financial community of the USA wanted an end to the strike. The president wanted an end to the strike. This time, the local community, the church, and the state supported local strikers. Shop owners and farmers helped the strikers survive. The coal operators were forced to talk with the union.

On October 3, 1902, President Roosevelt invited Mitchell and the presidents of the involved companies to the White House. This was the first time a president interfered in a union strike. The operators refused to recognize the UMWA. Most of the public in the Northeast favored the UMWA.

Morison quotes President Roosevelt: "The great coal-mining and coal-carrying companies, which employed their tens of thousands, could easily dispense with the services of any particular miner. The miner, on the other hand, could not dispense with the companies. He needed a job, his wife and children would starve if he did not get one. His labor was not like most commodities—a mere thing: it was part of a living, breathing human being. The workman saw that the labor problem was not only an economic but also a moral, a human problem."[66]

The miners needed to secure their human rights. Corporations had the combined wealth of many companies and thousands of shareholders. They could afford lawyers. They hired detectives and strikebreakers.

On the 6th of October, Governor Stone sent 12,000 National Guard men into the anthracite region to maintain order and protect mine workers who worked.

Two weeks later, J. Pierpont Morgan resolved the 163-day Anthracite Coal Strike by pressing George Baer to agree to arbitration. The United Mine Workers returned to work before negotiations were completed. The following morning, President Roosevelt met the commissioners and asked them to establish good relations between the employers and the workers. Roosevelt appointed seven commissioners to lead the arbitration process. The hearings lasted three months.

During the arbitration hearings at the Scranton Courthouse, the commissioners heard evidence of terrible conditions, but they found the conditions in the mines satisfactory. This meant the claims of the miners were only partly justified. The miners were given a 10% increase in wages. They were awarded a nine-hour day instead of the standard ten hours. The arbitration board retained the power to settle future labor disputes. Although the Anthracite Commission criticized child labor and changed some laws, children continued to work in the mines. One of every nine workers was a boy between the ages of seven and sixteen. The operators still refused to recognize the UMWA, yet Mitchell believed the creation of a six-man arbitration board to settle disputes was the most important gain.

When the strike finally came to an end, businessmen, conservatives, and the president all praised Mitchell as a hero, while socialists and many of the mine workers were outraged. During the strike, President Roosevelt described Mitchell as an earnest gentleman. After the Great Strike, they became genuine friends.

Labor peace came to the coal fields in the valley after the strike. The company stores that overpriced the miners and held them in their system by providing credit were gone. The company police remained. The Pennsylvania State Archives has no record of the Pennsylvania Department of Labor and Industry before 1926. When coal companies were dissolved, records of the UMWA were also lost or destroyed.

A direct consequence of the strike of 1902 was the creation of the Pennsylvania State Police on May 2, 1905. The department became the first organization of uniformed police in the United States. At first, organized labor feared the state police, so they were limited by law to only 228 men to patrol Pennsylvania's entire 45,000 square miles.

After the Anthracite Strike of 1902, Roosevelt used the federal government to improve the standard of living for all Americans. Progress was made by the advocates of progressivism, who fought for better living conditions for the masses, especially laborers in factories and mines. Progressivism led to the formation of the NAACP by W.E.B. DuBois in 1905. The Pure Food and Drug Act in 1906 forbade selling impure foods and required a list of ingredients on foods and drugs. The strike also helped women in America gain universal suffrage in 1920.

CHAPTER 16

The Information Revolutions

Advertisers, media, governments, and private groups use techniques to influence your motives and behavior. They want to change your feelings and manipulate your decisions. They target your subconscious drives so you desire to buy their products. Hidden subliminal messages influence your attitudes.

The key is to develop your own clear thinking and bring it into your willpower through your actions. You learn to make your own decisions and act upon them. A large part of your will is in your subconscious, which is the unconscious part of your being. The subconscious will has many important sides to it. One side includes your instinctive actions that take place automatically without even thinking. When you are hungry, you look for food. Another side includes your drives to actions that you may choose. Pay attention to the motives for your actions, your wishes, and your decisions.

Within your subconscious will also lies your destiny. It guides you to the people you need to meet and the experiences you need to have. With it, you take part in the interests that you are passionate about. Engaging your thinking more powerfully into your will helps you identify what is going on in your subconscious and in your destiny. You take part in your learning processes. You decide which people you want to be with, the

Strive for Insight

work you want to do, and how you want to play. Therefore, it is important to connect with the impulses in your will and make decisions. When you strive for more insight in history, you discover how you are influenced by the actions of other people.

The will is so powerful that you can project it into every activity of your senses. You can learn to take a more active part in your processes of seeing, touching, hearing, smelling, and tasting. You may practice your skills in artistic activities like music, painting, drawing, sculpting, and handicrafts. You can also be active in your physical body through work, dance, sports, outdooring, and much more. In your social activities, you learn to respect, to trust, to connect with others. All of this takes place within your will. You can also learn to unite yourself with your ideals and to create inner freedom. In this way, you go much deeper into life than any information machine ever can. If you pay attention to your decisions and your actions, you go deeper into your being in a healthy way.

In the previous chapters, you learned how people have changed from century to century. Empires, slavery, enlightenment, and human rights have changed.

A very important change is the fact that many people now feel responsible for others. They are genuinely interested in neighbors and friends. The education, health, and the quality of life of others become important for you.

On the other hand, you can learn from people who spread lies and harm. Their lies aim to divert your attention so that you lose the context in which you are thinking and feeling.

If ideas do not become ideals, empty rooms in your soul are created where very negative forces can flow in like air into a bicycle pump. If we no longer share our lives with others, if we become poisoned by lies, isolated in our dogmas, and paralyzed in our will, our lives become weakened.

Our most important communication weaves from person to person. It is spoken and heard. Other important communication takes place with the body and in our senses. Each person communicates with her soul and unique spirit.

Your soul has three distinctive powers: thinking; feeling; and willing.

The Information Revolutions

The combination of sounds and pictures in your soul is a source of creativity and information. We all want a daily dosage of sounds and pictures. When pictures and sounds are brought together, they strengthen each other. Pictures are an outward experience, music and sound an inward experience. Music inspires our feelings. We become energized. It makes us want to dance. Nothing can replace live music, where sound and pictures work together!

When we see a lightning storm, we experience it directly in our senses. The sky lights up, then the thunder rolls. They awaken feelings. Some feel fear in a storm, while others become excited. Our feelings of the lightning and thunder become mental images. They are carried by the nervous system to the neural networks in our brains, where they become memories. We remember them when we choose to, or they pop up instinctively when we see the next flash of lightning. These natural and human experiences are very different from mechanical experiences.

Information Machines in the 20th Century

Once electricity became available, mankind quickly made artificial environments. Communication also became artificial, a copy of the real model in nature or in man. To improve our communication, we have developed mechanical information machines with artificial sound, artificial moving pictures, artificial intelligence, and artificial neural networks. What was called applied science in the Industrial Revolution is now called technology. Information technology, IT, has become a dominant form of technology in the 21st Century. How did we get here?

Since 1893, when Edison built the first movie studio in West Orange, New Jersey, new machines have appeared regularly. Auguste and Louis Lumière built the first public presentation of moving pictures in Paris in 1895. The global telegraph network was established in 1902. GE's first radio broadcast was in 1905. Universal Pictures started movie production in 1912. On January 22, 1914, the first wireless message from a moving train was sent thirty-five miles east of Scranton to the *New York Times* in New York. That same year, Charlie Chaplin's figure, the Tramp, appeared in *Kid Auto Races At Venice*.

In 1915, the first transcontinental long distance telephone call was completed between Alexander G. Bell and his assistant, Thomas Watson. GE set up the first coast to coast AM radio network in 1920. In 1928, George Eastman and Edison displayed the first large film camera. That year, Mickey Mouse cartoons started with *Steamboat Willie*. Walt Disney understood that people craved a daily dosage of sound and pictures.

In the 1930s, GE experimented with audio and video broadcasts. NBC sent television broadcasts using antennas from Philadelphia to Schenectady, New York, in 1940. NBC launched their first regularly operating television network in 1947 between New York, Philadelphia, Schenectady, and Washington, D.C.

A revolution in the flow of information took place when televisions in our homes continually manufactured vivid, repetitive pictures. These machine-generated images became mental images in our minds and our memories. The artificial images are created by someone else. All artificial images we have experienced continue to influence us to this day. The TV advertisements of Ford trucks in 1965 are still in my memory. To discover my own mental images and my own imagination, I must separate the machine-generated images in my mind from my own images. I learn how to be conscious of my own power of imagination, which creates healthy mental images in me. I actively use my senses.

Towards the end of the century, after Americans had listened to transistor radios, record players, tape decks, and walkman, the bold and loud boomboxes linked us to breakdancing and graffiti in New York City. The box came in a hard metal casing, with speakers protected by silvery-black grilles and lots of clunky knobs and buttons. And at the heart of every box was a cassette deck that created instant, loud gatherings on subway platforms and crowded city sidewalks. Wherever you took it, you had an instant party. Then hip-hop went mainstream.

Propaganda, Consumer Relations, and Dogma

Where there is great progress in history, there is also the potential for great abuse of the human being. At the Paris Peace talks in Versailles in 1918, Edward Bernays worked as a propagandist for President Woodrow Wilson. His job was to spread Wilson's ideas of "making the world safe for democracy." This was the motto for the Fourteen Points plan, in which Wilson proposed more power to national states. Bernays realized if he could spread propaganda in war time, he could also spread propaganda in times of peace. He returned to New York and substituted the unpopular word "propaganda" for "counsel of consumer relations." He became a public relations consultant.

One big advantage for Edward Bernays was his uncle in Vienna, Dr. Sigmund Freud. Dr. Freud had a theory of how the human mind works. He said he had discovered hidden sexual and aggressive forces inside the subconscious will and the human mind that bring destruction of individuals and the masses if not controlled. His method was to analyze dreams and associations from the instinctual forces in the subconscious animal side of the human being. Information can stimulate irrational forces and manipulate human consciousness.

This theory was accepted by science and academia. It became a dogma. The Oxford Dictionary defines dogma as a belief or set of beliefs held by an authority or group which others are expected to accept without argument. We risk being dogmatic by insisting our beliefs are right and others should accept them without providing other opinions or evidence. In a moment of brutal honesty, Freud admitted to his pupil, C.G. Jung, that he had created a dogma about the hidden sexual and aggressive forces.

Jung explains: "The devaluation of the psyche and other resistances to psychological enlightenment are based in large measure on fear—on panic fear of the discoveries that might be made in the realm of the unconscious. These fears are found not only among persons who are frightened by the picture Freud painted of the unconscious, they also troubled the originator of psychoanalysis himself, who confessed to me that it was necessary to make a dogma of his sexual theory because this was the sole bulwark of reason against a possible 'eruption of the black flood of occultism.' In these words, Freud was expressing his conviction that the unconscious still harbored many things that might lend themselves to *occult* interpretation, as is the case."[67]

Freud's official motive for creating his sexual dogma was to provide a rational barrier to the black flood of occultism in the Nazi Regime across Europe. The word "occult" has many interpretations. It can mean "hidden from the eye or beyond understanding." It can also represent the mysterious or supernatural. Nevertheless, Freud entered many regions of the occult as he developed a science of the subconscious. He incorrectly interpreted the unconscious will as something negative and destructive, mostly filled with sexual suppression and destruction. Unfortunately, his dogma of sexual fixation prevented his followers and millions of people from discovering the positive sides of the subconscious.

Bernays decided to use his uncle's theories to teach corporations and politicians in America how to control the masses in a democracy. The idea was to connect the mass-production of products in the commerce revolutions to the desires of millions of people living in American cities by spreading targeted information.

How do you influence millions of people? In 1923, Bernays argued in his book, *Crystallizing Public Opinion*, that people constantly seek information about the world. The public relations consultant spread symbolic images that link the masses. The images create a group identity by emphasizing change—new technology, new music, new fashion. The images are driven by universal instincts such as sex, anger, and hate. The messages may be lies or half-truths. They are often abusive. The subliminal images are based on group psychology. Crowds exaggerate the individual's urges. People lose their inhibitions and become even more angry at other groups.

The companies learned to capture people's attention! For example, they sold cars not because people needed a new car but because it made them look good and feel good. The goal was to change commerce by changing the way people think about buying and selling. They created unconscious American consumers.

The subliminal messages are also used in politics. The elite manage the psychological feelings of the masses. They appeal to the animal desires of the public, using the science of psychology to develop strategies for social control. Bernays and many students of his work thought the average citizen was stupid and that democracy was not a good idea. One excuse they gave for their manipulative actions was that animal forces in individuals and the irrational forces of the masses must be kept under control or they will lead societies into destruction. Their propaganda was designed in a way that the emotional response limited people's choices to act or not act. The more emotional you were, the faster you reacted with an automatic response. The masses did not understand.

To this day, public relations consultants suggest to your subconscious what you should think and do. They unlock your desires. This is called suggestion.

Manipulated Communication Can Lead to Violence

When did this manipulation of the individual's subconsciousness begin? Edward Bernays became a pioneer of public relations in 1929. His first advertising campaign to train people to desire things they do not need was paid for by the American Tobacco Company. At that time, it was taboo for women to smoke in America. The tobacco industry was missing half of their customers. Bernays staged a consumer spectacle: women pulled out cigarettes during the Easter Day Parade on Fifth Avenue in New York. After that, many American women started to smoke.

The United Fruit Company hired Bernays to increase the sale of bananas in the 1950s. The government of Guatemala wanted to control their own bananas. Earning $100,000 a year, he promoted the scare of communism in Guatemala to convince the US to take over the country and continue the sale of bananas.

When the Nazis came to power in 1933, Joseph Goebbels led the Reich Ministry of Public Enlightenment and Propaganda. He controlled the media, arts, news, and all other information in Germany. This unleashed a violent communication revolution. Goebbels had studied Bernays' books and put the ideas to work. He became an expert at lying and spreading harm to millions of people. With propaganda, Goebbels attacked the Jewish people, the Christians, communists, and anyone else who did not agree with the Nazis. Using the techniques of Edward Bernays, he produced massive propaganda campaigns using censorship, parades, gramophone recordings, silent films, and rallies.

During World War II, Alan Turing worked as a decryption expert at Bletchley Park, England, to produce Ultra Intelligence. He made advances to cryptanalysis while deciphering some of the secret messages of the Nazis, the Enigma deciphering machine. He designed the *bombe*, an electrical-mechanical device that could find settings of the Enigma machine. Turing figured out the indicator procedure used by the Nazi Navy. He developed a statistical procedure to make better use of the *bombes* after understanding the cam settings of the wheels of the Nazi cipher machine, the Lorenz SZ. Turing's work inspired those who built the Colossus computer, the first programmable digital electronic computer for decryption.

Computers and the Internet

After the USA dropped two atomic bombs on Japan, the military was looking for a way to survive a nuclear attack. One solution was to build the internet on a decentralized system to withstand an attack. In 1969, the Defense Department's Advanced Research Projects Agency (DARPA) played a key role in launching a new information revolution, the Internet Network (ARPANET). Leonard Kleinrock and J.C.R. Licklider provided the standard protocols that are shared online every day.

Global networking become a reality in 1973 as the University College of London and the Royal Radar Establishment in Norway connected to ARPANET. One year later, the first Internet Service Provider (ISP), known as Telenet, became the first commercial version of ARPANET. University computer scientists were given networking services on the Computer Science Network in 1981.

In 1986, the National Science Foundation (NSF) created NSFNET to connect supercomputer centers with regional research and education networks. This placed the Internet all over the United States.

From their garage in Los Altos, California, Steve Wozniak and Steve Jobs produced their first computer with a typewriter-like keyboard and a regular TV as a screen. In 1976, they christened it Apple I. The Apple II debuted at the West Coast Computer Fair of April 1977. It had color graphics and tape-based storage. Over the next sixteen years, Apple would sell 6 million Apple II machines.

In Palo Alto, California, Xerox PARC was a research center exploring new technologies such as optical media, Ethernet, laser printers, and interface design. Jobs was granted three days at the center. He wanted something more intuitive than a text-based machine. He liked the Xerox

The Information Revolutions

Alto, which worked in a user-centric manner. It had a mouse to navigate and click on the screen.

In 1981, Jobs became so involved with his work on his computer, Lisa, that he bypassed management. Therefore, Michael Scott, Apple's CEO, removed Jobs from research and development within the company. Lisa was launched in 1983, with its graphical user interface (GUI) in place. Macintosh System Software allowed for overlapping windows. Susan Kane developed a visual language of onscreen icons that have since become classics. The Macintosh went on sale in January 1984, priced at $2,495. That same year, Apple shipped 70,000 units.

Meanwhile, in August 1980, Bill Gates and Paul Allen signed a very successful agreement with IBM. They agreed to help IBM build a disk operating system for Project Chess, their first PC. The agreement allowed Microsoft to keep the operating system and to license it as MS-DOS to other companies besides IBM. Revenue for Microsoft increased to $140 million in 1985. IBM lost control of the PC platform.

In March 1985, the board of Apple urged CEO John Sculley to remove Steve Jobs from the Macintosh team. Jobs resigned from Apple and founded NeXT, a company that would build workstations for use in academia.

At Microsoft, the Windows operating system appeared as an add-on to DOS in 1985. Microsoft was gearing up for Windows 3, a direct competitor to the all-graphical OS System. The graphical design language had been implemented with icons in place of program names in Windows Explorer.

1989 is the year the World Wide Web was founded. At the European Organization for Nuclear Research (CERN) in Switzerland, a project called ENQUIRE was started by British scientist Tim Berners-Lee. He wanted to make the Internet available to the public. His goal was to link information and let users browse as they will. At that time, there were no emails, no reliable websites, no html, no space you could click through. Berners-Lee was frustrated, so he decided to build the first Web browser, WorldWideWeb (WWW), on one of Steve Job's NeXT computers. In 1990, his first web page was a guide to the WWW, written in HTML.

In 1993, CERN placed its WWW technology in the public domain.

Strive for Insight

They gave it away to the common-wealth of the world! The number of websites soon reached 600. The White House and the United Nations went online. Mosaic 1.0 became the first web browser for the public. By 1994, 11 million American households were online.

1995 was a breakthrough year for the Internet. Eighteen million American homes were online. Amazon.com opened for business, billing itself as "Earth's Biggest Bookstore." Netscape went public. Microsoft released Windows 95 and the first version of Internet Explorer. America Online and Prodigy provided Internet access.

NeXTSTEP was launched by Job's new company in 1996. Apple purchased NeXT in 1997 for $429 million in cash, plus 1.5 million shares of Apple stock. Steve Jobs became CEO of Apple, twelve years after leaving the company.

In 1997, the Google search engine was born. Netflix was founded as a company that sent DVDs by mail. AOL bought the Netscape browser. Yahoo acquired GeoCities for $3.6 billion. Napster provided high-speed networks in college dormitories. Many colleges banned the service and it was later shut down for enabling the illegal sharing of music files.

Apple had its own productivity applications in Pages, Numbers, and Keynote, but Microsoft's Word, Excel, and PowerPoint remained industry standards. Apple needed Microsoft Office onboard, especially for business users. Jobs asked Gates to keep developing Office for Mac for at least the next five years. In 1997, Gates agreed, and, at the same time, Microsoft bought $150 million worth of non-voting Apple stock, thereby securing its future. In return, Apple unseated Netscape as the Mac's default browser and installed Internet Explorer in its place (until 2003). In addition to computers, Apple was working on its own browser, Safari, as well as digital cameras, video consoles, TV appliances, and CD players.

Back in the 1920s, Americans shared information via postcards, letters, newspapers, magazines, radio, plays, cinema, and direct mail. As of 1990, information spread via TV, fax machines, and newspapers. By the year 2000, the Internet had taken over.

The Information Revolutions

Information Machines in the 21st Century

In the 21st century, our senses and ability to pay attention in the real world became colonized by the digital world, especially by our pocket devices. We use them to access music, stores, movies, news, dating, photography, computer games, financial transactions, and social media.

By 2000, 40 million Americans had purchased a product online. Internet companies bought media companies. AOL acquired Time Warner for $165 billion.

In 2003, Skype was launched. One year later, the multiplayer online role-playing game World of Warcraft was launched. YouTube was founded on Valentine's Day. Harvard student Mark Zuckerberg launched Facebook that year.

Social Media

On September 5, 2006, the algorithmically tailored Facebook News Feed was launched. Since then, users receive a wave of information with built-in monitors of their choices to determine their future experiences. Users were given a passive role in seeking information. Artificial Intelligence (AI) controlled what people saw and copied their responses. Since then, millions of teens have been manipulated on their digital landscape, which changes regularly. They receive huge amounts of information, but do they understand the larger context of the information?

Twitter was also launched in 2006. Then Apple changed the wireless device market by releasing its first iPhone in 2007.

Big Companies Swallowed the Smaller Companies

In business, the big companies swallow the smaller companies. As of 2021, Google had acquired 242 companies, including YouTube for $1.65 billion in 2006. Facebook acquired roughly eighty-nine companies, including Instagram for $1 billion in 2012 and WhatsApp for $19 billion two years later.

Microsoft has acquired about 225 companies, including Skype for $8.5 billion in 2011, Nokia Mobile Hardware for 3.8 billion euros in 2013, Yahoo for $4.5 billion in 2015, and LinkedIn for $26.2 billion in

2016. Apple has acquired more than one hundred companies since 2015. Amazon has bought 104 companies since 1994. Tesla founder Elon Musk bought Twitter in 2022 for $44 billion. Just to mention a few!

Opensource and Real-time Information

In addition to propriety software, anyone can inspect, modify, and enhance opensource software (OSS). Computer programmers use the code to change how a piece of software works. It enables honest and accurate public information. Nobody claims they own your private information or tracks your behavior to sell it to other companies or governments. The Mozilla browser is opensource. On Microsoft's cloud, Azure, the opensource operating system Linux is more widely used than Windows. The international space station runs on OSS systems.

Real-time information is delivered immediately after it has been collected. It is the right information at the right time in the right quantity. It provides genuine information used for tracking or navigating.

Financial transactions and information about the markets are in real time. Some of the Federal Reserve Banks of America have made real-time databases available for people to track accurate economic data.

The mail is traced using real time. If you lose your iPhone, you need to track it. In sports, real-time information gives you the live status and then the results. At train stations and airports, traveler information is displayed real time.

An area of importance is called Application Programmers Interface (API). It allows two applications to share information. Real time must be automatic so you receive the right information. Deviation information is extremely important when maintaining the flow of correct information. AI can find patterns in the API, but is unable to add anything new to the flow of information.

Artificial Intelligence and Deep-learning

At a workshop in Florence, Italy, in October 2012, a turning point for deep-learning was reached. Fei-Fei Li, founder of the annual ImageNet computer vision contest, announced that two of Geoffrey Hinton's students invented software that identified objects with almost twice the accuracy of human competitors. ImageNet is an online database of millions of images, all labelled by hand. For any given word, such as "balloon," ImageNet contains 700 images. Further use of deep-learning "brought further rapid improvements, producing an accuracy of 96% in the ImageNet Challenge in 2015 and surpassing humans for the first time."[68]

Shortly thereafter, at the University of Montreal, Yoshua Bengio stated that deep-learning used huge amounts of computing power and vast quantities of training data to renew the old idea of artificial neural networks (ANNs). These are biologically inspired networks of artificial neurons. In a biological brain, each neuron can be triggered by other neurons whose outputs feed into it. In turn, its own output can then trigger other neurons. ANNs are simulated in software. A simple ANN has an input layer of neurons where data can be fed into the network, an output layer where results come out, and possibly a couple of hidden layers in the middle where information is processed.

AI techniques enable computers to mimic human intelligence using machine logic, if-then rules, decision trees, and machine learning. Machine learning is when the computer performs tasks based on data from previous searches and other user behavior. The machines reportedly improve themselves based on the information that has been programmed.

Deep-learning is a subset of machine learning composed of algorithms that permit software to train itself to perform tasks, like speech and image recognition, by exposing artificial neural networks to vast amounts of data. In 2020, most of the deep-learning applications were used in search, email, maps, translations, YouTube, speech recognition, self-driving cars, drones, and robotics. ChatGPT is a generative, pre-trained transformer (GPT). In November 2022, experts claimed ChatGPT could solve problems for humanity and find better ways of using human willpower and creativity. They promised to build a machine that can do anything the human brain can do.

The battle for control of the electronic cloud is on. Google, Facebook, IBM, Amazon, and Microsoft are setting up ecosystems for AI services in the cloud. They will apply it to every industry that works with genes, images, and language.

Strive for Insight

Artificial neural nets are good at recognizing patterns, but they cannot reason as the human being does with real neural networks in the brain.

The Surveillance Industry

Every time you log onto Facebook, Instagram, and other sources of social media they collect information about your behavior. They learn where you go, where you live, how you shop, how much money you have, and much more. Companies claim they own your personal data and sell it to other companies.

Information is no longer totally in the private sector. In 2013, Edward Snowden, a computer expert for the CIA and the National Security Agency (NSA), stole over one million documents and took them to Hong Kong. At the age of twenty-nine, Snowden proved the government had destroyed the notion of the free market. That is why Snowden is wanted as a traitor and a thief of government property. He considers himself a whistleblower protected by American law.

The government and the companies that cooperated broke American law that protects us against government breach of privacy. The civil justice system is ingrained in the Constitution. It is important for combating tyranny and building a democratic society. The Fourth Amendment reads: "The right of the people to be secure in their persons, houses, papers, and effects, against unreasonable searches and seizures, shall not be violated, and no warrants shall issue, but upon probable cause, supported by oath or affirmation, and particularly describing the place to be searched, and the persons or things to be seized."

Although the WWW is the most powerful mechanical medium for knowledge, communications, and commerce in the world, Tim Berners-Lee is convinced the original spirit of helping people has been undermined by mechanisms that control how people act, what they see, and for spying.

Everyone owns the right to her own knowledge, experience, and expertise. Injustice occurs when these rights are abused. Surveillance capitalists assert ownership rights over personal information. Shoshana

Zuboff raises many important questions about the information society: How is knowledge distributed? Who has the authority to distribute it? Who protects that authority?

Civil Rights Online

By 2013, internet companies, including Google, Facebook, YouTube, Twitter, and telecom companies, made it possible for new internet companies to steal human experience and turn it into proprietary data.

Zuboff writes: "The license to steal came with a price, binding the executives to the continued patronage of elected officials and regulators as well as the sustained ignorance, or at least learned resignation, of users. The doctrine was, after all, a political doctrine, and its defense would require a future of political maneuvering, appeasement, engagement and investment."[69]

Our information civilization needs to be grounded in democracy. Zuboff challenges us to create a new charter of rights. "We need legal frameworks that interrupt and outlaw the massive-scale extraction of human experience. Laws that stop data collection would end surveillance capitalism's illegitimate supply chains. The algorithms that recommend, micro-target and manipulate, and the millions of behavioral predictions pushed out by the second cannot exist without the trillions of data points fed to them each day."[70]

We are challenged to decide which form of communication is most important. A lot of information we receive each day is pure illusion. Machines act as they are directed. History will continue to document the changes in the machine-driven artificial communication, as well as genuinely human live communication.

CHAPTER 17

The Financial Revolutions

When you are trying to understand the financial revolutions, continue to ask four important questions: Where is the gold? Who is printing the money? Who is giving credit? How does the country regulate financial activity? The answers change from revolution to revolution.

In this century, you are challenged to think of finances not only in millions, but in billions and trillions. Your forebearers were not challenged in this way. National debt, budgets, world trade, and investments are now in the trillions.

How many millions of dollars are in one billion dollars? One thousand. How many billions of dollars are in one trillion dollars? One thousand. No wonder figures in the billions and trillions stretch our imagination!

If there were such a thing as a one million dollar bill, you would need to multiply that by one million to reach one trillion. Multiply one trillion with twenty-eight and you reach the amount of our national debt in 2021. The equation: $\$28 \times 10^6 \times 10^6 = \$28 \times 10^{12}$. Notice what takes place in your consciousness when you use these numbers. It is hard to remain focused, let alone understand.

Strive for Insight

Money and numbers are always very difficult, not to mention the laws that must be followed and the methods used in finance. You may want to work on this chapter step by step with a teacher, your parents, or your friends.

Financial Revolution 1 was the Revolutionary War and the formation of a new country. We addressed this in Chapters 6 and 7.

Now we will look at six other financial revolutions. Three of them are major wars: the American Civil War; WWI; and WWII. The other three include the Great Depression, the Casino Economy, and the National Debt.

Revolution 2—The American Civil War

In a major war, the country's entire population, natural resources, and financial resources are used to build a war machine. If you win the war, you determine the future, if you lose the war, you suffer tremendous damage and it takes years for the nation to rebuild a peacetime economy.

When war breaks out, a country has four choices to raise money: increase taxes; borrow by selling war bonds to individuals and banks; borrow abroad; or print money. If the government prints money, it does not have to pay interest as it does when it borrows money.

At the start of the Civil War, the Union Defense Committee of Safety was formed on Wall Street to organize the war effort financially. The Union needed troops sent to the front, weapons, ammunition, ships, food, and other war materials.

The North decided on a combination of taxing, borrowing, and printing money. On July 15, 1861, Congress authorized Secretary of the Treasury Salmon Chase to float loans up to $150 million. Chase developed the income tax system that we still use today. In addition to income, most everything was taxed—railroads, ferries, documents, and all products sold. The Treasury borrowed money by selling bonds to banks, who kept them as reserves or sold them to their customers. The government paid back the bonds with interest.

Both the North and the South used the quickest way to raise money—printing their own paper money. This was fast, but limited. If a country prints too much money in relation to the services and goods being sold, the value of the money will decrease and foreigners will prefer to sell their products for gold. To buy with gold means shipping your gold abroad. When money was based on gold, traders calculated future costs and profits more easily, knowing the value of the money was stable. But the gold standard made it hard to fight a major war. As of 1861, the North was off the gold standard.

A revolution began when the North issued $450 million in paper money called greenbacks. There was no gold or silver behind that sum, only the promise of the government to pay.

During the Civil War, the most important American banking merchant in London was George Peabody. In 1838, he started a merchant bank to help Europeans invest in the United States and vice versa. In 1854, Peabody had chosen Junius Spencer Morgan to be his partner in London. Together they sold stocks, engaged in foreign currency exchange, extended banking credits, then brokered railroads, iron, and other commodities. President Lincoln had given the task of selling war bonds to banker Jay Cooke in Philadelphia. The buyers in London for these bonds were George Peabody and Junius Morgan.

Historian Ron Chernow wrote about the Morgan relationship to the Atlantic Trade Triangle during the Civil War. "Despite his Yankee sympathies, Morgan was stymied in undertaking Union financing. After southern banks drained their deposits from the North, Lincoln cast about for new sources of funds. With Lancashire textile mills closely allied with southern cotton plantations, the City (financial district in London) was cool to any large-scale operation for the North."[71]

The North soon broke the Southern control of the Atlantic Trade Triangle and supplied England with cotton during the war. The slave colonies in the Southern states were removed and the North acquired the share of the trade triangles owned by Southern merchants and bankers. The Asian Trade Triangle with India and China continued uninterrupted throughout the war.

The son of Junius Morgan, J.P. Morgan, started his own company in New York in 1864, J. Pierpont Morgan & Company. He helped his father enable wealthy Europeans to invest in the United States during the Civil War. The economy was booming. Heavy industry and railroads needed capital. Who gave the credit? The bankers. Who gave the credit to sovereign nations? The bankers. Who soon controlled the heavy industries and the railroad commerce? The bankers.

In 1862, the national debt was $324 million. After the war, the national debt had risen to $2,755 million. In 1869, Congress promised to pay the interest and principal of government bonds in gold. The credit of the country was again on the gold standard. By the end of the century, the Civil War was paid for.

Economic Panics and Crises Between the Revolutions

There is a difference between major financial revolutions and regular economic crises that are an ordinary part of the business boom and bust cycle. The major revolutions occur over many years and change the way the economy is driven. The economic crises or banking panics are necessary adjustments after irresponsible spending, speculation, or inflation. The American economy has experienced a long series of national banking panics or crises roughly every twenty years—in 1797, 1819, 1837, 1856, 1873, 1895, 1907, 1971, and 1987.

Let us consider the panics of 1873, 1895, and 1907, leading up to World War I. The Morgans wanted to enter the international banking market. The war between Germany and France in 1871 provided an opportunity. They gave the French government a war loan and earned 1.5 million British pounds. Now Pierpont had the power of London finance behind him while creating deals in New York.

After the Germans defeated the French in 1871, Chancellor Bismarck sent his personal banker to negotiate the reparations with France. The French provisional government offered an indemnity of 1.5 billion francs. Bismarck knew France was the richest country in Europe, and demanded that 5 billion francs be paid to the Germans. Forty-six years later, the French would remember this when Germany lost World War I and was forced to pay enormous reparations in 1921.

The war reparations from France gave the Germans billions of francs to invest in their commerce revolutions and in American railroad stocks. Then came the market crash in 1873 due to unsound railroad speculation.

The Financial Revolutions

The Jay Cooke Bank failed in Philadelphia, and European investors lost $600 million worth of railroad stocks. That year, J.P. Morgan personally earned one million dollars.

If anyone knew where the gold was, it was J.P. Morgan. He knew how much was being shipped on the ocean liners between New York and London, and how much was in Europe and the USA at any time. Much to Morgan's approval, the US resumed the gold standard in 1879.

One of Morgan's finest moments in gold deals came in the panic of 1895. In the American West and the South, farmers were very much in debt for their land and operations. Prices for their products were low. Their Populist Party wanted the government to leave the gold standard. By January 1895, the gold reserves dipped below $68 million. If the supply ran out, the dollar could no longer be redeemed for gold. The country would collapse financially. The Rothschild agent in New York, August Belmont, and J.P. Morgan left for Washington by train to meet the president. The bankers wanted a private bond issue. The populists wanted a public bond issue. With Morgan sitting silently at the meeting in the White House, a clerk came in and informed President Cleveland that the reserves for the entire country had fallen to $9 million. Morgan told Cleveland he knew of a draft that would demand $10 million worth of gold. If that draft were placed demanding $10 million worth of gold, the country would go bankrupt.

J.P. Morgan proposed the Houses of Morgan and Rothschild bring in $65 million worth of gold from Europe. He also promised to rig the flow of gold, so it would not flow back to Europe. Morgan told President Cleveland the government could buy the gold using an old statute from the Civil War. The deal was made. J.P. Morgan had acted as the national bank of the United States.

By 1907, company after company had merged to form massive trusts. Local industries were swallowed up by national enterprises. For example, the steel industry left Scranton. Morgan dominated railroads and steel. The Rockefellers dominated oil and gas. Other trusts dominated the sugar, whiskey, copper, coal, glass, and farming machinery industries. What should they do with the profits? Investments exploded on

Wall Street. Banks loaned large sums of money. Irresponsible, overextended trust companies crashed. Once again, the panic was managed by one man acting as the national bank: Mr. J.P. Morgan.

The Federal Reserve Bank Becomes the New Central Bank in America

Politicians and bankers were faced with new questions: Who should print our money? How should short-term cash be supplied to banks? Who should regulate the flow of credit? Should the stock market be regulated by the federal government? How can we create a new central bank, known as the Federal Reserve System, to stabilize the use of money? Who should own it?

Morgan wanted the central bank to be modelled on the Bank of England, a privately-owned bank started in 1694. The Populist Movement and the Democrats wanted it to be run by the government. The Houses of Morgan, Goldman Sachs, Rockefeller, Lehman Brothers, and Kuhn Loebs of New York; the Rothschilds of Paris and London; and the Warburgs of Hamburg would not put their gold supplies and their future earnings into a national bank in America without increasing their power.

The Federal Reserve Act of 1913 created the Federal Reserve System (the Fed), a privately-owned government agency that regulates the American financial system and the broader economy. The new central bank is a system of private banks with a board of commercial bankers at the top. It became the private bank of choice for central banks all over the world.

The Fed provided loans. The payment of interest on the loans reduced the money supply and slowed economic activity. In this system, recovery comes only when new loans are taken out that are at least equal to the interest to be paid. The system is designed for boom-and-bust economies that regularly collapse and are bailed out.

The Fed prints our money. The Treasury uses taxpayer money to pay the Fed interest on the money the Fed has printed for us. The Fed system devises economic policy with currency to grow or shrink the economy.

The Financial Revolutions

Revolution 3—World War I

Before WWI, you could turn in any Bank of England note, which is paper money, to the Bank of England and receive English gold coins. You could send the gold coins to any country you liked. Even checks could be converted to gold. If the country needed more gold, it was brought in from abroad. The gold that arrived in England by ship was used as reserves against the notes or as deposits in the bank. The balance between gold and the Bank of England notes depended on how the Bank of England created credit by spending and lending. Businessmen objected to the gold standard as it depended too much on the amount of gold being dug up on foreign soil. The politicians found it simpler to make money. This changed during the financial revolution of World War I.

During the war, everyone was asked to turn in their gold coins and use the new Treasury notes instead. British gold was then sent abroad to buy war materials.

The government printed money and created credit. Soon that money lost its value. Prices rose in England.

In America, the income tax had been stopped in the 1870s. It did not return until the Sixteenth Amendment was ratified on February 3, 1913. The personal income tax law was signed that October by President Wilson. Exclusions from income taxes were quickly developed. State and local bonds were not taxed. Life insurance and inheritance were not taxed.

In 1917, US government war expenditures doubled. The money-printing press was run by the Fed as of 1913, so the government had two options: raise taxes or borrow money. The borrowing was in the form of war bonds sold to individuals and companies. Because of the war, taxes on imports brought in little money. The best source of quick income for the Wilson Administration was income tax. They lowered the exemption for income tax from three thousand to one thousand dollars. The government brought in twice as much tax revenue. Since then, income tax has dominated the American tax structure.

After any war, war debt is a major issue. From Morison, we have reliable numbers for Allied debt during World War I: "The United States government had lent to the Allies something over $7 billion, practically all of which was spent in the United States. These were the original war debts but after the armistice loans and credits to the sum of $3.24 billion more were extended for use at peace."[72]

Reparations for war damage paid by a defeated Germany and Austria-Hungary to the Allies were fixed in 1921 at $33 billion. This was impossible for the Germans and Austrians to pay. By 1923, both countries were in default. Their ability to buy and sell products was undermined by hyper-inflation we cannot imagine. Economist Hartley Withers wrote, "In August 1923 the German mark fell to about a two-millionth of its pre-war value in sterling, being dealt in, or quoted, at 40 million to the pound."[73] This made it very difficult to build a democracy in Germany—it made it easier for the Nazis to take over in 1933.

The Germans paid their reparations until 1928. When the 1929 stock market crash dried up German loans in America, the country defaulted again. The Young Plan reduced Germany's total reparations bill to $27 billion over fifty-nine years. The Germans borrowed even more money in the United States, and paid their bills until 1931. Then the Great Depression hit both countries and Germany stopped payments. We learn from Morison that in 1931, "Altogether Germany had paid in reparations $4,475,000,000 and had borrowed in the United States $2,475,000,000. During this same period the Allies had paid to the United States only $2,606,340,000. The United States therefore had paid over half the reparations bill and almost the whole war debt bill; the Allied nations who had based their war debt payments on German reparations were almost $2 billion to the good."[74]

The New York Federal Reserve Bank (NY Fed) took part in the reconstruction of Europe. Together with the Bank of England, their dream was to become two autonomous central banks conducting global monetary policy without governmental regulation. The NY Fed played a special role in the Fed system by dealing with European central banks and foreign exchange. All New York banks wanted free trade, unregulated flow of capital, balanced federal budgets, and stable currencies.

The three-leaved clover—J.P Morgan and Company, the NY Fed, and Monty Norman from the Bank of England—wanted exchange rates in currency tied to the gold standard. In London, Englishman Teddy

Grenfell acted as the go-between for Wall Street and the Bank of England. Grenfell was not only a director of the Bank of England, but a conservative Member of Parliament. Ben Strong, chairman of the Fed in Washington, also favored the gold standard. Treasury Secretary Andrew Mellon told Norman he approved of J.P. Morgan and Company and the NY Fed helping the British Empire go back to the gold standard.

Chernow writes, "Either Norman had to maintain high interest rates in London—drawing money into the pound—or Strong had to keep rates low in New York—making dollar investments attractive."[75] Ben Strong lowered American interest rates and held them low even during the 1929 Wall Street Crash.

The British Empire needed credit to defend the pound against attacks. The Fed System could not give credit to central banks in other countries. Strong provided $200 million credit to the Bank of England. J.P. Morgan & Company provided $100 million credit to the British Treasury. Winston Churchill was Chancellor of the Exchequer when the empire resumed the gold standard in April 1925.

The British Commonwealth of Nations was formed in 1926 when the British Empire was slowly falling apart. Remember, in this book I use a hyphen between *common* and *wealth* when I refer to the common good, the common-wealth in America.

Revolution 4—The Great Depression

By 1920, the national debt stood at $24 billion. President Taft appointed Andrew Mellon as Secretary of the Treasury. Mellon had financed Gulf Oil and Alcoa. He was the son of Thomas Mellon, a Scotch-Irish banker in Pittsburgh who had financed the empires of Andrew Carnegie and Henry Frick.

In 1924, Andrew Mellon wrote a book entitled *Taxation, the People's Business*. Historian John Steele Gordon quotes the secretary, "... since the war, two guiding principles have dominated the financial policy of the Government. One is the balancing of the budget, and the other is the payment of the public debt. Both are in line with the fundamental policy of the government since its beginning."[76]

Under Mellon, US government spending was cut in half by 1927.

Strive for Insight

The national debt was reduced to $16 billion in 1930. Mellon was convinced if you reduce the taxation on the rich, the companies will build more capital and increase investment. The economy will grow, wages will increase, and the government will receive more revenue. Taxes were reduced in the 1920s, but the revenue from income tax remained stable. The rich paid even more income tax than previously.

In America we have two separate economies: the real economy and the Wall Street economy. These two economies do not always work together. On Wall Street, banks and companies make money on money. In the real economy, we work for a living and pay taxes. The real economy not only deals with money but with people, homes, products, and natural resources. In early 1929, the real economy slowed down, though the Fed was charging low interest rates and the stock market was booming. To buy a stock you only needed 10% of the price in cash. The rest could be loaned. Speculators loaned large amounts of money to buy stocks. Bankers could borrow money from the Fed at 5% interest and their brokers could loan the money to speculators at 12%.

Knowing the crash was inevitable, some investors moved large funds from New York to London beforehand. In 1929, the Fed and the Treasury did next to nothing to prevent bank failures. This caused drastic contraction of credit, business activity, and employment. The Fed kept flooding the market with money while the value of the money sank. The liquidity in the banking system dried up. Banks could make no more loans. To protect America's gold position, the Fed allowed the banks to collapse. The country sank from recession into the Great Depression.

By 1932, the national debt was at $19 billion. That year, Franklin Roosevelt was elected president. To help 13 million unemployed Americans, he announced the New Deal to employ America's workers.

How should the financial activity in the country be regulated? New initiatives were taken to protect Americans. The Glass-Steagall Act of 1933 created the Federal Deposit Insurance Company (FDIC) to insure bank deposits. The act prohibited banks from both accepting deposits and underwriting securities. Banks could not underwrite securities as investment banks do, nor could they underwrite insurance. This act required investment banks to be limited to "capital market" activities, while other banks could only engage in commercial banking. Commercial banks offered savings accounts, checking accounts, mortgages, personal loans, and credit cards. Commercial banks could take in deposits, while investment banks could not. The Glass-Steagall Act of 1933 prohibited investment banks from having a controlling interest in commercial banks. It also forbade the NY Fed from negotiating with foreign banks. From now on, the Fed board in Washington would do that.

In 1935, Roosevelt increased government revenues with taxes on incomes of the rich. The Revenue Act of 1935 demanded 13% tax on income. Corporate income taxes reached 40%.

Revolution 5—World War II

From 1941 to 1945, our country's entire population, natural resources, and financial resources were used to build another war machine. Once again, we must ask where the gold was. The Gold Standard Act of 1900 made gold the only standard for redeeming money in the US. On April 19, 1933, the US abandoned the gold standard within the country but continued to use it for international transactions. Then, in 1944, forty-four nations met at Bretton Woods, New Hampshire, to set up a new international monetary system. They wanted stable exchange rates. Countries agreed to use the dollar for international accounts. They established a fixed rate of thirty-five dollars per ounce of gold, to be redeemed by the government. They owned over half of the world's gold reserves—574 million ounces. Foreign currencies were pegged to the dollar and the US would back every dollar used abroad.

Major changes in the world financial regulation started in 1946. The privately-owned Bank of England, established in 1694, was nationalized in 1946. In America, the Employment Act of 1946 directed the Fed to balance two goals: full employment and low inflation. Five years later, the Monetary Accord Act of 1951 gave the Fed more independence from the Treasury. The Fed was no longer responsible for keeping interest rates low.

Strive for Insight

Revolution 6—The Casino Economy

Journalist and biographer Ron Chernow dates the beginning of the Casino Economy Age to 1948. At that time, governments, rather than private banks, assumed financial leadership. The central banks and huge private banks could no longer function as sovereign states. Enormous capital markets opened as monster-sized companies in the American Empire spread around the world—Mobil, GE, GM, Ford, Monsanto, IBM, and many more. They received their investment money abroad.

In the Casino Age, new types of banking emerged. Insurance companies provided cash to their customers. Major corporations opened their own banking services. They raised money with their own bond issues or used earnings to finance expansion. Corporations also sold commercial paper at low interest. Banks became dependent on their larger clients. The traditional merchant banks were no longer focused on issuing securities—they began hostile takeovers of other companies. Banks also made loans, not based on assets but on money. Their traders bought money cheaply in the marketplace or secured higher interest on the loans given.

The Fed approved of banking in Europe, where the Glass-Steagall Act did not regulate activities. American banks looked for multinational customers. Investment banks raided other banks' clients.

Back home, we can turn to a fictitious family from Ohio, the Hawkins, as an example. In 1992, they received a housing loan from their local bank. They had decided to pursue the American Dream of owning their own property. Their income was too low to pay back such a loan, but the local bank gave them a twenty-five-year loan at high risk.

In 1998, President Clinton decided to give all Americans the opportunity to buy their own homes. The Federal National Mortgage Association, known as Fannie Mae, was forced to invest at least 50% of their loans in low-income customers.

In 1999, the local bank in Ohio considered twenty-five years too long to wait for a return on their investment in the Hawkins family. They sold the loan to Fannie Mae. The Hawkins' housing loan cost Fannie Mae half the value of the interest the family should pay on the loan. The local bank no longer had to deal with the risk involved with the Hawkins family, but they had earned half of the interest. Now the bank had more capital with which it could loan money to other families with high risk. Family after family in America joined the Hawkins in this housing marketplace.

The Glass-Steagall bank regulation was repealed in 1999 when President Clinton signed the Gramm-Leach-Bliley Act (GLBA). This deregulated the banks, removing the difference between investment banks and commercial banks. GLBA also authorized financial holding companies to control the stock of many companies. Now investment banks also provided commercial banking services. They could loan money and keep the value of the money in their bank. This enabled enormous speculation. The Fed became one of the major players. The government could not control the casino.

Meanwhile, the Hawkins had no idea how politics were changing in New York and Washington. As of 2000, the banking system was so far deregulated that investment banks bought the Hawkins loan from Fannie Mae and then sold it as part of an investment package to hedge funds, retirement funds, organizations, and townships. The family did not realize they were locked into a housing bubble that would lead to a world financial breakdown. How did the meltdown unfold?

First, the investment banks combined various commercial real estate loans, housing loans, car loans, credit card debt, and other types of loans into new financial instruments. These were bundled together in packages they called Collateralized Debt Obligations (CDOs). Officially, the CDOs were called structured debt, or derivatives, but the banks named them "surprise packages." No one fully understood the real value of these good and bad loans. Huge insurance companies, such as American Internationals Group (AIG), sold insurance to the investment banks in order to help them cover their risk.

Then, in 2002, the investment banks had trouble selling their surprise packages. They were forced to keep them, but they did not want them on their accounting records. How did they hide the packages? One way was to move them over to other companies they owned. These legal companies were hidden from the government in tax paradises such as Luxembourg, Bermuda, and the Cayman Islands. The banks' accountants no longer saw the total risk the investment banks still owned. The risk was not on their books, not in their financial balances, but on an island far away!

The banks continued to build their hidden risk. In the Casino Economy, everyone thought that housing prices would never fall. If they did, the toxic packages would be exposed and the risk unveiled. The poison would spread into the healthy parts of the economy and the whole financial system might fail.

In 2003, the Fed lowered the key rate to 1%, the lowest level in forty-five years. The key rate defines what the Fed charges the government and the banks to loan money. The low rate gave the sellers of CDOs their primetime! Financial advisors ranked CDOs very high. Housing loans increased.

How much credit should the investment banks be allowed to give? Was there a limit to how much debt they could carry? In 2004, five gigantic investment banks were allowed to have as much debt as they wanted: Goldman Sachs; Merrill Lynch; Lehman Brothers; Bear Sterns; and Morgan Stanley.

Let us sidetrack to the local amusement park, where you can jump on a plastic horse on the old-fashioned carousel and ride it up and down and roundabout while you listen to the romantic music and dream away. In the Casino Economy, millions of American families were riding a debt carousel until the motor began to sputter. Then the machine stopped and they had to face reality.

By the end of 2005, the Fed had adjusted the key rate to 5.25%. Now the Hawkins family in Ohio could no longer pay the interest on their loan. They tried to keep their house for two more years. Many Americans were in the same boat.

As the prices for houses grew, the debt grew along with it. The high-risk mortgages rose in value from roughly $100 billion in 2005 to $600 billion in 2006.

The casino economy was huge in 2006. According to Niall Ferguson, "The measured economic output of the entire world was worth around $48.6 trillion. The total market capitalization of the world's stock markets was $50.6 trillion, 4% larger. The total value of domestic and international bonds was $67.9 trillion, 40% larger . . . Every day $3.1 trillion changed hands on foreign-exchange markets. Every month $5.8 trillion changed hands on global stock markets. And all the time new financial instruments were evolving. The volume of *derivatives*—contracts such as options and swaps—grew even faster, so that by the end of 2006 their notional value was just over $400 trillion."[77]

This market crashed rapidly. According to the Bank for International Settlements (BIS) in Switzerland, credit-default swaps totaled $58 trillion in 2007. They had fallen from $400 trillion the year before.

On August 18, 2007, Fed Chairman Ben S. Bernanke reduced the key rate 0.5% to 4.75%. He stated that the private $2 trillion subprime mortgage market was no problem, nor was the entire US mortgage market, estimated to be $10 trillion. The Fed failed to stop the toxic mortgages.

In the fall of 2007, the housing bubble burst! Millions of homeowners in America could no longer pay the interest and installments on their loans. The banks took over their properties. Housing prices sank as houses were put up for sale by the banks. Four million existing homes were for sale and 2.2 million were vacant. In January 2008, the Hawkins family lost their house, their private finances were amiss, and they had a large debt. Their jobs soon disappeared. Soon their grandmother's retirement fund would also disappear.

On the national stage, a large investment bank in New York, Bear Stearns, was having serious liquidity problems. Saying they needed to prevent the global capital markets system from collapsing, Treasury Secretary Henry M. Paulson, Fed Chairman Bernanke, and NY Fed Chairman Timothy Geithner decided to have the Fed provide a $30 billion line of credit to Bear Stearns. But the market responded poorly. On March 16, they arranged for the outright sale of Bear Stearns to JPMorgan Chase at two dollars a share. They decided the Fed would underwrite $29 billion in losses on $30 billion of Bear's bad assets. For the first time in the history of America, the federal government would not let a big Wall Street securities firm fail.

In June 2008, Treasury Secretary Paulsen invited key players to Washington to brainstorm which emergency powers the government might want at its disposal to confront the upcoming crisis. Geithner proposed asking Congress to give the president broad power to guarantee all the debt in the banking system. Participants protested! It was politically impossible because it could put taxpayers and their common-wealth on the hook for trillions of dollars. In July 2008, Congress increased the amount of debt the US government could carry to $10.6 trillion.

The problems snowballed. Lehman Brothers in New York had a very large position of sub-prime mortgages. In the second quarter of 2008, the company lost $2.8 billion and was forced to sell off $6 billion worth of assets to compensate for the losses. Their stock price fell 73% as credit markets tightened. On Sunday, September 14, neither New York Fed Chief Geithner nor Treasury Secretary Paulson offered support to Barclay Bank's bid for Lehmans. On September 15, Lehman Brothers Investment Bank filed for bankruptcy protection. Lehman Brothers became the largest bankruptcy in history, with a debt of $613 billion and assets of $639 billion. They owned close to one thousand companies around the world.

JPMorgan Chase received a $3 billion loan from the Fed. Goldman Sachs became a Fed-regulated depository-bank holding company during the crisis. From March 2008 to May 2009, the Fed extended a cumulative total of nearly $9 trillion in short-term loans to eighteen financial institutions under a credit program.

Trade on the stock market in the USA caused pandemonium in Japan, China, England, and Germany. Panic set in. Afraid of toxic assets, the banks hoarded their money and refused to make loans. Billions of dollars were frozen by investors. Hedge funds were short of cash. More selling occurred as the downward cycle grew.

The cash flow between large and small banks was choked off. On September 18, 2008, President Bush announced the $700 billion Troubled Asset Relief Program (TARP) from the Treasury. Each of the big five investment banks was either sold or converted into holding companies to receive federal assistance. More than one quarter of the bailout funds went to three financial institutions: Goldman Sachs, Merrill Lynch, and Deutsche Bank, a foreign bank operating in America. These institutions were loaned money for their credit-swaps and securities-lending programs. Fannie Mae and Freddie Mac received support. AIG, Goldman Sachs, and Citigroup were rescued while Lehmans was allowed to fail. Taxpayers gained ownership in the country's leading financial institutions.

In 2008, Barack Obama was elected president. He brought in former JPMorgan executive William Daley as chief of staff in the White House. Former New York Fed Director Geithner replaced Paulsen as Treasury Secretary. Obama also brought back Larry Sumner from the Clinton Administration as his chief financial advisor. They designed new methods of mastering a future financial crisis by giving the Fed more power.

Jamie Dimon, CEO of JPMorgan Chase, agreed in late October 2013, to pay a fine of $13 billion on civil charges. Dimon accepted this civil settlement in order to stop the criminal investigation of his bank. The government claimed the bank committed fraud in its mortgage-based securities. They had lied to their customers. Four billion dollars of the fine was paid to swindled homeowners in the inner cities.

Housing bubbles affect the real economy because the speculation is based on credit given to families. Every businessman in America knew it was only a matter of time before the financial housing bubble would explode, leaving millions of Americans in the real economy with no savings, no homes, and no jobs.

A legend in Italy tells us where the word "bankruptcy" arose. Eight hundred years ago, the money dealers would set up marble tables in the city square. The table was called a "banca." If they were declared bankrupt, an official smashed the marble table in small pieces with a sledgehammer. Their bank was then "banca rota"!

Since 2007, 9 million more American families have become unemployed. Americans lost a quarter of their net worth. Families like the Hawkins lost everything. The people who created and managed the casino lost nothing. The Department of Justice convicted none of the players in the casino system of 2008. The wizards of Goldman Sachs, who also led the Treasury, made sure the big banks were bailed out. The banks received full value on the dollar they had speculated.

Strive for Insight

The collapse in the financial markets in 2008 exposed the weakness in the Casino Economy. Who could save the system when it crashed? It was the taxpayers, the stable common-wealth of America.

Soon, many industries were facing bankruptcy. The CEOs of Ford, Chrysler, and General Motors flew to Washington and demanded $25 billion of taxpayer money to avoid bankruptcy. They were trying to avoid the sledgehammer. The large companies received survival packages. They paid bonuses to their executives with taxpayer money while millions of taxpayers lost their savings, their homes, and their jobs. Once again, many investors knew the crash was inevitable. They moved large funds from America to tax havens and foreign countries beforehand. Private industry was bailed out; the American people were hit by the sledgehammers!

Revolution 7—The National Debt

The Casino Era continues to this day. It works hand in hand with our national debt. The banks are still not regulated as they were under Glass-Steagall.

The spending goes on! In 1936, John Maynard Keynes published *The General Theory of Employment, Interest, and Money*. His philosophy was not based on balancing the budget and paying down the national debt. He proposed the government should spend to strengthen the economy. If the country faces inflation, the government can reduce the supply of money, raise taxes, and reduce government spending. If the economy is too slow, the government can increase the money supply, reduce taxes, and increase government spending. He argued the national debt does not really matter because a nation can borrow from itself.

Another serious problem with debt is that individuals and corporations have stopped paying billions of dollars of taxes into the common-wealth of our country. Lobbyists develop loopholes in the tax code so fewer taxes are paid. Companies move to foreign lands where taxes are low. Politicians run the USA on increased national debt.

The Revenue Act of 1942 converted the income tax into a mass tax, also for the middle class. Historian John Steele Gordon calls income tax a social-engineering device to make the rich pay their share of federal expenses. The rich move their assets and hide their income. State and local bonds are tax exempt.

The national deficit increased by $211 billion during World War II. By 1946, the national debt stood at $269 billion. By 1960, the national debt rose to $286 billion. By 1970, public debt from the Vietnam War had grown tremendously. The Fed increased monetary inflation. Then in 1971, President Nixon cancelled the international convertibility of the dollar to gold. The Bretton Woods system was replaced with floating currencies in 1973. Since then, the value of the currency changes depending on demand, not on gold. In the 1980s, new techniques in the Casino Economy were established—interest swaps, currency swaps, and packaged loans. Global buyouts became popular.

President Reagan lowered taxes while bringing in more money to the government. Reagan cut off federal funding to local government. Then he cut the budgets for Medicaid, food stamps, education programs, and the Environmental Protection Agency. Defense spending added to national debt. To cover Reagan's budget deficits, the United States borrowed at home and abroad. Under Reagan, the national debt rose from $977 billion to $2.85 trillion.

According to research by the Institute of International Finance in 2019, the total public and private sector debt in the United States amounted to $70 trillion. In 2022, the Statista Research Department determined the total United States public and private sector debt to be $88.2 trillion. In 2023, the US Treasury estimated the federal debt to be $31.3 trillion.

The American Taxpayer Carries the Real Economy

The people of America create the real value with their work, their family, and their social engagement on the local and national stages. The people of the world create the real value where they live.

As I mentioned previously, in the Casino Economy, banks and companies make money on money. In the real economy, we work for a living and pay taxes. The real economy not only deals with money, but with people, homes, products, and natural resources. It includes the common good for all citizens.

Strive for Insight

The foundation of our common-wealth in America are the United States Constitution and our state constitutions. Local governments are also driven by our American common-wealth. The US Treasury collects our taxes. The US military defends our shores. Our police and the press protect our human rights. It is in your interest that the citizens of your city or town receive a good education, retirement, proper healthcare, clean water, public transportation, broadband, bridges, highways, parks, and legal services. These are the social goods of the real economy that improve our democracy. In response to the Declaration of Independence two-hundred and fifty years ago in 1776, the preamble to the U.S. Constitution reads:

"We the People of the United States, in order to form a more perfect Union, establish justice, insure domestic tranquility, provide for the common defense, promote the general welfare, and secure the blessings of liberty to ourselves and our posterity, do ordain and establish this Constitution for the United States of America."

Afterword

In this book, we viewed history on the local stage in the Great Valley of Northeastern Pennsylvania, on the national stage of the United States of America, and on the world stage. We learned about the growth of science and colonization, the enlightenments, the political revolutions, common-wealth, money, and wars. The creation of civil liberties and human rights are golden threads on all three stages.

There is a fourth stage. The fourth stage is you!

Every day, you live on the individual stage of history. Both rivers of time flow through you, carrying your destiny within your subconscious will. With your mind, you make conscious decisions and build the concepts of your ideas and ideals. In your feelings, you follow your unique learning style. With your actions, you take part in history.

Although the individual stage has been active in you from the beginning of the book, I chose not to emphasize it, hoping you would discover it for yourself. If you want to learn more about the individual stage, read the summary of many ideas in your life in the Index to Ideas on page 338, The Individual Stage of History, conflicts, etc. There you will find the parts of the book where this stage is specifically addressed. Reread those parts and judge the ideas and events to see how history works in you. Then develop your own meaningful context of your individual stage. By striving for insight, you develop new concepts and ideas. You learn to judge what is true and what is not true.

Bibliography

Aster, Howard and Xu Mingqiang, *China, Images of a Civilization*, Foreign Languages Press, First Edition, Beijing, 2010.

Athearn, Robert G., *William Tecumseh Sherman and the Settlement of the West*, University of Oklahoma Press, Norman, 1956.

Aurand, Harold W., *Anthracite Heritage Museum and Scranton Iron Furnaces*, Stackpole Books, Mechanicsburg, PA, 2002.

Bailey, Thomas A., *The American Spirit, United States History as Seen by Contemporaries*. Volume II, D. C. Heath and Company, Boston, 1963.

Bailyn, Bernard, *The Ideological Origins of the American Revolution*. Cambridge: Belknap Press of Harvard University Press, 1967.

Baldwin, Neil, *Edison, Inventing the Century*, Hyperion, New York, 1995.

Barr, James, *A Line In The Sand*, Simon & Schuster, New York, 2011.

Bates, Samuel P., *History of Pennsylvania Volunteers, 1861-5*; Harrisburg, 1868-1871.

Beard, Charles A. and Mary R., *The Rise of American Civilization*, The Macmillan Company, New York, 1930.

Beck, John, *The Story of Scranton, Never Before In History*, Windsor Publications, 1986.

Bradley, Omar N., *A Soldier's Story*, The Modern Library, New York, 1999.

Bradsby, G. C., *History of Luzerne County Pennsylvania*, S. B. Nelson & Co., Publishers, 1893.

Brown, Dee, *Bury My Heart at Wounded Knee*, Holt, Rinehart & Winston, New York, 1970.

Brown, Patrick, *Industrial Pioneers, Scranton Pennsylvania, and the Transformation of America, 1846- 1902*, Tribute Books, Archbald, Pennsylvania, 2010.

Carson, Rachel, *Silent Spring*, Houghton Mifflin, Boston, 1962.

Cary, John, *Joseph Warren*, University of Illinois Press, Urbana, 1961.

Catton, Bruce, *Glory Road, The Army of the Potomac Trilogy*, An Anchor Book, New York, 1952.

Chaplin, Charles, *My Autobiography*, Modern Classics, London, 1964.

Chernow, Ron, *The House of Morgan, An American Banking Dynasty and the Rise of Modern Finance*, Grove Press, New York, 1990.

Chernow, Ron, *Alexander Hamilton*, Penguin Books, New York, 2004.

Clarke, Peter, *The Last Thousand Days of the British Empire: Churchill, Roosevelt, and the Birth of the Pax Americana*, Bloomsbury Press, London, 2008.

Conway, Moncure Daniel, *Emerson at Home and Abroad*, Trübner & Co., Ludgate Hill, London, 1883.

Corey, Lewis, *The House of Morgan: A Social Biography of the Masters of Money*, G. Howard Watt, Van Rees Press, New York, 1939.

Crosby, David, *The Lackawanna Railroad In Northeastern Pennsylvania*, Arcadia Publishing, Charleston, SC, 2014.

Dalrymple, William, *The Anarchy, The East India Company, Corporate Violence, and the Pillage of an Empire*. Bloomsbury, 2019.

Dickens, Charles, *American Notes*, Estes & Lauriat, Boston, 1890.

Drimmer, Melvin, *Black History: A Reappraisal*, Anchor Books, 1969.

Dunbar-Ortiz, Roxanne, *An Indigenous Peoples' History of the United States*, Beacon Press, Boston, 2014.

Dunn, Josephine M. and Kashuba, Cheryl A., *The Women of Scranton, 1880—1935*, Arcadia Publishing, 2007.

Dyer, Frederick H., *A Compendium of the War of the Rebellion Compiled and Arranged from Official Records of the Federal and Confederate Armies*, The Dyer Publishing Company Des Moines, Iowa, 1908.

Earle, Kathleen A., *An Early History of the Wyoming Valley*, The History Press, Charleston, SC, 2022.

Bibliography

Farrand, Max, *The Framing Of The Constitution Of The United States*, Yale University Press, New Haven, 1913.

Farrington, Benjamin, *The Philosophy of Francis Bacon*, Liverpool University Press, 1964.

Folsom Jr., Burton W., *Urban Capitalists*, The University of Scranton Press, Scranton, 2000.

Forbes, Esther, *Paul Revere & The World He Lived In*, Houghton Mifflin Company, Boston, 1942.

Forman, Samuel A., *Dr. Joseph Warren*, Pelican Publishing Company, Gretna, Louisiana, 2011.

Fraser Steve and Gary Gerstle, *Ruling America, A History of Wealth and Power in a Democracy*, Harvard University Press, Cambridge, Massachusetts 2005.

Frothingham, Richard, *Life and Times of Joseph Warren*, Boston: Little, Brown, & Co; 1865.

Gallagher, John, *The Battle of Brooklyn, 1776*, De Capo Press, 2001.

Gandhi, Mohandas, T*he Story of My Experiments with Truth*, Public Affairs Press, Washington D.C. 1948.

Glickman, Jay L. *Painted In Blood: Remember Wyoming!* Affiliated Writers of America, Inc. Cody, Wyoming, 1997.

Gobodo-Madikizela, Pumla, *A Human Being Died That Night: A South African Story of Forgiveness*. Houghton Mifflin, Boston, 2003.

Gordon, John Steele, *Hamilton's Blessing, The Extraordinary Life and Times of Our National Debt*, Walker and Company, New York, 1997.

Guthman, Edwin and Shulman, Jeffrey, editors, *Robert Kennedy in His Own Words*, Bantam Press, New York, 1988.

Halberstam, David, *The Best and the Brightest*, Greenwich, Connecticut, Fawcett Publications, 1973.

Hamilton, Alexander, "Report on Public Credit", in *Writings*, edited by Joanne B. Freeman, Library of America, New York Literary Classics of the United States, 1999.

Harris, Ben and Raatz, Stephan, *United States Armed Forces, A Salute to America's Heros*, Centennial Media, New York, New York, 2017.

Harris, Howard, editor, *Keystone of Democracy*. Commonwealth of Pennsylvania Harrisburg, 1999.

Hart, B. H. Liddell, *Sherman, Soldier, Realist, American*, Dodd, Mead & Company, New York, 1929.

Hawke, David Freeman, *Those Tremendous Mountains, The Story of the Lewis and Clark Expedition*, W.W. Norton & Company, New York, 1980.

Heffner, Richard D., *A Documentary History of the United States*, A Mentor Book, New American Library, New York, 1952.

Hitchcock, Col. Frederick L, *War From The Inside, The Story of the 132nd Regiment Pennsylvania Volunteers Infantry in the War for the Suppression of the Rebellion*, J. P. Lippincott Company, Philadelphia, 1904.

Hitchcock, Col. Frederick L, *History of Scranton and its People*, Volume I, Lewis Historical Publishing Company, 1914.

Hodas, Daniel, *The Business Career of Moses Taylor*, New York University Press,1976.

Hourani, Albert, *A History of the Arab Peoples*, Warner Books, New York, 1991.

Hopkins, J. Castell, *French Canada and the St. Lawrence*, The John C. Winston Co, Philadelphia, 1913.

Hudson, Michael, *Super Imperialism*, Pluto Press, New York, 1972.

Inglis, Brian, *The Opium War*, Hodder and Stoughton, London, 1979.

Jacobs, Jane, *The Death and Life of Great American Cities*, Vintage Books, New York,1961.

Jensen, Merrill, *The New Nation, A History of the United States During the Confederation 1781—1789*, A Vintage Book, New York, 1950.

Josephy, Jr, Alvin M., *The Indian Heritage of America*, Alfred A. Knopf, New York, 1971.

Kissinger, Henry, *World Order*, Penguin Books, London, 2014.

Lama, Dalai and Tutu, Desmond, *The Book of Joy*, Penguin Random House, New York, 2016.

Logan, Samuel C., *The Life of Thomas Dickson: A Memorial*, Leopold Classic Library, Scranton, PA. 1888.

Longstreet, James, *From Manassas To Appomattox, Memories Of The Civil War In America*, J. B. Lippincott Company, Philadelphia, 1896.

Lucas, Henry S., *A Short History of Civilization*, McGraw-Hill Book Company, New York, 1943.

Bibliography

Mandela, Nelson, *Long Walk To Freedom*, Back Bay Books, Boston, 1995.
Mandela, Nelson, *Notes To The Future*, Atria Books, New York, 2012.
Mapp, Jr., Alf J., *Thomas Jefferson, A Strange Case of Mistaken Identity*, Madison Books, New York, 1987.
Marshall III, Joseph M., *The Journey of Crazy Horse*, Penguin Books, New York, 2004.
Marye, William B., *Warriors Paths, Pennsylvania Archeologist, 13-14*, 1943—1944.
McClellan, H. B., *The Life and Campaigns of Major-General J. E. B. Stuart*, Houghton Mifflin and Company, Richmond, VA, 1885.
McDonnel, Michael A., *Masters of Empire*, Hill and Wang, New York, 2015.
McLuhan, Marshall, *Understanding Media: The Extensions of Man*, Allen Lane Penguin Books, London, 1964.
Morison, Samuel Eliot and Commager, Henry Steele, *The Growth of the American Republic*, Volume Two, Oxford University Press, New York, 1940.
Morison, Samuel Eliot, *Sources & Documents illustrating the American Revolution 1764 -1788 and the formation of the Federal Constitution*, second edition, Oxford, University Press, New York, reprint 1972.
Morton, A. L., *The Industrial Revolution*, Anglo-American Reader II, J. W. Cappelens Forlag, Oslo,1963.
Nehru, Jawaharlal, *Glimpses of World History*, Asia Publishing House, London, 1934.
Neihardt, John G., *Black Elk Speaks*, William Morris & Company, Now Pocket Books, New York, 1932.
Oates, Stephen B., *Let The Trumpet Sound*, Search Press, London, 1982.
Obama, Barack, *A Promised Land*, Viking, Penguin Random House, New York, 2020.
Palladino, Grace, *Another Civil War, Labor, Capital, and the State in the Anthracite Regions of Pennsylvania 1840-68*, University of Illinois Press, Chicago, 1990.
Palmer, Charles, *Reparations for African-Americans: It's about more than slavery*, Sermon, Grosse Pointe Unitarian Church, February 2, 2020

Pecora, Ferdinand, *Wall Street Under Oath: The Story of Our Modern Money Changers*, Simon and Schuster, New York, 1939.

Pinson, Koppel S., *Modern Germany, Its History and Civilization*, The Macmillan Company, New York, 1966.

Poliniak, Louis, *When Coal Was King, Mining Pennsylvania's Anthracite*, Applied Arts Publishers, Lebanon, Pennsylvania, 1970.

Powderly, Terrence V., *The Path I Trod*, Columbia University Press, New York, 1940.

Powell, John Wesley, *The Exploration of the Colorado River and Its Canyons*, 1895. Simon and Brown, 2013.

Richter, Daniel K. and Merrell, James H., *Beyond the Covenant Chain: The Iroquois and Their neighbors in North America, 1600-1900*, Syracuse University Press, Syracuse, 1987.

Rossiter, Clinton, editor, *The Federalist Papers*, Alexander Hamilton, James Madison,

John Jay, A Mentor Book, New American Library, New York, 1961.

Ruth, Philip, *Of Pulleys and Ropes and Gear*, The Wayne County Historical Society, Honesdale, 1997.

Sandbu, Martin, *Europe's Orphan, The Future of the Euro and the Politics of Debt*, Princeton University Press, Princeton, 2015.

Scherer, Joanna Cohan, *Indians*, Crown Publishers, Inc. New York. 1973.

Schlesinger, Arthur, *Prelude to Independence, The Newspaper War on Boston, 1764—1774*, Greenwood Press, 1979.

Schurz, Carl, *The Reminiscences of Carl Schurz*, Volume Three, The McClure Company, New York, 1907.

Shaara, Jeff, *Gods and Generals*, Ballentine Books, New York, 1996.

Shaara, Jeff, *The Glorious Cause*, A Ballantine Book, New York, 2002.

Sherman, William T., *Memoirs of General W. T. Sherman*, D. Appleton & Co., New York, 1889.

Shilts, Randy, *And The Band Played On, Politics, People And The Aids Epidemic*, Penguin Books, New York, 1987.

Simpson, J.A. and Weiner, E.S.C., *Oxford English Dictionary*, Second Edition, Claredon Press, Oxford, 1953.

Bibliography

Snyder, Timothy, *The Road to Unfreedom, Russia, Europe, America*, Bodley Head Publishing, 2018.

Sperber, Jonathan, *The European Revolutions 1848—1851*, Cambridge University Press, 1994.

Stanley, Jason, *How Fascism Works, The Politics of Us and Them*: Random House, New York, 2020.

Stanley, Sir Henry Morton, *The Autobiography of Sir Henry Morton Stanley*, Houghton Mifflin, Boston, 1909.

Sumner, William Graham, *The Forgotten Man*, Yale University Press, New Haven, 1919.

Taylor, A. J. P., *Bismarck, The Man and the Statesman*, Vintage Books, New York, 1955.

Tesla, Nikola, *My Inventions, The Autobiography of Nikola Tesla*, Experimenter Publishing Company, New York, 1919.

Treese, Lorett, *The Storm Gathering: The Penn Family and the American Revolution*, Keystone Books, Penn State University Press, 1992.

Wallace, Paul A. W., *Indian Paths of Pennsylvania*, Harrisburg Pennsylvania Historical and Museum Commission, 1971.

Washington, James M., editor, *A Testament Of Hope, The Essential Writings of Martin Luther King Jr.*, Harper & Row, San Francisco, 1986.

Waters, Frank, *The Book of the Hopi*, Viking Penguin Books, New York, 1963.

Wember, Valentin, *Ein welthistorischer Kampf*, Stratosverlag, Tübingen, 2022.

Wilkerson, Isabel, *Caste, The Origins of Our Discontent*, Random House, New York, 2020.

Williamson, James R and Fossler, Linda A., *The Susquehanna Frontier: Northeastern Pennsylvania during the Revolutionary Years*, Wilkes University Press, Wilkes-Barre, PA, 1997.

Withers, Hartley, *Bankers and Credit*, Eveleigh Nash & Grayson Limited, London, 1924.

Wolf, George D., *William Warren Scranton, Pennsylvania Statesman*, A Keystone Book, 1981.

Woodward, C. Vann, *The Strange Career of Jim Crow*, Oxford University Press, New York, 1955.

Wright Jr., Robert K., *The Continental Army*, Center of Military History, United States Army, Washington, D.C. 2006.

Wright, John R., *Archeology in the Minisink Today*, Newsletter of Delaware Water Gap National Recreation Area, Vol. 25 No 2. Summer 2003.

Wulf, Andrea, *Magnificent Rebels, The First Romantics and the Invention of the Self*, First Vintage Books, New York, 2023.

Zweig, Stefan, *Marie Antoinette*, Garden City Publishing, New York, 1932.

Magazines

Das Deutsche Kaiserreich, 1871 bis 1914: Der Weg in die Moderne, Der Spiegel, Geschichte, Nr. 3, 2013. *Die Revolution Von 1848, als Deutschland die Freiheit Entdeckte*, Der Spiegel, Geschichte, Nr. 3, 2014. *Die Weimarer Republikk, Deutschlands erste Demokratie*, Der Spiegel, Geschichte, Nr. 5, 2014. *Die Bombe, Das Zeitalter der Nuklearen Bedrohung*, Der Spiegel, Geschichte, August, 2015. *Die Kelten*, Der Spiegel, Geschichte, Nr. 5, 2017. *Das Britische Empire, Die unsichtbare Hand*, Der Spiegel Geschichte, Michael Sontheimer, Januar, 2013. *The Miners of Scranton*, Harper's New Monthly Magazine. Volume 55, Issue 330, November 1877. Nichols, George Ward, "The Indian: What We Should Do With Him" Harper's New Monthly Magazine, Vol XI (December, 2869—May 1870) p. 372-79.

Newspapers

Aftenposten, Akwesasne Notes, Chinadaily.com, Financial Times, Morgenbladet

New York Times, The Times-Tribune *Scranton 150 Years*, The Times-Tribune, George V. Lynett Jr., publisher, 2016.

Websites

History.com, Brittanica.com, GE.com, NASA.gov, Wikipedia.com EXplorePAhistory.com

Bibliography

Documentaries

A&E, Biography, *J. Pierpont Morgan, Emperor of Wall Street*, 1996.

Apple TV+, Documentary, *Lincoln`s Dilemma*, 2020

Blanchard, Pascal & Korn-Brzoza, David, *Decolonisation, du sang et des larmes*, A French Documentary, Cinétévé, 2020.

Burns, Ric, *New York*, American Experience, PBS Home Video, 2003.

Cattier, Daniel, *Slavery Routes*, a French Documentary, Studio Mikros Image, CNC. 2018.

Curtis, Adam, *The Century of the Self*, BBC, 2002.

Doran, Kristin, *Innovation & Enterprise, The Story of Gentex Corporation*, WVIA Public Media, 2014.

Eagle Media Productions, *American Civil War, A Union Divided*, Ltd. 2003.

Evans, Harold, *The American Century, Volume IV, 1963—1989*, Audio Rennaissance, 1998.

Jones, Julian, *Rise of the Nazis*, BBC Documentary, 2019.

Gooder, Barak, *Woodstock: Three Days That Defined A Generation*, PBS America, 2019.

Index to Ideas

You may want to write an essay on one of the topics in this book. Or you just may want to understand the context of the ideas better. To do so, you first collect the information that appears to you as conclusions in history. Once you collect the relevant information, you judge it from many sides—the positive sides and the negative sides.

The next step is to build concepts by bringing your judgments and conclusions into a meaningful relationship. Now you are approaching the flow of ideas that drive history. You notice how ideas have developed from century to century, from generation to generation, from country to country. When your individual concepts are filled with the ideas in history, you begin to understand the context. This not only increases your awareness, but it develops your personality. Through independent, critical thinking, you gain a feeling for what people have contributed on the stages of history. When you not only understand the ideas, but you connect your will to them, they grow in your real life. The ideas become your ideals.

To help you get started, I have categorized conclusions on the Individual Stage of History, the Common-wealth, Civil Rights and Segregation, the United States Constitution, and the American Empire. And then I added other topics you might want to work with.

Strive for Insight

Your Individual Stage of History

Preface, IX–XI, time, IX; consciousness; IX; conflicts, IX; context, IX; destiny, X; starting point, X; learning process, X; sacrifice, X; thankfulness, X; responsibility X; choices, XI; limitations, XI;

insight, XI; Universal Human Rights, 46-47; love, 46; clear thinking, 289; subliminal messages, 289; motives, 289; subconscious will, 289; decisions, 290; lies and harm, 290; dogma, 290; ideas, 290; ideals, 290; communication, 290; thinking, feeling, willing, 290; sounds and pictures, 291; artificial environments, 291; repetitive pictures, 291; healthy mental images, 291; power of imagination, 291; abuse of the human being, 291; dogmas of sexual fixation, 294; group psychology, 294;

Afterward, take part in history, 325; truth, 325

Four Important Topics Bundled

Our Common-wealth
Definition and foundation of, 324; electrified public transportation, 21; State Police, 22; Women`s Suffrage, 23; Scranton Railway Company abandons serve, 23; Federal Works Programs Administration, 24; New York Subway, 26; New York wharves, tunnels, bridges, 26; streetcar systems and railways dismantled, 27; Public Utility Holding Company Act of 1935, 27; Central Park, 28; F.K. Olmstead designs park, 192; La Guardia`s public programs, 28; Robert Moses, highways, 28; Universal Human Rights, 46; Civil Rights Act of 1964, 62; Title One, 70; Title Two, 71; Cross Bronx Expressway in 1955, 71; Penn Station, demolished in 1963, 71; Lackawanna River Conservation Association, 77; The Six Nations Confederacy, 93; The Declaration of Independence, 107; Commonwealth of Pennsylvania, 107–109; 127; The Constitution of the United States, 135-137; Difference between the Commonwealth of Australia and common-wealth in the USA, 233; weakened after the Civil War, 217; Powdery, Terrence, 278-274; George, Henry wrote *Progress and Poverty*, 1879, 275; Norwegian Government Pension Fund, 275; Pennsylvania State Police, 287; Mellon, Andrew, T, wrote *Taxation, the People's Business*, 1924, 313; the real economy, 314; the New Deal, 314; the Revenue Act of 1935, 315; the Revenue Act of 1942, 322; national deficit, 2020, 323; taxpayers, 323

The Constitution of the United States of America
Presidential oath, 20; new executive war powers in Tonkin Resolution, 50; Constitutional Convention, in 1787, 132-138; Articles of Confederation, 132; The Founding Fathers, 132; John Locke, 132; Voltaire, 132; Montesquieu, checks and balances, 133; New Jersey Plan, 133; Virginia Plan, 133; Articles of the Constitution, 135 - 138; Congress, compromise on, 133 ; executive power, 134; judicial branch, 133; restrictions on the states, 134; Federalists 134; 139; Republicans, 134; 139; United States of America, ratified, 134; Articles of the Constitution, 136; Amendments to

Index to Ideas

the Constitution since 1791, 136; the first ten amendments are called Bill of Rights, 135-136; First, 135; Second, 135; and controversy thereof, 137; Third, 135; Fourth,136; 302; Fifth, 136; Sixth, 136; Seventh, 136; Eighth, 136; Ninth, 136; Tenth, 136; Eleventh, 136; Twelfth, 136; Thirteenth, 58; 136; and 1865, 223; Fourteenth, 137; and in 1868, 221; 223; Fifteenth, 61; 137; and in 1870, 221, 223; Sixteenth, 137; and income tax in 1913, 311; Seventeenth, 137; Eighteenth, prohibition in 1920, 24; Nineteenth Amendment, 23; First Congress, 138

Commerce Clause, 255; Preamble to the Constitution, 324

Civil Rights and Segregation
Black Lives Matter, 16; Segregation, 26; 58; Jim Crow laws, 26; 58; Louisiana Black Codes, 220; disenfranchisement, 221; see Naturalization Act of 1870; NAACP, 26; 61; 288; W.E.B. Du Bois, 26;288; Compromise of 1877, 221; Civil Rights Act of 1875, 221; Plessy v. Ferguson, legalized segregation, 26, Harlan, Justice, against Plessy v. Ferguson; 26; KKK Act of 1871, 220; Wilkerson, Isabel, historian wrote, *Caste, The Origins of Our Discontent*, 59, South African Segregation, 59; Gobodo-Madikiizela, Pumla, wrote *A Human Being Died That Night*, 59, Mandela, Nelson, 59; Tutu, Archbishop Desmond, Reconciliation, 59, civil liberties, 61; Cornell Law School Legal Information Institute, 61, Voting Rights Act of 1965, 61, Brown vs. Board of Education decision in 1954, 62; 101st Airborne Division in Little Rock, Arkansas, 62; Cumming v, Richmond decision, 1899, 62; Parks, Rosa and Montgomery bus boycott, 62, Browder v. Gayle, 1956 decision desegregated buses, 62; March On Washington, August 28, 1964, 62; Civil Rights Act of 1964, Malcolm X, 64; Watts riots, 64; Carmichael, Stokely, 64; Black Power, 64; Black Panthers, 64; King Jr., Martin Luther creates Washington Spring Project, 1968, 65; Title One, Slum Clearance Bill of 1948, 70; Title Two, 70; Women`s Liberation, 72; Gay Rights, 73

The American Empire

Native Americans
Government schools, 27; The Indian Citizen Act of 1924, 27; Wheeler-Howard Act of 1934 promoted self-government, 27; *The Book of the Hopi*, 57; Termination Act of 1953 to end all agreements, 67; Indian Relocation Act, 1956, 67; AIM, 67; Means, Russel, 67; Trail of Broken Treaties of 1972, 67; Wounded Knee, site of 1890 massacre, 67; Pine Ridge, South Dakota, 68; Peltier, Leonard, 68; the Iroquois, 91-95; Sullivan's expedition, 1779, 122-124; Cherokee forefathers, 164; Treaty of Greenville of 1795, 165; manifest destiny, 244; Jackson, President Andrew *Indian Removal Act,1830*, 245; Indian colonial wars east of Mississippi, 245, Cherokee Nation vs. Georgia, 245; Van Buren, President Martin, evicted Cherokee on *The Trails of Tears*, 1838, 246; Indian colonial wars west of the Mississippi, 248, Indian Appropriations Act of 1871, 249; Black Elk, 249; Crazy Horse, 249; Chief Joseph, 250, Dawes Act of 1886, 250; Curtis Act of 1898, 251; Killing off the buffalo, 225; Native American population, 226

Strive for Insight

Colonization abroad
Minh, Ho Chi, 48; American War in Vietnam 1954—1975, 49-53; domino theory, 49; Republic of South Vietnam founded in 1956, 49; President John F. Kennedy, 49; Gulf of Tonkin Resolution, of 1964, allowed presidents to wage war without Congressional approval, 50; Vietcong invade South Vietnam in 1964, Joint Chiefs of Staff escalate war in 1964, 50; Operation Rolling Thunder, B-52 bombing raids February, 1965, 50; Johnson, President Lyndon, 50; Governor Scranton evaluates the war, 50; Rostow, W. W., 50; Rusk, Dean, 50; Bundy, McGeorge, 50; Taylor, Maxwell, 50; Martin Luther King Jr. speaks against war at Riverside Church, 1967, 51; McNamara commissioned the *Report of the Office of the Secretary of Defense Vietnam Task Force*, known as the *Pentagon Papers*, 51; Vietnam Veterans Against the War, 51; Tet Offensive, January to March, 1968, 52; Củ Chi underground tunnels, 52; Nixon invaded Cambodia, in April 1970; Kent State and Jackson State students killed, 52; Ellsberg, Daniel, *Pentagon Papers*, June 13, 1971, agent orange, 53; Operation Linebacker with napalm bombs, 53; in May, 1975 the Vietnam War ended. 53; Spanish-American War of 1898, 244

The American Empire in Business
Turning point in 1945, 45; the Marschall Plan, 48; military coup in Chile, 51; Cuban sugar plantations, 244; United Fruit Company, 244; Phelps Dodge in Peru and the Congo, 244; Amalgamated Copper in Chile and Mexico 1899, 244; Panama Canal seized in 1902, 244; Bretton Woods, 315; Employment Act of 1946, 315; The Federal Reserve Bank, 310; Casino Economy, 316; Glass Steagall Act of 1933 regulation repealed in 1999, 317; CDOs, 317; high risk mortgages, 319; housing bubble burst in 2007, 319; $700 billion TARP, 320; Lehman Brothers, 320; JP Morgan Chase, 320; Goldman Sachs, 320; tax havens, 322; individuals and corporations no longer pay taxes into the Common-wealth, 322; national deficits, 323; the real economy, 324

Other Topics to Write About

WWII in Europe
Old empires fall, 28; Treaty of Versailles, 33; Germans and Austrians pay WWI war reparations, 33; fascist National Socialist German Workers Party, (NS) 36; Hitler, Adolf elected Prime Minister in 1933, 36; secret military police, Gestapo, developed by Goering, Herman, 37; SA, a militia commanded by E. Röhm, 37; Himmler, Heinrich, SS commander, 37; Poland, invaded by Nazis in 1939.39; Nazi Final Solution Movement, 39; Heisenberg developed Nazi nuclear weapon program, 39; Nazis invaded Denmark, Norway, France, Belgium, Luxembourg, and the Netherlands in 1940,39; Bombing of London, 39; Nazis invaded Greece and Yugoslavia, then the Soviet Union, 39; Yalta Conference in February 1945, 42; Allied civilian bombing of Dresden on February 13, 1945, 42; Patton, General George, crossed the Rhine on March 22, 42; Bradley, General Omar, quot. 42; Soviet Red Army, General Zhukov and General Konev, 42; Simpson, General, Ninth Army reached the river Elbe, 42;, Battle of Berlin, 43; Goebbels, Nazi Propaganda Minister Joseph, 295

Index to Ideas

WW II against Japan
Tojo, General Hideki, 40; Pearl Harbor, 40; Japanese take Guam, the Wake Islands, the Philippines, Burma, the Dutch East Indies, the Malay Peninsula, 40; Japanese captured Rangoon, Singapore, and Jakarta, 40; Solomon Islands, Guadalcanal attacked in February,40; New Georgia fell, 40; Bougainville, 41; Edward Steven Walker in 12th Marines, Third Division, 41; Guam, Iwo Jima, 41; Operation Olympic, planned attack on the Island of Japan, ch2; Hiroshima bomb, August 5, 1945, 43; and, *Fat Man*, exploded over Nagasaki August 8, 1945, 45; Japanese surrender, September 2, 1945, 45

The American Revolution
The Boston Massacre, 102; Stamp Act of 1765, 102; King George III, 102; Adams, Samuel, 103; Warren, Dr. Joseph, quot. Suffolk Resolves, 103; at Bunker Hill, 106; Sons of Liberty in Boston 103; at Boston Tea Party, 103 and in Connecticut, 106; Continental Congress, First, 103, and Second, at York, 113; Revere, Paul, 104; Henry, Patrick, 104; Adams, John, 105; Declaration of Independence, 107, answered by Preamble, 324; missing from National Archives, 121; Hamilton, Alexander, gunner, 112, founded Bank of New York, 131; first Treasury Secretary, 138; emigrates from West Indies, 163

The Continental Army
Putnam, Colonel Israel, at Bunker Hill, 105, at Battle of Brooklyn, 109; Washington, General George, commander-in-chief, 106; military weapons, 110, Durkee, Major John, in Wyoming, 100; at Bunker Hill, 105; at Brooklyn, 109; at Trenton, 111; at Monmouth Courthouse, 117; Robert Durkee, 110, Samuel Ransom, 110; at Valley Forge, 115; two Wyoming Companies, 111; Battle of Wyoming, 120-121; Connecticut, 24th Regiment of Militia, Butler, Captain Zebulon, in Wyoming, 101; in Connecticut Line, 112, at Battle of Wyoming, 118- 121; Hartley, Colonel Thomas, designated to Wyoming, 115; Greene, Major General Nathanial, 111; as Quartermaster, 114; in Carolina,124; Knox, General Henry 111, and Siege of Yorktown, 126; Steuben, General Fredrick von, drillmaster at Valley Forge, 115; Varnum, General James, of Connecticut, 114, Wayne, Major General Anthony, 117, at Yorktown, 125; at Battle of Fallen Timbers, 165; Denison, Colonel Nathan, commander at Forty Fort, 116, Gates, Horatio, at Saratoga, 113; abandoned Washington at Trenton, 118; as President of the Board of War, 118; lost Battle of Camden, 124; Lafayette, General Marquis de, at Monmouth 117, at Yorktown, 125; Lee, Major General Charles, American traitor, 118; Arnold, Benedict, American traitor, 125; Marion, General Francis, known as the Swamp Fox, 125; Morgan, General Daniel, 124; Lee, General Henry, 125; Rochambeau, French General, at Yorktown, 125

The British Army
Gage, British Commander, Thomas, 101; Howe, British Commander, William, 112; Clinton, British Commander, 116; Cornwalls, Lord Charles, at Princeton, 111; chased Americans in Carolinas, 124; surrendered at Yorktown, 125; later Governor of India, 160, Burgoyne, General John defeated at Saratoga, 113; Fort Niagara, 115, Butler, John, Tory from Connecticut, 115

Strive for Insight

Some Revolutionary War Battles
Concord and Lexington, 105; Bunker Hil, 106; Siege of Boston, 109; Battle of Brooklyn, 109; Battle of Fort Washington, 110; Princeton, 111; Brandywine, 112; Fort Mifflin, 113; Battles at Saratoga, 113; two Westmoreland Companies at Battles of Millstone, Round Rock, and Germantown, 114; Monmouth Courthouse, 117; Battle of Wyoming, 118–122; Sullivan`s March, 122, Washington`s orders, 123; Cowpens, 125, Guilford Court, 125; Siege of Yorktown, 125

The American Civil War
The Union
Hitchcock, Colonel Richard, wrote *War From the Inside, the Story of the 132nd Pennsylvania Volunteers*, his company from Scranton at Antietam, 199, at Fredericksburg, 205, at Chancellorsville, 206; quot. on Ligget`s Gap, 186, in 1877 strike, 282; Lincoln, President Abraham, at Cooper Union, 192; Army of the Potomac, 203; McClellan, General George B. on Virginia peninsula, 203; Lincoln replaced McClellan, 204; pro-slavery Union General, 204; McClellan replaced again after Antietam, 205; Emancipation Proclamation, 201-202; Burnside, General Ambrose, at Fredericksburg, Virginia, 204; French, General William, H., 206; Hooker, Major General Joseph, at Chancellorsville, 207; Sedgewick, General John, 207; Meade, General Geore G., command of the Army of the Potomac, 208; Buford, Major General John, 210; Fitzgerald, Richard, Captain in 17th Pennsylvania Cavalry, 210, bar in Scranton, 232; Schurz, Major General Carl, at Gettysburg, 210; quot. 211; in German Revolution of 1848, 197; meets Bismarck in Berlin, 262; Chamberlain, Colonel Joshua L. at Little Round Top, 211; and at Appomattox, 216; Howard, General Oliver, O., at Gettysburg, 210; Freedmen`s Bureau, 219; captured Chief Joseph, 250, Grant, Ulysses S., 215; at Appomattox, 216; President of the USA, 220; Sherman, General William T., march to the Sea 1864; ignored prisoners at Andersonville, 213; military Governor, 219; sent to St. Louis after the war, 247; Sheridan, Major General Philip, 215; Indian Wars, 248; Willard, Captain E. N., 215; Captain of USCT from Luzerne County, Appomattox campaign, 215; Chase, Salmon, Treasury Secretary, 222; helped by Moses Taylor, 228; developed income tax, 306

The Confederacy
Secession of Southern States, 202; Jefferson Davis, 214; Lee, Confederate General, Robert E., son of Henry Lee, 125, at Antietam, 201; resigns from Union Army, 202, saves Richmond, 203; at Fredericksburg, 205-207; at Chancellorsville, 207; Gettysburg, 209-212; at Petersburg, surrender at Appomattox Courthouse, 216; Jackson, Thomas, 'Stonewall' attacked near Harper`s Ferry, 203; died at Chancellorsville, 207-208; Longstreet, Lieutenant General James, quot. at Fredericksburg, 206; at Gettysburg, 212; Pickett, Major General George, E. at Fredericksburg, 207, at Gettysburg, 212; Hood, General John B. at Fredericksburg, 207; at Gettysburg, in Atlanta campaign, Hill, Lieutenant J. P., at Gettysburg, 210 and 212; Stuart, J. E. B., at Carlisle, 209, absent at Gettysburg, 210-211

Index to Ideas

Some Civil War Battles
Fort Sumter, 202; Manassas, First, 203; Peninsula Campaign, 203; Antietam Creek, 199-201; Fredericksburg, 204-207; Chancellorsville, 207; Lee in Pennsylvania, 20 -212; Gettysburg, 210-212; Vicksburg, 212; Atlanta campaign, 212-215; Battle of the Wilderness, 213; Cold Harbor, 213; Petersburg, 213

The British Empire in the Atlantic Trade Triangle
The empires fell, 28, empires fight in WWI, 29-33; Prime Minister Loyd George gives Palestine to the Jewish people, 32; Balfour Declaration of 1917, 32; Spanish Armada defeated in 1588, 153; East India Company (EIC) founded in 1600, 153; 159; The Royal African Company, (RAC) in 1660, 153; Hudson`s Bay Company in 1670, 154; in Caribbean, 154, colonization of Ireland, 156; potato famine in Ireland, 234; Atlantic Trade Triangle, 158; broken in 1862, 218

Double Trade Triangles, 161; triangles drive industrial revolution, 167; the American side of the triangles, 176; effect of Erie Canal and New York City, 177, world trade, 177; cotton production in the USA on trade routes, 189; Battle of Trafalgar, 233; British North America Act, 234, Charter Act of 1813, 234; Irish Land league, 273; British Commonwealth of Nations, 313; End of the Empire 1945

The British Empire in the Asian Trade Triangle
Indian national Congress, 35; Ghandi`s Salt March of 1931, 35; Clive, Robert, ruler of Bengali, 159; EIC enters China in 1637; British drug cartel, in Canton, China, 160; Inglis, Brian, quot. 236; double trade triangles from British perspective, 237; First British Chinese Opium War, in 1839, 238; Second Opium War in 1856, 239; New South Wales, 233; Commonwealth of Australia in 1901; Charter Act of 1813 where British government takes over opium trade, 236; EIC dissolved in 1858, 236; Suez canal opened, 1869, 236; Government India Act. 1858, 236; Treaty of Nanjing, 238; Queen Victoria`s birthday, 1897

French Empire
The French Empire dissolves in 1945, 34, 48-49; Chad, Cameroon, Congo freed in 1960, Gabon, Algeria in 1962, Morocco in 1956, Tunisia in 1956, and Senegal independence, 48; Syria and Libanon independent in 1946, 48; French Indochina War, 1945-1954,49; Colonies in Caribbean, 154; slave ports in France, 154; New France, 155; The Sun King established Black Codes in Colonial Ordinance of 1685, 155; French East India Company, 156; French West Indies Company on Guadeloupe, 144, French and Indian War, 156; in Vietnam, 243

Saint Dominique Revolution
Slave revolt for twelve years starting in 1791, 144; France declared war on Britain in 1793, 144; Toussaint Louverture commanded revolt, 144; Napoleon sent troops and dogs, 145; Dessalines, Jacques, new commander of revolt, 145; French expelled at Battle of Vertieres in 1803, 145; Dessaline

Changes name to Haiti, 145; Haiti paid reparations to France as of 1825; Atlantic Trade Triangle Empires sent coffee production to Brazil, sugar to Cuba, and Cotton to North America, 145; new colonization of the USA, 145; Louisiana Purchase of 1803, 145; Lewis and Clark Expedition, 145

Ottoman Empire
Hourani, Historian Albert, quot. 240; Empire from 1413, 240; House of Osmani, 244; trade taken by Europeans in 1800, 240; won Crimean War in 1856, 241; defeated by the British in 1917, 31; 241; Sykes-Picot agreement, 9; 11; 38

The Chinese Revolution
Taiping Rebellion in 1864, 239; USA Open Door Policy, 239; the Boxer rebellion, 240; foreign opium trade ended in 1910, 240; Communists led by Mao Zedung and Zhou Enlai in civil war against Chiang Kai Shek and Kuomintang National Army, 34; Chinese socialism, December 1952, 54; Great Leap Forward, 1958-1960, 54; People's Republic of China, declared by Mao Zedong October 1, 1949 at Tiananmen Gate, Beijing, 54; Cultural Revolution, 55; Tiananmen Square, 1989, 55; Hong Kong, administrative region in 1997, 55

Enlightenment in England
Bacon, Sir Francis, wrote, *Separation of Sciences and New Organon* in 1620, 148; Locke, John, wrote, *The Second Treatise of Government*, 132; Newton, Sir Isaac, defined laws of planetary motion, 148; The Royal Society of London, 149

Enlightenment in France
Voltaire, French advocate for human rights, 132; Montesquieu, French author of *The Spirit of Laws*. defining checks and balances in government, 133; Lafayette, Marquis de Declaration of the Rights of Man in 1789, 142; imprisoned, 143; Liberty, Equality, and Brotherhood, 142

Enlightenment in Germany
Lessing, Gotthold Ephriam, wrote *The Education of the Human Race*. 173; Mozart, Wolfgang Amadeus, *The Magic Flute*, 173, Schiller, Friedrich, *The Esthetic Education of Mankind*, 174; Beethoven, Ludwig van, *Symphony No. 9*, 174, Kant, Immanuel, wrote *Critique of Pure Reason*, 175; Herder, Johann, 175; Fichte, Johann Gottlieb, 175; Goethe, Johann Wolfgang von, wrote *Faust*, 175; and *Theory of Colors* in 1810, 150, Hegel, Georg Wilhelm, wrote *Science of Logic*, 175, unsuccessful German Revolution in 1848, 196-188; Waldorf School in Stuttgart, Germany, Rudolf Steiner and Anthroposophy, 34

Enlightenment in American
Carson, Rachel, aquatic biologist, warned of DDT and phosphates in, *A Silent Spring*, 63; and 193; Black Elk, wrote *Black Elk Speaks*, 249; and 193; Thoreau, Henry David, wrote *On the Duty of Civil Disobedience*, quot. on, 193; inspired Tolstoi, 194; quot. from Gandhi, 194; influenced, M. L. King, quot. 195; Peabody, Elizabeth, 195; Fuller, Sarah

Index to Ideas

Margaret, wrote, *Women in the Nineteenth Century*, 195; Emerson, Ralph Waldo, wrote *Representative Men* and *Self Reliance*, 195; and quot. on slavery, 196; Whitman, Walt, published, *Leaves of Grass*, 196, Frederick Douglass, quot. 218; North Star, 196

Science
Cosmology, 20; Atomic bomb over Hiroshima, 43 ; and over Nagasaki, 45; atomic bomb development in Germany, 39; bomb development in the USA.40; Atomic power in China,7 ; NASA, 68; Project Mercury-Atlas, 68; Gemini Missions, 68; Space Lab, 68; Venus 8, 68; Viking 2 on Mars, 68; Voyager 1 passed Saturn, 68; Wisconsin Ice Age, 81; Allegheny Plateau, 81; Mississippian geological era,82 ; Pennsylvanian geological period, 82; Permian geological period, plate tectonics, ch4; oxygen, 82; carbon, 82; anthracite coal, 82; bituminous coal, 82; water gap geology, 83; and 185; Powell, John Wesley, explores Colorado River, 226; National Geographical Society, 227; Webb telescope, 20

Scientists
Einstein, Albert, 40; and 264; Steiner, Rudolf, founder of Waldorf School and Anthroposophy, 34; Plato wrote, *Allegory of the Caves*, 148; Aristoteles, *Categories*, 148; Bacon, Francis, 147; Royal Society of London, 149, Newton on planetary motion, 148; Harvey, William, on blood and calculus, 149; Boyle, Robert on particles, 149; Franklin, Benjamin, started the American Philosophical Society in 1743, 149; Galvani, Luigi, on electricity,149; Volta, Allesandro, on electricity and batteries, 149; Dalton, John on atomic theory, 150; Priestley, Joseph, on CO_2,150; Davy, Sir Humphry on electrochemistry, 159; Faraday, Michael, on electromagnetism, 150; Goethe, Wolfgang von, on botany, and geology, 150; Tull, Jethro, sewing seeds, 168; Townsend, Lord, fertilizers, 168, Young, Arthur, on new land distribution, 168; Darwin, Charles, wrote *The Descent of Man*, 234; Curie, Marie, 264; Born, Max, wrote, *Atomic Physics*, 264- 265; Hilbert, David, 264; Hubble, Edwin, 265; Klein, Felix, 264; Minkowski, Hermann, 264; Planck, Max, 264; Rutherford, Ernest, 264; Thomson, J.J. 264; Heisenberg, Werner, 265; Oppenheimer. J. Robert, 265; Bohr, Niles, 266; Freud, Sigmund, 293; Jung, C.G. quot., 293

Inventors of Machines
New machines, 151; Newcomen, Thomas, constructs a steam engine, 168; Kay, John, the flying shuttle, 169; Arkwright, Richard, initial spinning machine,169; Hargreave, James, spinning jenny, 169; Crompton, Samuel, the mule stool, 170; Cartwright, Edmund, power loom, 170; Watt, James and Boulton, Mathew build cylinders and pistons, 170; Wilkinson, John, boring lathe, 170

Trevethick, first working railway, 170; Stephensen, George and son Stephenson, Robert built locomotives for first steam railway, 170; Whitney, Eli patented the cotton gin, 176, Fitch, John, the steamboat, 176; McCormick, Cyrus, mechanical reaper, 177, Wright, Benjamin, the Erie Canal, 177; T-rail production in Scranton, 194; Cort, Henry, refined cast iron, 185; Brown, Moses, hired Samuel Slater to set up spinning mill; 190, Cooper, Peter, produced glue, 190; Steinways build pianos, 190; Singer, Isaac produces sewing machines, 190; Scranton brothers produced T-rails and railroads, 190; Edison, Thomas, ch2, car production in Germany 263; Bessemer converters, 267

Strive for Insight

Railroads
Delaware and Hudson Gravity Railroad, 188; Liggets Gap Railroad, 166; Lackawanna and Western Railroad, 186; Pennsylvania Gravity Railroad, 187; Delaware, Lackawanna and Western Railroad, D.L.&W, 187 and 267; Dickson, Thomas, with brothers John and George, build locomotives, 188; Dickson Manufacturing Company, 231; Lackawanna and Bloomsburg Railroad, 230; Transcontinental railroads, 225; Central Railroad of New Jersey, 229, 267; Erie Railroad, 229,. 267; Delaware and Hudson Railway, 267; Gotthard Tunnel and Railway, 263; New York, Ontario, and Western Railroad, 267; the Sherman Anti-Trust Act of 1890, 256;

Electric rail transportation
Scranton Railway Company, 21; abandoned in 1923, 23; suburban lines cut back in 1929; electric trolleys in Scranton, 268; Scranton-Wilkes Barre Laurel Line, 22; electric service ended in 1952, 75; the Interstate Commerce Act of 1887, 256

Electricity
Edison, Thomas, in Wyoming State, 256; movie studio, 291; Edison Electric Light Company of 1881, 257; Pearl Street Station, 257; Westinghouse, George, 257-258; Tesla, Nikola, 257; alternative current (AC), 258; war of the currents, 258; General Electric Company, 1892, 258; 292, and GE.com, 260; Electric streetcars and subways in New York, 259; Eastman, George, 259; nuclear energy, 259; eCommerce, 261; Amazon, 262, cloud services, 262; health services, 262

Labor
Powderly, Terrence, apprentice to James Dickenon, quot.188; lawyer, 189; Mayor of Scranton in 1878, 273; quot. 275; Grand Master Knights of Labor, 280-281; *The Scranton Miner* in 1877, Harper's New Monthly Magazine, 276; coal breakers, 277, breaker boys, 278;; the American football, 278; Nippers, 278; mule drivers, 279, child labor, 21; in mills, 279; Haymarket Square and Pullman Strike, 281; WBA, 281; Lackawanna Iron and Coal Company riot, 282, and strike in 1877, 282; Mitchell, John, President of UMWA in 1899, 284; UMA records destroyed,287; Anthracite Strike of 1902, 285-287, Roosevelt, President Theodore quot. 286;

Capital and Capitalism
Middle Class, 3; the richest 400 Americans, 18; The Sherman Anti-Trust Act of 1890, 256; on ownership, 282; definition of capital and capitalism, 283; Social Darwinism, 283; Sumner, William Graham, 283; welfare state, 283; communism, 283; Marx, Karl, wrote *Capital, a Critique of Political Economy*, 283; stockholders, 283; corporations, 284; cartels, 284; Anthracite Combine, 284; Baer, George F., 285; J. P. Morgan 286; 307-308; big fish swallow smaller fish, 299; war reparations, 308; trusts, 309; Rockefellers, 309; Morgan, J.P. Wall Street, 228, and 257; Morgan, Junius S., 307; House of Morgan, 309, House of Rothschild, 309, Morison, Samuel on war debt, quot. 311; Bank of England, 311; Winston, Churchill, 313; credit, 313; New York Federal Reserve Bank, 313; the Glass-Steagall Act of 1933; 314; FDIC, 314; President Clinton signed Gramm-Leach

Index to Ideas

Bliley Act of 1999, 317; CDOs 317; Niall Ferguson quot. 318; TARP, 320; Treasury Secretary Paulson, 320; J. P. Morgan Chase, 321; Goldman Sachs, 321; Keynes, John M., wrote *The General Theory of Employment, Interest, and Money*, 322

Information Technology in the Twentieth Century

Turing, Alan produced Ultra Intelligence, 295, DARPA, 296; ISP, 296; Internet, 296; Wozniak, Steve and Jobs, Steve produced Apple computer in 1976, 296 ;Xerox PARC, 296; Macintosh Systems Software, 297; Gates, Bill, and Allen, Paul, kept operating system MS-DOS, 297; Microsoft Windows 3, 297; World Wide Web, Tim Berners-Lee at CERN, 297; Job`s NeXTSTEP, 298; Google started in 1997, 298; Microsoft Internet Explorer, 298

Information Technology in the Twenty-First Century

AOL bought Time Warner, 299; Skype started in 2003; World of Warcraft in 2004; YouTube and Facebook 2004, 299; social media, twitter in 2006, 299; the iPhone in 2007, 299; opensource software, 300; application programmers interface, (API), 300; ImageNet Contest in 2012, 300; deep-learning, 301; artificial neural networks, 301; artificial intelligence, 301; ChatGPT, 301; cloud technology, 301; National Security Agency, 302; civil rights online, 303; Zuboff, Shoshana, quot. 303

Culture and the Arts

Shakespeare, William, wrote *As You Like it.*, IX; Armstrong, Louis, Hughes, Langston, Baker, Josephine, Chaplin movies *City Lights* and *Modern Times*, Cotton Club, Ellington, Duke, Guthrie, Woody, wrote *This Land is Your Land*, and autobiography, *Bound For Glory*, Washington, Booker T., all on, 26; Breaking Benjamin, 3; Dylan, Bob and Baez, Joan, 62, Woodstock Generation, 69, Credence Clearwater Revival, 69; Havens, Richie, 69, Hendrix, Jimi, 70; Poli Theaters in Scranton and Wilkes-Barre, 270, Vaudeville in Scranton, 270, Buffalo Bill Cody, Mae West, W. C. Fields, Houdini, Will Rogers, Groucho Marx, Buster Keaton, Jack Benny, and Fred Astaire, all in Scranton, 270

General Index

African slave routes, 151
Ali, succeeds Prophet Mohammed, 8
Ali, Muhammed, Heavyweight Champion of the World, 65
Al Qaida, 13, in Afghanistan, 57
American Record Corp, in Scranton, 22
Anthracite coal industry apex in Scranton, 23; end of, 24
Antoinette, Marie, Queen of France, 140
Arab Spring, 11
Aster, John Jacob, 177; 244

Bank of America, formed in 1781, 131
Bank of the United States, First, in 1791, 138
Bank for International Settlements, 319
Bank of New York, formed in 1784, 131
Barre, Isaac, 100
Berlin, Wall, 54
Bernays, Edward, nephew of Dr. Freud, 292; wrote *Crystallizing Public Opinion*, 294-295
Biden, Joe Jr., 22
Bismarck, Otto, von, 308
Blair, John, 187; 191
Bosak, Michael, 269
Brazil, sugar in 1515, 152; then coffee production, 145
Brown, Patrick, quot., 184
Brule, Etienne, 94
Buddha, 89
Bush, President George W., 13; and 320

Carbondale, 1
Catton, Historian Bruce, 204
Celts, 156
Champlain, Samuel de, 94
Chernow, Ron, Historian, quot. 307; quot. 313
CIA, 302
Climate crisis, 17
Cognetti, Mayor Page Gebhardt, 2
Colorado River, 17; 226
Cooke, Jay, bank panic of 1873, 231; 307
Covid-19, 12

D&H Canal, 180
Delaware River, 83; 183
Delaware Water Gap, 4; 80
Dodge, William Earle, 183
Dust storm, Oklahoma and Kansas, 28

East-Jerusalem. Israel officially annexed in 1980, 56
Egypt, Sunni majority in, 8; Arab Spring, 10; in Arab coalition, 55
Eisenhower, President Dwight D., 62; 67
Electoral College, certificates, 18
European Economic Community, 48

Federal Bureau of Justice Statistics, 15
First National Bank of Scranton, 222
First Bank of the United States in 1791, 139
Folsom, Burton, Historian, 266
Fort Augusta, 97

349

Franklin, Colonel John, 128
French Revolution, a social revolution, 140; King Louis XVI executed, 140; Versailles, 140,
Friendly Sons of St. Patrick of Lackawanna County, 22

Gaza, 9-10
Geisinger Commonwealth School of Medicine, 5
Geithner, Timothy, Treasury Secretary, 319
General Motors Company in 1906, 261
General Silk Importing Company, in Carbondale, 23
Gentex Corporation, 3; 76
Glen Canyon, 227
Glickman, Jay, Historian, wrote, *Remember Wyoming*, guot. 115; gap in Papers of Continental Congress, 121
Gorbachev, Mikhail ended the Cold War in 1991, 54
Gordon, John Steele, wrote *Hamilton's Blessing, The Extraordinary Life and Times of Our National Debt*, 322
Grand Central Station, in New York, 25
Great Depression, 28; 313
Great Valley, 2; chapter 61-87; 93

Hamas, 7, 9
Harley Davidson, 5
Harrisburg, 4; in Civil War, 209
Hefner, Richard, historian, quot. 222
Hollister, Isaac, quot. 98
Homeland Security, Department of, 18
Hussein, Saddam, 14, President of Iraq in 1979, 56

Iaccavazzi, Cosmo, 77
Immigrants, in New York City, 25; first wave to Scranton, 184; during Civil War, 221; in 1875, 228; Irish to New York and Scranton, 187; 269
Institute on Taxation and Economic Policy, 18
Institute of International Finance, 323
Interstate Commerce Act, 1887, 256

Iraq, Shia majority in, 8; Refugees from, 11; Sykes-Picot Agreement, 31
Iranian Revolution, in 1979, 56
Islamic State, 10; 13
Israel, State of, 9-10; 55

Jacobs, Jane, 71
Jinping, Xi, 6
Jerusalem, 55
Johns Hopkins University Covid Resource Center,12
Johnson, President Andrew, 219; 220

Kennedy, Robert F., 63
Keystone State, 271
Khrushchev, Nikita, 54
King Charles II, 96
King's College, 5
Klots Throwing Company, 22; 24; 268
Kurds, Sunni Islam majority of, 9; Minority in Iraq,15; excluded from Sykes-Picot, 31
Kuwait, Shia Muslim minority in, 8

Lackawanna Avenue, 185
Lackawanna Iron & Steel in 1899, 269
Lackawanna River, 77; 91
Lackawanna Valley, 1, 186, and painting by George Inness in National Gallery in D.C. 229
Lenin, Vladimir, 32
Louis XIV, the Sun King of France, 141
Louis XVI, King of France, alliance with Americans, 113; executed, 140
Luzerne County, 128
Maastricht Treaty, created Parliament, European Bank, and Euro, 48
Marasco, Ralph, 3
Marcellus Shale, 5
Marshall Plan, in Europe 1948, 48
Mayer, Timmy, 77
McCarthy, Senator Joseph, House Committee on Un-American, 58
McGrath, Judith Ann, 2
Minisink Island, 90
Mohammed Ibn Saud, 8
Mohammed Ibn Wahhab, 8

General Index

Morrill Tariff, 222
Moses, Robert, 71
Murrow, Edward R., 58

Nanjing, China, 34
National Banking Acts of 1863 and 1864, 222
National Security Agency, 14; 302
National Security Act of 1947, 57
NATO, 53
Nehru, Jawaharlel, on types of revolutions, 143
Neoconservatives, 74
NEPA, 2
New York City, population, 25; subway, 25; 177; needed coal, 179; wealth and poverty in, 227; Wall Street, 227; 257; Metropolitan, Museum of, 228

Obama, President Barack, 9; 15; 321
Operation Iraqi Freedom, 15, 20
Palestine, 8; Sykes-Picot Agreement in 1916, 31; riots, 38
Patriot Act, 15
Paulson, Henry M., Treasury Secretary, 319
Penn Station, in New York, 71
Penn, John, of Stoke, in 1776, 109
Penn, John, the Governor, 101, last governor, 109
Penn, William, in 1681, 98; two grandsons in 1776, 109
Penn, Admiral Sir, 96; 155
Pennsylvania, State of, 1; 4
Pennsylvania State Police, 22; formation of, 287
Pennsylvania Power and Light, 4
Philadelphia, First Continental Congress, 103
Phuc, Kim, 53
Prison System, 15
Profit Muhammed, 9
Public Utility Holding Company Act of 1935, 27

Refugee Crisis, 16
Robling, John, built Brooklyn Bridge, 228

Roosevelt President Franklin, 314
Roosevelt, President Theodore, Empire, 244; Anthracite Coal Strike, 286

Salman, Saudi King, 9
Saudi Arabia, Sunni Muslim majority, 8; oil, 38
Saquoit Silk Manufacturing Company, 268
Scranton Button Co. 22; 269
Scranton, city of, population, 21; in 1870, 230; in 1900 and 1941, 269
Scranton Railway Company, 21,
Scranton, University of, 2; 270
Scranton Wilkes Barrie Airport, 1; 271
Scranton, Joseph H., 184, 191
Scranton, George, 183; elected to Congress, 188
Scranton, Seldon, 183; returns to New Jersey, 188
Scranton Steel, 267
Scranton, William Walker, 267; strike in 1877, 282
Scranton, Walter, 267
Scranton, William Warren., 76
September 11, 2001, 17
Shia Muslims, 9
Shikallamy Swatana, Oneida chief, 93
Shilts, Randy, 73
Shohola-Minisink Path, 90
Slocum, Francis, 122
Snowden, Edward, 302
Spain, in South America, 152; popes in Rome, 153, in Cuba, 153
Stanley, Henry Morgan, in Congo, Africa, 242; lecture in Scranton, 268
St. Thomas College in 1888, 269
Stock Market, crash of 1929, 28; 313
Sunni Wahhabism 9; and 13
Susquehanna River, 4, into Chesapeake Bay, 85, Wyomink people, 91, flow, 185
Susquehanna Company, 97
Susquehanna-Roseland power line, 6
Syria, Shia Muslim minority in, 8; Arab Spring, 10; Sykes-Picot Agreement, 31

Taylor, Moses, entrepreneur, 190-191, in Civil War, 228; donated Moses Taylor Hospital, 267
Terrorism, war on, 14
Textiles industry, in Scranton, 24; in New York, 25
The Office, NBC sit-com, 1
Triangle Shirt Waist Company, in New York, 25
Trump, President Donald, 17
Turkey, Sunni Muslim majority in, 8; Sykes-Picot Agreement, 31
Ukraine, invasion of 13-14; hunger returns in 1930s, 39
Union of Soviet Socialist Republics, 34
United Nations, 15
Universal Declaration of Human Rights, 46
US Census, 19

Vera Institute of Justice, 16

West Bank, ;, 55
Wikileaks, 14
Wilkes, John, 100
Wilkes-Barre, 1; 21; 101; elites of, 178; 266
Wilson, President Woodrow, 311
Withers, Hartley, quot., 312
Woolworth, Charles, in Scranton, 267
World Economic Forum, 12
World Trade Center, 13
World's Fair in Queens, 1939, 28
Wyoming Valley, 86; 97; 102; painting, *The Valley of Wyoming*, by Jasper Francis Cropsey, 228

Zarathustra, 89
Zexu, Lin, Imperial Commissioner, 238

Notes

Chapter 1 The Twenty-First Century
1. Constitution Annotated, Analysis and Interpreptation of the U.S. Constitution. See constituion.congress.gov.

Chapter 2 The Twentieth Century 1900—1945
2. Samuel Eliot Morison, and Henry Steele Commager, The Growth of the American Republic, New York, Oxford University Press, 1940, p. 553.
3. IBID, p. 491.
4. Charles Chaplin, My Autobiography, London, Modern Classics, 1964, p. 337.
5. Omar N. Bradley, A Soldier's Story, New York, The Modern Library, 1999, p. 531.

Chapter 3 The Twentieth Century 1945—1999
6. Universal Declaration of Human Rights, UN.org.
7. James M. Washington, editor, A Testament Of Hope, The Essential Writings of Martin Luther King Jr., San Francisco, Harper & Row, 1986, p. 238.
8. IBID, p.240.
9. Kim Phúc, Wikipedia.
10. Albert Hourani, A History of the Arab Peoples, New York, Warner Books, 1991, p. 446.
11. Frank Waters, Book of the Hopi, New York, Viking Penguin Books, 1963, p. 21.
12. Isabel Wilkerson, Caste, The Origins of Our Discontent, New York, Random House, 2020, p.18.
13. Pumla Gobodo-Madikizela, A Human Being Died That Night, A South African Story of Forgiveness, Houghton Mufflin Company, Boston, 2003, p.118
14. Palmer, Charles, Reparations for African-Americans: It's about more than slavery, Sermon, Grosse Pointe Unitarian Church, February 2, 2020. See United States v. Reese, 92 Reports 214, 1875.
15. Rachel Carson, Silent Spring, Boston, Houghton Mifflin, 1962, p.25.

16. Martin Luther King Jr., Showdown for Nonviolence, Look Magazine, April 16, 1968, ps. 23-25.
17. Peltier, Leonard, Sacrifice, a song by Robbie Robertson, in album Contact From the Underworld of Redboy, Capital Records, 1998.
18. Randy Silts, And The Band Played On, Politics, People And The Aids Epidemic, New York, Penguin Books, 1987, p. XXI.
19. A Brief Narrative of the Captivity of Isaac Hollister, Who Was taken by the Indians, A.D. 1763. Evans Early American Imprint Collection, https://quod.lib.umich.edu.
20. John Cary, Joseph Warren, chapter IV "A Pen For Propaganda" Urbana, University of Illinois Press, 1961.
21. The Avalon Project, Constitution of Pennsylvania-September 28, 1776, Yale Law School,. https://avalon.law.yale.edu/18th_century/pa08.asp
22. Jay L. Glickman, Painted In Blood: Remember Wyoming! America's First Civil War, Cody, Wyoming, Affiliated Writers of America, Inc. 1997, p. 87.
23. IBID, p. 100.
24. IBID, p. 185.

Chapter 7 Political Revolutions in the Eighteenth Century

25. Jawaharlal Nehru, Glimpses of World History, Being further letters to his daughter, written in prison, and containing a rambling account of history for young people. chapter: Europe Facing Great Upheaval, September 24,1932, London, Asia Publishing House, London, 1934.

Chapter 8 Science and Colonization in the Seventeenth and Eighteenth Centuries

26. Daniel Cattier, Slavery Routes, a French Documentary, Sudio Mikros Image, CNC. 2018.
27. Ric Burns, New York, Episode One, American Experience, PBS Home Video, 2003.
28. Alvin M. Josephy, Jr, The Indian Heritage of America, New York, Alfred A. Knopf, 1971, page 107.
29. IBID, page 316.

Chapter 10 The Industrial Revolution in America

30. Patrick Brown, Industrial Pioneers, Scranton Pennsylvania and the Transformation of America, 1846- 1902, Archbald, Pennsylvania, Tribute Books, 2010, p. 2.
31. Col. Frederick Hitchcock, History of Scranton and Its People, Lewis Historical Publishing Company, 1914, p. 42.
32. Terrence Powderly, The Path I Trod, New York, Columbia University Press,1940. p. 19.
33. Adam Rothman, The Slave Power in the United States 1783—1865, in Ruling America, edited by Steve Fraser & Gary Gerstle. Cambridge, Massachusetts, Harvard University, Press, 2005., p. 68.
34. Henry David Thoreau, Resistance to Civil Government, Æstethic Papers, 1849, p. 5.
35. IBID, page 17.

Notes

36. Mahatma Gandhi, For Passive Resistance, The Indian Opinion, October 26, 1907.
37. Martin Luther King Jr. The Autobiography of Martin Luther King Jr., New York, Warner Books, 1998.
38. Moncure Daniel Conway, Emerson at Home and Abroad, London, Trübner & Co., Ludgate Hill,1883, p. 223

Chapter 11 The American Civil War

39. Col. Frederick L. Hitchcock, War From The Inside, Chapter V, The Battle of Antietam, Philadelphia, J. P. Lippincott Company, 1904, ps. 55-58.
40. IBID, p. 116.
41. James Longstreet, From Manassas to Appomattox, Memoirs of the Civil War in America, p. 310. Philadelphia, J. B. Lippincott Company, 1896.
42. Col. Frederick L. Hitchcock, War From The Inside, Chapter XV, The Battle of Chancellorsville, Philadelphia, J. P. Lippincott Company, 1904, p. 200.
43. Carl Schurz, The Reminiscences of Carl Schurz, Volume Three, New York, The McClure Company, 1913. ps 7-11.
44. Paul Kensey, West Point Classmates—Civil War Enemies, October 2002, www.americancivilwar.asn.au.

Chapter 12 Reconstruction and the American West

45. . Frederick Douglass, The Life and Times of Frederick Douglass: From 1817-1882, London, Christian Age Office, 1882.
46. Richard D. Heffner, A Documentary History of the United States, New York, A Mentor Book, New American Library, 1952, p. 165.
47. Morison, Samuel Eliot and Commager, Henry Steel, The Growth of the American Republic, New York, Oxford University Press, 1940, p. 95.
48. IBID p. 98.
49. John Wesley Powell, The Exploration of the Colorado River and Its Canyons, 1895. Simon and Brown, 2013, p. 233.
50. IBID, p. 242.
51. Terrence V. Powderly, The Path I Trod, New York, Columbia University Press, 1940, p. 27.
52. IBID, p. 43.

Chapter 13 Colonial Empires in the Nineteenth Century

53. Brian Inglis, The Opium War, London, Hodder and Stoughton, 1979, p. 51.
54. IBID, p. 55.
55. Albert Hourani, A History of the Arab Peoples, New York, Warner Books, 1991, p. 215.
56. William T. Sherman, Memoirs of General W. T. Sherman, Volume I, Chapter 26, After The War, New York, D. Appleton and Company, 1889.
57. IBID, Chapter 26.
58. John G Neihardt, Black Elk Speaks, New York, William Morris & Company, New Pocket Books, 1932, p. 72.

Chapter 14 The Commerce Revolutions

59. Cornell Law School, Legal Information Institute, Sherman Antitrust Act, law.cornell.edu
60. Carl Schurz, The Reminiscences of Carl Schurz, Volume Three, New York, The McClure Company, 1907, p. 278.
61. Burton W. Folsom, Jr., Urban Capitalists, Scranton, The University of Scranton Press, 2000, p. 85.

Chapter 15 Land, Labor, Capital, and the Great Anthracite Strike of 1902

62. Terrence V. Powderly, The Path I Trod, New York, Columbia University Press, 1940, p. 76.
63. IBID, p. 276.
64. Unknown author, The Scranton Miner, article in Harper's New Monthly Magazine, New York, November, 1877.
65. Samuel Eliot Morison, and Henry Steele Commager, The Growth of the American Republic, New York, Oxford University Press, 1940, p. 149.
66. IBID, p. 155.

Chapter 16 The Information Revolutions

67. C. G. Jung, The Undiscovered Self, translated by R.F.C. Hull, Princeton University Press, 1957, p.28.
68. The Economist, Special Report, Artificial Intelligence, June 2016. p. 2.
69. Shoshana Zuboff, The Coup We Are Not Talking Abou, NY Times, Jan. 29, 2021. p. 3.
70. IBID, p. 11.

Chapter 17 The Financial Revolutions

71. Ron Chernow, The House of Morgan, An American Banking Dynasty and the Rise of Modern Finance, New York, Grove Press, 1990, p.13.
72. Samuel Eliot Morison, and Henry Steele Commager, The Growth of the American Republic, New York, Oxford University Press, 1940, p. 502.
73. Hartley Withers, Bankers and Credit, London, Eveleigh Nash & Grayson Limited, 1924, p. 2.
74. Samuel Eliot Morison, and Henry Steele Commager, The Growth of the American Republic, New York, Oxford University Press,1940, p. 504.
75. Ron Chernow, The House of Morgan, An American Banking Dynasty and the Rise of Modern Finance, New York, Grove Press, 1990, p. 275.
76. John Steele Gordon, Hamilton's Blessing, The Extraordinary Life and Times of Our National Debt, New York, Walker and Company, 1997, p. 110.
77. Niall Ferguson, Wall Street Lays Another Egg, New York Times, December 2008.

Born in Scranton, Pennsylvania in 1953, Ted Warren majored in European History at Harvard College before studying in Marburg, Germany. He ended up teaching History and English for thirty-three years to grades six through twelve at Waldorf Schools in Oslo, Norway and Princeton, New Jersey.

Contact me at www.teenage-edge.org

www.ingramcontent.com/pod-product-compliance
Lightning Source LLC
Chambersburg PA
CBHW031138020426
42333CB00013B/429